Making Publics in
Early Modern Europe

Routledge Studies in Renaissance Literature and Culture

Making Publics in Early Modern Europe

People, Things, Forms of Knowledge

Edited by Bronwen Wilson and Paul Yachnin

Routledge
Taylor & Francis Group
New York   London

First published 2010
by Routledge
711 Third Avenue, New York, NY 10017

Simultaneously published in the UK
by Routledge
2 Park Square, Milton Park, Abingdon, Oxon OX14 4RN

Routledge is an imprint of the Taylor & Francis Group, an informa business

First issued in paperback 2011

Library of Congress Cataloging-in-Publication Data
   Making publics in early modern Europe : people, things, forms of knowledge / edited by Bronwen Wilson and Paul Yachnin.
      p. cm. — (Routledge studies in Renaissance literature and culture ; 13)
      Includes bibliographical references and index.
   1. European literature—Renaissance, 1450–1600—History and criticism.   2. European literature—17th century—History and criticism.   3. Europe—Intellectual life—16th century.   4. Europe—Intellectual life—17th century.   5. Social action in literature.   6. Political culture—Europe—History.   7. Literature and society—Europe—History.   8. Politics and literature—Europe—History.   I. Wilson, Bronwen.   II. Yachnin, Paul Edward, 1953–
   PN721.M35 2010
   809'.93355—dc22
   2009028312

ISBN10: 0-415-80589-9 (hbk)
ISBN10: 0-415-89608-8 (pbk)
ISBN10: 0-203-86135-3 (ebk)

ISBN13: 978-0-415-80589-6 (hbk)
ISBN13: 978-0-415-89608-5 (pbk)
ISBN13: 978-0-203-86135-6 (ebk)

In Memory of Richard Helgerson

"constant zeale, and courage bold"

The half-line is from Edmund Spenser's *Faerie Queene,* book 1, canto 8, stanza 40. It describes Arthur, the Knight of Magnificence, as he rescues the distraught Red Cross Knight. The *Faerie Queene* was one of the many works that Richard Helgerson wrote about.

Contents

Figures

Tables

Acknowledgments

This volume is the work of many hands. It is a particularly worthwhile book, we think, because in it historical and theoretical researchers (we are using these terms roughly) get along together and work collaboratively toward the common goal of rethinking public life in early modern Europe. We hope that you will agree that the book achieves a high degree of complexity, variety, and concert. In the course of reading it, you will no doubt notice that not all the contributors write about publics and public making in the same way, but we also hope that you will get the impression that their differences, which are indeed persistent, are nevertheless substantial and productive. In this sense, the book can be seen as an extended conversation among people who like and respect each other; who, while they do not necessarily agree with each other, have yet learned a great deal about each other's methodologies and areas of interest; and who share a belief in the value of the study of the public-making capacities of works of art, music, theater, literature, mathematics, science, geography, and religion.

In view of the highly collaborative nature of this book, the editors' and contributors' primary debt must be to each other and to the Making Publics (MaPs) research team as a whole, not all of whom are represented here. It is also important to note that the team includes graduate student associates (GSAs), postdoctoral fellows, and summer seminarians. Their hard work and intellectual creativity have certainly contributed to what you will find here that is insightful or revelatory. Our thanks to Heather Muckart, a GSA of the project, for her intelligent assistance with editing and formatting the book. (Our younger colleagues are not to be held accountable for anything that is ill-conceived or just wrong.) Marlene Eberhart happens to be the project manager as well as a postdoctoral fellow; the fact that we are grateful for her excellent administration of the project should not distract us from acknowledging her considerable scholarly input to MaPs.

We are delighted to be able to thank the Social Sciences and Humanities Research Council of Canada for its splendid support of our work—and not just financial support either. We thank our partner institutions also for their financial, logistical, and moral support: University of California–Santa Barbara, University of Michigan, Queen's University, University of

Alberta, University of Mississippi, Reed College, MIT, and Concordia University. The administrators and staff of McGill University, the lead institution in the MaPs project, have been unfailingly generous in their support. We are grateful to them.

Introduction

Bronwen Wilson and Paul Yachnin

PUBLICS, CULTURE, ASSOCIATION

This book is about how concatenations of people, things, and forms of knowledge created "publics" in early modern Europe and how publics changed the shape of early modern society. Our focus is not exactly the publics themselves but rather the phenomenon that we call "making publics"—the active creation of new forms of association that allowed people to connect with others in ways not rooted in family, rank, or vocation, but rather founded in voluntary groupings built on the shared interests, tastes, commitments, and desires of individuals. By creating new forms of public association, cultural producers and consumers in effect challenged dominant ideas about just who could be a public person, greatly expanded the resources of public life for ordinary people in their own time, and developed ideas and practices that have helped to create the political culture of modernity.

Among the early modern cultural producers that we consider are poets, painters, theologians, mathematicians, travel writers, musicians, printers, globe makers, theatrical players, and many others. Even though their various works, publications, and performances did change the nature of the *polis,* the purposes of early modern artistic and intellectual producers were by no means always directly political; their inventiveness emerged from a complex of motives including sheer curiosity and creativity, the need to make a livelihood, a desire for fame, as well as sometimes an aspiration to reimagine or even transform the world. Those on the demand side were no more wholly bent on fundamental social or political change than were their supply-side counterparts. Those who by their acquisition, enjoyment, and manifold uses of works of art, craft, and intellect contributed fundamentally to the processes of public making included, among others, Catholics who attended Mass in the *huiskerken* (house churches) of Protestant Amsterdam, bourgeoisie who frequented the "salons" of sixteenth-century France, Shakespeare's playgoers and readers, Italian customers for printed music, and English provincial buyers of hand-crafted portraits. Note also that the boundary between producers and consumers tended to be highly porous in early modernity: some publics, such as the huiskerk-goers or the French salons, simply were not organized around a bipartite model of cultural production and consumption; others, such as theatrical, literary, or scientific publics, featured a relatively low threshold for entry into the company of producers. Shakespeare, for example, must have started out as a playgoer before he became a player and dramatist.

None of these people could have done any public making at all without public things: the material basis of the growth of the groups of "makers" and "partakers" (to use two characteristically early modern terms) included a vast array of built, written, printed, crafted, performed, and painted things that were made public and thereby became capable of small- and large-scale movement at the same time that they made it possible for their makers and partakers to develop an enhanced public life. It is also worth noting that while we focus on national or even local public making, we bear in mind that the expansion of publicity was an international innovation enabled by cross-border traffic in cultural goods of many different kinds.

The forms of knowledge that developed from and contributed to public making included new areas of expertise and evaluative standards specific to cultural products such as painting, music, theater, cartography, and poetry; new kinds of practical knowledge (know-how about musical and theatrical performance, calculation, navigation, and so on); new critical modes of understanding the historical and political world; and new kinds of geographical, mathematical, and theological knowledge as well as attendant modes of analysis and judgment. Importantly, while these new forms of knowledge were distinctively public and open to debate, they were concerned with accounts of the person as well as with descriptions of the world; the private, interior lives of people and the connections between private and public were key areas of concern in early modern portraiture, poetry, theater, mathematics, and theology. The expansion of public life was inseparable from the increase in new ways of describing and experiencing private life; in early modernity, as in all periods from antiquity to modernity, the domains of the public and private have been mutually constituting. One additional form of knowledge that played a significant role in public making was the self-awareness on the part of makers and partakers about their creation of and participation in public activities and exchanges. There can be no public where there is not also an active idea among the participants that they are doing something public—something open to others and potentially boundless in its effects.

The many new ways of "coming out" for both people and things and the attendant new ways of thinking about things, personhood, association, and the world brought about major changes in the private and public existence of early modern Europeans including those, like commoners and women, who would have discovered new paths toward a kind of public life as well as innovative ways of describing and experiencing their inner lives. In this volume, we attempt to develop analyses of a representative sampling of cases of early modern public making that will suggest something about the rich inventiveness and formative social power of artistic and intellectual publication and public making of all stripes in the period. We offer this book in the hope that it will help to deepen the modern understanding of the social and political dimensions of artistic and intellectual work generally, encourage others to think about early modern intellectual and cultural life in terms of public making, and contribute to a renewed interdisciplinary understanding of the most salient features of early modern European culture.

That word "culture" is an important part of what this book is about. Some years ago, Raymond Williams pointed out that "culture" was at first primarily a noun of process, nurture, or making:

> Culture in all its early uses was a noun of process: the tending of something, basically crops or animals. . . . This provided a further basis for the important next stage of meaning, by metaphor. From [the early sixteenth century] the tending of natural growth was extended to a process of human development, and this, alongside the original meaning in husbandry, was the main sense until [the late eighteenth century] and [early nineteenth century]. Thus More: "to the culture and profit of their minds"; Bacon: "the culture and manurance of minds" . . . At various points in this development two crucial changes occurred: first, a degree of habituation to the metaphor, which made the sense of human tending direct; second, an extension of particular processes to a general process, which the word could abstractly carry.[1]

Over approximately the past thirty years, the word "culture" in early modern studies has lost this sense of the processual or of active making and has begun to look more and more like something already made and firmly set in place. "Culture" has emerged in the work of New Historicism and various kinds of materialist criticism as a system or structure in which people, practices, and texts are imbricated. On this account, people, practices, and texts may reinscribe or resist the power of the social formation (and they may do both), but they are bound to operate in terms of certain nearly insurmountable strictures and limits, which belong to the whole-cloth composition of "culture." While we certainly do not claim that people are able freely and without impediment to make their world up solely according to their needs, desires, or ideals, we do want to shift the angle of view very substantially so that it becomes easier to see how individual and collective social actors are able to develop new and culturally innovative forms of public expression, identity, space, and action.

Closely akin to "culture" is the word "social," which has also come to stand for a system or structure by which the meaning of people, texts, and practices tends to be determined and the sphere of their action circum-scribed. In order to see past this misleading assumption about the struc-turedness and givenness of the social, we can recruit another word, one that is featured in the name of the project ("Making Publics: Media, Mar-kets, and Association in Early Modern Europe") and one that has gained currency in the Actor-Network-Theory (ANT) developed by Bruno Latour. Like Latour, the contributors to this volume are not focused on "the social" conceived of as a quasi-metaphysical structure that is assumed to be always already in place; we are far more interested in a view of the social that is suggested by the word "association," a term that suggests how people and things are involved in shifting chains of exchange and action. Here is Latour on how changing associations themselves comprise the social:

> For ANT . . . the definition of the term [social] is different: it doesn't designate a domain of reality or some particular item, but rather is the name of a movement, a displacement, a transformation, a translation, an enrollment. It is an association between entities which are in no way recognizable as being social in the ordinary manner, *except* during the brief moment when they are reshuffled together. . . . Thus, social, for ANT, is the name of a type of momentary association which is charac-terized by the way it gathers together into new shapes.[2]

Attending to "association," we suggest, opens up the possibility of seeing how social change is brought about by people who, while not necessarily bent on innovation, nevertheless find themselves involved with new people, practices, or things in ways that modify the way they relate to others, the world, and themselves and that thereby introduce new associations into society. The idea of association also makes visible how change is fomented by the social agency of things themselves in their interactions with people. Indeed, we might say that "the social" is not the condition of living inside a system of given relations and behaviors, but rather that it is the moment of formative change itself; or we might say that we are being truly social or cultural only when we are engaged in processes of reassembly—taking part in emerging and shifting concatenations of things, people, and forms of knowledge.

On this account, a focus on public making is valuable because it is able to recapture an idea of individual and collective agency as fundamental to how culture and society work and how they change. It can also be illumi-nating about what we might call the materiality of early modern public-ity; after all, it was the movement itself of poetry, plays, printed music, globes, maps, and portraits, among many other created things, that facili-tated the rapid expansion of public life. Indeed, it might be argued that the increased mobility of things themselves created public life in early modern culture. And culture, we suggest, is a made thing also, or something always being made; and culture conceived in these terms, as a thinker like Hannah

Arendt might argue, is the site of true publicity because it is the space for original, self-disclosing speech and action with others.[3]

PUBLICS, THE PUBLIC, AND PUBLIC MAKING

We have left so far untouched the central question with which we have to deal: what is a public? In order to answer this question, let us consider first the relationship between publics and the public. "*The* public," Michael Warner tells us, "is a kind of social totality. Its most common sense is that of the people in general. It might be the people organized as the nation, the commonwealth, the city, the state, or some other community. . . . But in each case, the public, as a people, is thought to include everyone within the field in question."[4] The public or the public sphere is an indispensable and powerfully influential idea—a way of conceiving of the social world, rather than a measurable reality. The idea of "the public" or "the world" motivates public making since it provides individual makers with a promise that they might achieve boundlessness or even immortality and since it offers groups of people a picture of themselves as boundlessly inclusive and influential. We suggest, however, that "the public" is in reality a congeries of publics—just as (to cite Latour again) what is usually called "society" is in truth an aggregation of mobile associations.

Another way to think about this question is in terms of spatiality. Traditionally, the space of the public has been characterized as unified and uniform—an open, visible, inclusive space in which people engage in what Jürgen Habermas calls "rational-critical debate."[5] Charles Taylor's recent discussion of the public sphere develops a valuable idea of "the public" as a formative feature of the social imaginary of the West, and he is illuminating about the interplay between the material and the ideological in the creation of what he calls "common space":

> A public sphere can only exist if it is imagined as such. Unless all the dispersed discussions are seen by their participants as linked in one great exchange, there can be no sense of their upshot as "public opinion." This doesn't mean that imagination is all-powerful here. There are objective conditions; internal: for instance, that the fragmentary local discussions inter-refer; external: there had to be printed materials, circulating from a plurality of independent sources, for there to be the bases of what could be seen as a common discussion.[6]

Taylor's use of phrases such as "dispersed discussions" and "fragmentary local discussions" suggests that he is taking for granted the preexistence of the very public whose coming into being he is supposed to be explaining, and also suggests that the characteristic activity that makes the participants members of the public in the first place can include little outside of debate and discussion. An analysis of early modern works of art and intellect and the fields of activity that grew up around them suggests, however, that the formative work of public making is far less unified and uniform than has been thought and also that forms of public expression, identity, and action include poetry, play, and performance (to mention only a few forms) as well as rational debate.

"A public sphere," Craig Calhoun says, "comprises an indefinite number of more or less overlapping publics, some ephemeral, some enduring, and some shaped by struggle against the dominant organization of others."[7] The space of public life on a grand scale may accordingly be imagined as a contact zone where different publics encounter each other, but irregularly, unpredictably, and at odd angles. Publics may come into conflict because they are competing for customers or resources; but their struggles as well as their alliances are founded primarily in their working assumption that they are competing for the attention and approval of "the public," a totality that is conjured into existence on the strength of each public's address to "the world" and each one's aspiration toward growth. What has been called the public sphere is, in this view, a misrecognition of the jostling interactivity of publics that develop differing, competing forms of public expression and action. But the misrecognition itself is telling since the idea of "the public" is formative of individual publics; they bend their address toward the commonweal as it is traditionally understood even though their actual membership remains sectoral.

It is important, therefore, to understand the plural and multiform nature of public space, and necessary also to take account of the multiple kinds of expression that take place within this aggregation of spaces. We miss something fundamental about the formation of public life around works of art and intellect if we fold their various practices into an account of particular rational debates about matters of public concern (just as we mistake their nature if we view them as outside of politics altogether). Nancy Fraser has critiqued the Kantian ideal of rational debate developed by Habermas on the grounds that "the public sphere" installs a false inclusiveness in the interests of the ruling fraction by promoting a certain kind of expression (that is, rational debate) as normative.[8] Warner also calls into question an idea of publicity that excludes many sorts of public expression as well as the people who make them:

> In *The Structural Transformation of the Public Sphere,* Habermas speaks of "people's public use of their reason." But what counts as a use of reason? . . . Movements around gender and sexuality seek to transform fundamental styles of embodiment, identity, and social relations. . . . Because this is a field that people want to transform, it is not possible to assume the habitus according to which rational-critical debate is a neutral, relatively disembodied procedure for addressing common concerns, while embodied life is assumed to be private, local,

or merely affective and expressive. The styles by which people assume public relevance are themselves contested.[9]

The contributors to this volume take further Fraser's and Warner's critique of the uniformity and unity of the Habermasian public sphere by developing case histories of public making in a range of more and less political activities—from, on one side, the activist work of Protestant polemicists and the intermittently political literary salons to, on the other, the publics around printed motets, theatrical performances, and melancholy lyric poetry. At the far end of this range, public formation does not engage with politics at the level of ideology or action but rather achieves its sociopolitical effects by way of changing available and normative forms of speech, practice, and association. That people in 1600 somehow evaded their working-day tasks, went to the Globe to see *Hamlet,* and then talked about the play and the performance is, in this view, an event of diffuse but significant consequence for the early modern polity.

* * *

One way of thinking about early modern publics is as dynamic social entities that are constituted in part by the making public of particular kinds of made things along with their makers and partakers. (By the way, this statement makes it sound as if the public were an already-existing space into which things and people could be inducted, but in fact public making is a process by which social and material relations are reassembled, so that a public space, as it were, is created where one did not exist before.) We can add that, once creating the means for coming out in public ceases to be central to the things and the people who make them and enjoy them, then we might have a number of social entities such as academies, clubs, or societies, but we no longer have a public. Publics also develop durable languages, standards of judgment, criteria for belonging, and representative works or performances or ideas, but once making things and people public ceases to be central, what remains are precisely those features transformed into the lineaments of an institution: technical languages, evaluative rules, forms of credentialization, canons of works and writings.

The approach that we take is post-Habermasian because, as we have seen, it focuses on a plurality of publics rather than on a single public sphere, because it is interested in accidental and unintended outcomes as much as in intended ones, and because it is interested in the realm of art on its own aesthetic, evaluative, and affective terms rather than in art as instrumental to the emergence of rational public debate. However, the contributors to this volume also bear in mind the continuing value of Habermas's emphasis on the public sphere, since we know that if we lose sight of how publics relate to the broader social formation, we will be at risk of producing something like a historical sociology of early modern hobbies and hobby collectivities.

Also important is Habermas's brilliant insight into the crucial interactivity of privacy and publicity in the formation of what he characterizes as the modern public domain, an event that he locates in the eighteenth century. The "bourgeois public sphere," he says, is "the sphere of private people come together as a public; they soon claimed the public sphere regulated from above against the public authorities themselves."[10] He grounds modern publicity itself in domestic life and the private experience of reading: "The sphere of the public arose in the broader strata of the bourgeoisie as an expansion and at the same time completion of the intimate sphere of the conjugal family. . . . And as the subjectivity of the privatized individual was related from the very start to publicity, so both were conjoined in literature that had become 'fiction.'"[11] It is important to note that the primary meaning of the word "private" in early modernity (a meaning still current in modern English) had mainly to do with "privation" rather than with the authority and value of untrammeled inwardness. This privative meaning of "private" is well captured by how Antony petitions Octavius Caesar in Shakespeare's *Antony and Cleopatra* to allow him to leave public life and to live out his natural days as a nobody: "To let him breathe between the heavens and the earth, / A private man in Athens."[12] In Antony's case, the privative life of a private man records a social distinction and also marks the threshold of humanity itself, since a life reduced to "breath[ing] between the heavens and the earth" is the life more of an animal than of a man.

Publics in early modernity could augment and refashion the public sphere because they were able to introduce increasing numbers of "private" persons into public space, speech, and action by inviting them to take part in forms of association that were both public and not public—public in the sense of being open to strangers and oriented, if fitfully, toward political matters; and not public because of the nonpurposiveness of their political dimension and because of their distance from what counted as real public speech and action in early modern society—real public speech and action having to take place within a sphere defined largely by the social elite. Early modern publics were thus easier of access than was the public sphere itself. But publics were not merely gathering places for those excluded from public life on a grand scale. Importantly, publics contested the exclusionary nature of early modern publicity itself. They were able to do this because publics then as now retain an aspiration toward growth and public action (if they did not aspire to broader public relevance and membership, they would of course resemble private clubs). Publics, we might say, have the capacity to pass in and out of the state of publicity; it is precisely this shiftiness or hybridity vis-à-vis the realms of the private and public that allows publics to reshape the public sphere. Publics in early modern Europe enhanced the meaning and experience of private life and contributed to a formative change in the relationship between the private and the public by binding them together in a new complex interrelationship. Insofar as publics and public making were necessarily innovative in terms of language, practice, identity, and social imagining and transgressive of long-standing boundaries of rank, gender, personhood, and access to public life on a grand scale, they were the principal drivers of structural and ideological change in the early modern public sphere.

EARLY MODERN PUBLICS (AND THE PRIVATE) IN HISTORY

Straddling the divide between antiquity and the modern age, early modern public making was harnessed to the traditions, authorities, and forms of behavior of the past as it also initiated some of the lineaments to which future forms and expressions of public life were to become tethered. Equally important is the historical distinctiveness of early modern publics: how they stood apart from but also impinged upon entrenched and emerging institutions and practices, thereby putting pressure on or reorganizing what constituted earlier conditions and arrangements of private and public. The pivotal changes that define the period—the Reformation and responses to it, the discovery of worlds previously unknown to Europeans, and formation of the modern nation-state—are important factors of the historical picture. These do not emerge as the principal causes of early modern public making, however; nor for that matter do the intentions or actions of the familiar protagonists whose lives dominate early modern histories (although those individuals and their works are not excluded from the processes we are describing). Instead, the evidence for public making is more likely to be found in and given impetus by the agency of made things.

Those things, importantly, are never originary or original. A sonnet, a performance of *Hamlet,* or a treatise on globes or physiognomy, might have readers or an audience, but single works reveal little about publics precisely because publics are discursive: their makeup is always in flux, and they become visible over time, their constituencies and concerns evolving historically and meandering geographically. The same holds for artifacts, texts, and forms of knowledge that require us to attend to their mobility from place to place, and to their translation into new forms and diverse media. Evidence may be fragmentary, sometimes appearing through the part of a work that breaks off, such as a line from *Hamlet* that is copied into a commonplace book. But that fragment contributes to a picture of a public fostered by a play whose relevance extends beyond the script or the performance. *Hamlet,* not Shakespeare, has become something that matters.[13] Central to early modern public making, then, is the reorientation of relations to objects and to others through this discursive process: through the rhetoric of texts, forms of address, translations, the possibilities of media, and the evolving historical significance of phenomena such as melancholy, physiognomy, letters, algebra, globes, or motets. The causes of historical change thereby emerge in the possibilities of representation, whether intended, structural, or latent, to foster interests and investments, to prompt debate and communication, and to gather people together.

The distinctiveness of early modern public making emerges with greater clarity when brought into comparison with earlier historical arrangements of the public and the private. Thus the following offers some perspectives on social configurations in the ancient Greek world, and more briefly in the Roman and medieval contexts, in order to cast a different light on theoretical issues described above. Given the extensive historical literature and depth of scholarly debates, not to mention constraints of space and expertise, any account of the history of what constitutes the public, or publics, will be limited and open to debate. Nevertheless it is hoped that some account of earlier formations, historiographical for the most part, helps to bring forward the mechanisms that resonate with or stand apart from early modern publics; that is, why discussion, appearances, permanence, associations, culture, and representation matter. Arendt is therefore a key interlocutor, partly because her account of the public and private realms has been particularly influential, but also because she elucidates the stakes of public life, stakes that are bound up with speech and with things that are made.

That public life opens up possibilities for political action as well as the potential for repressing this, through, say, acting in the name of the public, is a prevailing theme in the writing of many scholars already cited, including Arendt and Habermas, for whom political conditions demanded a response. *The Structural Transformation of the Public Sphere* became extraordinarily influential following its translation into English in 1989, but its initial publication in 1962 was prompted by the conditions of postwar Germany, what Habermas describes in the book as the disintegration of the character of public debate and publicity, and later, in *Technik und Wissenschaft als "Ideologie,"* as the "scientization of politics."[14] That context fueled his engagement with the emergence and normalization of a bourgeois public sphere, an ideal of liberty fostered through rational communication, and the subordination of private interests in favor of consensus building. Habermas was influenced by Arendt, of course, whose book, *The Human Condition,* published in 1958, was also a response to the war, but in her case it was the atrocities of the Holocaust that led her to counter the social realm of modernity and the nation-state with the public realm of the Greek polis. Her pessimistic and critical view of the social realm that swells following the epistemological break with Cartesian skepticism is contrasted with the public realm, an ideal for politics (the word derives from the enfranchisement of belonging to a polis) in which freedom, communication, virtue, and permanence are fostered.[15] "To be political," she writes, that is "to live in a *polis,* meant that everything was decided through words and persuasion and not through force and violence."[16]

Against the polis, Arendt pits the private realm of the *oikos* (house-hold, house, or family), which she describes as a place of deprivation and necessity where humans are the same as animals. This is the place of the social, where women are relegated, and where violence against slaves demonstrates "the despotic, and subhuman sphere in which freedom does not exist," to use Judith Swanson's words.[17] The private realm is "the darkness of sheltered existence," according to Arendt, which existed only "for the sake of the 'good life' in the *polis*."[18] Habermas echoes this language and emphasis on the foundational role of the private realm in his contrast between the "freedom and permanence" that characterized public life and the "necessity and transitoriness [that] remained immersed in the obscurity of the private sphere."[19] Ownership of the household, the family, and slave labor were essential for status, but status accrued to individuals in the public realm. The household, where desire and human needs were "shamefully hidden," was set apart from politics where self-interpretation and virtues were rendered visible "in the light of the public sphere."[20] Individuals defined themselves and were judged in public, particularly through speech, practices, and common action. Thus the household was the other as well as the ground of the public realm, and the latter a space of appearances in which people communicated, acted, and made things that endured and thereby confirmed reality.

There have of course been challenges to Arendt's emphasis on the separation of the public and private realms, and those terms of reference. For Swanson, who questions the extent of Aristotle's contempt for the private sphere, the use of the terms public and private is partly a projection of a modern liberal understanding of the terms. This kind of antagonistic relation between two bounded spheres is fostered by defensive imagery, such as fences and shields, which are deployed respectively by Thomas Hobbes and John Locke. Instead Swanson highlights the reciprocity between the two realms. The term *idios,* for example, is often interpreted as "private" or "one's own," whereas Aristotle, she proposes, usually means "what is not common, public, or relative to the public."[21] The private for Aristotle is defined by the "activities that ordinarily go on within it," such as economic ones but also activities that cultivate virtues in a place that is "uncompromised by prevailing morality" and the potential corruption of common opinion.[22] The private is the place in which friendship and philosophy are fostered, both of which "can transform common opinion," and thus serve the public.[23]

Nicholas Jones identifies associations as a mechanism through which the public and private permeated each other, noting that the terms, like voluntary and involuntary, are modern and not fully translatable to ancient Greece.[24] Athenian society was characterized by diverse groups and associations (what Aristotle called *koinoniai*) comprised of a range of professions and practices, from soldiers and sailors, to business partnerships and travelers, to burial societies, pirates, and traders.[25] Their constituencies and functions fluctuated: some were public, with all citizens belonging; some were quasi-public, such as schools, clubs, and associations; and some were private. Some had voluntary participation and others not; some endured, while others were short-lived. The function of some were expressive and others instrumental; and some included foreigners, and others women. Moreover some public associations engaged in private business and vice versa. Reciprocity between these associations and institutions was a central feature of Greek public life, playing an intermediate role by responding to the government (an idea anticipated by Aristotle's theory but not known to him), and thereby fostering stability and the evolving nature of the state.[26] Thus, Jones proposes we understand "'public' and 'private' not as mutually exclusive 'either/or' alternatives but rather as opposing extremes on a continuum possessing infinite intermediate gradations."[27]

An intriguing point of comparison with early modern publics are *hetairia,* voluntary associations of men who gathered for political and sometimes subversive and also violent ends.[28] These could be aristocrats who, threatened by and antagonistic to egalitarian politics, claimed to have influence in private and public life. The symposium is one example: a club of elite men gathering for dinner, performances, and discourse that concluded with drunken revelry and a street procession. Bonding provided a means of manifesting their aristocratic solidarity.[29] Ideological in their orientation, these associations resonate with the competing, plural, unofficial, and politically oppositional publics seen in the early modern period. Impinging on public life, the private associations of the Greek hetairia prompt consideration of Habermas's insight about the orientation of the privatized individual toward publicity. This turning to publicity is central to the artifacts, ideas, and publics in early modern Europe where it is staged repeatedly, for example, in the orientation of the playhouse and the salon to the court and to the city (Chapters 5 and 3), or in the publication of private letters or sonnets (Chapters 4 and 11).

Fluctuating participation in Greek associations, their reciprocal involvement in public life and potentially moderating effects, and the productive and disruptive ways in which they came into contact with private life, can also be compared with early modern publics. The sixteenth-century salon at Poitiers, for example, consisted of the bourgeois women who hosted the gatherings along with poets, lawyers, as well as visitors sometimes from the court. The private space, its semipublic readings, and the subsequent publication of those works for readers in Paris and elsewhere operated independently of the court, but also in response to it (Chapter 3). The example of the salon elucidates an important difference: in contrast to Greek associations that were organized by categories, such as occupation, cultic affiliation, or social status, the constituencies of early modern publics were inherently fluctuating and heterogeneous, their constituencies separated in place and time. To think of this in a different way: in contrast to Athenian society, the public realm (or for that matter public spaces) in early modern Europe was not prior to or enabling of publics, which came into being instead in the interstices of institutions that claimed to represent the commonweal, in the academies and salons that operated on the fringes of the court or city (Chapters 3 and 10), for instance, or in the house churches where Catholics gathered for Mass in Calvinist Amsterdam (Chapter 1). Spaces were *made* public by the actions and practices carried out there. This also pertains to some of the artifacts discussed in this volume, such as the compilation of texts brought together by Richard Hakluyt for his *Principal Navigations,* or the engravings of artwork collected by the Holmes (Chapters 9 and 7). Each collection is compiled by individuals from a range of sources, thereby bringing together a plurality of perspectives and condensing what is at stake (colonialism in one case and pictorial style in the other) for the unified purpose of collective persuasion. Exemplary of a new kind of object, which is itself a kind of public space (what goes into the work is different from what comes out), these compendia have an address that is both unifying and multiple.

It is worth observing here that one of the features of a democracy like Athens was its proclivity to publish acts in manuscripts or inscriptions for its citizens.[30] Literature was another manifestation of the "freedom to express oneself politically," as Jones notes.[31] While there are some parallels between "democracy" and political expression in early modern political theory, the cause-and-effect relation is sometimes inverted. For instance it was constraints on religion imposed by the French state in the early sixteenth century, fueled in part by the Affair of the Placards, that led, perhaps ironically, to the translation and circulation of seditious religious pamphlets in England (Chapter 2). Instead of the public sphere operating on its own accord, it was the agency of print that enabled new uses and forms of expression and public making. Print is a factor, on some level, in almost all the chapters in this volume, and one that paves the way for the literary and critical character of the eighteenth century.

This brings us back to Arendt's emphasis on the public realm as a space in which one is seen and heard by others who are unequal and anonymous, a plurality in which everyone has a different perspective.[32] The public realm for her constitutes our reality through the multiple viewpoints that it brings to the "thing character" of the world. People make things that give the world its objective character and that condition their makers. Note that acts and laws are also made things that bind individuals together through their enduring character.[33] Permanence is thus central to Arendt's concept of the public realm, the notion that there are things that "stand against" and stabilize human life. A table, for example, organizes the ways in which the people seated around it hear and see each other, but for that arrangement to constitute a public, the table must endure. Like the table, which "relates and separates men at the same time," the public realm "gathers us together."[34] The members of a public are always in flux, then, but the space in which they appear for Arendt is determined by the permanent status of the made thing, a permanence that is bound up with the public's interest in its memory created by the desire to transcend its own mortality.

Fundamentally different, then, is the picture developed in this volume, for it is often precisely the gap between the enduring and the ephemeral that comes forward, the transformation of one kind of object or idea into another that distinguishes the agency of early modern objects to assemble people. Consider for example how the projection of the world is translated into a printed map with gores (triangular points) from which to make globes that will appear in visual imagery and in treatises, both of which are dispersed and yet bound to the objects that generated them (Chapter 8). The globe has become an object that matters, but it is the globe as a concept that brings people together, a process of public making fueled by intermediality (the interconnectedness of media) and the migration from one form into another, and from one place into another. Another example is the translation of algebra into legal formulations of personhood (Chapter 12). Or consider again the new continental style for painting that circulates in engravings in London that are collected by the Holmes for use in Chester; the prints offer examples of a new style for painted portraits in a provincial context where portraiture was used to forge and give collective expression to local public officials (Chapter 7). The places of early modern public making also differ in important ways from ancient examples; in contrast to spaces such as the agora (marketplace) or court, early modern spaces emerge as substitutes (the huiskerk) or contact zones (the salon in the bourgeois home in Poitiers). Note however that both examples maintain some relation to the Greek sense in which the public sphere was constituted by acts or speech.[35]

The investment in permanence and the objective world of things in the Greek world reemerges in Roman sources. When Cicero was writing at the end of the republic, citizenship was granted to people living far from the political center with Rome thereby resembling a nation-state in its unusually expansive political system.[36] Nevertheless Roman political ideas had relatively little impact on later periods since there was no central text.[37] If Roman political thinking can be characterized by its "striking unoriginality," Dean Hammer finds its relevance in how it is taken up by modern scholars, including Arendt, through its attentiveness to the world and to "world-building."[38] In contrast to the utopic republics of Plato and Aristotle, Roman authors convey an interest in *terra ricognita*, "to know again, to recognize the world that we inhabit."[39] Instead of ideals, it is the tangibility of the world that stands out—the objectivity that characterizes the construction of architectural monuments and the embodied experience of rituals and festivals. Like the visibility of the public realm in the Greek world, the light of the objective world imbues these artifacts with an "illuminating quality," according to Hammer, "an image used by both Arendt and Cicero" that attests to an enduring presence of the past.[40]

These are ideas brought forward in the *Tusculan Disputations,* composed around 45 BCE, where Cicero responds to the change from republic to monarchy by exploring the loss of bearings. Already this was a concern in his *De re publica (On the Commonwealth)*, written in the years following the renewal of the triumvirate in 56 BCE where he describes the failure of the political system of the republic as well as "the loss of traditions by which individuals orient themselves in the world."[41] Looking back at the real and the stable, Hammer continues, referring to Livy, "human artifacts that surround us provide a foundation . . . by which we relate not just to those things, but also to each other."[42] Like Arendt's table, the artifacts fabricated by humans endure and condition each other in the public realm.

In Cicero Arendt finds a way to counter the philosopher's departure from the world for the contemplative life (she is thinking of Plato), by returning philosophy to the world through the cultivation of culture. The latter springs from *colere,* a Roman word meaning "to cultivate, to dwell, to take care, to tend and preserve."[43] For Hammer, "this suggests a disposition of care for the things of the world that humans have made: momentous buildings, works of art, political institutions, and laws."[44] Arguing against the conflict between art and politics, Arendt writes that made things "share with political 'products,' words and deeds, the quality that they are in need of some public space where they can appear and be seen."[45] What mediates this conflict, she adds, "is the *cultura animi,*" the cultivated mind and the freedom of the humanist whose judgment lies "beyond the coercion" imposed by the disciplines of the scientist, the philosopher, the artist.[46] Arendt's use of Cicero to appeal to the responsibility of philosophy and humanism to foster the relation between the acts of politics and making things stands against private ownership of the latter. Note how the private remains the precondition for the public realm, which endures because of the permanence of things found in sensorial and embodied experience, characteristics as already suggested that differ from the discursive, intermedial, and virtual nature of early modern publics and their relations to made things.

In ancient Rome, the normative power of the Greek ideal was maintained in the concept of *res publica.* Meaning "public issue" or "public matter," and also "the common wealth," this usage reappears in early modern Europe.[47] In medieval Europe, however, when public life was subordinated to the individual rights that characterize the feudal system, the Roman distinction between private and public was familiar, but not used with any consistency. The "common good" was no longer a political ideal, and instead an exclusive sphere associated with the common interests of private individuals. And the private realm of the Greek world was transformed into the secular realm. Domestic authority in the manor was not the same as private authority in the Greek world; nor did feudal organizations operate in conjunction with public authority or liberty. Indeed the "hallmark" of feudalism, according to Arendt, "was the absorption of all activities into the household sphere, where they had only private significance, and consequently the very absence of a public realm."[48]

Impetus for another transformation in relations between public and private can be found in the later Middle Ages when the theoretical ideals of Plato and Aristotle were subordinated to legal concepts that were useful for the practice of politics.[49] Even after the recovery of Aristotle's *Politics* in the late thirteenth century, it was Roman law—the will of the people during the Roman Empire—that served as a precedent for new representative assemblies and for emerging ideas of the state, an entity that claimed rights to maintain public welfare.[50] It is not easy "to distinguish between the public and private," as Gaines Post observed some time ago, given the variety of terms being used in the twelfth and thirteenth centuries: "public," "common utility," "reason of the *status*," "public welfare."[51] These terms were developed into "the early modern theory of public law and the State" that was deployed by rulers and popes "to justify their claim to an authority that represented the public and common welfare."[52]

That authority can be understood as "a kind of status attribute," according to Habermas, like the ducal seal, which was one of the attributes described as "public": "Lordship was something publicly represented. This *publicness* (or *publicity*) *of representation* was not constituted as a social realm, that is, as a public sphere ... representation pretended to make something invisible visible through the public presence of the person of the lord."[53] Publicity was making visible, but it was harnessed to the lord himself, investing him with authority and represented to the people. Habermas underlines the "staging of the publicity involved in representation" through objects (badges, seals, clothes) and modes of behavior (gestures, rhetoric).[54] This code of conduct is crucial to the history of public life since it is where virtue lies. Aristotle's virtues, once fostered in the private sphere, as noted earlier, were transmuted into forms of expression such as chivalry and courtesy during the Middle Ages.

In the early modern period, the maintenance of existing institutions through the use of representative publicity comes under pressure sometimes from the appropriation of those very codes of behavior. This is precisely what is staged in the playhouse, where the diversity of roles—status, occupation, gender—played by the performers commingles with an audience with its own plurality of perspectives (Chapter 5). Or consider how anticlerical rhetoric deployed in placards in France and printed pamphlets in England fostered public participation that undermined the public authority claimed by the church and state, compelling them to muster counter-arguments (Chapter 2). Representative publicity is also interrogated through new spaces for gatherings in which the mixture of individuals blurs the boundaries between the private and public, exemplified again in the salon and the huiskerk, or through the theorizing of forms of behavior, such as melancholy and dissimulation, that challenge the transparency of appearances and forge interiority as a form of self-defense against increasing public visibility in the court and city (Chapters 10 and 11).

Roman law also contributed to the dissolution of the power of the church and to the emergence of city-states. The terms public and private were drawn from Roman law to organize the universities, guilds, corporations, towns, and communes that accompanied growing urbanization.[55] Increasing trade was one development that provided grounds for exploration, colonialism, and the commercial economy that ensued in the early modern period. This transformed modes of production into a capitalist system in which state authorities were increasingly facilitating private individuals—what Habermas calls "the privatization of the process of economic reproduction."[56] He continues:

> The economic activity that had become private had to be oriented toward a commodity market that had expanded under public direction and supervision; the economic conditions under which this activity now took place lay outside the confines of the single household; for the first time they were of general interest.[57]

This account evokes Arendt's view of the modern age in which the private and public have been subsumed into the social realm, and where the public (the political realm) and the private interpenetrate.[58] Humans are no longer judged by their speech and actions but by their labors, which are quickly consumed and produce nothing that lasts. The rise of private interests becomes the only thing people have in common.[59]

The reorientation of economic interests and labor were changes, like the Reformation and colonialism, that cut deep and wide in the period. Those experiences were not modern, however, according to Arendt, but rooted in tradition since the pathos of novelty was absent.[60] More important for understanding the radical break is Galileo's demonstration of the heliocentric system with the telescope. Not only is this event a cause of change; it is symbolic of the rupture itself. For Galileo confirmed what his predecessors had already imagined: the telescope verified the fact that the earth moves around the sun by making it visible to the human eye and thus understood "with the certainty of sense perceptions."[61] The event's significance lies not in the novelty of the instrument (something available only to hindsight), nor in the ideas of the astronomer, nor in the conventionality of the scientific demonstration. It was antique knowledge that Galileo adopted, the Archimedean viewpoint that enabled him to stand "outside of nature itself" looking back at the earth.[62] The telescope (a material object, a made thing), and Galileo's demonstration (his action, done in front of others), is symbolic of the change to the Modern Age because it embodies the very process of reorientation that it both describes (Archimedes' transcendental point of view) and causes: the splitting of objects from subjects that initiates our alienation from the world. The durability and tangibility of things fabricated in the Greek and Roman worlds—what gave those worlds their objective character and defined their reality[63]—has been inverted by objectifying things, by turning them into products of labor, or objects of knowledge. For Arendt, the telescope thematizes the turn toward the social realm of modernity when reality was no longer confirmed by the multiple perspectives that make up the public realm.

However as we have already suggested, the chapters in this volume often challenge or complicate this view (while recognizing the historical conditions that fueled it), by attending, as Arendt does, to the reorientation of individuals to others through made things, spaces, artifacts, and forms of knowledge that give voice to or address multiple perspectives. This recalls an important characteristic shared by the public realm in antiquity and early modern public making: that actions, people, and things are made visible. More striking in the early modern period, however, is the dynamic relation between public visibility and privacy, with the former contributing to the fracturing of social coherence (as this also opened up access to forms of public life for groups previously excluded). Precisely because individuals were increasingly defined by doing things in front of others, long-standing claims to knowledge about the body, such as melancholy, physiognomy, and interiority, were increasingly redefined in terms that call attention to the divide between public appearances and private personhood, terms such as deception, concealment, blackness, and trust (Chapters 10–12). Recall also the house church where the Catholic Mass is hidden from view, but knowledge of it circulates in public as an open secret (Chapter 1).

Mobility, we note again, is a theme that runs throughout the essays. Public making is not simply a result of the dissemination of *Hamlet*, engravings, globes, or melancholy; it is their movement and translation into different media and into diverse places that make them visible and that create multiple perspectives. Another example is the composing of motets in early sixteenth-century Venice (Chapter 6). Initially manuscript, motets were published in a new format and circulated, the music appearing later in Germany where it had been copied from print back into manuscript. The motet, like the globe, the portrait, or *Hamlet,* had become a thing instead of an object; no longer rooted to one place, the motet had become meta-topical, actively taken up in different places, the public it generated coming into visibility across time and space. This process invites us to think of publics as spaces of agency with fluctuating intensities.

Arendt's poignant account of the telescope reasserts the crucial relation between the material world and public life as it also brings us back to the divide between antiquity and modernity that the early modern period straddles. For it is this historical position that activated early modern public making: the shuttle between traditional authorities and forms of knowledge and new uses for them. Literary and artistic producers and consumers initially developed their public, associative identity on the authority of their experiences within well-established, and typically hierarchical, relationships (patron-client relations, guilds, family, courts). The expression of that authority and knowledge—from styles for portraiture to religious tracts—within a context that consisted of strangers and often crossed geographical boundaries, fueled discussion and debate about terms of reference and rules for action. Early modern publics and the things around which they came together opened up possibilities for exploring tensions wrought by religious conflict or between diverse status groups in the playhouse, or negotiating between urban life in London and provincial towns, or between interiority and worldliness. In doing so, early modern public making brings forward the power of the material world to orient the social life of individuals, thereby disclosing possibilities for politics.

NOTES

1. Raymond Williams, *Keywords: A Vocabulary of Culture and Society* (1976; expanded ed., London: Fontana, 1983), 87–88.
2. Emphasis in the original; Bruno Latour, *Reassembling the Social: An Introduction to Actor-Network-Theory* (Oxford: Oxford University Press, 2005), 64–65.
3. Hannah Arendt, *The Human Condition* (Chicago: University of Chicago Press, 1998).
4. Emphasis in the original; Michael Warner, *Publics and Counterpublics* (New York: Zone Books, 2002), 65.
5. Jürgen Habermas, *The Structural Transformation of the Public Sphere: An Inquiry into a Category of Bourgeois Society*, trans. Thomas Burger (Cambridge, MA: MIT Press, 1991), 51.
6. Charles Taylor, *A Secular Age* (Cambridge, MA: Harvard University Press, 2007), 186.
7. Craig Calhoun, "Imagining Solidarity: Cosmopolitanism, Constitutional Patriotism, and the Public Sphere," *Public Culture* 14, no. 1 (2002): 162.
8. Nancy Fraser, "Rethinking the Public Sphere: A Contribution to the Critique of Actually Existing Democracy," in *Habermas and the Public Sphere*, ed. Craig Calhoun (Cambridge, MA: MIT Press, 1992), 109–42, esp. 112–18.
9. Warner, *Publics*, 51.
10. Habermas, *Public Sphere*, 27.
11. Ibid., 50.
12. *Antony and Cleopatra*, 3.12.14–15, in *The Riverside Shakespeare*, textual ed. G. Blakemore Evans, 2nd ed. (Boston: Houghton Mifflin, 1997).
13. Bruno Latour, "Why Has Critique Run Out of Steam? From Matters of Fact to Matters of Concern," *Critical Inquiry* 30, no. 2 (2004), 225–48.
14. Habermas, *Public Sphere*, see esp. 247–50; Jürgen Habermas, *Technik und Wissenschaft als "Ideologie"* (Frankfurt am Main: Suhrkamp, 1968). Reference in Ken Hirschkop, "Justice and Drama: On Bakhtin as a Complement to Habermas," in *After Habermas: New Perspectives on the Public Sphere*, ed. Nick Crossley, Jürgen Habermas, and John Michael Roberts (Malden, MA: Wiley-Blackwell, 2004), 49.
15. Nicholas F. Jones, *The Associations of Classical Athens: The Response to Democracy* (New York: Oxford University Press, 1999), 288.

16. Arendt, *The Human Condition*, 26.
17. Judith Swanson, *The Public and the Private in Aristotle's Political Philosophy* (Ithaca, NY: Cornell University Press, 1992), 9; in reference to Arendt, *The Human Condition*, 24–38, 45–46, 71–84. On Aristotle's view of women as intellectually inferior and thus unable to participate in politics, Swanson proposes that their role in the household "helps to bring about harmony between the public and the private" (45).
18. Arendt, *The Human Condition*, 37.
19. Habermas, *Public Sphere*, 3.
20. Ibid., 3–4.
21. Swanson, *Public and the Private*, 2.
22. Ibid. Public debate in Aristotle, according to Swanson, seeks "the protection and provision of the private" partly to foster virtue (186). Moreover humans are "not simply political animals, . . . (in the sense of inclined toward others), but, insofar as they have a divine element in them, also intensely private beings" (206).
23. Ibid., 3. On friendship, see 180–83, where she states that "Aristotle believes that the standards for public interpersonal conduct should be lower than those for private interpersonal" (180).
24. Jones, *Associations*, 33.
25. See Ibid., 2–4. This is not in Aristotle's model, Jones posits, because his isolation from government precluded any understanding of the relation between its institutions and the associations, although his political theory anticipated it in the *koinoniai*, which he described loosely as communities (30).
26. Ibid., 6–7, 18–21.
27. Ibid., 31.
28. Ibid. Jones adds that "the *heratiari*, or voluntary associations, although initially the preserve of men, extended to 'outsiders,' notably women and foreigners" (4).
29. Ibid., 85–87.
30. Nicholas F. Jones, *Politics and Society in Ancient Greece* (Westport, CT: Praeger, 2008), 2, 7, 14–15.
31. Ibid., 7.
32. Arendt, *The Human Condition*, 57.
33. Calhoun, "Imagining Solidarity," 170.
34. Arendt, *The Human Condition*, 52, 55.
35. Habermas, *Public Sphere*, 3.
36. Fergus Millar, *The Roman Republic in Political Thought* (Hanover, NH: Brandeis University Press, 2002), 3.
37. Ibid., 5.
38. Dean Hammer, *Roman Political Thought and the Modern Theoretical Imagination* (Norman: University of Oklahoma Press, 2008), 4.
39. Ibid., 6.
40. Ibid., 8–9.
41. Ibid., 38.
42. Ibid., 7.
43. Hannah Arendt, *Between Past and Future* (Harmondsworth: Penguin, 1968), 211; cited in Hammer, *Roman Political Thought*, 54.
44. Hammer, *Roman Political Thought*, 42; For Arendt's discussion on this see, *Between Past and Future*, 224–26.
45. Arendt, *Between Past and Future*, 218.
46. Ibid., 218, 225–26.
47. Habermas, *Public Sphere*, 4.
48. Arendt, *The Human Condition*, 34–35.

49. Gaines Post, *Studies in Medieval Legal Thought: Public Law and the State, 1100–1322* (Princeton, NJ: Princeton University Press, 1964), vii.
50. Ibid., 11–12, 7–8; Also Habermas, *Public Sphere*, 4.
51. Post, *Medieval Legal Thought*, 7.
52. Ibid., 8–9. Later Post expands on this: "Although normally *status* meant the condition or standing of individuals, classes, or regions, in connection with the public law it meant the common welfare and public utility of the whole community of the kingdom. . . . And the terms would be called, in seventeenth-century England, the commonweal, the Commonwealth, or the State of the Commonwealth." Post, *Medieval Legal Thought*, 222–23.
53. Emphasis in the original; Habermas, *Public Sphere*, 7. Medieval documents attest to the correspondence between "lordly" and *publicus* and "publicare meant to claim for the lord" (6).
54. Ibid., 7–8.
55. Post, *Medieval Legal Thought*, 564.
56. Habermas, *Public Sphere*, 19.
57. Ibid.
58. Arendt, *The Human Condition*, 33.
59. Ibid., 22, 46.
60. Ibid., 248–49.
61. Ibid., 259. Isabelle Stengers offers an alternative account of Galileo in whom she finds a model for what she calls the "cosmopolitical proposal." Instead of the facts of his experiments, Galileo exemplifies the linkages, networks, and the questioning of authority that she ascribes to open-ended participatory assemblages. Isabelle Stengers, "The Cosmopolitical Proposal," in *Making Things Public: Atmospheres of Democracy*, ed. Bruno Latour and Peter Weibel (Cambridge, MA: MIT Press, 2005).
62. Arendt, *The Human Condition*, 265.
63. Ibid., 137.

Part I

People

1 Religion Inside Out
Dutch House Churches and the Making of Publics in the Dutch Republic

Steven Mullaney, Angela Vanhaelen, and Joseph Ward

When visiting Amsterdam in 1663, Balthasar de Monconys, counselor to the king of France, attended a Roman Catholic Mass. As De Monconys describes it, the religious service took place "in a middle-class home, where one entered and exited only two at a time."[1] This brief and cryptic comment is intriguing: Celebration of the Mass had been outlawed in the northern Netherlands since 1581, yet De Monconys, a stranger in the Calvinist city, seemed to have had no trouble discovering a place where he could observe the forbidden practices of his faith. Like many Roman Catholic visitors, he found a Dutch *huiskerk,* or house church. Open to local and foreign Catholics, yet shrouded with at least the semblance of secrecy, these private spaces allowed the maintenance of banned religious practices and identities. Sir William Temple, British ambassador to the Netherlands and keen observer of its social customs, described this particular form of Dutch religious tolerance in this way: "Every man enjoys the free exercise [of religion] in his own Chamber, or his own House, unquestioned and unespied."[2] According to both De Monconys and Temple, then, within the Calvinist Dutch Republic, diverse religious groups could actively practice their faith in a manner that was both clandestine *and* licensed.

Analysis of the interlinked tensions between openness and secrecy and orthodoxy and dissent is one of the threads that run through this essay, which seeks to address larger questions: how does the peculiar social formation of the house church contribute to early modern definitions of a public? Could worshipers attending Mass in a huiskerk constitute a public? In working through these issues, we encountered a series of oppositions, and the essay explores the complex relations between tolerance and divisiveness, between actual and virtual publics, and between the private and public spheres. How did small local gatherings of the faithful conceive of themselves in connection or in counterdistinction to a larger virtual public? And what were the links between private space, private identity, and the making of a public? As we thought through these interrelated questions, we discovered that the case of the Dutch house church offers more insights into the potential ways that a public emerges, coalesces, interacts, and grows or fades away, than the familiar, classic, Habermasian version of an Enlightenment "bourgeois" public sphere. Our immediate focus is religion, our larger enterprise, the making of early modern publics and other forms of public sociability. The case of the house church demonstrates how the particular forms of public assembly that emerged in the post-Reformation period sometimes produced mutations in private as well as public spaces, even hybrid articulations of private and public as a single, paradoxical entity, and suggests that early modern publics owed some of their character and vitality to such mutations or hybridities.

THE HUISKERK

As Temple noted, the Dutch guaranteed freedom of conscience to each individual, as long as that freedom was exercised in private. Citizens were not required to attend services at the official Calvinist church, but no other public churches were allowed in Dutch towns and cities—that is to say, no other openly identified and outwardly identifiable places of worship, no buildings adorned with crosses or signs or any other architectural markers of faith, were allowed. The private household chapels that emerged in the late sixteenth century were originally known as huiskerken or house churches. Modern scholars often refer to them as *schuilkerken,* hidden churches, but the term is an anachronistic one, dating from the Catholic emancipation movement of the nineteenth century. Its suggestion of a hidden or clandestine activity is in many ways misleading,[3] especially if it encourages an oversimplification of a phenomenon that looks to be a complex permutation within, and between, the private and public realms of early modern Europe. In densely populated urban neighborhoods, most residents knew of the existence of a house church, even if those who attended did so discreetly, entering and exiting only two at a time. Indeed, huiskerken were such "open secrets" that Calvinist magistrates sometimes played a role in the selection of a new priest.[4] Hidden in plain sight, these were not the clandestine or illicit spaces that the anachronistic, nineteenth-century term schuilkerken would suggest. Their full ambiguity as religious spaces and sociological entities is well captured, in fact, by the term the period used for them: they were house churches, home-chapels, a new conundrum in the social *habitus* involving a significant expansion of the private or domestic realm to include activities formerly understood as public, in the sense of open, manifest, officially promulgated, or out in the public eye.

As legal preserves for the exercise of a free religious conscience, huiskerken were originally intended to serve individual families and not larger groups. Thus they were exactly what their name suggests: rooms (or spaces within rooms) in the family home where those who lived in the house could worship in private. If equipped with an altar, family income and the overall size of the domicile would determine whether the altar was portable or fixed, the room fully devoted to the celebration of the Mass or designed to allow for multiple uses. A huiskerk as such would be strictly a family affair, a private, domestic space in which a single houschold could practice a form of worship no longer allowed in public. In many cities, however, huiskerken evolved into much larger places of communal worship, located not in the family residence but in other kinds of buildings designated for the purpose,[5] where multiple families, indeed an entire congregation or parish, could meet for Mass and share in the communal experience of faith.

On the outside, such huiskerken were anonymous structures, undistinguished from the residences or warehouses alongside them, whose everyday facades they adopted as their own. Inside, however, they could be large and lavishly appointed spaces, graced with all the rich Baroque adornment—from altar to rosewood tabernacle, separate side pews for prominent parishioners, carved panels and oil paintings—that one would expect in a Catholic church of the period. In some cases, the walls were hung with paintings specially commissioned for the purpose, depicting scenes from biblical history or the lives of local saints, which were of pointed significance to a shuttered Catholicism, denied any overt or public recognition of their long history in the Netherlands.[6] In such artwork, collective memory combined with worship in the space of the huiskerk, embodying a new, quasi-clandestine and quasi-licensed sense of community and identity. And the community involved could be quite substantial. Some huiskerken, such as "the Hart" in Amsterdam, seated over 150 people. This is quite possibly the church attended by De Monconys. By 1700, there were about twenty Roman Catholic house churches in Amsterdam alone, eleven in Utrecht, and seven in Haarlem.[7]

It was not just the Roman Catholics who established these quasi-hidden churches; almost every non-Calvinist religious group in the Republic relied on some form of house church for the continuance of their specific religious practices.[8] Moreover, as Benjamin Kaplan has recently pointed out, the Dutch house church had thousands of counterparts throughout Europe, making it clear that such permutations in what is private and what is public—and what is significantly or ambiguously in-between—were key components in the practice of religious tolerance.[9] The development of private churches in the Netherlands thus suggests one way that the accommodation of religious dissent and difference could precipitate the emergence of new forms of public association and collective identity.

TOLERANCE AND DIVISIVENESS IN THE POST-REFORMATION PERIOD

The Reformation was divisive on many levels: it divided states; it divided communities; it divided selves. Diarmaid MacCulloch suggests that during the sixteenth century, Latin or Western Christendom, "previously unified by the pope's symbolic leadership and by possession of that common Latin culture, was torn apart by deep disagreements about how human beings should exercise the power of God in the world, arguments even about what it was to be human. It was a process of extreme mental and physical violence."[10] As a statement intended to set the stage for a grand narrative of the Reformation, MacCulloch's assertion seems apt. The sixteenth and seventeenth centuries were a time when "religious discourse was a, if not the, predominant means by which individuals defined and debated issues" in public.[11] Throughout Europe, the period of the Reformation and Counter-Reformation changed forever the ways in which private individuals negotiated their sense of collective identity. This was the period when European Christendom fractured along fault lines that divided one realm from another, one region from another, one town, one generation, one neighbor, and one family member from another. Emergent Protestantism(s) and retrenching Catholicism(s) redefined the virtual as well as the physical spaces in which religious faith could be practiced. New dimensions opened up within the social imaginary; new forms of public sociability developed, while older or traditional forms were eliminated or driven under cover or out of sight. New kinds of affiliation evolved on every level of the social, from the familial to the regional to the national. The period was one of intensely rooted contradictions that conditioned not only what was debated in public but also what and how people thought of themselves in relation to others, whether kin or neighbor or stranger, whether fellow members of "the" one true faith (in all its fragmented multiplicity) or followers of another Christianity, another equally exclusive, absolute, and monotheistic rival. Each country, each town or city or local community, indeed, each family and individual experienced its own kind and range of changes, but it is safe to say that no one alive at the time in Europe was untouched by such transformations of religious beliefs and practices.

The fragmentation of religion contributed to a public political discourse that was messy, volatile, fractious, and contentious.[12] It was a great deal more heterogeneous and multivocal and included a far wider range of social classes than the Habermasian model. "It is important to acknowledge the existence of *competing* publics," as Geoff Eley has suggested, "not just later in the nineteenth century, when Habermas sees a fragmentation of the classical liberal model of *Öffentlichkeit*, but at every stage in the history of the public sphere and, indeed, from the very beginning."[13] A public sphere is born from a productive disunity rather than a preexisting consensus; it emerges only when significant difference and disagreement exists among differing interests and groups, with diverse, partisan, and conflicting collective identities. "If people have the same views," notes Craig Calhoun, "no public sphere is needed."[14] A public sphere is the product of competing publics and hence, implicitly, of counterpublics, too. For the early modern period, it is especially important to keep in mind the fact that each of these publics and counterpublics had histories of their own and independent existences, whether or not they ever achieved, in conflict and concert with one another, the kind of synaptic density that can be called, according to one definition or the other, "a" or even "the" public sphere.

It is not unusual, among English historians at any rate, to emphasize the emergence of Protestantism, with its dismantling of priestly power, vernacular translation of scripture, and other assertions of lay authority, as a key factor in the development of new forms of public debate and identity. The place and practice of Catholicism in the Dutch Republic, however, offers an illuminating contrast. In its struggle for freedom from Roman Catholic Spain, the Republic declared itself a Protestant state. The Dutch Reformation was in part a political reformation; introduced by those in power, it did not seek the widespread support of the Dutch populace.[15] Calvinism was the official religion, which served to uphold and justify political power, yet it remained a minority religion: much of the population was Catholic and was allowed to remain so.[16]

In England, Catholic worship also was officially banned when a modified Calvinism became the law of the land. Catholicism was uprooted and effaced from the physical and ecclesiastical landscape in the decades before the Elizabethan compromise defined the Church of England as an official and established Protestant faith. Much of the infrastructure of Catholicism was eradicated over the thirty years that preceded Elizabeth's accession, from the dissolution of monasteries under Henry VIII to the many reforms under Edward VI, which included the elimination of chantries, the purgation of purgatory from reformed cosmology, and the adoption of regular (Protestant) religious instruction for all. The intent—to erase prominent aspects of Catholic faith and ecclesiastical authority from the land and its collective memory—was clear. Nonetheless, England also evolved a version of de facto religious tolerance. Although officially intolerant of rival Christianities, Elizabethan England set the bar for religious compliance quite low: as long as one attended an Anglican service once a month, the authorities would usually not inquire further into one's actual beliefs or private practices. It was a Reformation version of a "don't ask, don't tell" policy, an officially prescribed hypocrisy. As a well-understood but uncodified policy, it allowed communities to keep the peace and maintain the appearance of an ordered and unified orthodoxy while avoiding the need to police the private beliefs of its residents.

Such policies of tolerance lead us to rethink MacCulloch's emphasis on violence and discord, for as a description of how many Europeans experienced the events of the sixteenth and seventeenth centuries at the local level, this formulation leaves much to be desired. In particular, MacCulloch's insistence on the divisiveness of change overlooks the considerable body of research developed by scholars working across Europe that stresses the multiple ways that early modern people tolerated and accommodated difference. Often, in the context of the Reformation, the term tolerance is used to describe these kinds of relations between members of rival religious groupings. In addition to the English and Dutch examples, one could point to the kind of political relations that emerged in the Holy Roman Empire after the Peace of Augsburg or in France after the Edict of Nantes. Gregory Hanlon suggests that we consider tolerance to mean "a mutual interaction and integration of competing confessional groups into the fabric of daily social, political, and economic activity within a local community."[17] His research cautions scholars against assuming that violence was the normal form of interaction across confessional lines during the Reformation and indicates that complicities and compromises might have been the norm in many local contexts.[18]

Complicity and compromise—this describes well the situation that engendered Dutch house churches. Religious historian Joke Spaans attributes the absence of violent religious conflict in the Netherlands in part to the policies of secular authorities, who systematically de-emphasized boundaries between religious groups.[19] The ideal of religious peace was central to political stability and the formation of a unified and disciplined society, and such concerns probably played a role in the maintenance of Roman Catholic worship alongside the established Reformed church.[20] In fact, Catholics were not allowed to worship in public primarily because they were seen as a *politically* oppositional group. Especially during the war with Spain, authorities worked to render Roman Catholicism politically docile for fear that the sizable Catholic population might ally with the enemy.[21] Intolerance and insistence on confessional difference certainly did exist, but there also is much evidence to suggest the practical day-to-day functioning of interconfessional relationships.[22] This was not a society of rigid religious oppositions; in the everyday lives of the cities especially, there was much contact between different religious groups—for instance, in civic militias, guilds, *gebuurten* (neighborhood organizations), extended kinship, and even intimate family groups.[23]

People with diverse religious affiliations also encountered each other in church. Another form of licensed tolerance was the distinction made within the Reformed Church between *lidmaten,* full members, and *liefhebbers,* sympathizers who attended services but did not take communion and were not full members.[24] Although political office and civil service were in theory restricted to members of the Reformed church, in practice, full participation in civic life was open to a much wider group.[25] This category of liefhebber allowed the non-Reformed to belong to the established church and thus to hold political offices and participate in public life. The remarks of a seventeenth-century Calvinist about the identity of the liefhebber are illuminating: "It often appears that among the persons who call themselves *liefhebbers* lurk Catholics, Mennonites, Libertines and atheists."[26] This has important implications for our understanding of an early modern public. It implies that a Roman Catholic who celebrated Mass at a huiskerk also might regularly attend the Reformed church. As Harold Love suggests, when thinking about an early modern public, it is crucial to acknowledge the existence of a "considerable number of discrete publics and the fact that members of these publics were usually also members of other publics." This "means breaking down the notion of a public sphere into the lesser domains, agencies, and practices out of which it perpetually composed and recomposed itself."[27] The Dutch practices of tolerance thus allowed for an ideal of a civil society comprised of diverse persons and groups, including dissenting religious sects.

Huiskerken occupied a paradoxical place in Dutch society. While they were allowed in order to accommodate and therefore de-emphasize religious differences, these sites also sharpened awareness of the existence of distinct religious groups with identities that dissented from the imposed orthodoxy. If a distinct type of public emerged within the bounds of the huiskerk, it was a public that was never completely walled off from other kinds of publics. These were sites of contained difference rather than resistance. As such, they defined a group identity that was at once separate and integrated, oppositional and quasi-licensed, excluded and included in civic life. Hidden and in view, the house church was an open secret characterized by the facade of the private enclosing the rich splendor and extravagance of a newly conceived site of public assembly. The identity that such a congregation develops is different from the one that a Catholic congregation might develop in a chapel in Naples or Rome. Although the ritual of the Mass is too reproducible to constitute the discursive self-definition that a full-fledged public needs, the experience of the service under these conditions imposes a collective identity in addition to and collateral with the religious communion. As Michel de Certeau has argued, hidden churches were defined, not so much by doctrines or ideologies, but as "a practical way of resisting the surrounding milieu."[28] This contributes, or could contribute, to a bond with, and a strong if implicit inclusion of, those who are not present: the larger congregation of the faithful, whether persecuted or tolerated.

THE INTERACTIONS OF ACTUAL AND VIRTUAL PUBLICS

Were these spaces conducive to the formation of the entity, yet to be defined adequately, that we have referred to as a public, or a counterpublic? Normally such terms are not used for congregations of the faithful gathered together for the purpose of worship, especially when the religion involved is one with such a long and international history. Publics are not usually regarded as official entities, organized by either a state or an institutionalized religion; they are, in Craig Calhoun's terms, "self-organized fields of discourse in which participation is not based primarily on personal connections and is always in principle open to strangers."[29] Michael Warner places an even greater emphasis on a public as a self-organized relation among strangers, structured by what he calls a "stranger sociability" or "environment of strangerhood":

> The modern social imaginary does not make sense without strangers. A nation or public or market in which everyone could be known personally would be no nation or public or market at all. This constitutive and normative environment of strangerhood is more, too, than an objectively describable *gesellschaft;* it requires our constant imagining.[30]

Publics are focused gatherings, to borrow a concept from Erving Goffman, but unlike the face-to-face, actual encounters that Goffman studied, a public is a focused gathering that necessarily includes a virtual dimension, an audience of others—strangers who are no longer aliens or exotics but are, in a sense, versions of the self—who are included in its discursive address but are not present. Indeed, a public need not involve an actual, physical gathering but does need to involve a virtual, discursive gathering, and a public can be formed and operate entirely in and as this virtual space of discourse. Just as some gatherings can be too focused to qualify as a public—closed or secret societies, clubs, or other associations, for example, which are not open even in principle to strangers—some can be too unfocused, such as a crowd or a mob.

In the case of the Dutch huiskerken, a virtual public may have included strangers such as the French king's representative, De Monconys. It also encompassed other shuttered or repressed Catholics. The huiskerken should be considered in the broader context of Counter-Reformation efforts to minister to the oppressed faithful and reconvert Protestant lands such as the Dutch Republic. The priests who performed the Mass and offered sacraments and pastoral care to Roman Catholics inside private dwellings were part of the Holland Mission, a movement that attempted to harden confessional distinctions with the Republic and maintain strong connections with Roman Catholics across Europe.[31] Imagining a community that contrasted rather sharply with the everyday ecumenicity of the Dutch cities and the ways that Roman Catholics had adapted to the new political and religious reality, the aims of the Holland Mission were based on utopian hopes for the complete restoration of the Roman Catholic Church.[32] The Mission provided a virtual dimension, linking the huiskerken to a larger imagined community of beleaguered Catholics across Europe.

Publics are special kinds of focused gatherings, then, with a virtual as well as, or even in place of, an actual audience. They are, in this sense, imaginary communities, and as such, they exist "precisely because they are imagined; they are real because they are treated as real."[33] They are an integral part of what some would call the social imaginary, a concept derived from Cornelius Castoriadis and defined by Charles Taylor in terms that resonate with our customary understandings of a culture's social habitus: the social imaginary, Taylor suggests, "is that common understanding that makes possible common practices and a widely shared sense of legitimacy."[34] Publics are also not strictly rational or critical sociological entities; they are not strictly governed by explicit discursive networks, but are also performative and productive processes, "'world-making' in Hannah Arendt's sense."[35] Publics respond to changes in material, actual, face-to-face associations and gatherings, and the relationship between the material world and the quasi-virtual world of publics is also fully recursive. As Calhoun puts it, "New ways of imagining identity, interests, and solidarity make possible new material forms of social relations."[36] In this way, the small group who gathered in a room of a private dwelling expanded out to connect with a larger imagined community.

PRIVATE AND PUBLIC SPHERES

The defining activity of the house church is the communal, ritual experience of a shared faith that remains within the dictates of the Roman Catholic Church's larger sphere of public authority. Yet that experience takes place in a space that has oddly, weirdly, metamorphosed to resemble neither public nor private, interior nor exterior, but something different and new, at least, to the exercise of the Catholic faith in early modern Holland. We sometimes forget a paradox at the heart of the Habermasian public sphere, which is that it first develops not in the public realm at all but in the private, domestic realm. His virtual public realm enclosed within the actual private sphere of the family, situated as an alternative to and hence, in an inescapable sense, in opposition to the *res publica* of state and official church authorities. In Habermas's terms,

> The sphere of the public arose . . . as an expansion and at the same time completion of the intimate sphere of the conjugal family. Living room and *salon* were under the same roof; and just as the privacy of the one was oriented toward the public nature of the other, . . . the subjectivity of the privatized individual was related from the very start to publicity.[37]

In his excellent overview of huiskerken, Benjamin Kaplan has argued that they served primarily as a reinforcement of a boundary between the private and the public, an expansion of the private space for worship that reinforced and prolonged the "representative publicity" of the official, Calvinist church.[38] We would argue that huiskerken did indeed perform an expansion of the private but of a more paradoxical order—one that involves the creation of a new dimension within the private or domestic realm. If "house church" is a conundrum or portmanteau word, the sociological entity to which it refers is a conundrum or portmanteau creature as well. It is as if a single room in a home were discovered to house, in a Mobius strip sort of way, another room within it, and that this second, interior space also violated the normal laws of physics by being larger than the space in which it was contained. In the huiskerk, private space opens up into, opens up as, public space in this fashion, creating the possibility, at any rate, that private individuals gathered together within such a space might come together as public individuals, too.

Publics need not form in such circumstances, and different kinds of religious gatherings—in other countries, subject to other cultural and legal contexts—will need to be examined in their own right. Huiskerken cannot serve as typical examples of the emergence of public identities in religious congregations. However, we can draw a limited general insight that has some bearing on the period of the Reformation and Counter-Reformation in Europe: when an actual religious congregation is forced into an oppositional relation to an orthodoxy, a virtual, public audience is more likely to develop alongside the communal audience of the Mass than when that communal audience represents such an orthodoxy. As imaginary communities, publics emerge as tangential formations to official gatherings, alongside of, outside of, or beneath the fully overt association or group or congregation. In the religious climate of the period, all congregations, whether orthodox or banned, were in some sense thus embattled; what this means is that any congregation could, under the right circumstances, contribute to new senses of a shared, public, or collective identity.

When we began, we doubted whether a religious congregation could be a public. The complexity of religious discourse and practice in the period has caused us to rethink this assumption and to adopt a more flexible, nuanced understanding of publics and counterpublics in operation. Thus we have moved toward a more fluid notion of what a public is. It is self-organized, but can also flow in and out of an officially organized group. What matters is that there is a complex interaction or dialectic between a private realm and a growing sense of public identity dependent on that private realm in some fashion. This seems to imply in some fashion an oppositional vector or impetus. It does for Habermas, too. The Habermasian public sphere develops within the private in opposition to, and as an alternative to, the state monopoly on self-representation. This is why many theorists talk of counterpublics in the same breath as publics, because all publics are in a sense counterpublics, when viewed aright—from the proper, which is to say oppositional, point of view.

NOTES

1. "dans une maison bourgeoise, où l'on entroit et sortoit secrettement deux seulement à la fois." Balthasar de Monconys, *Journal des voyages de monsieur de Monconys, conseiller du roi en ses conseils d'estat et privé. Seconde partie. Voyage d'Angleterre, Païs-Bas, Allemagne et Italie* (Lyon: Horace Boisat and Georges Remeus, 1666), 161.

2. William Temple, quoted in George Clark, ed., *Observations upon the United Provinces of the Netherlands, 1673* (Oxford: Clarendon Press, 1972), 104.

3. On these debates, see Benjamin J. Kaplan, "Fictions of Privacy: House Chapels and the Spatial Accommodation of Religious Dissent in Early Modern Europe," *American Historical Review* 1, no. 4 (2002): 1034–35.

4. Ibid., 1034.

5. Xander van Eck, "Dreaming of an Eternally Catholic Utrecht during Protestant Rule," *Simiolus* 30, no. 1–2 (2003): 22. Van Eck describes a converted school building.

6. For specific art historical studies on the decoration of the house churches, see the work of Xander van Eck.

7. Kaplan, "Fictions of Privacy," 1034.

8. Ibid. Jews were the notable exception, being allowed to build quite lavish synagogues in cities such as Amsterdam.

9. Ibid., 1035.

10. Diarmaid MacCulloch, *The Reformation* (New York: Viking, 2004), xix.

11. David Zaret, "Religion, Science, and Printing in the Public Spheres in Seventeenth-Century England," in *Habermas and the Public Sphere*, ed. Craig Calhoun (Cambridge, MA: MIT Press, 1992), 213.

12. A growing number of scholars have associated such characteristics with the emergence of a genuine public sphere in England by the 1640s, albeit a public sphere that is decidedly un-Habermasian in its conflictual nature and social range of representation. See for example David Norbrook, *Writing the English Republic: Poetry, Rhetoric and Politics, 1627–1660* (Cambridge: Cambridge University Press, 1999).

13. Emphasis in the original; Geoff Eley, "Nations, Publics, and Political Cultures: Placing Habermas in the Nineteenth Century," in Calhoun, *Habermas and the Public Sphere*, 306.

14. Craig Calhoun, "Imagining Solidarity: Cosmopolitanism, Constitutional Patriotism, and the Public Sphere," *Public Culture* 14, no. 1 (2002): 165.

15. Joke Spaans, "Catholicism and Resistance to the Reformation in the Northern Netherlands," in *Reformation, Revolt and Civil War in France and the Netherlands, 1555–1585*, ed. Philip Benedict et al. (Amsterdam: Royal Netherlands Academy of Arts and Sciences, 1999), 176:150.

16. In the late sixteenth and early seventeenth centuries, Catholics comprised approximately half of the population of the United Provinces. In the second half of the 1600s, there was decline in the number of Catholics, possibly spurred by greater public acceptance of the Reformed Church, combined with clerical disputes. By the early eighteenth century, Catholics made up one-third of the population. See Charles H. Parker, "Obedience with an Attitude: Laity and Clergy in the Dutch Catholic Church of the Seventeenth Century," in *The Low Countries as a Crossroads of Religious Beliefs*, ed. Arie-Jan Gelderblom et al. (Leiden: Brill, 2004), 182.

17. Gregory Hanlon, *Confession and Community in Seventeenth-Century France: Catholic and Protestant Coexistence in Aquitaine* (Philadelphia: University of Pennsylvania Press, 1993), 1.

18. Ibid., 5.

19. Joke Spaans, "Violent Dreams, Peaceful Coexistence: On the Absence of Religious Violence in the Dutch Republic," *De Zeventiende Eeuw* 18, no. 2 (2003): 157.

20. Ibid., 154; Heinz Schilling, "Confessional Europe," in *Handbook of European History, 1400–1600: Late Middle Ages, Renaissance and Reformation; Visions, Programs and Outcomes*, ed. Thomas A. Brady et al. (Leiden: Brill, 1995), 2:643.

21. Alistair Duke, *Reformation and Revolt in the Low Countries* (London: Hambledon Press, 1990), 273.
22. Judith Pollmann, "The Bond of Christian Piety: The Individual Practice of Tolerance and Intolerance in the Dutch Republic," in *Calvinism and Religious Toleration in the Dutch Golden Age,* ed. Ronnie Po-Chia Hsia and Henk van Nierop (Cambridge: Cambridge University Press, 2002), 57.
23. Willem Frijhoff, "The Threshold of Toleration. Interconfessional Conviviality in Holland during the Early Modern Period," in *Embodied Belief: Ten Essays on Religious Culture in the Dutch Republic* (Hilversum: Verloren, 2002), 41; Pollmann, "Bond of Christian Piety," 55–57.
24. Duke, *Reformation and Revolt,* 288; Spaans, "Catholicism and Resistance," 161.
25. Spaans, "Violent Dreams," 158.
26. Quoted in Benjamin J. Kaplan, "Confessionalism and Its Limits: Religion in Utrecht, 1600–1650," in *Masters of Light: Dutch Painters in Utrecht during the Golden Age,* exhibition catalog, ed. Joneath Spicer et al. (Baltimore: Walters Art Gallery; San Francisco: Fine Arts Museum of San Francisco; New Haven, CT: Yale University Press, 1997), 68.
27. Harold Love, "How Music Created a Public," *Criticism* 46, no. 2 (2004): 259–60.
28. Michel de Certeau, *The Writing of History,* trans. Tom Conley (New York: Columbia University Press, 1988), 166.
29. Calhoun, "Imagining Solidarity," 162.
30. Michael Warner, "Publics and Counterpublics," *Quarterly Journal of Speech* 88, no. 4 (2002): 417.
31. Christine Kooi, "'A Serpent in the Bosom of Our Dear Fatherland': Reformed Reaction to the Holland Mission in the Seventeenth Century," in *The Low Countries as a Crossroads of Religious Beliefs,* ed. Arie-Jan Gelderblom et al. (Leiden: Brill, 2004), 165–76; Spaans, "Catholicism and Resistance," 161.
32. Frijhoff, *Embodied Belief,* 158, 165.
33. Calhoun, "Imagining Solidarity," 152.
34. Charles Taylor, "Modern Social Imaginaries," *Public Culture* 14, no. 1 (2002): 106.
35. Hannah Arendt, *The Human Condition* (1958; reprint, Chicago: University of Chicago Press, 1971), esp. 51–55. See also Calhoun, "Imagining Solidarity," 148.
36. Calhoun, "Imagining Solidarity," 149.
37. Jürgen Habermas, *The Structural Transformation of the Public Sphere: An Inquiry into a Category of Bourgeois Society,* trans. Thomas Burger (Cambridge, MA: MIT Press, 1989), 50. Habermas provides a diagram of the emergence of the public sphere within the private realm, ibid., 30.
38. Kaplan, "Fictions of Privacy," 1061.

2   Emerging Publics of Religious Reform in the 1530s

The Affair of the Placards and the Publication of Antoine de Marcourt's *Livre des marchans*

Torrance Kirby

AFFAIR OF THE PLACARDS

One of the most dramatic and influential events of the early stages of Reformation in France—the notorious "Affair of the Placards"—occurred during the night of October 17, 1534. In the city of Paris as well as in other principal centers—including Orleans, Blois, Tours, and Rouen—placards proclaiming *"Articles veritables sur les horribles, grandz et importables abuz de la Messe papalle"* were posted in highly visible public venues, including the door of the king's own bedchamber at the Château d'Amboise.[1] The putative author of the placard, Antoine de Marcourt, was a member of the French evangelical-humanist avant-garde in the circle of Guillaume Briconnet, otherwise known as the "cercle" or "groupe de Meaux."[2] Members of the circle had lately come to view Martin Luther's proposals for reform of the church and its teachings with considerable favor. Marcourt's placard served to focus the reformers' mounting criticism of traditional religion on the ritual central to the church's own practice and self-understanding in the form of a direct appeal to popular judgment. In a classic early instance of challenge to the reigning paradigm of "representative publicity," Marcourt's appeal to public opinion in his attack on the doctrine of the Mass was interpreted by both the religious and civil establishment not only as a challenge to received church dogma, but also, owing to the provocative manner of its publication, as a direct assault on the authority of the monarchy itself.[3] King Francis, the Archbishop of Paris, the doctors of the Sorbonne, and other leading clergy of the realm closed ranks and together mounted a swift and ferocious response aimed at quelling this upstart attempt to sway public opinion over the heads of the establishment. Many of the religious reformers associated with criticism of the church and the traditional teachings were either executed for sedition or driven into exile. Marcourt himself fled France along with other leading members of the circle of reformers, including Jean Calvin. In a dramatic and equally public response to the placards, Francis and his court processed solemnly through the streets of the capital, the ritual purpose of which was to purify the capital from the "pollution" of the placards. Francis himself processed beneath a canopy carried by peers of the realm in the place where onlookers would normally expect to view the Host in a Corpus Christi procession; thereby the establishment underscored the intimate association of monarchical and sacramental "presence" and linked in dramatic fashion the definition of representative publicity with fundamental ontological claims.[4]

The posting of Marcourt's placard and the official response to it both provide theatrical manifestations of prominent sixteenth-century impulses to define religious identity through direct popular appeal. Marcourt evidently hoped that by publicizing his evangelical objections to the doctrine and practice of the Mass he would win over his fellow subjects to the cause of religious reform. Through this attempt to bring about a popular reform of French religious identity on the basis of argumentation and interpretation in public space unconstrained by the official imprimatur of crown, church, and university, the posting of the placards exemplifies an early expression of what has been called the early modern "culture of persuasion"—namely, the endeavor to address the "public" through an appeal to "public reason" in aid of achieving a manifestly "public good."[5] Indeed, in the context of the explosive political dimension of the ensuing confrontation with the political and religious establishment of France, the "Affair of the Placards" neatly illustrates an early instance of direct challenge to what Habermas has identified as "representative publicity" (here embodied in the authority of crown and church) by an emerging "public sphere" grounded in a rhetoric of popular persuasion developed by a particular group of religious activists.[6]

Prior to the posting of the placards, Francis I had shown considerable favor toward *les évangéliques* and the reforming humanists of the *groupe de Meaux;* both he and his sister Marguerite of Navarre had shown marked support for Erasmus, Lefèvre d'Étaples, and Gérard Roussel and their followers, while Francis had even exiled the conservative Noël Béda to Mont-St-Michel in May of 1533. After the infamous placards, a veritable sea change in the climate of religious reform can be discerned. Sharper lines of distinction emerge between the moderate humanism of the Erasmian reformers and more radical "sacramentarian" Protestants. By calling for radical religious reform through an open appeal to popular judgment, Marcourt played a key role in precipitating a controversy that was to alter decisively (and perhaps irrevocably) the course of the Reformation in France. The posting of Marcourt's placard in 1534 is without doubt a key dramatic episode in the unfolding of the Reformation in France, and serves to highlight the emergence in the early modern period of a new and popular sense of "public" over against a much older and hieratic sense embodied in the institutions of monarch and church.

MEANWHILE, ACROSS THE ENGLISH CHANNEL . . .

Forty years ago in his magisterial study *English Humanists and Reformation Politics,* James McConica observed that the English reform movement under Henry VIII and Edward VI is closely bound to the complexities of pan-European currents of religious reform: "The closer the examination," claims McConica, "the more apparent is the difficulty of separating English developments from those on the Continent."[7] Particular support for this claim can be discerned in the history of the publication in English translation of tracts by Marcourt. The first wave of French radical evangelical propaganda swept across *La Manche* and up the Thames estuary in the summer of 1534—in the same year as the Affair of the Placards. On August 24 an anonymous English translation of Marcourt's rollicking Rabelaisian spoof on ecclesiastical abuses was published in London by Thomas Godfray under the title *The Boke of Marchauntes.*[8] This was almost twelve months to the day from the publication of the original French text of *Le livre des marchans* by Pierre de Vingle in Neuchâtel.[9] In her landmark study *Antoine Marcourt: reformateur et pamphlétaire,* Gabrielle Berthoud observes that *Le livre des marchans* is Marcourt's most popular and best-known work.[10] In his assumed Rabelaisian identity—namely, "the lorde Pantapole, right expert in suche busynesse, nere neyghbour vnto the lorde Pantagrule"—Marcourt sets himself up as the one who sells all—*celui qui "vend de tout"*[11]—the wholesaler, as it were, who seeks to undercut the ecclesiastical "middleman." In this allusion Marcourt's satirical form and the evangelical intent are fused together. According to the central thrust of the satire, the entrepreneurial role of the priestly "merchant" was that of a retailer, whose task is to distribute the spiritual "goods" of divine grace incrementally.

In the early 1530s England was in the throes of radical constitutional transformation. Henry's chief minister, Chancellor Thomas Cromwell, simultaneously managed both the intricacies of the legislative program and a highly sophisticated propaganda campaign through the press in support of the reformist constitutional agenda then before Parliament.[12] Cromwell's use of the printing press obviously targets growth of a public favorable to reform through maximum possible exposure of an argument. Such a religious public may have as its goal the creation of a new, reformed religious establishment—which was in fact attained in England under Edward VI (1547–1553), but not so in France under Edward's contemporary, Henri II (1547–1559). In the case of England the emergent public sympathetic to religious reform comes to be situated, at least temporarily, within the field of royal power, in large part owing to the political success of the reform; it is an arrangement that suggests well the social mobility and organizational flexibility of public making. On the other hand, lack of political success may arguably have had the effect of the institutionalizing a dissenting public of like-minded people in France—that is, the Huguenots—whose self-organizing field of discourse might aspire to grow but would remain forever under the threat of the dominant political power. Comparison of the radically differing receptions of Marcourt in France and England can therefore offer instruction on the question of the effects of growth and respectability on an emerging public. Over time, a public formed out of religious dissent may (or may not, as the case may be) find itself absorbed into the established forms of institutional life.

A PUBLIC OF PUBLISHERS ON THE FRINGES OF THE COURT

Close linkage of the publishing trade to the corridors of power was intrinsic to the success of Henry VIII's constitutional revolution. It has been argued that many of the pamphlets of the early 1530s epitomize the substance of the constitutional legislation passed by the Reformation Parliament.[13] Thomas Godfray's list of published titles suggests that he was evidently an important player in Thomas Cromwell's circle, a group that also included printers Robert Redman, John Mychell, and Thomas Berthelet.[14] Godfray published numerous books that contributed directly to the advancement of Cromwell's propaganda campaign and were associated with some of the principal prophets and propagandists of the Tudor revolution, including William Tyndale, John Frith, Christopher St. German, and William Marshall.[15]

The printers, authors, and certain members of the Privy Council associated within this tightly knit circle of friendship, patronage, and personal connection in a gray area at the edges of the court effectively comprised a public of like-minded members united by the common purpose of promoting religious change.[16] In England of the 1530s, the promotion of radical religious reform on continental models was definitely on the cultural fringe. In contrast to members of publics described in several other chapters in this volume (see Chapters 5 and 8, for example), many of the evangelical avant-garde could hardly be described as disinterested players, especially when they were prepared to go to the stake for their religious persuasion (Simon Fish, William Tyndale, and others). Yet from the standpoint of the established institutions of the Tudor commonwealth, their voluntary association for the purpose of publishing political and religious tracts manifests a certain degree of ambivalence when compared with the situation in France. King Henry simultaneously approved *and* disapproved of these religious radicals and their newfangled doctrines. Approval stemmed from their willingness to promote Henry's cause of Caesaro-Papism, while disapproval arose from their tendency to undermine core Catholic teachings. In short, Henry quite liked evangelical politics, but had his doubts about their sacramental radicalism. Unlike France, the continued toleration of religious radicals is largely owing to an emerging distinction in England between the political and religious elements of the controversy. In short, the ambivalence of the king's religious orientation—he was against the papacy yet, at the same time, in favor of Catholic teaching—had the noteworthy yet unintended effect of defining Cromwell's stable of propagandists as simultaneously both inside and outside the establishment. This is clearly a case of a public emerging as a "dynamic system of discourse" on the fringes of the circles of power—in a manner analogous to François Rouget's salons "au marge de la Cour."[17]

The publisher Thomas Godfray contributed to the advancement of Thomas Cromwell's simultaneous campaign of constitutional and religious reform in the mid- to late 1530s, but at arm's length from the Crown. While Thomas Berthelet was officially the king's printer, Godfray's press published numerous books that contributed directly to the advancement of Cromwell's propaganda campaign and was associated with some of the more radical evangelical prophets and propagandists of the Tudor revolution, including works by William Tyndale, John Frith, Christopher St. German, William Marshall, and Clement Armstrong, most of whom embraced theological opinions anathema to the king. This circle of authors, translators, and their common publisher, Godfray, composed a voluntary association—a public—consisting of what we might call the Tudor evangelical avant-garde whose main object was to prod the government to move toward a radical political break with the Roman hierarchy and to a theological break with the old religion. Cromwell's circle faced the problem of Henry's ready acceptance of the former goal but his reluctance to proceed with the latter.

The radical reformers whose works and translations were published by Godfray could hardly be said to be involved in the enterprise principally for money or even preferment. Indeed the evidence suggests that King Henry looked askance at the more radical literary productions of the evangelical radicals, and some of the group were actually hounded to their deaths by official government policy. The tension between Cromwell's own more advanced Protestant position and the king's religious conservatism helps to explain the chancellor's employment of a semiofficial press attached to Cromwell's interest but not having the direct imprimatur of the royal printer. Nonetheless, in a letter to Cromwell, William Marshall indicates that he is relying on Cromwell's promise of a subsidy of twenty pounds for printing his translation of Marsilius of Padua's treatise on constitutional theory in support of royal supremacy.[18] While Marshall was well known for his advanced Protestant opinions, there was certainly a cash nexus here for a "grubstreet" translator promoting the Crown's interest.

Godfray published twenty titles sporadically between the years 1530 and 1536. Among those that link him in diverse ways to the reforming interest are two important works by William Tyndale, *The Obedience of a Christian Man* and *Pathway into the Holy Scripture,* both unequivocally evangelical pieces by the great translator of the Bible.[19] Tyndale's treatise on obedience draws an explicit connection between evangelical teaching concerning justification by faith alone and divinely derived authority exercised by the godly prince over both church and commonwealth. Richard Rex has shown that Tyndale had a critical influence on the chief propagandists of the Henrician regime, especially through his demonstration of the theological ground of the royal supremacy.[20] Rex maintains that "Tyndale's primary motive in writing *Obedience* was to defend the new learning against the charge that 'it causeth insurrection and teacheth people to disobey their heads and governors, and moveth them to rise against their prince.'"[21] In a vein of argument closely analogous to Tyndale's political theology, the *Boke of Marchauntes* launches an impassioned appeal to the secular rulers to correct the abuses of the clergy. Marcourt urges that the care of religion be taken under the direct control of the civil power as the corrective for long-standing ecclesiastical abuses.

Common lawyer and political theorist of the Tudor state Christopher St. German was another key player in Cromwell's circle of religious and constitutional reformers. St. German's sustained literary attack on the papacy resulted in a series of pamphlets with an increasingly sharp edge. While several of St. German's contributions to the propaganda campaign were published by the king's printer, Thomas Berthelet,[22] one of the common lawyer's more strident pieces, *An Answer to a Letter,* was farmed out for publication in 1535 by Thomas Godfray.[23] In *An Answer* St. German sets out to redefine the nature of the church in a manner consistent with the king's claim to the *plenitudo potestatis.* Not only do kings exercise the "cure of souls" but they are also the final arbiters of both doctrine and the interpretation of the scriptures.

In his appeal to the model of the virtuous Old Testament kings whose care was for both the honor of God and the good governance of the people, Marcourt's polemic is in accord with the approach taken by Tyndale, St. German, and other leading Tudor propagandists of the royal supremacy. In the case of another propagandist of Cromwell's circle, Clement Armstrong, Ethan Shagan has suggested that religious radicalism is by no means necessarily opposed to authoritarian political theology as has been frequently asserted.[24] Like Marcourt a full-blown sacramentarian opponent of the Mass—an extremely radical position to hold in England in the 1530s, and anathema to King Henry himself—Armstrong nonetheless defined the church as "the congregation of all men in a realm congregated as in the body of one man, which one man is the king's body wherein all people his subjects are as his bodily members . . . like as the king is the Church, so the Church is the king."[25] In the case of Clement Armstrong, Shagan has shown how Henry VIII's antipapal maneuvers of the early 1530s were received and embraced by London's radical Protestant public. Far from eroding the authority of princes, the assertion of a radical evangelical agenda could go hand in hand with a revolutionary extension of royal powers. For Marcourt as for Armstrong and others in the circle of Thomas Cromwell, the royal supremacy served to promote radical doctrinal reform. That Marcourt's satire on such key questions of religious and political reform should be in basic accord with the English avant-garde comprising Tyndale, St. German, and Armstrong—not to mention Martin Bucer and Marsilius of Padua, whose writings were also published by Godfray—challenges deeply rooted historiographical assumptions about the Reformation in both England and France.

In view of the variety of genres yet common underlying polemical thrust of books published by Thomas Godfray in the period 1533–1536, the appearance among them of the Rabelaisian anticlerical satire of a radical evangelical of Marcourt's stripe appears wholly in keeping with the constitutional aims of Cromwell's literary campaign if not wholly consistent with the more conservative doctrinal policies of the king. Marcourt, like Tyndale and Armstrong, is associated with extreme theological radicalism. The *Articles veritables* published as the placard of October 1534 confirm his radical Sacramentarian leaning which, like Armstrong's, could not have been reconciled under any circumstances with the official position on the Mass and the real presence countenanced by King Henry. It is nonetheless plain that the *Boke of Marchauntes* lends solid support to the new ideology of secular and secularizing authority unfolding in the agenda of the Reformation Parliament and its accompanying propaganda.

The open publication of Marcourt's book by Thomas Godfray contrasts sharply with the attempt at concealment of the publisher's identity and the place of publication in Pierre de Vingle's two French editions of 1533 and 1534.[26] One small but revealing piece of evidence of this discrepancy in the reception of Marcourt's satire on the two sides of the Channel is discernible in a rhetorical modification in translation of the use of the personal pronoun. In the peroration of the appeal to the Princes in the original French edition of 1533, Marcourt writes "O, si ainsi promptz et vigilans *vous* estiez à procurer l'honneur de Dieu comme sont promptz et diligentz ces convoiteux marchans de estre apres leur cas pour bien garder que rien ne leur eschappe, las que la chose iroit bien."[27] The rhetorical effect is admonitory, perhaps even reproving—a voice of protest addressing the powers that be. In the English translation of Godfray's 1534 edition, the pronoun is shifted from the second person to the first: "O lorde / if *we* were so prompt and wakinge for to procure the honour of god / as these covetouse marchantes be prompte and diligent / for to be about theyr maters / and to be well ware that nothinge escape theym: Helas all wolde goo well."[28] The shift from "vous" to "nous" (from "you" to "we") suggests an assumed element of common purpose between author and the intended audience of the apology. This subtle discrepancy of translation points to a whole world of difference between the public receptions of Marcourt's pamphlet in England and France. In England, at least during the mid-1530s, the "representative publicity" of the monarchy does *not* regard itself as under threat by the voice of public religious protest, whereas the very opposite condition prevails in France. The consequence is the flourishing of Cromwell's public of pamphleteers and publishers at the margin of the English Court, while in France the voice of religious protest is compelled to flee the realm for the safety of foreign parts.

A generation later in *Actes and Monuments*,[29] John Foxe mentions the *Boke of Marchauntes* as having been included in a list of books prohibited by Henry VIII in a Proclamation issued in 1546 two years after the theology faculty of Paris had issued France's first index of prohibited books.[30] Accompanied by a list of other avant-garde evangelical writings by such reformers as Miles Coverdale, George Joye, William Tyndale, John Frith, William Turner, and Robert Barnes, among others, *The Boke of Marchauntes* was publicly consigned to a bonfire at Paul's Cross.[31] The Proclamation classifies the books into order according to author and includes *The Boke of Marchauntes* within a subsection of titles attributed to William Turner including his notorious satire *The huntyng & fyndyng out of the Romishe fox* and his translation of *A comparison betwene the olde learnynge and the newe*,[32] a French edition of the latter having been published also by Pierre de Vingle in Neuchâtel in 1534.[33] This Proclamation in Bonner's Register may well be our best contemporary clue to the identity of the translator. It is interesting to note that the item immediately preceding *The Boke of Marchauntes* in the list of prohibited books attached to the Royal Injunction is *The Summe of the holye Scripture*,[34] an English translation of *De Summa der Godeliker Scrifturen*. Originally composed in Dutch and published in Leiden in 1523, this work has been attributed to Henricus Bomelius (or Hendrik von Bommel), an evangelical preacher in the region of the Lower Rhine and pastor of the Brethren of the Common Life.[35] An English translation is attributed to another evangelical firebrand, Simon Fish, author of the popular evangelical satire *Supplicacyon for the beggars*, first circulated in the spring of 1529 and a copy of which Anne Boleyn is said to have presented to Henry VIII.[36] Both Simon Fish and John Frith were engaged in polemics with Sir Thomas More concerning the doctrine of purgatory, and thus serve to highlight the developing rift between Erasmian humanist and radical evangelical approaches to religious reform. And, as Isabelle Crevier-Denommé has shown, the French translation, published by Vingle under the title *Summe de l'escripture saincte*, provides yet another instance of links between England and Marcourt's publisher in Neuchâtel.[37] Here again we witness the impossibility of separating developments in the course of the Reformation in England from events on the continent, and the existence of an engaged public that transcends national and linguistic boundaries.

McConica's claim in *English Humanists and Reformation Politics* that the humanist evangelicals of Henry's reign "declined the general heterodoxy of the Protestant reformers" and embraced the middle way of Erasmian moderation as "the very formula of the Henrician Church" does seem now a rather unlikely reading of the rough-and-tumble polemical environment that witnessed the making public of Marcourt's satire.[38] Thomas Godfray's press played a key role in Cromwell's antipapal campaign from 1533 onward, and the *Boke of Marchaunts* was one among numerous publications by French evangelical radicals enlisted in support of Thomas Cromwell's strategy for constitutional and religious reform. England's reformist humanism had its "evangelical moment" in the 1530s and then reverted to a more consciously conservative mode in the decade following. From the fall of Thomas Cromwell in 1540 until the death of Henry in January 1547, the Church of England came to be dominated by the spirit of a conservative Erasmian humanism such as it had known prior to 1533,[39] while during the same period of the middle 1540s France witnessed a severe repression of heresy and rigorous enforcement of Catholic orthodoxy.[40] With the accession of Edward VI, "the young Josiah," the climate shifted once again, and the *Boke of Marchauntes* was resurrected phoenixlike from the ashes in its second English edition only months after perishing in the flames at Paul's Cross. Within a year continental evangelical theologians Martin Bucer from Strasbourg and the Florentine Peter Martyr Vermigli would be installed in Cambridge and Oxford respectively as the king's professors of divinity. Those in France who longed for a ruler who would emulate the idol-smashing boy-king of ancient Judah would have to wait until the accession of Francis II in 1559 and then Charles IX in 1560 only to have their hopes of a thorough reform of church and doctrine dashed in the wake of the Colloquy of Poissy (1561).[41]

THE POPULAR VOICE OF RELIGIOUS REFORM

The tide of religious reform was far from attaining equilibrium on either side of the Channel. There was a virtual flood of evangelical propaganda in England in the 1530s. Unlike France where, after the Day of the Placards in October 1534, every attempt is made by government to squelch the voice of reform, the Tudor regime is willing to allow this voice a hearing, though at a respectable distance from the Crown. The evangelical circle around Thomas Cromwell acquires a voice through various presses, those of a more moderate tone through the royal printer and those of a more radical bent through presses with only quasi-official sanction, as with the press of Thomas Godfray, publisher of Marcourt's satire. In the case of the French printer Pierre de Vingle, on the other hand, while forced expulsion from the realm of France creates a more negative delimitation of the actual site of production, the pamphlets are nonetheless distributed to an eager French-reading public wherever they may be found. Indeed it is especially interesting to observe the broadly international dimension of mid-sixteenth-century religious propaganda. Tracts appearing in Germany, Holland, and France are translated and appear in England in very short order. The public in search of religious transformation transcends national, political, and linguistic boundaries, and thus presses *beyond* the limits imposed by individual states. The virtual public space of popular religious reform becomes increasingly international in scope as the sixteenth century unfolds.

What then are the leading characteristics of the nascent public of avant-garde evangelicals at the periphery of King Henry VIII's court in the 1530s, the public that has its center in the group of propagandists associated with the circle of Thomas Cromwell? The avant-garde circle around Thomas Cromwell seeks a reform of both the church and the civil constitution, but does so from outside the established institutions themselves by means of persuasion in the popular press. The English press of the 1530s arguably denotes an emergent civil society with competing ideologies, a situation owing in large part to the fluctuating state of official religious policy at the time in Parliament and at court. The fall of Cromwell in 1540 is accompanied by a spectacular drop in the volume of polemical books published. It is not until after the accession of the Protestant Edward VI in 1547 that the volume of publication regains the level attained in the mid-1530s. In this we have a rough indicator of the Crown's power to permit or to suppress an incipient public discourse founded upon religious dissent.

Their common interest is in the promotion of radical constitutional and religious agenda of reform through the agency of semiofficial printers, including Thomas Godfray. The political dimension of the propaganda machine in Cromwell's circle of religious radicals is fairly self-evident. It might be argued that the overtly political purpose of religious persuasion is so explicit as to disqualify the web of friendship, patronage, and personal connection to which a printer like Thomas Godfray is attached from identification as a disinterested public, although it would certainly be difficult to label this phenomenon without appealing to some analogous category. It would certainly be a mistake to exclude an explicit political dimension to all species of early modern publics when some clearly appear either in the process of the dissolution of one establishment or in the inauguration of another—such as is the case of England in the mid-1530s and later throughout the reign of Edward VI.

The evangelical radicals in both England and France are unquestionably engaged, to borrow a key idea from Charles Taylor, in a very elaborate exercise of social imagining.[42] Marcourt, moreover, imagines the benefits of religion taken under the care of the civil power. The *Boke of Marchaunts* proposes such radical constitutional revision based on evangelical religious reform. In doing so, the author has set himself outside established institutional structures. The preferred mode of revolution is through the printed word—the tracts, the placards, the subversive religious songs. The aim is to achieve constitutional revolution through persuasion—a frequent epigraph on books published by Vingle, Marcourt's original publisher in Neuchâtel, is "lisez et puis jugez."

As we have seen, one of Godfray's notable publications was the English translation of Antoine de Marcourt's Rabelaisian spoof on ecclesiastical hierarchy, first secretively published in French by Pierre de Vingle at Neuchâ-tel in October 1533. The characteristic medium of the evangelical avant-garde is print. However, this allows diverse modes of expression including theological tracts (e.g., Marcourt's *Declaration of the Masse*), satire (*Boke of Marchaunts*, Tyndale's *Parable of the Wicked Mammon*), sermons, carols and hymns (*Noelz nouveaux*), and "picture books" with wood-cut images (*Les faictz du Jesus Christ et du pape*).

The press of Thomas Godfray thus constitutes a "semiofficial" public functioning in fairly close proximity to the court through its association with the circle of Chancellor Thomas Cromwell, but does not possess the official status of "king's printer." The point of publishing radical evangeli-cal and political tracts by those close to the seat of power was to influence the constitutional course of events through what Michael Warner charac-terizes as a self-organized field of discourse.[43] The field is open in principle to strangers on the condition that they subscribe to the tenets promoted by the public in question. It may well be ephemeral in view of its ultimate prospects for success—those who find themselves at the fringes of political power (such as the evangelical radicals of Cromwell's circle in the 1530s) may find themselves forming a new Establishment over time (such as in fact was accomplished by them at the accession of Edward VI). To become the establishment in no way detracts from its erstwhile status as a public at an earlier stage. This exemplifies the diachronic nature of publics: they are not static entities, but come into being and can evolve into something that may no longer be a public in a formal sense.[44]

CONCLUSION

Throughout England's radical religious and constitutional transformation of the 1530s, Henry's chief minister Thomas Cromwell simultaneously managed both the intricacies of the legislative program and a highly sophis-ticated propaganda campaign through pulpit and press in support of the constitutional agenda before Parliament. The substance of the pamphlets of the early 1530s in many respects epitomizes the legislation passed by the Reformation Parliament.[46] What, then, is the significance of Cromwell's resorting to private presses in order to justify a new definition of religious identity? The older order defined by monarchical and ecclesiastical "repre-sentative publicity" is no longer assumed as simply hegemonic, but must give an account of itself by reasoned argument; there is a revolutionary break with long-held assumptions concerning the nature of the church and its relation to political power, of the relation between religion and the primary social structures, and also of the relation between the conscience of the individual subject and constituted political authority. The crucial element in this new relation is especially evident in the perceived need for the encouragement of a public campaign of persuasion. As with Marcourt's ill-fated placard, such a campaign assumes that the moral force of religious identity rests not upon its intrinsic given-ness, but rather upon active recognition, assent, and embrace by its adherents. The importance of subjective appropriation of the new framework—namely through persuasion—and the consequent definition of the communal identity have become intrinsic to the subsistence of that framework. This is the sense of the importance attached to a "culture of persuasion" and to Cromwell's avant-garde "public" of propagandist, printers, and publishers who largely brought it into existence.

NOTES

1. The placard was formally titled *Articles veritables sur les horribles, grandz et importables abuz de la messe papalle, inventee directement contre la saincte cene de Jesus Christ* (Neuchâtel: Pierre de Vingle, 1534). Marcourt's sharp polemic against the Catholic doctrine of the Mass was posted throughout Paris as well as at the château of Amboise where King François I was then residing. See Francis Higman, "De l'affaire des Placards aux nicodémites: le movement évangélique français sous François Ier," in *Lire et découvrir: la circulation des idées au temps de la Réforme* (Geneva: Droz, 1998), 619–25.
2. On the groupe de Meaux, see Arlette Jouanna, *La France de la renaissance, histoire et dictionnaire* (Paris: Éditions Robert Laffont, 2001), 300ff.
3. For a full account of Marcourt's career, see Gabrielle Berthoud, *Antoine Marcourt: Réformateur et pamphlétaire du "livre des marchans" aux placards de 1534* (Geneva: Droz, 1973).
4. Christopher Elwood, *The Body Broken: The Calvinist Doctrine of the Eucharist and the Symbolization of Power in Sixteenth-Century France* (New York: Oxford University Press, 1999), 27–55.
5. See Andrew Pettegree, *Reformation and the Culture of Persuasion* (Cambridge: Cambridge University Press, 2005).
6. Jürgen Habermas, *The Structural Transformation of the Public Sphere* (Cambridge: Polity, 1989), 7, 8.
7. James Kelsey McConica, *English Humanists and Reformation Politics under Henry VIII and Edward VI* (Oxford: Oxford University Press, 1965), 6.
8. Antoine de Marcourt, *The Boke of Marchauntes, right necessarye vnto all folkes. Newly made by the lorde Pantapole, right expert in suche busynesse, nere neyghbour vnto the lorde Pantagrul* (London: Thomas Godfraye, *cum priuilegio Regali*, 1534).
9. The original text was published by Vingle on August 22, 1533, under the title *Le livre des marchans, fort utile a toutes gens nouvellement composé par le sire Pantapole, bien expert en tel affaire, prochain voysin du seigneur Pantagruel*. According to Gabrielle Berthoud, "le *Livre des Marchans* est l'œuvre la plus poplaire et, apparemment, la mieux connue de l'auteur des Placards." See Berthoud, *Antoine Marcourt*, 111.
10. Ibid.,111, 149ff.
11. See ibid., 111. Berthoud, however, does not provide the precise Greek etymology of this Rabelaisian name. The Greek πάντα (panta) is "all" and πώλης (poles) is "dealer," "seller," or "purveyor." According to Anne Lake Prescott, Marcourt's assumed identity is the first printed allusion to Rabelais in English. See Anne Lake Prescott, *Imagining Rabelais in Renaissance England* (New Haven, CT: Yale University Press, 1998), 17.

12. See Robert Hutchinson, *Thomas Cromwell: The Rise and Fall of Henry VIII's Most Notorious Minister* (London: Weidenfeld and Nicolson, 2007); G. R. Elton, *Reform and Reformation: England 1509–1558* (Cambridge, MA: Harvard University Press, 1977), 157: "Cromwell obtained a grip on the press in latter part of 1533. Under his patronage a very different body of writers and writings took over the task of discussing the issues of the day; production turned from controversy to constructive thought."

13. According to Franklin Le Van Baumer, Henry VIII and Cromwell devoted almost as much attention to the printing press as to the parliamentary session. See Franklin Le Van Baumer, *The Early Tudor Theory of Kingship* (New York: Russell and Russell, 1966), 35–84. See p. 39: "Henry VIII exercised a dictatorship of the press which, judged by its results, was just about as effective as any western Europe has ever seen. The opposition, denied the use of the English printing press, was either driven abroad to publish, or else forced to circulate its views in manuscript."

14. See J. Christopher Warner, *Henry VIII's Divorce: Literature and the Politics of the Printing Press* (Woodbridge, Suffolk: Boydell Press, 1998).

15. An anonymous *Panegyric of King Henry VIII as the abolisher of papist abuses* (London: Thomas Godfray, 1537) is identified in the Short Title Catalogue (2nd ed.) 13089a as published by Thomas Godfray; see also Bodleian Library, Douce Fragm. fol. 51 (10). This short piece of just three leaves may be consulted at *Early English Books Online*.

16. Andrew Pettegree, "Printing and the Reformation: The English Exception," in *The Beginnings of English Protestantism*, ed. Peter Marshall and Alex Ryrie (Cambridge: Cambridge University Press, 2002), 173. See also Warner, *Henry VIII's Divorce*.

17. See François Rouget, "Academies, Circles, 'Salons,' and the Emergence of the Premodern 'Literary Public Sphere' in Sixteenth-Century France," Chapter 3, this text.

18. In a letter to Cromwell, Marshall indicates that he is relying on Cromwell's promise of a subsidy for the printing of his translation of Marsilius's work. See J. S. Brewer, R. H. Brodie, and J. Gairdner, eds., *Letters and Papers, Foreign and Domestic of the Reign of Henry VIII, 1509–1547* (London, 1862–1932), 7:423.

19. William Tyndale, *The obedyence of a Chrysten man: and howe Chrysten rulers ought to gouerne, wherin also (yf thou marke dilygently) thou shalte fynde eyes to perceyue the craftye conueyaunce of all iugglers* (London: Thomas Godfray?, 1536); William Tyndale, *A Pathway i[n]to the Holy Scripture* (London: Thomas Godfray, 1536?); and a modern edition of the latter, P. E. Satterthwaite and D. F. Wright, eds., *A Pathway into the Holy Scripture* (Grand Rapids, MI: Eerdmans, 1994).

20. Richard Rex, "Crisis of Obedience: God's Word and Henry's Reformation," *The Historical Journal* 39, no. 4 (1996): 863–67.

21. Ibid., 866.

22. Christopher St. German, *A treatise concernynge the diuision betwene the spiritualtie and temporaltie* (London: Thomas Berthelet, 1532?); Christopher St. German, *Salem and Bizance* (London: Thomas Berthelet, 1533).

23. Christopher St. German, *An answere to a letter* (London: Thomas Godfray *cum priuilegio*, 1535); see also Christopher St. German, *A treatyse concernige the powre of the clergye and the lawes of the realme* (London: Thomas Godfray, 1535?).

24. Ethan Shagan, "Clement Armstrong and the Godly Commonwealth: Radical Religion in Early Tudor England," in *The Beginnings of English Protestantism*, 61. Shagan argues that "it is a commonplace of scholarly analyses of the

'radical Reformation' that radical theology required churches to be organised 'on the principle of voluntary association' [quoting George Williams, *The Radical Reformation*, xxviii] and that radicals 'disdained a settled relationship with secular society' . . . yet in Armstrong's case we have what seems to be an authoritarian and hyper-institutionalist concoction mixed from many of the same elements found in the Anabaptist theological brew. In the English Reformation 'radical' and 'magisterial' cannot function as simple antonyms. . . . In England of the early 1530s . . . the hopes of a small evangelical minority lay in the policies of a mercurial king who had begun making dark threats against the pope and the clergy." See p. 78.

25. Public Record Office, State Papers, Theological Tracts 6/11, 199v. Cited in Shagan, "Clement Armstrong," 74.

26. See Berthoud, *Antoine Marcourt*, 141: "Godfray, on l'a vu, n'a dissimulé ni son nom, ni son adresse, mais n'a pas renonce totalement pour autant aux indications fictives de Pierre de Vingle. . . . D'autre part, 'l'Imprimé à Corinthe' est devenu 'Written at Corinthe, by your frende and lover (out of frenche) Thorny, wyld, wedy, harletry.' Le traducteur ne s'est malheureusement pas trahi advantage par ces mots énigmatiques."

27. Marcourt, *Livre des marchans* (1533), ci v (my italics). I am grateful to Isabelle Crevier-Denommé for drawing this critical discrepancy in the translation to my attention.

28. My emphasis; Marcourt, *Boke of Marchauntes*, ciii r.

29. John Foxe, *Actes and monuments of these latter and perillous dayes, touching matters of the Church, wherein ar comprehended and described the great persecutions [and] horrible troubles, that haue bene wrought and practised by the Romishe prelates, speciallye in this realme of England and Scotlande.* . . . (London: John Day, *cum privilegio Regiae Maiestatis*, 1563).

30. The Royal Proclamation, issued on 8 July 1546, is included in the Bonner Register, followed by Edmund Bonner's own certificate to the Privy Council confirming execution of the order together with a list of prohibited books, Guildhall MS 9531/12, pt1, fol. 91r: "The king's most excellent majesty—understanding how, under pretence of expounding and declaring the truth of God's Scripture, divers lewd and evil-disposed persons have taken upon them to utter and sow abroad, by books imprinted in the English tongue, sundry pernicious and detestable errors and heresies, not only contrary to the laws of this realm, but also repugnant to the true sense of God's law and his word . . . His majesty straitly chargeth and commandeth, that no person or persons, of what estate, degree, or condition soever he or they be, from the day of this proclamation, presume to bring any manner of English book, concerning any manner of Christian religion, printed in the parts beyond the seas, into this realm." See P. L. Hughes and J. F. Larkin, eds., *Tudor Royal Proclamations* (New Haven, CT: Yale University Press, 1964), 1:373–76. The catalog of prohibited books is recorded only in the first edition of Foxe, *Actes and monuments* (1563), 573–74. On the Paris index see Philip Benedict and Virginia Reinburg, "Religion and the Sacred," in *Renaissance and Reformation France, 1500–1648*, ed. Mack P. Holt (Oxford: Oxford University Press, 2002), 139.

31. See Edmund Bonner, *Certificatorium factum dominis de privato consilio regio super concrematione quorundam librorum prohibitorum*, Guildhall MS 9531/12, fol. 91v; repr. *Actes and Monuments* (London: Adam and Company, 1873), appendix to vol. 5, no. xviii.

32. William Turner, *The huntyng & fyndyng out of the Romishe fox whiche more then seuen yeares hath bene hyd among the bisshoppes of Englong [sic] after that the Kynges hyghnes had comma[n]ded hym to be dryuen out*

of hys realme (Imprynted at Basyl [i.e., Bonn: L. Mylius], 1543). Rhegius, *A co[m]parison betwene the olde learnynge [and] the newe, translated out of latin in Englysh by Wyliam Turner* (Southward: James Nicolson, 1537).

33. William Turner, *Doctrine nouvelle et ancienne* (Neuchâtel: Pierre de Vingle, 1534), a translation of Urbanus Rhegius, *Nova doctrina et veterem collatio* (Augsburg: Simprecht Ruff, 1526).

34. Henricus Bomelius, *The summe of the holye scripture: and ordinarye of the Christen teachyng, the true Christen faithe* (Antwerp?: s.n., 1529). Reprinted again after the accession of Edward VI under the title *The summe of the holy Scripture, and ordinarye of the Chrystian teaching* (n.p., 1548). See modern facsimile version edited by Robert Peters, *The Sum of the Holy Scripture and a Supplication for the Beggars 1529* (Menston: Scolar Press, 1973).

35. Henricus Bomelius, *De Summa der Godliker Scrifturen (1523)*, ed. Johannes Trapman (Leiden: Elve/Labor Vincit, 1978). Published anonymously in 1523, the *Summa* was a free translation by Bomelius of his Latin work *Oeconomica christiana*, which was not published until 1527.

36. Simon Fish, *The summe of the holye scripture: and ordinarye of the Christian teachyng* (Antwerp: s.n., 1529). See John N. King, "John Day: Master Printer of the English Reformation," in *The Beginnings of English Protestantism*, 184. See also Robert Peters's introductory note to the Scolar Press facsimile edition of *The sum of the holy Scripture*, n. 34 in this chapter. Simon Fish, *A supplication of the poore commons. Wherunto is added the Supplicacyon for the beggers* (London: John Day and William Seres?, 1546). Sir Thomas More engaged Fish in defense of the doctrine of Purgatory as he did John Frith. See Thomas More, *The supplycacyon of soulys made by syr Thomas More knight. . . . Agaynst the supplycacyon of beggars* (London: William Rastell, 1529). Another of Thomas Godfray's publications resonates to some extent with the social satire of Fish's *Supplication*. See William Marshall's translation of the Spanish Erasmian Juan Luis Vives's *Forma subventionis pauperum* (1526); *The forme and maner of subue[n]tion or helping for pore people, deuysed and practysed i[n] the cytie of Hypres in Flaunders, whiche forme is auctorised by the Emperour, [and] approued by the facultie of diuinitie in Paris. Cu[m] priuilegio regali* (London: Thomas Godfray, 1535). Juan Luis Vives, *De subventione pauperum sive de humanis necessitatibus, libri II*, ed. C. Matheeussen and C. Fantazzi (Leiden: E. J. Brill, 2002).

37. Isabelle Crevier-Denommé, "Les changements doctrinaux dans les versions de la *Summe de l'escripture saincte* (1529–1539)." Paper presented at the annual meeting of the Renaissance Society of America, Cambridge, UK.

38. McConica, *English Humanists*, 10, 11.

39. For a penetrating analysis of the situation of Reform in the years immediately preceding the accession of Edward VI, see Alec Ryrie, "The Strange Death of Lutheran England," *Journal of Ecclesiastical History* 53, no. 1 (2002): 83–92. As Ryrie sums it up, there is a significant division of opinion in the interpretation of this period. Richard Rex sees it as an almost fully-fledged Counter-Reformation while Eamon Duffy regards the Reforming party as biding their time in anticipation of the succession. (Nothing succeeds like succession?) See Rex, *Henry VIII*, 144; and Eamon Duffy, *The Stripping of the Altars* (New Haven, CT: Yale University Press, 1992), 424–47. On this historiographical divergence, see Ryrie, "Strange Death," 83.

40. Benedict and Reinburg, "Religion and the Sacred," 139.

41. Philip Benedict, "The Wars of Religion, 1562–1598," in *Renaissance and Reformation France, 1500–1648*, 150.

42. See Charles Taylor, *Modern Social Imaginaries* (Durham, NC: Duke University Press, 2005).
43. For this view of publics, see Michael Warner, *Publics and Counterpublics* (New York: Zone Books, 2002), 67–74.
44. My thanks to Angela Vanhaelen for this observation.
45. G. R. Elton, *Reform and Reformation: England 1509–1558* (Cambridge, MA: Harvard University Press, 1977), 157: "Cromwell obtained a grip on the press in latter part of 1533. Under his patronage a very different body of writers and writings took over the task of discussing the issues of the day; production turned from controversy to constructive thought."

3 Academies, Circles, "Salons," and the Emergence of the Premodern "Literary Public Sphere" in Sixteenth-Century France[1]

François Rouget

During the sixteenth century, under the influence of an Italian humanism that offered new forms of literary sociability, France, especially in its big urban centers, witnessed the emergence and organization of new cultural groups.[2] Originating from social classes that were becoming more and more diverse (an "amalgam"[3] of nobility, civil officers, officers de robe, bourgeoisie), the members of these new gatherings would come together on the initiative of a patron of the arts or of an intellectual to debate a diversity of questions from moral philosophy to music, touching on such subjects as love poetry and theology. These formal groups, like the Académie de Poésie et Musique (the Academy of Poetry and Music), or more informal ones, such as the humanist salons of Catherine de Clermont, duchess of Retz, and Madeleine and Catherine Des Roches, multiplied around 1550 and even shared each other's members. They were characterized by a mobility of affiliation and the eclecticism of their activities. In spite of the extreme diversity of their origins, education, and intellectual interests, the members met out of the sole desire to participate in forms of exchange: public debate, discussion concerning sometimes sensitive subject matter (power, religion), public presentation, and individual and collective creation of poetry, musical airs, and so forth. To a high degree, the participants found in these gatherings a place for cultural experimentation and for the first semipublic reception of their artistic and intellectual productions. Between the court, where a prescribed and explicit political culture was controlled by the king, and the general public who had access to public forms of culture (including books, civic holidays, and fairs), the gatherings— which brought together a crop of associations: academies, circles, salons, *puys*, courts—made up a specific sphere, a semipublic, semiprivate "contact zone."[4] This was an intermediate space: open, marked by the mobility of its members, and by the liberty of the subject matter they debated.[5] Devoted to the education of its members and to the exchange of ideas, these gatherings "in the entourage of the Court"[6] have a good claim to have been places of passage on the fringes of institutionalized academies with which they competed, and places of emancipation where women often played a leading role.[7] Because of their interconnection, these groups set out new paradigms for the production, consumption, and circulation of culture in the sixteenth century.

I would like to reflect on the modernity of gatherings in order to understand better the formation of these groups, the nature of their activities, the relationship between participating actors and spectators, and the methods of circulation. To do this, I will first examine the terms of reference for these groups and then propose a means to categorize them. The chapter will examine the nature of these gatherings, their origins, and the social characteristics of their members. It will also suggest the motives for encouraging member participation in one or many cultural groups along with members' levels of participation. Finally, we will see which activities were common or specific to these groups or cultural assemblies; which topics of discussion were chosen; how the subject matter was produced and how it entered into debate; and how the material supports (books, concerts, etc.) of these exchanges found their way into circulation.

THE ASSEMBLIES AND THEIR PUBLICS: A PROBLEM OF TERMINOLOGY AND OF TYPOLOGY

The groups of cultural partnership that we observe in France in the sixteenth century are most commonly defined by the generic term "assemblies." If they emulate the model of the Italian academies of the Quattrocentro (the Accademia Platonica in Florence, for example), they almost never employ the term "academy," with the exceptions of the Académie des Jeux Floraux in Toulouse (the Academy of Floral Games), and two academies that were established during the reigns of Charles IX (Academie de Poésie et Musique, 1570) and his brother Henri III (commonly known as the Académie du Palais because its members would usually meet at the Louvre).[8] We notice straight away that the French term "académie" signals its status as an institutional model under the influence of a central or regional power. This aspect differentiates the French academies from their Italian models, which were constituted according to the "free meeting of great minds," according to André Chastel,[9] and which, in the absence of statutes, were granted the freedom to address philosophical, moral, and religious questions.

In fact, the Italian model seems to find its equivalent in other literary gatherings that were forged as a result of the initiatives of a curious bourgeois, Jean Brinon in Vilennes, a humanist protecting the learned, Jean de Morel in Paris, and women, from the bourgeoisie of the provinces (the Des Roches ladies), to aristocrats (the princesses Marguerite de Navarre, Marguerite de Valois, and Marguerite de Savoie), to wives of royal officers (like Catherine de Retz and Madeleine de L'Aubespine-Villeroy). As noted by L. Clark Keating, these circles multiplied after 1550, offering a new model of literary sociability on the fringes of the court that both furthered and challenged its cultural activities.[10] Whether they belonged to the sphere of the court or not, the members of these assemblies—which we have the habit of calling "circles," "salons," and "academies" in order to designate the gatherings of humanists, courtesans or socialites, and scholars—mix with one another and often frequent many assemblies. In terms of structure, the assemblies may be classified in three categories. Chronologically, humanist circles precede formal academies that seem to develop in France after 1570. The society of humanists emerges around 1550 on the initiative of influential bourgeoisie who acquired power through official and administrative positions ("charges"). Morel, who came to Paris as a young man and who later became a petitioner of the king, is a good example.[11] He became widely acquainted with humanists such as Erasmus along with rising poets (Pierre de Ronsard, Joachim Du Bellay, Jean Dorat), and his house in Paris became a site of intellectual exchange, which contributed to the education of his daughters. At that time, another law officer at the Parliament of Paris, Brinon, started to gather mostly established poets in his castle of Vilennes.[12] Renowned for his extreme generosity, Brinon was the center of a cultural group that celebrated him as a new Maecenas. The benefactors of his patronage depicted his house as a space that was dedicated to poetry and the exchange of ideas, a public place that fostered all kinds of literary expression. In a sense, the new assemblies formed by these bourgeois noblemen signal the emergence of a new class of men whose wealth allowed them to enter the aristocracy and imitate aristocratic and court cultural activities. Thus the bourgeois salons tended to compete with the culture of courts; they shared similar interests as well as participants. While Dorat and Ronsard frequented the Morel and Brinon circles, they were also the favorite poets of Marguerite de France, sister of King Henri II, who entertained and offered protection to artists in her entourage. Once established in Savoie and Piedmont after her marriage to Philibert-Emmanuel of Savoie in 1559, she would continue to receive artists, in addition to prosecuting reformers at her court.

This type of cultural public constitutes a second category that was situated at the margins of the royal court under the supervision of the king and his administration. Of course these circles, under the protection of royalty, had existed since the beginning of aristocracy: the "cercle de Meaux" with Marguerite de Navarre, the circle of Marguerite de France, and later the one of Marguerite de Valois.[13] These assemblies were simply the cultural element of court life and the traditional aspect of aristocratic representation. But around 1570, a category of noble men and women chose to surround themselves with groups of artists to create Parisian salons. The most famous ones are the salons of Nicolas of Neuville, *sieur* of Villeroy, powerful secretary of state of Charles IX, and his wife Madeleine de L'Aubespine, who supported the work of poets such as Ronsard, Philippe Desportes, and Amadis Jamyn in their castle of Conflans, not far from Paris.[14] At the same time, Catherine de Clermont, *maréchale de Retz,* and her husband, the commander of the royal army, received the same company in their Parisian residence and their estate in Île-de-France.[15] These two salons illustrate the emergence of a peripheral court culture, positioned on the boundaries of the royal court, where literature was not the production of a public or the official representation of the monarchy, but merely an occasional activity to entertain patrons through discussions of preofficial/public production of works in more private spaces. A common element seems to place these salons or gatherings in the same category: the prominent role of a female patron. Emerging on the fringes of the court, the gathering is a contact zone controlled by noble and bourgeois women. Besides the salons of the monarchy (Marguerite de Savoie, Marguerite de Valois), and of the high aristocracy (Retz, Villeroy), which were mainly based in Île-de-France due to their patrons' part-time residences at the royal court, we observe the emergence of bourgeois salons in Paris (Morel, Brinon) as well as in the provinces. As early as 1540–1550, in Lyon, the poet Louise Labé was renowned for entertaining the regional poets in her salon. Twenty years later, two bourgeois ladies from Poitiers, Catherine and Madeleine Des Roches, created a famous salon that became the center of cultural life in Poitou, receiving visiting humanists and law officers (including Étienne Pasquier, Antoine Loisel, Nicolas Rapin, and Scévole de Sainte-Marthe) during the "Grands Jours" in 1579 when lawyers and jurists were sent to Poitiers to ease the burden of the local courts.[16] The Des Roches salon served as a meeting point between Paris and its provinces; it was a semipublic place through which were disseminated cultural products such as readings, discussions, and concerts that arrived from Paris. After the Grands Jours, the Des Roches ladies collected all the poems written by visiting poets to Poitiers that were published in Paris. Thus, they were able to reverse what had been a cultural shift to Paris and also enlarge their audience by reaching a virtual public through print. By reaching out to a local public and encouraging, in their own salon, a form of poetry that fostered public debate—between lawyers and poets, for example, over recognized topics—the Des Roches were emulating the kinds of philosophical exchanges that were taking place in the formal academies.

These constitute the third category of assemblies that partake in the literary public sphere where two academies must be mentioned in particular.[17] Devoted to poetry, the first is the Académie des Jeux Floraux in Toulouse, which was governed by strict regulations by elected members belonging to the influential bourgeois of Southern France.[18] The other one is the Académie du Palais (the Palace Academy), created by King Henri III, which brought together court members, humanists, and poets twice a week in the Louvre to debate ethics and eloquence.[19] The Académie du Palais, defined by its semiformal constitution, possessed neither institutional status nor a permanent location. The speakers were asked to educate the king and his audience, an act that was probably rewarded financially. They spoke at lunchtime in the royal palace and met irregularly in different locations, such as Ollainville from 1576 to 1579. The Académie was, like the assemblies of the other two groups, and in spite of its royal patronage, a semipublic, semiprivate space that was open to participants of varying social and intellectual backgrounds who were also partakers of other circles and salons.

To sum up, the core of all these groups can be defined by a specific kind of participation that Christian Bec characterizes as "informality and variation amongst poets, jurists, philosophers, doctors and cultivated bourgeois, who discuss varied philosophical subjects."[20] These assemblies can be understood, then, as publics, groups that consisted of strangers and whose membership rosters fluctuated freely. In their own ways, these publics suggest an increasingly popular and general passion for knowledge and for education of the mind. All of this was carried out in a leisurely environment that preferred relaxation and intellectual exchange, inspired by Plato, which arrived by way of Italian humanism. In this respect, the intimacy of the salons and the circles contrasts sharply with the ritual involved in meetings of the academies, which remained concerned with maintaining a certain level of formality in their debates.

These diverse gatherings were significantly different from the groups that existed within the earlier and contemporary cultural tradition of the court. What distinguishes these new groups is their acceptance of the social diversity of participants, their mobility within an arena removed from royal power, the absence of governing statutes, and the emergence or renewal of a short-lived, timely, and collective framework for cultural consumption.

The aforementioned reassessment of assemblies—albeit the term is an expansive one—confirms that "the concept of the 'public sphere' is elastic,"[21] which is essential to the nature of publics as we define them in this study. The assemblies should be considered meeting places for exchanges between spectators and actors, producers and consumers of cultural life. It is within these assemblies, in the space of one session, that the social and political differences of the diverse members begin to blur, yielding a place for the exercise of thought and ideological debate.

THE PUBLICS OF THE ASSEMBLIES: PLACES, AFFILIATION, AND RECRUITMENT

One of the pressing questions, of course, is the formation of these publics. Who took part in these literary assemblies? How frequent were the meetings and how long did they last? How did members become integrated in them? What role did social affinities, networks of sociability, and popularity-seeking tactics play in their formation? And, ultimately, which role was reserved for the initiator or the patron of the assembly in the recruitment of members? These are some of the central questions of this study to which I will now try to respond. All of these questions relate *in fine* back to the question about origins. Why do we observe, from the year 1550, and especially between 1565 and 1580, the emergence of new cultural and noninstitutionalized associations, which organize collective activities under the protection of certain individuals in private urban spaces?

A closer look at the composition of these publics—at the social status of members, in particular—can help answer this question. We must, however, take into consideration the intentions of the assemblies' initiators, patrons, or intellectual guides, which vary between groups and depend on whether the group is a humanist coterie, an elite salon, or a royal academy. Questions about the composition of these assemblies lead to a number of reflections.

First, we note a large diversity in the social status of participants. Major or minor nobility, bourgeois, or humble servants, all seem to have been selected or co-opted because of their affiliation with an influential member, or follower. Thus it is not surprising to find in these publics learned poets, such as Philippe Desportes, protégé of the Villeroy, and his rival Ronsard, who belonged to other influential circles. Another example is Jamyn, who served as secretary to Ronsard, yet who took advantage of his participation in the salon of the Villeroys around 1570 to assert his status as a poet and to break free from the tutelage of Ronsard. It is these same scholars who debate important subjects at the salon of Catherine de Retz, a woman who becomes influential because of the military functions performed by her admiral husband. At the same time, between 1576 and 1579, these men and their female patrons continue to regularly attend the formal sessions of the Académie du Palais to expatiate upon moral philosophy before the king.

The archives reveal that the individuals who participated in these assemblies tended also to frequent a number of other ones. It is often the same individuals, then, who attended a variety of assemblies, either by choice or because they were solicited by organizers because of their oratory talents, reputation at court, literary work, or a common servitorship to princely families, aristocrats, or prelates. They all, therefore, knew each other and took advantage of their status as writers to impress one another in the elite salons, which, in addition to extending the cultural activities of the court, provided these writers with an arena for the initial circulation, and even creation of poetry, musical airs, and other forms of cultural production. The relative modesty in the social status of the more widely known participants is a common feature of these gatherings. But such an understanding leaves other participants unaccounted for, such as bourgeois and noblemen whose names and identification are rarely known and often veiled. At the salon of Dictynne, which is to say that of Catherine de Retz, the ladies employ borrowed, mythological names (Marguerite de Valois, Henriette de Clèves, Madeleine de L'Aubespine-Villeroy, Hélène de Surgères), while the majority of the participants remain anonymous, just like the poems that were later transcribed by a secretary in the album for Retz. The compilation of dedicatory notes in the works of contemporaries allows us to reconstitute this circle, which includes poets such as Pontus de Tyard, Étienne Du Tronchet, Ronsard, Jamyn, Antoine de Laval, Desportes, Jean-Antoine de

Baïf, Flaminio de Birague, Jean Bertaut, Rapin, and Jean Passerat, along with musicians such as Adrian Le Roy, among many others.[22]

Whereas the participants of the Parisian salons were recruited from individuals at court, those in the provincial salons came from both the city and the region. Around 1570 to 1580, for example, the salon of the Des Roches ladies in Poitiers welcomed local writers, while also remaining open to visitors. In 1579, for instance, the salon hosted the court on a sojourn, which made for intense poetic activity administered by the ladies and their admirers, such as Pasquier and Sainte-Marthe. What becomes evident is the mobility, social as well as spatial, of the participants. These assemblies, which are constituted by a more affluent sociocultural demographic, mix rather liberally, interpenetrating other gatherings, while their cultural products also circulate within this larger public of potential participants. Parisian and provincial culture are at odds since the provincial salons seek novelties from the capital city in order to introduce them into the provinces. This relaying of information is transmitted through the circulation of books (bilateral, like many provincial centers such as Poitiers, Bourges, Lyon, Rouen, and so forth, disseminating their products in Paris), the itinerant character of the court (in Île-de-France, in France during the royal Entries, the Royal Tour in 1564–1565, and so on), and the increased mobility of scholars whose pedagogical, diplomatic, and administrative functions lead to the communication of current events.

Whether chosen, elected, co-opted, or recommended by some members, these participants frequented the assemblies on their own initiative in hope of finding some sort of profit (monetary, protection, support) or forum for intellectual conviviality. With the exception of the members of the Académie du Palais, who were directly solicited by the king, the participants engaged in largely carefree activities in these assemblies. It was their shared tastes and interests that brought them together to forge a community. The participants' association in small groups, as miniature images of the royal court, permitted them to debate in public and allowed everyone a voice. This open discussion took precedence over monologist discourse, a format that was mirrored in the convivial scenes recounted in the philosophical dialogues of the time described by Tyard, Guy de Bruès, Jacques Tahureau, and Pasquier, and in *L'Heptaméron* by Marguerite de Navarre. The pleasure of conversation is founded on a *locus amœnus* and a spiritual fraternity that allowed everyone to exercise a certain degree of influence on the assembly. In the absence of documents that would allow us to reconstitute either the ways in which the sessions unfolded or the roles of members, we are able to offer some suggestions that can be traced in written testimonials, dedications, and correspondence. The information contained in these documents sheds light on the aspirations, tastes, and preoccupations of these proto-publics but, alas, a large component is left unresolved, such as their productive activities and their modes of participation.

THE ACTIVITIES OF THE PUBLICS OF THE
ASSEMBLIES: PRODUCTION AND CIRCULATION—
THE CASE OF THE POETIC ALBUMS

Since the assemblies' activities were essentially of an oral nature, involving musical performances, lectures, recitations, and discussions that link them to the dual courtly tradition—medieval and humanist—of the Renaissance, it seems perilous and perhaps futile to attempt to describe with any precision the relationships between actors and spectators, as well as the degree of participation of individual members. In the quasi-absence of statutes and other historical records[23] that would clarify the precise objectives of these gatherings, we must reconstruct their activities and production from extant documents. This is a risky task because the documents (letters, albums, memoirs, etc.) offer only a distorted image of the event that is removed from its actual performance. Indeed, how do these written documents, often composed long after the texts were produced and performed, reproduce the salons' settings and ambiance fully and with accuracy? If the essential goal of the assemblies was to meet and exchange ideas held in common, it becomes difficult, then, to relate accurately the activities of individual participants.

We thus offer a number of hypotheses that will elucidate the production and circulation of cultural activities in an attempt to categorize the assemblies' activities according to the type of assembly. First, we can deduce from archival documents that the groups' principal function was to meet in order to perform a verbal and oral activity; participants attended the assemblies to discuss, debate, recite poetry, and play music. Both the performance and the reception of these kinds of intellectual activities meant that the separation between actors and spectators was often indistinguishable, perhaps even nonexistent, since each individual was encouraged to play both roles. The point, moreover, was the immediacy of the event, *hic et nunc,* even when the forms of cultural representation, such as texts or musical compositions, were prepared or performed before the meetings. What is important is that they were intended to be presented to a public.

One particularly intriguing document describes the Grands Jours of 1579, when jurists, lawyers, and poets from Paris and Poitiers met to celebrate the presence of a flea on the breast of Catherine Des Roches. This incident elicited responses in a host of languages, including French, Latin, Greek, and Italian, and participants competed with one another, through their texts, as if at court. These responses generated debate about the flea's characteristics and the virtues of its mistress. What is suggested here is that the display of eloquence, which fused judiciary rhetoric with amorous themes, served to reactivate the tradition of a collective, and, to some degree, a spontaneous kind of oral poetic expression.[24] This culture is ultimately not that different from the culture at court since it is motivated by circumstance. What separates the two, however, is the framework of their performance, which is restricted in the salons and widespread at court, along with their degree of formality, informal in the salons and solemn at the court.

My second point concerns the memorization or the documentation of the groups' intellectual activities. The texts, which were produced more or less spontaneously, were compiled to form albums. The existence of these objects is a result of the desire of the patron to conserve a written trace of the group's activities, and thus the albums constitute, in my opinion, the central point of my study of publics in sixteenth-century France. They are significant precisely because the cultural products of these assemblies were public representations, which were not, in fact, destined for publication. These albums are reminiscent of the *album amicorum* in which the book's owner collected friendly testimonials, literary or not, from occasional guests. These inscriptions were often composed a considerable time after the meetings had ended.

What is intriguing about these albums, and different from the *album amicorum,* is that they were compiled by and for women, princesses or bourgeois ladies. The recopied texts are often anonymous and serve for the sole interest and use of the albums' owners. They are collections made specifically for private use. Whatever their contexts (Royal Academies, Marguerite de France Savoie's and Marguerite de Valois's courts, Louise de Coligny's court, Madeleine de L'Aubespine-Villeroy's and Catherine de Retz's salons), these handwritten albums have remained unpublished until recently.[25] Without them, we would know nearly nothing of the nature of the groups' activities. From these texts, we discover that discussions centered primarily on the analysis of the passions through poetic, theological, and musical discourse.

My third remark concerns the mode of intellectual production along with its conservation and circulation. Produced in situ, in the salons, and also outside the gatherings, the collective cultural activities were often diffused elsewhere, thereby extending the public for them beyond the framework of the salon. Intellectual production was thus intended for immediate circulation within the salons, but it could also by distributed by others through print and material means. For example, dedications to the Retz family appear in an array of printed materials: the songs of Guillaume Costeley by Adrian Le Roy and Robert Ballard (1570), the *Nouvelles Œuvres poétiques* by Tyard (1573), the *Lettres amoureuses* by Du Tronchet (1573), and also poems by Ronsard, Desportes, Jamyn, and Baïf, to the Villeroy.[26] All these specifically indicate the circumstances of their composition and the identity of the patron. Once read, recited, and performed in the salons, the texts and melodies would sometimes experience a second life, usually after a period of time, through their circulation in the form of a book. For example, some of Ronsard's and Desportes's poems are found in the Villeroy, Retz, and Valois albums, and the poems were eventually modified in the published *works* of the poets. Also, Jacques de Sourdrai, at the likely request of the Des Roches ladies, undertook the collection and publication of the poems in 1582 that had been presented three years earlier in their salon in Poitiers.[27] However, by no means is there a clear norm; the texts and melodies presented in the semipublic space of the salons, along with most of the salons' cultural production, were kept only in manuscripts, such as the albums. Often the identity of the authors who wrote texts for these albums can be discovered only in the printed versions of these texts. And this identification is not always feasible. We might think, for example, of the speeches given at the Académie du Palais, of which many—signed or not—were transcribed in handwritten albums.[28] Rare are those that go on to be published. Only Jacques Davy Du Perron and Jamyn decided to circulate their albums to a larger public, compiling their manuscript records in their entirety in print. The other contributors, Ronsard and Desportes, never incorporated their speeches in their printed *works*. For them, without question, these texts strayed from their principal interest, which was poetry. This is why their poetic contributions to the handwritten albums can also be found later in their editions of poetry in, at times, modified form. The experience of the poem was thereby doubled: first, through its presentation to and reception by the assembly in the semipublic context of the salons, and then later by a wider public. Many of the poems by Ronsard, for instance, were produced first for the Villeroy and then later incorporated into his *works*. We can say the same for Desportes, Jamyn and Baïf, and Honoré d'Urfé, who—at the Parisian salon of Marguerite de Valois, in the early 1600s—introduced the *galant* genre of the *pastorale* and the *style précieux*. We can therefore consider the assemblies as experimental laboratories for cultural production that was often fugitive, which was the same effect as found at court, before which unpublished works were often presented, either read and sung. Before circulating a cultural product to a large public—to consumers of the printed book, for example—artists could present their work to a chosen public within the space of the salon. This public, in turn, could immediately intervene in the reception and in the potential correction of the work's presentation. The variations in certain poems by Ronsard between the handwritten and printed versions seem to support this hypothesis. The artistic production is thus informed, modified, and finalized by the group's initiators who, intriguingly, as we have seen, were mostly women who were often of diverse social status.

CONCLUSION

The key concepts of mobility, openness, and community help to explain the phenomenon of cultural assemblies in France during the second half of the sixteenth century: spatial mobility resulting from changes in the salons' meeting places; openness to the exchange of ideas by members of varying backgrounds; and a community gathered around initiators who stimulated debate.[29]

The existence of these groups is, of course, hardly surprising. There is a long history of princes surrounding themselves with communities of intellectuals and artists to enhance their own prestige. The constitution of publics is thus intimately related to the exercise of aristocratic power. However, what changes in France in the sixteenth century is the rise in numbers of, and interplay between, publics and how they come to function. The Italian model is undoubtedly a determining factor in the increase in French salons. But that is not all. With the dual phenomenon of the continual centralization of royal power and its increasing influence—due to political and religious disputes and the ascension of urbane bourgeoisie, political culture is no longer the sole responsibility of the Crown. We can therefore examine the developments since the reign of François I, who instigated a royal and cultural program in the service of his European political ambitions. Under the reign of the last Valois kings (Charles IX and Henri III), the court did not lose all of its glamour, but cultural and intellectual debates were now expressed in new arenas. The great princes and princesses favored the protection of counselors who were also intellectuals and artists; Guy Du Faur de Pibrac, Agrippa d'Aubigné, Ronsard, and Desportes were connected to Marguerite de Valois's salon, while Du Bellay, Antoine de Chandieu, and Michel de L'Hospital enlivened the circle of Marguerite de Savoie. These salons underwent geographical changes, moving from Paris to the regions of Île-de-France, Navarre, Savoie, and Poitou. With this decentering of culture, and its relative democratization through the inclusion of a larger part of the bourgeoisie, central power was decidedly weakened.[30] Is it for this reason that Henri III, from the time of his accession to the throne, attempted to recapture the political and cultural initiative of the kingdom? Indeed, under Henri III, we witness the creation of the Académie du Palais at the Louvre—the center of power—where important intellectuals of the time (including Ronsard, Desportes, and Pibrac) as well as their female patrons (Retz, Valois, and Madame de Lignerolles) came together in debate. This was his way of exercising control over his subjects: to recover the cultural initiative of his rivals by taking the ascendancy over debates by defining the nature and focus of debates around his own priorities (ethics and political philosophy). The political culture of Henri III can therefore be perceived as a strategic plan to reinforce centralized power at a moment when France was torn apart by major civil disputes. This royal policy, in turn, was intended to offset the initiatives of the princes and princesses whose assemblies were competing directly with the court. Indeed, under the reign of Louis XIII, the court had already begun to give way to the cultural politics of the state, a feat that would encounter its climax under the rule of Louis XIV.

NOTES

1. Jürgen Habermas uses the expression "literary public sphere" to define the cultural category of the bourgeois social sphere in the seventeenth century; see Jürgen Habermas, *The Structural Transformation of the Public Sphere* (Boston: MIT Press, 1989). I am indebted to Habermas's categorization in my analysis of the emergence of the early modern semipublic literary milieu.

2. The best reference book on this history of French humanism and Academies is the one by Frances Yates, *The French Academies of the Sixteenth Century* (London: Warburg Institute, University of London, 1947). For the influence of the Italian academies, see chapter 1 ("Italian Academies and French Academies," pp. 1–13). In addition, L. Clark Keating has studied more extensively the bourgeois cultural assemblies in his monograph, which is the revised version of his Ph.D. thesis, L. Clark Keating, *Studies on the Literary Salon in France, 1550–1615* (Cambridge, MA: Harvard University Press, 1941). Keating summarizes the influence of Italian humanism (pp. 11–19) and devotes only a few pages to the French Royal Academies, ca. 1570–1579 (pp. 70–81). Since the publication of these two books in 1947 and 1941, respectively, a new extensive monograph has been dedicated to the cultural academies and salons in Renaissance Europe: Marc Deramaix, Perrine Galand-Hallyn, Ginette Vagenheim, and Jean Vignes, eds. *Les Académies dans l'Europe humaniste: idéaux et pratiques* (Geneva: Drosz, 2008).

3. Joseph Loewenstein and Paul Stevens, "Charting Habermas's 'Literary' or 'Precursor' Public Sphere," *Criticism* 46, no. 2 (2004): 201.

4. A. E. B. Coldiron, "Public Sphere/Contact Zone: Habermas, Early Print, and Verse Translation," *Criticism* 46, no. 2 (2004): 207.

5. On this aspect, see Habermas, *Structural Transformation,* 23: "This stratum of 'bourgeois' was the real carrier of the public, which from the outset was a reading public. . . . Their commanding status in the new sphere of civil society led instead to a tension between 'town' and 'court.'" Habermas underlines both the discontinuity between the two social groups (bourgeois vs. aristocrats), overlapping social spaces (court vs. cities), and the continuity of the two by the existence of a zone of contact (ibid., 29). It must be recalled that the separation of aristocrats and bourgeois in the cultural public sphere tends to be reduced in the Renaissance and that the courtier-artist, because of his spatial and social mobility, crosses the class boundaries and disseminates cultural products on each side. See Peter Burke, "L'homme de cour," in *L'homme de la Renaissance,* ed. E. Garin (Paris: Le Seuil, 2002; Rome-Bari: G. Laterza and Figli, 1988), 167–72. Citations are to the Le Seuil edition. Also see Jean Balsamo, "Société et culture de cour au XVIe siècle," in *Histoire de la France littéraire, naissances, renaissances. Moyen âge-XVIe siècle,* ed. Frank Lestringant and Michel Zink (Paris: PUF, t.1, 2006), 646–66.

6. Keating, *Studies on the Literary Salon,* 70.

7. The public of these salons can be defined by the modern sense of the "public" according to Michael Warner, "Publics and Counterpublics," *Quarterly Journal of Speech* 88, no. 4 (2002): 410–54. As he notes on p. 414: "A public organizes itself independently of state institutions, law, formal frameworks of citizenship, or preexisting institutions such as the church."

8. This is why Yates's book on French academies, in sticking to associations designated as "academies," offers only a reduced panorama of the cultural associative life of the Renaissance. On this point, see Yvonne Bellenger, "Des académies italiennes à celles de France au XVIe siècle," in *Rapporti e scambi tra umanesimo italiano ed umanesimo europeo,* ed. Luisa Rotondi Secchi Tarugi (Milan: Nuovi Orizzonti, 2001), 11–22.

9. André Chastel evokes "une réunion libre de beaux esprits," in André Chastel, *Marsile Ficin et l'art* (Geneva: Droz, 1975), 9.

10. Op. cit., 20.

11. On Morel, see Keating, *Studies on the Literary Salon,* 22–38; and Philip Ford, "An Early French Renaissance Salon: The Morel Household," in *Renaissance and Reformation/Renaissance et Réforme* 28, no. 1 (2004): 9–20.

12. We know very little about the cultural activities of Brinon's circle; see Pierre de Nolhac, *Ronsard et l'humanisme* (Paris: H. Champion, 1966), 16–21; and Josef Isjewijn, Gilbert Tournoy, and Marcus De Schepper, "Jean Dorat and His *Tumulus Brynonis*," in *Neo-Latin and the Vernacular in Renaissance France*, ed. Grahame Castor and Terence Cave (Oxford: Clarendon Press, 1984), 129–55. Brinon was recognized as a man of spirit, a collector of books, but almost all the poets of his time dedicated many poetical pieces and sometimes—like Ronsard in his *Meslanges* of 1555—books to him. Brinon died in 1555 in a state of absolute poverty.

13. See Eugénie Droz, "Marguerite de Valois's Album of Verse," in *Aspects of the Renaissance. International Conference on the Meaning of the Renaissance (1964)*, ed. Archibald Ross Lewis (Austin: University of Texas Press, 1967), 87–100; and Éliane Viennot, *Marguerite de Valois: "la reine Margot"* (Paris: Perrin, coll. Tempus, 2005), 263–65, 275–77.

14. On the Villeroys and their salon, see Keating, *Studies on the Literary Salon*, 81–103; many poems of praise in honor of the Villeroys are copied in the "album de vers manuscrit" studied by Pierre Champion, *Contribution à l'histoire de la société polie: Ronsard et Villeroy, les secrétaires du roi et les poètes d'après le manuscrit français 1663 de la Bibliothèque nationale* (Paris: É. Champion, 1925).

15. See Keating, *Studies on the Literary Salon*, 103–25; and the Introduction by Colette Winn and François Rouget of the critical edition of Catherine de Clermont and Maréchale de Retz, *Album de poésies*, ed. Colette Winn and François Rouget (Paris: H. Champion, 2004), 16–23. Recently, Emmanuel Buron has argued that the Retz household had never been the center of a salon ("Le mythe du salon de la maréchale de Retz," in Emmanuel Buron, *Henri III mécène des arts, des sciences et des lettres*, ed. Isabelle de Conihout et al. [Paris: Presses de l'Université de Paris-Sorbonne, 2006], 306–15). Buron's assertion is not convincing because of its anachronistic interpretation of the term salon.

16. See Keating, *Studies on the Literary Salon*, 49–69; George E. Diller, *Les dames des roches. Étude sur la vie littéraire à Poitiers dans la deuxième moitié du XVIe siècle* (Paris: Droz, 1936); Jean Brunel, *Un poitevin poète, humaniste et soldat à l'époque des guerres de religion. Nicolas Rapin (1539–1608)* (Paris: H. Champion, 2 t., 2002), 280–309; Anne Larsen, "Catherine Des Roches, the Pastoral, and Salon Poetics," in *Women Writers in Pre-Revolutionary France: Strategies of Emancipation*, ed. Colette Winn and Donna Kuizenga (New York: Garland, 1997), 227–41; and Kendall B. Tarte, *Writing Places: Sixteenth-Century City Culture and the Des Roches Salon* (Newark: University of Delaware Press, 2007).

17. We could also mention the *puys*, these assemblies vibrant in Normandy and Picardie that gathered poets who would compete once or a few times per year to celebrate Jesus and Mary at the important dates of the Christian calendar (Christmas, Easter, and so forth). In spite of their institutionalized aspect and their popularity throughout the eighteenth century, these *confréries* are part of a medieval and semisecular, semiclerical tradition, which differentiates them from the emergence of a literary public sphere that we observe in the Renaissance. On the history of the *puys*, see Gérard Gros, *Le poète, la Vierge et le prince du puy: étude sur les puys marials de la France du nord du XIVe siècle à la Renaissance* (Paris: Klincksieck, 1992); and the remarks of Bruno Petey-Girard, "Rêve académique, goût du prince et mécénat royal au XVIe siècle," in *Travaux de Littérature* 19 (2006): 101.

18. See Isabelle Luciani, "Jeux floraux et 'humanisme civique' au XVIe siècle: entre enjeux de pouvoir et expérience du politique," in *L'Humanisme à Toulouse (1480–1596), Actes du colloque international de Toulouse (2004)*, ed. Nathalie Dauvois (Paris: H. Champion, 2006), 301–35.

19. Since the early studies by Keating and Yates, Robert J. Sealy has more recently brought many new documents in Robert J. Sealy, *The Palace Academy of Henry III* (Geneva: Droz, 1981).

20. Christian Bec, "L'humanisme littéraire," in *Précis de littérature italienne* (Paris: Presses Universitaires de France, 1982), 130.

21. Coldiron, "Public Sphere," 207.

22. Audrey Boucaut has succeeded in reconstituting such circles from dedicatory pieces in early music printed books; see Audrey Boucaut, "Utilisateurs et mécènes de la musique imprimée à Paris au XVIe siècle: étude des dédicaces des éditions d'Adrian Le Roy et Robert Ballard," *Seizième Siècle* 2 (2006): 243–313.

23. Even though the one of the Académie du Palais, written by Ph. Desportes, has been lost, the *statuts* of the Academie de Poésie et Musique of Baïf and Thibault de Courville, the Académie des Jeux Floraux, and the *puys* have been preserved and recovered by historians. See Édouard Frémy, *Origines de l'académie française. L'Académie des derniers Valois* (Paris: E. Leroux, 1887), 39–42; François de Gélis, *Histoire critique des jeux floraux depuis leur origine jusqu'à leur transformation en académie, 1323–1694* (1912; reprint, Geneva: Slatkine Reprints, 1981); Gros, *Le poète*.

24. The medieval tradition of *débats d'amour* (love debates) was quite vivid at the beginning of the sixteenth century, whose best and most popular example is the *Arrests d'amour* of Martial d'Auvergne. Neglected and rejected by the poets of "La Pléiade" around 1550, it seemed to have a revival under the reign of Henri III. The *"dialogues," "debats,"* and *"responces"* are symptomatic of the emergence of a new courtly, oral, and collective salon esthetics in 1570–1580.

25. To date, only the *Album de poésies* of Retz has been the subject of a modern edition (Retz, *Album de poesies*). The album of Marguerite de Berry was recently studied by François Rouget, "Marguerite de Berry et sa cour en savoie d'après son album de vers," *Revue d'histoire littéraire de la France* 1 (2006): 3–16; and the one of Valois has been studied by Droz ("Marguerite de Valois") and will be published soon by Winn and Rouget (Paris: Les Classiques Garnier, in press). The album of Louise de Coligny has been documented by Anton Gerard Van Hamel, "L'album de Louise de Coligny," *Revue d'histoire littéraire de la France* 10 (1903): 232–55.

26. These pieces can be found in an album or anthology of Latin and French poetry put together by Nicolas de Neufville, Seigneur of Villeroy, around 1570–1571 (Bibliothèque nationale de France, département des manuscrits, fonds français 1663). It has been studied and partially edited by Champion, *Contribution à l'histoire*, 11–34.

27. The book was published in Paris by Abel l'Angelier in 1582. See Tarte, "From the Salon to the Page: Expressing Community in *La Puce de Madame des-Roches*," in *Writing Places*, 26–59.

28. Although most of these *"discours"* (speeches) were unpublished, there is a history of their circulation in the form of manuscripts (Copenhague, Thottshe Saml. 315; BnF, Fonds fr. 2585; N.A.F. 4655; manuscript copied for Marguerite de Valois, Wormsley Library). This leads me to suppose that these *"discours"* were certainly circulating among the public of the Académie du Palais and maybe beyond the space of the Louvre.

29. See Warner, "Publics and Counterpublic," 419: "In the self-understanding that makes them work, publics thus resemble the model of voluntary association that is so important to civil society," but Warner adds: "They are virtual entities, not voluntary associations." French Renaissance salons correspond to such "virtual entities."

30. In a sense, the publics of the salons can be seen and understood as "counterpublics." On the notion of "counterpublics," see Warner, "Publics and Counterpublics," 423–24.

4 Pietro Aretino, Thomas Nashe, and Early Modern Rhetorics of Public Address

Wes Folkerth

In addition to the idea of "the public" understood as the superset of all individuals in a given society, Michael Warner has suggested that we should also consider a more rhetorical notion of publics.[1] Publics in this rhetorically informed sense are discursively generated collectives that emerge as the result of being hailed or summoned into existence by the discourses that address them.[2] Observing that such utterances provisionally constitute their audiences in the very act of apostrophizing them, Warner sees this style of public making as intrinsically poetic, a "world-making" enterprise that is essentially "subjunctive-creative" in that the addressee of such utterances is, while remaining indeterminate and open, nevertheless provisionally constituted within the rhetoric of the discourse itself.[3] In the present chapter I consider the writings of Pietro Aretino and Thomas Nashe in light of Warner's work on publics. I wish to call attention to how the poetic, rhetorically generative dimension of this type of public making is readily observable in the writings of Aretino and Nashe, in the specific styles of address their discourses typically employ, and in the modes of audience engagement they seek to construct and maintain. The skill with which Aretino and Nashe (called the "true English Aretine" by his contemporary Thomas Lodge)[4] managed to project images of themselves as professional writers has been the subject of enduring critical attention, but what interests me here is how their works simultaneously project certain readerships, conjuring up imagined publics that are to a certain extent realized by virtue of the very act of their address.

THE SECRETARY OF THE WORLD: THE PRAGMATICS OF PUBLIC ADDRESS IN ARETINO'S LETTERS

In 1537 Pietro Aretino writes a letter to the humanist scholar Francesco Alunno in which he remarks with ostentatious bemusement on the variety of people who come to visit him. He notes the impressively broad spectrum of nations and social ranks they represent:

As a matter of fact, I don't believe that Rome itself ever saw such a conglomeration of people of different nationalities as burst into my house. To me come Turks, Jews, Frenchmen, Germans and Spaniards. You can imagine how many Italians there are. Of the plain people I will say nothing at all—except that it would be easier to woo you from your devotion to the Emperor than to see me for a single moment without soldiers, friars and priests surrounding me. For that reason, I have come to the conclusion that I am an oracle of truth, since everybody hies to me to relate the wrong done to him by this prince or that prelate. Yes, I am the secretary of the world, and so they address me in their superscriptions.[5]

The passage suggests not only the range of readership for Aretino's works, but the way these groups could attempt to speak to each other through him. They specifically look to Aretino to give wider public voice to their grievances. As members of his public, imagined readers and visitors, some of whom are strangers to Aretino, they recognize his capacity to influence opinion, and seek to mobilize that capacity in their own favor.

It seems probable that Aretino's personal history enabled him to appeal to and negotiate the various and often competing interests of the wide variety of publics he addresses in his writings. Born the son of a cobbler, the stories of his early life suggest an itinerancy that would have exhausted the hero of a picaresque novel. In the introduction to his edition of Aretino's letters, Thomas Caldecott Chubb notes that Aretino enrolled in school at an early age, was expelled, ran away to work as a bookbinder's assistant, then journeyed to Rome where he found employment as a household servant, a street singer, and an hostler. He also notes contemporary reports that Aretino subsequently wandered for a time impersonating a mendicant friar, then worked for a moneylender, as a tax collector, a mule skinner, a hangman's assistant, a galley slave, a miller, a courtier, and a pimp, among other things. In 1516, after publishing a satirical pamphlet on the passing of the pope's pet elephant, Aretino was engaged by Leo X to work in the papal household. From this point on Aretino would earn his living as a writer, and a comfortable living it came to be once he settled into the political sanctuary of Venice eleven years later in 1527.[6] The story of Aretino's early life, even if some of it is invented, the product of enemies' attempts to denigrate him, combines with the kinds of knowledge strewn about his writings to foster the impression that he possessed a familiar experience of the living practices of a wide spectrum of social actors, from pimps to the pope.

Even his literary output suggests a certain rootlessness. As Harald Hendrix observes in his account of Aretino's influence on the Elizabethans, what set Aretino apart from his contemporaries was the entrepreneurial initiative he brought to developing a career as professional writer.[7] Aretino identified and cultivated a variety of markets: His works include several comedies and a single tragedy; satirical *detournements* of contemporary events such as the aforementioned "Last Will and Testament of the Elephant"; parodic recastings of astrological prognostications that were then popular in print; satiric and nonsatiric poems addressed to prominent political figures; serious writings on religion; and more salacious works such as the *Ragionamenti* and his infamous poetic captions to the erotic paintings of Giulio Romano, which have continued to play a major role in his reputation down to the present day. He also regularly published collected volumes of his correspondence. These collections of letters were popular, and they best demonstrate the rhetorical sophistication he brought to managing his relations with the various individuals and communities that formed his public.

In the case of Aretino's letters, his readership has a dual nature; there are always two addressees. For each letter there is the initial private addressee, and then the wider reading public whose relation to the letters is of a more vicarious, and for Aretino an often frankly instrumental, nature. It is well known that Aretino derived much of his income from a particular form of patronage, a type of literary extortion.[8] The practice is exemplified in a letter to Agostino Ricchi of June 1537, in which Aretino quotes the Grand Master of France as having sent word to him that "if Aretino would consent to speak of the Emperor and my King according to the deserts of the former and the majesty of the latter, I would be willing to give him a life pension of 400 crowns."[9] In a great many of his letters, Aretino takes the opportunity to request that the eminent recipient honor a previous pledge of financial support. The publication of such letters serves to make these promises a matter of public record. It is clear that this testimonial function is far more important to Aretino than any income he might derive from the sale of his letters. Presumably the money involved in shaking down the reputations of aristocrats and eminent political or religious figures was much better than what he might expect from sales at the bookstalls. Later in June 1537 he writes to his publisher Francesco Marcolini:

> I hope God will grant that the courtesy of princes rewards me for the labor of writing, and not the small change of book buyers; for I would rather endure every hardship than to prostitute my genius by making it a day laborer of the liberal arts. It is obvious that those who write for money become hosts to, and even porters of their own infamy, and so if you want the advantage of profit, become a merchant. Frankly call yourself of a book pedlar, and lay the name of poet aside.[10]

Aretino's relationship with his readers is here exempted from the taint of mercenary considerations, a relationship in which the author barely condescends to accept the "small change" this public readership affords him. Rather, he publishes his private correspondence as a means of leveraging his claim to the support of wealthy patrons. By publishing letters to and about them, Aretino gives his audience the opportunity to become complicit in these power relationships. Each reader can become a part of a public, the leverage Aretino uses to compel wealthy patrons to honor their words.

Aretino's claim that he is wary of "prostituting his genius" bears further consideration given that so much of his published output is the result of making public that which is normally private. This is especially notable in his pornographic works, the *Ragionamenti* in particular, but the lurid strain can be found throughout his writing, and is, I would argue, one of its most consistent and compelling forms of appeal to the reader. The ability to "make public" becomes an important technique in this early phase of the early modern period. The public Aretino typically hails in his publications is summoned by the promise of salacious revelations—the bringing to the light of day that which is ordinarily obscured out of habit, custom, propriety, or shame. His claim to the title "secretary of the world" suggests not only his practice of writing letters for others, but also ironically recalls the older sense of the word that denotes the *secret* in "secretary," one who has been trusted with secrets.[11] Exposure is what Aretino traffics in; the public he calls into existence in his letters, and in many of his more popular works, is carefully developed to feed human curiosity—a far more bankable (and enduring, I would argue) commodity than the rational deliberation about common concerns that characterizes Jürgen Habermas's description of the eighteenth-century bourgeois public sphere.[12]

In many of his letters, Aretino contradicts his claim to Marcolini that he does not write for money, and in fact appears quite comfortable vaunting the naked exchange value of his good word, such as when he writes tauntingly in a letter to his rival Tasso that "I have made every Duke, Prince and Monarch that there is pay tribute to my genius. And that without running hither and thither, bowing the knee at court, or even stirring from where I am! Yet since my shop is the place where men from every corner of the globe buy fame, my portrait is much sought after in Persia and India, and my name esteemed there."[13] In a letter to Juneo Petreo from 1545, he remarks in more detail about the material evidence of his fame:

> I swear to you by the wings of steed Pegasus, that in this matter of my being famous, you don't know that half of it. As I have often said, I now say again that besides the medallions stamped or cast in gold, bronze, copper, lead, and plaster, I have had a lifelike copy made of my portrait which is on the facade of palaces and had it stamped on comb boxes, on the frames of mirrors and on majolica platters just like Caesar, Alexander, and Scipio. I affirm further that at Murano certain sorts of crystal vases are called Aretines, and Aretine they call a strain of ponies in honor of one Pope Clement gave me and I gave Duke Federigo. Moreover the little canal which bathes one of the sides of the house I live in on the Grand Canal is called Rio dell' Aretino, and not only do they speak of the Aretine style to the utter confusion

of pedagogues, but three of my housemaids and handmaidens who left me to become great ladies call themselves Aretines.[14]

The boastful quality of this passage is redeemed by Aretino's own delightful amazement at contemplating the material presence of his image in the world. Notwithstanding the sense of distance he is able to fashion between himself and his own fame, it is clear that the reputation Aretino is most careful to manage in his letters is of course his own. Time and again the readers of his letters, both the original "private" addressees and the subsequent larger readership, are encouraged to contemplate images of, and examples of, Aretino's fame and influence. In a letter to Modanese he notes how the street singers invoke his name: "But even as I write this to you, some intellectual snobs who see me writing it, heap scorn on me by saying that they have little respect for me because I now only allow myself to be, but rejoice at being, on the lips of your street singers."[15] He here scripts the very act of writing to Modanese into an event with its own audience (the "intellectual snobs"), and suggests that there will be a number of different, and even competing, audiences for the letter. Furthermore, we find here an attitude that Aretino is very careful to cultivate in other letters as well: controversy is not a thing to shy away from, but is rather the very source of his fame, and by extension his ability to project power and influence.

Frequently in Aretino's letters the original addressee is reminded that the letter may someday be published; in reading this future readers of the subsequently published letter are reminded that the mere prospect of their attention has had an effect even before they were aware of it themselves. This, I think, is Aretino's major contribution to the subject of early modern public formation: the instrumental and even systematic application of the awareness that an audience is not just witness to an event, but is possessed of judgment that can have an anticipatory effect on the behavior of others. A public, even as a purely notional entity, has a claim to power by virtue of its potential to render collective, and ostensibly normative, judgments. Pietro Aretino discovered a way, through corresponding with others and then repeating those utterances to a larger audience, of effectively harnessing the potential of this power. He uses this power to hold accountable those in positions of power, and he uses it for his own material benefit as well.

Michael Warner's argument that publics are hailed, or rhetorically conjured into existence by utterances that posit their existence, places an emphasis on the provisional, notional, or imagined nature of such entities. What Pietro Aretino's rhetorical practice in his letters suggests is that he was, as early as the first half of the sixteenth century, thinking several steps into this awareness, trading on the influence that these notional entities might be able to exert on his behalf in the court of public opinion. By composing letters, sending them to their recipients, and then subsequently sharing the same letters with a wider audience by publishing them in collections that include letters addressed to dozens of other originary addressees, Aretino's public address system plays both sides of the table. A single utterance can, in time, conjure up not just a single public, but multiple publics: the imagined public Aretino has in mind as he writes the letter; the imagined public the recipient is invited to consider while reading the letter; and the actual public that reads the published version of the letter.

NASHE AND THE POETICS OF PUBLIC ADDRESS

Thomas Nashe first published *The Unfortunate Traveller* in London in 1594. Set in the reign of Henry VIII, the narrative follows Jack Wilton, a page loosely engaged in the service of the earl of Surrey, as he travels throughout western Europe in the earlier sixteenth century, observing and wryly commenting on a wide variety of social and political situations. Jack participates in Henry's wars against the French, runs into academic communities in the Low Countries and Wittenberg, witnesses the tragic Anabaptist revolt at Leiden, and returns to England to find London beset by plague. He then sets off for Italy where he has numerous adventures, which include briefly living well above his social station by impersonating his noble master, and almost suffering vivisection at the hand of a physician. The episodic nature of the work leaves ample room for Nashe to interject with digression and commentary. One of the more notable of these digressions occurs when the narrator interrupts his tale in order to praise Pietro Aretino, who within the narrative is responsible for freeing the protagonist from an Italian prison. What makes the digression remarkable is the completely unreserved and enthusiastic nature of the narrator's praise for Aretino, who is described as "one of the wittiest knaues that euer God made," one whose "lyfe he contemned in comparison of the libertie of speech."[16] No other figure in the story receives such laudatory treatment. Nashe's reverential handling of this literary precursor is tied to his regard for Aretino's reputation as a model of the kind of social and political power a professional author should be capable of generating, and the influence such an author should be able to wield on the formation of public opinion and public taste. Considered from this professional perspective, it is fitting that Aretino is portrayed as an agent of liberation in Nashe's narrative.

As Aretino before him, Nashe forges his readership into an imagined public in the dedicatory apparatus of *The Unfortunate Traveller,* but due to the very different social and political climate within which Nashe writes, the wider public readership takes precedence over the sort of private patronage Aretino seeks and prefers. Nashe's book opens with what has to be one of the strangest dedications in Elizabethan literature. Addressed to aspiring literary patron Henry Wriothsley, the third earl of Southampton, the dedication is striking for its noncommittal tone and awkward impertinence. He opens by suggesting that the entire exercise is an empty convention:

> Ingenuous honorable Lord, I know not what blinde custome methodi-
> call antiquity hath thrust vpon vs, to dedicate such books as we publish
> to one great man or other; In which respect, least anie man should
> challenge these my papers as goods vncustomd, and so extend vppon
> them as forfeite to contempt, to the seale of your excellent censure, loe
> here I present them to be seene and allowed.[17]

It is difficult to imagine what Nashe thought Wriothsley would make of
this dedication, reading it and finding his role ascribed for him as that of
"one great man or other" called upon to participate in a literary ritual that
Nashe debases as "blinde custome." Nashe then runs with this already-
troubled word "custome," comparing the present work to goods that need
to pass through customs; amazingly, in the course of the metaphor, Wriothsley finds himself socially demoted from nobleman to government customs agent. Only midway through the dedication does Nashe employ any
conventional praise, when he writes "Incomprehensible is the height of your
spirit both in heroical resolution and matters of conceit. Vnrepriueably per-
isheth that booke whatsoeuer to wast paper, which on the diamond rocke
of your iudgement disasterly chanceth to be shipwrackt."[18] After comparing Wriothsley's sense of literary judgment to the scene of a naval catastro-
phe, the flattery halts abruptly when Nashe tactlessly delves into innuendo
concerning the young earl's rumored sexual proclivities: "A dere louer and
cherisher you are, as well of the louers of Poets, as of Poets themselues."[19]

The central question posed by the first dedication is why Nashe wrote
it and published it in the first place, since in it he as much as declares
that Wriothsley's support is unnecessary to him. He dismissively requests
Wriothsley to esteem the present work "as high or as low as you list," and
suggests that "of your gracious fauor I despaire not, for I am not altogether
Fames out-cast."[20] A strange mixture of pride, insecurity, and pointlessness
permeates the dedication to Wriothsley, informing and fueling its ambi-
guities. The subsequent omission of this dedication from the book's second
edition, coupled with its strange ambivalence, suggests Nashe felt that he
already had an audience willing to support his work. It is even possible to
imagine that this reading public—and not its direct addressee Wriothsley—
was the intended audience for the first dedication.

It is to Nashe's wider readership that the book's second dedication is
addressed. It is here that he is careful to construct his public in a certain
fashion. The second dedication is to "the dapper Monsieur Pages of the
Court,"[21] and the entire discursive register shifts abruptly to the language
of praise-abuse, a more typically winning style for Nashe as he imagines
a public—his readers and the relation they will have to his book. Here the
conventional modesty is both more artificial, and more effective, than in
the first dedication: "A proper fellow Page of yours called *Iack Wilton* by
me commends him vnto you, and hath bequeathed for wast paper here
amongst you certaine pages of his misfortunes."[22] In the first dedication

Nashe expresses a quaint fear that his work will become waste paper, but here among friends the humility rings more true, and instead of lamenting the possibility, he suggests numerous uses to which the waste pages could be put, keeping the preferences of his protagonist in mind. And whereas in the first dedication the wit is forced and weakly opportunistic, as in the careless punning on "custome," in the induction it flows with much greater imaginative vigor. Readers are enjoined to reimagine themselves according to Nashe's image of who they are, how they will rally around this text, and how they will value and defend it according to certain shared codes of behavior:

> *Memorandum,* euerie one of you after the perusing of this pamphlet is to prouide him a case of ponyardes, that if you come in companie with anie man which shall dispraise it or speak against it, you may straight crie *Sic respondeo,* and giue him the stockado. It standes not with your honours (I assure ye) to haue a gentleman and a page abusde in his absence.[23]

In addition, the community is enjoined, instead of swearing in men on a pantofle as they presently do, to use his book for that practice instead. It will also be accepted for them to use the book's cover as a platform to play false dice upon, and every time they pass a stationer's shop they are to doff their hats and reverently bend a leg to the book they know is there. The end of the induction sets up the implied communal, public situation of the narrative that is about to start: "Heighe passe, come alofte: euerie man of you take your places, and heare *Iack Wilton* tell his owne tale."[24]

In the dedicatory materials to *The Unfortunate Traveller,* nobleman Henry Wriothsley is the onlooker, the outsider, and not a privileged addressee. Instead, the privileged addressee of this discourse is Nashe's own public of pages—especially as he imagines and constructs it. Changes in the economics of the book trade, especially the decline in literary patronage that occurred in England in the 1590s, coupled with the rise of the professional author, made it possible and perhaps even necessary for a writer like Nashe to imagine his readers as a public, a community to which anyone could gain access, but that in this case implied a shared ethos and an at least virtual commitment to that ethos. It is of course unlikely that Nashe believed that his readership consisted wholly of the pages at court. Rather, the induction works as a kind of invitation to imaginatively become part of a public, a group of people with a shared perspective on the contemporary cultural and political situation. Nashe's unconventional use of the dedicatory apparatus in *The Unfortunate Traveller* suggests that the notion of publics, taken in the plural sense our research is tracking, was indeed well established at this time. A writer like Nashe could even expect his readers to be able to imagine themselves as part of such a public. Through that activity his readers would also be able to entertain certain oppositional social and political perspectives in a way that afforded them at least a provisional political agency.

THE INDIVIDUAL VOICE AND ITS PUBLICS

The rhetorical practices of Aretino and Nashe—their systems of public address—suggest that each had a keen sense not only of how to conjure up a public, but of the ways in which that imagined collectivity of anonymous individuals could be leveraged in support of social critique. For the readers of their texts, the opportunity to become a member of such a public presents access to an exciting new form of social agency. To this end, the rhetoric of both authors is conspiratorial in its address, and foregrounds the power of the professional author as a specialist in the print medium's new mechanisms for the construction and maintenance of public opinion (this is very probably how Nashe is drawn into the Marprelate controversy, for example, and it also explains the pseudonymous publication of the exchanges in that controversy).[25] Douglas Bruster has observed that the shift of sociocultural authority to the figure of professional writer was to some extent complete by Nashe's heyday in the mid-1590s, when "we see for the first time a significant number of readers and publishers placing as much importance on who had written a work as they did on what was in that work."[26] The author as public persona is anticipated in Aretino, who comes across in his writing as a new kind of public person: a commoner who has discovered how, like a monarch, to project his authority through material reiterations of his image and voice. As *The Unfortunate Traveller* suggests, Nashe consciously and overtly fashions himself as a professional writer in imitation of Aretino, though this imitation would always be incomplete, since circumstances dictated that he would never enjoy access to the necessary political sanctuary that Venice afforded Aretino.

The changing nature of literary patronage in the Renaissance, and the Elizabethan period more specifically, has been amply documented by critics such as Mark Thornton Burnett, Arthur Marotti, Katherine E. McLuskie, and Patricia Thomson.[27] These changes involved redefinitions of the social roles of, and redistributions of power between, authors, elite patrons, booksellers, and readers. Such changes affected all who would venture into print, however, and I do not wish to suggest that the differences between the public address systems of Nashe and Aretino can be explained exclusively or even primarily in structural terms. We also need to consider the contributions of personality and motivation, and it seems clear that there are important differences between these two figures that inflect their rhetorics of public address. For instance, it is clear that Nashe, for all of his rhetorical sophistication and critical sarcasm, is far more idealistic than Aretino, and that he has a less pragmatic outlook than his precursor. There is a greater sense of personal outrage in Nashe's work—social injustice and inequality are felt more keenly by him—whereas Aretino exposes inequity and injustice less out of a sense of his own moral outrage than as a way of activating an awareness, which he hopes to cash in on, of the implied disapproval of his implied audience. Ever the realist, Aretino is concerned with power and material comfort—unapologetically so. Nashe, bereft of both power and comfort, promotes social ideals in his work. Aretino appears comfortable with the corrupting effect of power, since it provides him with a seemingly inexhaustible resource with which to galvanize his audience. Nashe, on the other hand, writes in a satiric vein that purports to expose power's corrupting influence in the hope that social change might be effected. In sum, Aretino asks little of his public and in return receives all he needs. For his part, Nashe probably asks for more than it is in the nature of a public to be able to give.

While Michael Warner's rhetorical approach to the issue of publics and their formation highlights the social agency of the individual voice and the individual reader, it also suggests that publics are held together tentatively, by the same sorts of loose, unspoken contracts that we casually enter into in everyday communication. Aretino's and Nashe's rhetorics of public address indicate the nature of the contracts they wish to make with their readers. Aretino's practice in his published correspondence suggests that he is willing to allow his readers access to his public-making machinery for their benefit, if in return he can simply exploit their attention for his own. The result is the formation of a counterpublic that is strongly mediated by Aretino's authorial presence. For Nashe, the gesture of public address in *The Unfortunate Traveller* takes the form of an invitation for his readers to imagine themselves as other than they are, as pages in the presence of a fellow page. The result in Nashe's case is the formation of a virtual counterpublic that is encouraged to reflect upon the material form in which this mediation, and by extension the reader's implication in the discourse it presents, takes place.

NOTES

1. I wish to thank Karen Oberer, Jen Shea, Angela Vanhaelen, Myra Wright, Paul Yachnin, and especially Bronwen Wilson for their helpful and insightful comments on earlier versions of this essay.
2. Michael Warner, "Publics and Counterpublics," *Public Culture* 14, no. 1 (2002): 50.
3. Ibid., 82.
4. Thomas Lodge, *Wits Miserie, and the Worlds Madnesse Discouering the Deuils Incarnat of This Age* (London: Printed by Adam Islip, 1596).
5. Pietro Aretino, *The Letters of Pietro Aretino*, ed. and trans. Thomas Caldecott Chubb (Hamden, CT: Archon, 1967), 101–2.
6. See Thomas Caldecott Chubb's introduction to Aretino, *Letters*, 6–9.
7. See Harald Hendrix, "The Construction of an Author: Pietro Aretino and the Elizabethans," in *Betraying Our Selves: Forms of Self-Representation in*

Early Modern English Texts, ed. Henk Dragstra, Sheila Ottway, and Helen Wilcox (Basingstoke, UK: St. Martin's, 2000), 31–44.

8. See, for example, Jacob Burckhardt's estimation of Aretino in Jacob Burckhardt, *The Civilization of the Renaissance,* trans. Samuel George Chetwynd Middlemore (London: Phaidon, 1944), 100.

9. Aretino, *Letters,* 62.

10. Ibid., 66.

11. For the earlier sense, see *Oxford English Dictionary,* s.v. "Secretary," def. A1a.

12. See Jürgen Habermas, *The Structural Transformation of the Public Sphere: An Inquiry into a Category of Bourgeois Society,* trans. Thomas Burger (Cambridge: Polity, 1989).

13. Aretino, *Letters,* 284.

14. Ibid., 205.

15. Ibid., 216.

16. Thomas Nashe, *The Unfortunate Traveller,* in *The Works of Thomas Nashe,* ed. Ronald B. McKerrow (Oxford: Basil Blackwell, 1958), 2:264–65.

17. Ibid., 201.

18. Ibid.

19. Ibid.

20. Ibid., 201—2.

21. Ibid., 207.

22. Ibid.

23. Ibid.

24. Ibid., 208.

25. For more on the Martin Marprelate pamphlet wars and Nashe's purported role in them, see Donald J. McGinn, "Nashe's Share in the Marprelate Controversy," *PMLA* 59, no. 4 (1944): 952–84; and Joseph Black, "The Rhetoric of Reaction: The Martin Marprelate Tracts (1588–89), Anti-Martinism, and the Uses of Print in Early Modern England," *The Sixteenth Century Journal* 28, no. 3 (1997): 707–25.

26. Douglas Bruster, "The Structural Transformation of Print in Late Elizabethan England," in *Print, Manuscript, Performance: The Changing Relations of the Media in Early Modern England,* ed. Arthur F. Marotti and Michael D. Bristol (Columbus: Ohio State University Press, 2000), 59.

27. See Mark Thornton Burnett, "Apprentice Literature and the 'Crisis' of the 1590s," *The Yearbook of English Studies* 21 (1991): 27–38; Arthur Marotti, "Patronage, Poetry, and Print," *The Yearbook of English Studies* 21 (1991): 1–26; Kathleen E. McLuskie, "The Poets' Royal Exchange: Patronage and Commerce in Early Modern Drama," *The Yearbook of English Studies* 21 (1991): 53–62; and Patricia Thomson, "The Literature of Patronage, 1580–1630," *Essays in Criticism* 2 (1952): 267–84.

Part II
Things

5   *Hamlet* and the Social Thing in Early Modern England[1]

Paul Yachnin

My question in this chapter is, how can we best describe the political dimension of *Hamlet* in its own time? To answer that question, I take *Hamlet* as a representative instance of theatrical public making in early modern England. To what degree my account of the public made by *Hamlet* will be able to stand as an adequate description of the theatrical public as a whole, not to mention publics in general, must, I admit, remain to be seen. You might want perhaps to imagine my account of this particular play and its public making as an analysis of a cellular slice taken from the larger organism of early modern public making across a range of intellectual and artistic activities. Indeed what I do say is by no means all that might be said about public making or about the play itself. In what follows I focus down on one passage from *Hamlet,* on one early performance, and on one parodic response to the play in order to sketch some ideas about *Hamlet* in relation to public making and to what I am calling the social thing.

Since my focus is so local (though my goals are quite broad), I will not attempt to emulate some of the recent work on the play by scholars such as Stephen Greenblatt, Peter Lake, Andrew Hadfield, and Margreta de Grazia—Greenblatt in relation to the social trauma of the English Reformation; Lake in light of a history of the popular press, especially the many pamphlets that describe the instructive arc from crime to punishment and repentance; Hadfield in relation to the upsurge in interest in classical republicanism; and de Grazia across a range of political considerations, especially the nexus among land, entitlement, and identity.[2] Each of them has produced impressive historical scholarship, all of it aiming to answer more or less the same question that I am asking. They read *Hamlet* in relation to large-scale religious, literary (broadly defined), political, and ideological dimensions of the culture. My approach differs from theirs in part because I am paying attention to the local, social effects of the practices of playing, playgoing, reading, and writing in relation to *Hamlet*. My approach also differs from theirs because I am more interested in what the play does than in what it means. Indeed, my interest in what the play does depends on an idea that its social and political meaning is indeterminate, that it orchestrates a wide range of topics, and that it is able to anchor an expanding meta-topical network of performances, responses, and rewritings.

The idea of meta-topicality derives from Michael Warner, who says that a public "is the social space created by the reflexive circulation of discourse."[3] Meta-topicality also captures an essential and familiar feature of Shakespeare's art, which is that his plays are not theatricalized essays on particular topics but are instead imitations of actions that comprehend and are able to speak to a great range of interests and able also to do so with a high degree of self-awareness. The ideological pluralism and self-reflexiveness of a play like *Hamlet* is answerable to a range of critical responses, such as the ones by Greenblatt, Lake, Hadfield, and de Grazia; and pluralism also facilitates the wide-ranging circulation of *Hamlet*. That circulation, which is a process of making spin-offs of various kinds in textual, oral, and performative forms, has left in its wake an archival record of the creation of a social space of conversation. My argument identifies the political dimension of *Hamlet* not with its replaying of the social trauma of the Reformation, its engagement with the conventional morality of crime and punishment, its critical articulation of republicanism, or its investments in the landedness of personhood in early modernity. The political dimension of the play, I suggest, is bound up with its ability to cultivate public-making practices. *Hamlet*'s political effect and the political effects of artistic works generally in the period have therefore to do with the changes they were able to bring about in the structure of social and political relations rather than with their impact on social and political ideology. Ideas and practices are not, of course, entirely separable, but in the case of early modern public making, an articulate understanding of the growth and democratization of publicity tended to lag beyond the actual cultivation and expansion of new forms of public expression, identity, association, and action. That is why the emergence of public associations of playgoers in the period is routinely characterized and must to a degree have been experienced in traditional Christian-moralist terms, as what one contemporary called the "great resort and gathering together of all manner of vagrant and lewd persons."[4]

It also needs to be pointed out that the writing and first performance of *Hamlet* in around 1600 are not points of absolute origination since Shakespeare was adapting material that itself had a life in the theater and in print and since the dialogized meaning of the adapted material would have been part of the meaning of *Hamlet* from the moment of its inception. But *Hamlet* is nevertheless a work of such brilliant discursive orchestration and artistic originality that it can stand as a fountainhead. The record of dissemination, revision, response, and use that flows from 1600 and for the first twenty-five years only, includes performances in London, Oxford, and off the coast of Africa; the three early texts of the play (the first two quartos and the 1623 First Folio); bits of the text that find their way into other publications and plays (in *A Discourse of Marriage and Wiving* [1615], we find, set off in italics, "*In second husband let me be accurst, / None weds the second, but kills the first*");[5] standard stage properties that become Hamletized (the inky cloak and especially the skull, as in Thomas Middleton's *Revenger's Tragedy*); and the character of Hamlet himself (or a piece of him) that appears on stage, as we will see, as an overexcited footman in the play, *Eastward Ho!*

In this discussion, I want to consider not only the social agency of the playwright, players, playgoers, and readers, but also the social agency of the texts, textual bits, props, and costumes of *Hamlet* itself. To consider the agency of things as well as the agency of people is to take to heart Warner's simple but telling observation that a public is not "a really existing set of potentially numerable humans."[6] I take my cue here from Hannah Arendt's argument for the "thing character of the world," her claim that "the reality and reliability of the human world rest primarily on the fact that we are surrounded by things more permanent than the activity by which they were produced, and potentially even more permanent than the lives of their authors."[7] The world's thing character not only anchors "the unstable and mortal creature which is man," but also affords us the common objective reality that makes an authentically human lifeworld possible: "Only where things can be seen by many in a variety of aspects without changing their identity, so that those who are gathered around them know they see sameness in utter diversity, can worldly reality truly and reliably appear."[8] To Arendt's argument for the way things necessarily set the stage for a truly human world, we can add Bruno Latour's compelling case for the social agency of things themselves.

Latour argues that the dominant mode of sociological analysis, which relegates objects to mere materiality and instrumentality in the hands of humans and which trains its gaze on the interactions among people and on such metaphysical constructions as "the social compact" or "the social structure," is particularly well suited to the study of baboons but not to the study of humans.[9] "If sociologists had the privilege," he comments, "to watch more carefully baboons repairing their constantly decaying 'social structure,' they would have witnessed what incredible cost has been paid when the job is to maintain, for instance, social dominance with no *thing* at all, just social skills."[10] What makes, say, human relations of domination different from similar relations in the world of baboons are things— "entities," Latour says, "that don't sleep."[11] Latour suggests that the social world is best understood as a network of human and nonhuman actors (and this world, he insists, is not exclusively given over to relations of power):

> The main reason why objects had no chance to play any role before was not only due to the definition of the social used by sociologists, but also to the very definition of actors and agencies most often chosen. If action is limited a priori to what "intentional," "meaningful" humans do, it is hard to see how a hammer, a basket, a door closer, a cat, a rug, a mug, a list, or a tag could act. They might exist in the domain

of "material" causal relations, but not in the "reflexive" "symbolic" domain of social relations. But if we stick to our decision to start from the controversies about actors and agencies, then *any thing* that does modify a state of affairs by making a difference is an actor. . . . Thus, the questions to ask about any agent are simply the following: Does it make a difference in the course of some other agent's action or not? Is there some trial that allows someone to detect this difference?[12]

Hamlet is a particular kind of thing (a social thing), and one that, as we will see, is well characterized by Latour's idea of how things can become "matters of concern" (as opposed to "matters of fact"); but the basic thingness of the text needs to be taken into account in the story of how the play makes a public. The printed text, the written, printed, and borrowed bits of text, and the costumes and props take a full and robust part as "actors" in the public-making practices of writing, reading, publishing, playing, and playgoing.

I will come to *Hamlet* as a social thing, but first I want to imagine a moment in the first performance of the play at the Globe. The moment that I have in mind is from the fifth scene of the play. Hamlet has just ended his colloquy with his father's spirit. The soldiers and Horatio find him and, amid his wild and whirling words and the cries from the Ghost under the stage and as they shift their ground repeatedly, he makes them swear to silence about what they have just witnessed. Hamlet's words end the scene:

> Rest, rest, perturbed spirit! So, gentlemen,
> With all my love I do commend me to you,
> And what so poor a man as Hamlet is
> May do t' express his love and friending to you,
> God willing, shall not lack. Let us go in together,
> And still your fingers on your lips, I pray.
> The time is out of joint—O cursed spite,
> That ever I was born to set it right!
> Nay, come, let's go together. (1.5.182–90)[13]

The passage tells us something about the kind of public the play creates in the playhouse. The process starts when Richard Burbage cultivates the audience at the Globe by portraying a prince who cultivates a group of soldiers. His words conjure a collectivity on stage and off, one that crosses the boundaries of rank while carefully observing them. He describes himself as a poor man and addresses the soldiers as gentlemen (just as Shakespeare's prologues and epilogues typically address the audience as if they were gentles all); in deference to his rank, the soldiers hesitate before going in, so he invites them to leave the stage together with him. He speaks two lines of pseudo-soliloquy. The language of the lines draws on the mechanical arts of surgery and joinery and is expressive of the artisanal dimension of the playing company itself (not to mention the vocation of Hamlet's real father, the joiner and entrepreneur James Burbage).[14] By having a prince express self-doubt within the hearing of his social inferiors, Shakespeare creates a moment that is able to speak to the socially heterogeneous playgoers, seemingly able to unite them as a group invited to think through a problem and to form a judgment along with the protagonist, and able also to solicit from them a feeling of solidarity with the princely protagonist's task of bringing truth and justice to Denmark.

Hamlet in Elsinore is a man who is never able to go public, someone who feels his heart breaking because he must hold his tongue and someone whose dying wish is for someone else to go on living in pain in order to tell his, Hamlet's, story: "Report me and my cause aright / To the unsatisfied" (5.2.339–40), he says to his friend Horatio. Far from being the centerpiece in the emergence of a supposed bourgeois subjectivity, which is supposed to rob theater of its political force, Hamlet is the very figure of the individual's aspiration toward a full and active public life, and indeed a figure who represents and who has occasioned public, political talk and action in the real world.[15] This is more than a matter of Hamlet "going public" about the information that the new king is in fact a regicide. At stake is the reality of Hamlet's personhood: He needs to speak and act publicly so as to move out of his unstable private knowledge of himself and the world, including the secret he holds about the murder of his father, in order to *realize* who he is—both to make himself real and to secure his knowledge of himself. Arendt provides a radiant argument for the necessary relationship between publicity and personhood: "Action and speech are so closely related because the primordial and specifically human act must at the same time contain the answer to the question asked of every newcomer: 'Who are you?'"[16]

Of course, Hamlet in the playhouse is a man who is always already fully public, even and especially about his innermost thoughts. His soliloquies have a special power to gather the spectators into a judging and feeling community because these speeches have the authority of inner conviction or inner doubt, and because they are able to address the crowd one by one, as it were, each member of the audience as the prince's intimate interlocutor, and all of them freed from their social rank, gender, brand of Christianity, and profession in order to be able to take part in a collective process of deliberation that includes questions such as, is the specter that we see Hamlet's father's ghost or a demon in disguise? How are we to judge Hamlet's violent thoughts against his mother? How are we to judge his mother? Why kill Claudius when he might also be left to heaven? The most famous utterance in the play is an epitome of this relationship between private and public as a call to individual playgoers to think through a difficult question and to share equally in common cause with the protagonist. "To be or not to be" is intensely self-regarding and is also the perfect entry into a speech of debate-style deliberation. We might say that Shakespeare's design goes some way toward anticipating Habermas's emphasis on the formative place of private, equal individuals in the emergence of the public sphere:

> However much the . . . *salons* and coffee houses may have differed in the size and composition of their publics, the style of their proceedings, the climate of their debates . . . they all organized discussion among private people that tended to be ongoing . . . they preserved a kind of social intercourse that, far from presupposing the equality of status, disregarded status altogether. The tendency replaced the celebration of rank with a tact befitting equals. The parity on whose basis alone the authority of the better argument could assert itself against that of social hierarchy and in the end [could] carry the day meant, in the thought of the day, the parity of "common humanity."[17]

It is tempting to discover a full-fledged precursor of the Habermasian public sphere in a performance of *Hamlet* at Shakespeare's playhouse, circa 1600. The limitations of this picture of the play's creation of a social space where a heterogeneous audience comes together to take part in rational debate about matters of public import is suggested, of course, by, among other things, the play's own investments in elite culture and aristocratic charisma. What I have elsewhere called the populuxe theater (populuxe refers to popular versions of deluxe material and cultural goods or elite comportment or aristocratic forms of recreation) created a theatrical culture of emulation and masquerade that drew ordinary Londoners to the playhouse where they could drink in ersatz versions of courtly entertainment and could even hear something of court news, all provided to them in the poshest playhouse in Europe by the liveried servants of the Lord Chamberlain of England.[18] After all, the protagonist Hamlet, with whom playgoers are invited to feel intimate, is a prince. The spectators feel for him and they think with him, but they also want to feel like him and they are invited to emulate his princely pathos and tragic heroism. In the scene we have been looking at, we can note that the soldiers to whom Hamlet declares his friendship have seen but not heard the Ghost, whereas Hamlet has had a conversation with it. That difference is appropriate given Hamlet's special relationship with the spectral figure of his father, but it is also suggests the play's inattention to the basic informational conditions necessary for the realization of what Habermas calls a "public sphere of . . . rational-critical debate."[19]

I want to argue that *Hamlet* provides a case study of the process of coming out, which I think might be applicable to public making across a range of cultural and intellectual activities. *Hamlet*'s public, I suggest, is imaginary, virtual, and actual. It is imaginary in the sense that it is imagined within the playworld, which thereby invites the imaginative participation of the playgoers in the creation of a public in the playhouse. The playhouse public is not a mere fantasy, but it is hardly an undoubted reality either. It is in the realm of make-believe in as much as the theater represents itself as the purveyor of fiction and as powerless to effect any social ends except recreational ones. After all, there is no prince, no Denmark, and no struggle for truth and justice. Further, the playhouse public is fantastical because there is a poor fit between it as one of a plurality of publics in early modern London and the dominant early modern idea of the public as the whole commonwealth and as coterminous with public life as an attribute of the social elite (what Habermas calls "representative publicness"[20]), commoners and players being excluded from public discussion of public matters by royal proclamation.[21] Indeed, as I have suggested, a populuxe play like *Hamlet* reminds the playgoers of their exclusion from public life by inviting them to imagine their inclusion. And as I have argued elsewhere, the governmental regulation and marketplace commercialization of the drama combined to create a powerless theater, a theater whose activities were viewed as separate from and indeed as beneath the level of the operations of power.[22] I still think that this argument is correct as far as it goes, but I have come to understand that at the level of social and political imagining and also in terms of small-scale but formative innovations in the nature and accessibility of public space, speech, and action, the theater was very powerful indeed.

The playhouse audience begins to change into a theatrical public when the audience conceives of itself and makes itself into something more expansive, more productive, and more long-lasting than itself. In part, to be sure, the audience becomes a public merely by imagining itself as one. That act of imagining publicity is of a piece with its active creation. However, the audience's pleasure in the unfolding of the dramatic action and its collective thinking through of a matter of concern in solidarity with the protagonist is able to gain a greater degree of publicness because the pleasure and the thinking borne of the play *Hamlet* are disseminated beyond the walls of the playhouse into a space seemingly without boundaries, that is, the space of the public. As a matter of fact over the long term, the *Hamlet* of 1600 has entered precisely into such a boundless space: It is everywhere and for all time, a perfectly public, shared work of art. But in 1600 that high degree of publicity was long in the future. How, in the short term, did the audience of *Hamlet* become a virtual public?

Of course, audience members no doubt shared their affective and cognitive experience of the play with friends and family members who had not seen it, providing others with some knowledge and feeling about the play and engaging them in conversations about both its thematic content and the quality of the performance. But this kind of person-to-person dissemination would have had a relatively limited effect. More important by far are the texts of *Hamlet*. These include bits of the play that playgoers would have written in their table books and saved for later use in their own writing or conversation. This practice has been documented by Tiffany Stern and is gently mocked in the play when Hamlet says, "My tables. Meet it is I set it down / That one may smile, and smile, and be a villain . . . So, uncle, there you are" (1.5.107–10).[23] In addition, playgoers would have simply committed bits of the play, especially sent	entiae, to memory. In *A Nest of Ninnies* (1608), the actor Robert Armin wrote, "There are, as Hamlet says, things called whips in store," a misattribution of a phrase that is actually to be found in *The Spanish Tragedy,* which suggests the relative unreliability of memory in the process of transmission and dissemination and also, and more importantly, adumbrates a textual, public space in which *Hamlet* is inseparable from a canon of other plays and related writings.[24] Whether by way of physical tables or the table of memory, what is happening is a form of dissemination through a network of human and nonhuman actors—from the earlier, lost *Hamlet* play and myriad other printed, performed, and spoken sources to the playwright to the manuscript of the play *Hamlet* to the written parts for the actors to the performance itself, which depended on the actors' trained memories and a host of props, costumes, and the constructed space of the playhouse, to the textual or memorial recording practices of playgoers, readers, and writers, and then to their derivative or critical use of the play in a range of forms.

The reliability and commodity of textual reproduction made possible a remarkable early performance of *Hamlet* that took place on board a ship of the East India Company, the Red Dragon, on September 5, 1607, off the coast of Sierra Leone. The players were sailors and most of the playgoers also were sailors. Gary Taylor, who has written a history of this event, tells us that there were also visitors aboard for the performance—"four guests with filed teeth, plucked eyelashes, rings on their fingers and in their ears and noses, braided hair shaved into 'elegant patterns.'"[25] One of the spectators was Lucas Fernandez, a black African who was also the royal translator (mostly between the Africans and the Portuguese), a Catholic, and a favorite of Farim Buré, the ruler of the southern and eastern shores of the Sierra Leone estuary.[26] Taylor quotes from the diary of William Keeling, captain of the *Red Dragon:*

> Towards night, the King's interpreter came, and brought me a letter from the Portugal. . . . The bearer is a man of marvellous ready wit, and speaks in eloquent Portuguese. . . . I sent the interpreter, according to his desire, aboard the Hector [the *Red Dragon*'s sister ship], where he broke fast, and after came aboard me, where we gave *The Tragedy of Hamlet.*[27]

Taylor remarks on the appropriateness of the verb ("we gave *The Tragedy of Hamlet*"), especially in view of the custom of diplomatic entertainment in European courts and between European traders and their hosts in the East.[28] On this account the performance of *Hamlet* was a gift of welcome, able (if the performance were successful) to convey something about the beauty of English drama and the ease and effectiveness of English team-work and able thereby to help cultivate respect on the part of the Africans for the English traders.

My focus, however, is not on Shakespeare within a gift economy, but rather on the social thingness of *Hamlet,* as both text and performance within a system of exchange and theatrical production and publicity. The text of *Hamlet* (whether the first or second quarto is unknown) was an actor in this history. It was purchased and brought on the voyage, perhaps by the captain with a view toward keeping the crew from idleness and restlessness, which was a matter of great concern to naval officers and the trading companies that employed them, or perhaps by one of the sailors, someone with the foresight to lay in recreational stores for the long periods of shipboard idleness. The quarto would likely have been copied into parts, the parts committed to memory by the amateur players, and the play executed very generally after the fashion of the professional London company. The play was in fact performed twice on the *Red Dragon.* After the second performance, September 31, 1608, Keeling wrote in his diary, "I invited Captain Hawkins to a fish dinner, and had *Hamlet* acted aboard me, which I permit to keep my people from idleness and unlawful games or sleep."[29]

The quarto of *Hamlet* is a social thing because it enables the transmission of performance practices as well as the spread of the script itself. In a comic parody of the kind of amateur performance that took place on board the *Red Dragon* and the ways in which performance practice could become common property, the Citizen's Wife in Francis Beaumont's *The Knight of the Burning Pestle* interrupts the play that is supposed to be beginning in order to give her apprentice Rafe his hour upon the stage. "I pray you, youth, let him have a suit of reparel—I'll be sworn, gentlemen, my husband tells you true. He will act you sometimes at our house, that all the neighbours cry out on him. He will fetch you up a couraging part so in the garret that we are all as feared, I warrant you, that we quake again."[30]

Whether he provided the playbook to the sailors or not, it is striking that the captain of the *Red Dragon* thought that something like a stage play would serve the interests of good order on board ship, and it certainly should prompt us to reconsider the idea that the business elite was opposed to theater because they believed that playing and playgoing were idleness itself rather than a cure for idleness. There is of course no reason to think that the performance of *Hamlet* changed anything in the hierarchical organization or the social ideology on board ship, although it is certainly worth asking if the sailors shared with their captain a view of theatrical performance as a form of disciplinary recreation, especially since all of them would have been familiar with the charge that theater was slothful and sinful, and since many of them would have been at least occasional playgoers and would therefore have their experience of this *Hamlet* influenced by their recollection of watching it and other plays performed in London. The quarto edition of *Hamlet* thus carries the play to Africa and adds the sailors to the company of *Hamlet*'s public by involving them in a performance of the play and also, to some degree, in a critical debate about authority and playing, a debate that need not be explicit but that can be carried out in the performance itself and in the enjoying of the play.

The quarto edition of *Hamlet* is a social thing in that it is an agent capable of making a difference in the course of some other agent's action and because it can communicate the collective practices of playing and playgoing from the professional London stage to a group of sailor-actors on board a ship off the African coast. It is a social thing in a more urgent sense because, as a work of literature, it puts into circulation matters of social concern, including the duties of children to their parents, the inviolability of the monarch, the possibilities of social fairness and political justice, and the social place of theatrical performance. And because it thematizes the place of the stage, it is itself able to become a matter of concern. Here it is also useful to take note of Latour's account of how the objects of scientific knowledge have recently morphed into "matters of concern" (in a somewhat more complex sense of the phrase): "This has nothing to do with the 'interpretive flexibility' allowed by 'multiple points of views' [*sic*] taken on the 'same' thing. *It is the thing itself that has been allowed to be deployed as multiple* and thus allowed to be grasped through different viewpoints, before being possibly unified in some later stage depending on the abilities of the collective to unify them."[31] Because of its multiplicity, the play *Hamlet* stands in relation to its audience as a matter of concern rather than as an object of knowledge. Because of its meta-topicality—its ability to reflect on its own multiplicity and thereby to afford its spectators an image of their own interpretive activity—the concern that it embodies and arouses has a marked self-conscious and public quality.

Or consider this story that Homi Bhabha derives from historian Sir John Kaye's *History of the Indian Rebellion*, the story of how an ordinary *chapati* (flat bread) became an ominous thing of interest and focus of interpretive energy as it moved from village to village:

> From village to village, brought by one messenger and sent onward by another, passed a mysterious token in the shape of those flat cakes . . . which in their language are called chapatis. . . . The greater number looked upon it as a signal of warning and preparation, designed to tell the people that something great and portentous was about to happen, and to prompt them to be ready for the crisis. One great authority wrote to the Governor-General that he had been told that the chapati was the symbol of men's food, and that its circulation was intended to alarm and to influence men's minds by indicating to them that their means of subsistence would be taken from them, and to tell them therefore, to hold together. Others laughing to scorn this notion of the fiery cross, saw in it only a common superstition of the country. It was said that it was no unwonted thing for a Hindu, in whose family sickness had

broken out, to institute this transmission of chapatis, in the belief that it would carry off the disease. Then, again, it was believed by others . . . that the purpose attaching to the circulation [of the chapatis] was another fiction, that there was bone dust in them, and that the English had resorted to this supplementary method of defiling the people. . . . But whatsoever the real history of the movement, it had doubtless the effect of keeping alive much popular excitement in the districts through which the cakes were transmitted.[32]

Bhabha's reflections on the chapati's transformation from ordinary object-hood into a thing that stands apart, raising questions, soliciting theories, and gathering together the inhabitants of the disparate villages along its trajectory, can lead us away from mystifying formulations that attempt to explain the social agency of things such as *Hamlet* in terms of a human, intentional presence somehow bound like the genii within the materiality of the book. To recognize the social thingness of *Hamlet* is to begin to understand how the play is able to act upon people along quite unmagical lines and how texts can possess social agency. *Hamlet* is a chapati that is always already in movement, as it were, since controversy is build into it at the level of language. In broad terms, as Bakhtin has taught us, any utterance shares a socially meaningful relationship with others of its general kind:

Each utterance is filled with echoes and reverberations of other utterances to which it is related by the communality of the sphere of speech communication. Every utterance must be regarded primarily as a *response* to preceding utterances of the given sphere (we understand the word "response" here in the broadest sense). Each utterance refutes, affirms, supplements, and relies on the others, presupposes them to be known, and somehow takes them into account.[33]

The play's engagement with other utterances—including gestural as well as verbal expressions—is immense and complex and extends forward as well as backward in time. When Hamlet rehearses what is marked out by his performance as an antiquated vocabulary of revenge ("Bloody, bawdy villain! / Remorseless, treacherous, lecherous, kindless villain!" [2.2.580–1]), he is positioning himself in relation to earlier stage revengers; he is proleptically critiquing Laertes' conventional revenger language (4.5.132–7) (he will do the same face-to-face with Laertes in Ophelia's grave [5.1.274–84]); the play is situating itself as more verisimilar, more intelligent, and more responsive to moral ambiguity than the tragic drama that preceded it; and it is thereby raising questions about the moral value and social efficacy of violent revenge. "No texts themselves create publics," says Michael Warner, "but the concatenation of texts through time. Only when a previously existing discourse can be supposed, and when a responding discourse can be postulated, can a text address a public."[34] As a social thing, *Hamlet* is an expanding, multiple, meta-topical set of texts, performances, parodies, borrowings, critiques, props, and images—all sites of the interactivity of human and material agency—whose circulation beyond the walls of the Globe and the year 1600 was able to realize the public that was imagined in the first performance of the play and that was playfully enacted by the first audience.

Lastly is Ben Jonson, George Chapman, and John Marston's play, *Eastward Ho!* Here Hamlet is transformed into a footman who attends upon a woman named Gertrude (she actually sings a parody version of one of Ophelia's songs), who has recently married Sir Petronel Flash, a newly made knight. Lady Flash's imminent departure from London creates a bustle of preparation and a wave of excitement as the Londoners assemble to catch a glimpse of her:

Mistress Fond. Come, sweet Mistress Gazer, let's watch here, and see my Lady Flash take coach.
Mistress Gazer. O' my word, here's a most fine place to stand in. Did you see the new ship launched last day, Mistress Fond?
Mistress Fond. O God! and we citizens should lose such a sight!
Mistress Gazer. I warrant here will be double as many people to see her take coach as there were to see it take water.
Mistress Fond. O, she's married to a most fine castle i' th' country, they say.
Mistress Gazer. But there are no giants in the castle, are there?
Mistress Fond. O no; they say her knight killed 'em all, and therefore he was knighted.[35]

The two women are gazers, but they are not entirely fond, or "foolish." They are there to see Lady Flash take coach and they are also there to be seen seeing her, as if the looking relationship with gentry itself conferred a kind of public personhood. They also take their place in order to be able to comment on a public figure. Enamored of the spectacle of what they take to be an aristocratic woman, they nevertheless retain a critical faculty with respect to the object of their admiration, signaling a lively awareness of the appeal of property ("she's married to a most fine castle"), registering the operation of the network of rumor and talk ("they say . . . they say"), and deploying the forms of fairy tale ("they say her knight killed 'em all, and therefore he was knighted") in order to mock Lady Flash, her husband Petronel, and even the new king's widely criticized devaluing of honors. The scene provides a parodic version of some of the most salient features of early modern playgoing: the lure of looking that is tuned to the private person's desire to see the great personages and actions of the public world, the desire to be seen seeing, and the capacity of the theater to afford private persons the space in which to deliberate upon and to judge matters of public concern.

Hamlet's entrance is signaled by the direction, "Enter Hamlet, a footman, in haste." He says, "What, coachman! My lady's coach, for shame! / Her ladyship's ready to come down" (3.2.5–6). Potkin, a tankard-bearer, says, "'Sfoot, Hamlet, are you mad? Whither run you now?" (7–8). The play's mockery of Shakespeare's Hamlet's excited and ineffectual bustle about the stage, reminiscent surely of the end of Act 1 scene 5 in *Hamlet,* connects with its critique of the popular desire for the spectacle of aristocratic glamour. Jonson and his fellows develop a comic critique of the way Shakespeare's theater seeks to sell courtliness and intimacy with a fantasy prince to ordinary Londoners. *Eastward Ho!* cultivates its audience's aesthetic and political judgment about Shakespeare's play and thereby contributes to the development of a specifically theatrical public, a self-reflexive field of public discourse about the artistry and social politics of the drama itself.[36] It is an attack on Shakespeare's populuxe theatrical art, his trading on his company's connections with the court in order to impress what Hamlet himself calls "the groundlings," but it is also an extension of the play *Hamlet*'s imagining of a critical public, an extension in fact that helps to realize what the play *Hamlet* imagines. *Eastward Ho!* thus contributes to the creation of a virtual public space in which, first of all, public debate about theater, social rank, and authority could take place, and it serves to remind us that the public that *Hamlet* made must finally be joined to the theatrical public of early modern England, of which it was a part.

NOTES

1. I am happy to register my debt to Bronwen Wilson for her invaluable help with "thing theory," to Yael Margalit for her research assistance and for an insightful critique of an earlier version of this essay, and also to Albert Schultz, whose MaPs-sponsored workshop performance of Hamlet's soliloquies illuminated for me the play's dynamic orchestration of privacy and publicity.
2. Stephen Greenblatt, *Hamlet in Purgatory* (Princeton, NJ: Princeton University Press, 2002); Peter Lake, "Theatrical Appropriations: The First Time as Tragedy, the Second Time as Farce," in *The Antichrist's Lewd Hat: Protestants, Papists and Players in Post-Reformation England,* Peter Lake with Michael Questier (New Haven, CT: Yale University Press, 2002), 377–424; Andrew Hadfield, "The Radical *Hamlet,*" in *Shakespeare and Republicanism* (Cambridge: Cambridge University Press, 2005), 184–204; Margreta de Grazia, Hamlet *without Hamlet* (Cambridge: Cambridge University Press, 2007).
3. Michael Warner, *Publics and Counterpublics* (New York: Zone Books, 2002), 90.
4. From the petition of the inhabitants of the Blackfriars to the Privy Council (1596), in E. K. Chambers, *The Elizabethan Stage* (Oxford: Clarendon Press, 1923), 4:319.
5. Alexander Niccholes, *A Discourse of Marriage and Wiving* (London, 1615), 40.
6. Warner, *Publics and Counterpublics,* 68.

7. Hannah Arendt, *The Human Condition*, 2nd ed. (Chicago: University of Chicago Press, 1998), 93, 95–96.

8. Ibid., 136, 57.

9. Bruno Latour, *Reassembling the Social: An Introduction to Actor-Network-Theory* (Oxford: Oxford University Press, 2005), 70.

10. Emphasis in the original; ibid.

11. Emphasis in the original; ibid.

12. Ibid., 71.

13. All Shakespeare quotes are from G. Blakemore Evans, ed., *The Riverside Shakespeare*, 2nd textual ed. (Boston: Houghton Mifflin, 1997).

14. For more about the artisanal dimension of theatrical culture, see Paul Yachnin "'The Perfection of Ten': Populuxe Art and Artisanal Value in *Troilus and Cressida*," *Shakespeare Quarterly* 56 (2005): 306–25.

15. For brilliant and misleading cultural materialist arguments for the depoliticizing effect of Hamlet's private personhood, which is itself seen as an anachronistic imposition on the text, see Francis Barker, *The Private Tremulous Body: Essays on Subjection* (New York: Methuen, 1984); and, more recently, de Grazia, Hamlet *without Hamlet*. In contrast to these arguments, I think that it is precisely the private-public dynamic of Hamlet himself that has the capacity to galvanize an audience into a public, transforming a crowd of pleasure seekers into a political community. One modern instance of the political force of Hamlet's particular character dynamic were two series of performances of the play in Prague under the Nazis and then under Stalinist rule. In both cases, the audiences' identification with the hero's struggle spoke to national aspirations toward freedom and justice. See Jarka Burian, "Hamlet in Postwar Czech Theatre," in *Foreign Shakespeare: Contemporary Performance*, ed. Dennis Kennedy (Cambridge: Cambridge University Press, 1993), 195–210.

16. Arendt, *Human Condition*, 178. The idea of the necessary linkage between personhood and publicity is by no means a new one. Consider Ulysses' remarks to Achilles in Shakespeare's *Troilus and Cressida*: "no man is the lord of any thing, / Though in and of him there be much consisting, / Till he communicate his parts to others; / Nor doth he of himself know them for aught, / Till he behold them formed in th' applause / Where th' are extended" (3.3.115–20). Or consider the opening lines of *Hamlet*: "Who's there?" says one soldier. "Nay, answer me," says his counterpart, "Stand and unfold yourself."

17. Jürgen Habermas, *The Structural Transformation of the Public Sphere: An Inquiry into a Category of Bourgeois Society*, trans. Thomas Burger (Cambridge, MA: MIT Press, 1991), 36.

18. See Anthony Dawson and Paul Yachnin, "The Populuxe Theatre," in *The Culture of Playgoing in Shakespeare's England: A Collaborative Debate* (Cambridge: Cambridge University Press, 2001), 38–65.

19. Habermas, *Structural Transformation*, 51.

20. Ibid., 5.

21. See Paul L. Hughes and James F. Larkin, eds., *Tudor Royal Proclamations* (New Haven, CT: Yale University Press, 1969), 2:115.

22. See Paul Yachnin, "The Powerless Theater," in *Stage-Wrights: Shakespeare, Jonson, Middleton, and the Making of Theatrical Value* (Philadelphia: University of Pennsylvania Press, 1997), 1–24.

23. See Tiffany Stern, "Watching as Reading: The Audience and Written Text in Shakespeare's Playhouse," in *How to Do Things with Shakespeare: New Approaches, New Essays*, ed. Laurie Maguire (Oxford: Blackwell, 2008), 136–59. See also Douglas Bruster, *Quoting Shakespeare: Form and Culture*

in Early Modern Drama (Lincoln: University of Nebraska Press, 2000), 217–18, n. 28.

24. Robert Armin, *A Nest of Ninnies* (London, 1608), 50.

25. Gary Taylor, "*Hamlet* in Africa 1607," in *Travel Knowledge: European "Discoveries" in the Early Modern Period*, ed. Ivo Kamps and Jyotsna G. Singh (New York: Palgrave, 2001), 223.

26. Ibid., 226.

27. Quoted in ibid., 225.

28. Ibid., 232–33.

29. Quoted in David Farley-Hills, *Critical Responses to* Hamlet, *1600–1790* (New York: AMS, 1997), 8.

30. Francis Beaumont, *The Knight of the Burning Pestle*, ed. Michael Hattaway, 2nd ed. (London: A and C Black; New York: Norton, 2002), 1.1.67–72.

31. Latour, *Reassembling the Social*, 116 (italics in original).

32. Homi K. Bhabha, "By Bread Alone," in *The Location of Culture* (New York: Routledge, 1994), 201.

33. Emphasis in the original; M. M. Bakhtin, *Speech Genres and Other Late Essays*, ed. Caryl Emerson and Michael Holquist, trans. Vern W. McGee, (Austin: University of Texas Press, 1986), 91.

34. Warner, *Publics and Counterpublics*, 90.

35. George Chapman, Ben Jonson, and John Marston, *Eastward Ho!* ed. R. W. Van Fossen, Revels Plays (Manchester, UK: Manchester University Press, 1979), 3.2.13–21.

36. See Habermas, *Structural Transformation*, 39–40: "For the first time an audience gathered to listen to music as such—a public of music lovers to which anyone who was propertied and educated was admitted. Released from its functions in the service of social representation, art became an object of free choice and of changing preference. The 'taste' to which art was oriented from then on became manifest in the assessments of lay people who claimed no prerogative, since within a public everyone was entitled to judge."

6 Petrucci's Publics for the First Motet Prints

Julie E. Cumming

In 1501 Ottaviano Petrucci published the first book of polyphonic music printed with movable type. Over the next twenty years he published all the available genres of composed polyphony: *chansons, frottole, laude,* lute intabulations, Masses, other liturgical music, and motets.[1] Petrucci must have been aware of a demand for secular music, and his first book, the *Odhecaton,* was a collection of almost one hundred chansons. Masses by famous composers would have been another obvious choice for publication. But less clear are Petrucci's reasons for publishing motet anthologies: collections of polyphonic settings of sacred Latin texts. What was the market for Petrucci's motet prints? Did that market constitute a public, or publics? Did the existence of these new kinds of objects—printed motet anthologies—play a role in the formation of new publics?

In order to investigate these questions, I will look at a hypothetical market, an actual market, and a set of overlapping publics for the motet prints. First of all there is Petrucci's imagined market for the motet prints—the people that Petrucci thought might buy them, based on his knowledge of European society and markets for cultural goods before the appearance of the first of his prints. Then there is the actual market: the group of people who did in fact buy the prints. I will suggest that the actual market was somewhat different from Petrucci's imagined market.

A market does not equal a public, however, although it may be an important component of a public or publics.[2] As we investigate the imagined and actual markets, we will discover several groups of people with different uses for, or interests in, the motet books. Some of the members of these groups bought the books, but not all of them did. These groups of people, I propose, are the publics for the motet books—publics that together extend well beyond the actual market. Some of these publics, as we shall see, are new forms of association, called into existence by the advent of the printed motet book.

PETRUCCI AND THE MOTET

Petrucci published two series of motet prints, the first in Venice between 1502 and 1508, the second in Fossombrone between 1514 and 1519. I will

focus on the first series of five prints (see Table 6.1), although I will sometimes refer to information on the second series as well. In Venice Petrucci
worked with a music editor, Petrus Castellanus, the *maestro di cappella*
in the Dominican church of Santi Giovanni e Paolo, who must have had
a major role in imagining the market for the books, and in choosing the
music to be printed.[3] Any reference later to Petrucci should be taken as
referring to both men.

The motet circa 1500 was a Latin-texted vocal work, normally with a
preexistent sacred text (although some had new topical or laudatory political texts). The motets in the Petrucci collections, like most motets from
the period, are mostly for four voices (soprano, alto, tenor, bass), with text
provided in all parts. Some are simple homorhythmic prayer settings. Some
are extremely complex: long, multipartite pieces with conflicting rhythms,
varied textures, and esoteric centonate or classicizing Latin texts.

Johannes Tinctoris, a northern music theorist who worked in Naples,
described the motet in his dictionary of 1476: "A motet is a composition
of moderate length, to which words of any kind are set, but more often
those of a sacred nature." Almost thirty-five years later the Italian humanist Paolo Cortese emphasized the flexibility of the motet in a sacred context:
"Although mixed with the propitiatory singing [that is, the Mass], they
can be seen to be supernumerary and ingrafted, since for them there is free
option of choice." This seems to mean that while they can be performed
during Mass, motets are optional additions: Their texts and their location
in the service are a matter of choice.[4] Both Tinctoris and Cortese positioned
the motet in the middle of a hierarchy of musical genres, with the Mass
ordinary cycle at the top, and secular music at the bottom. The position
of the motet in the middle of the genre hierarchy is what makes possible
its range of musical styles and its functional flexibility—it can resemble a
humble secular song or a grand Mass movement. While on the one hand
it is hard to imagine any single group that would be interested in all the
motets in each collection, the variety of motets, on the other hand, also
suggests a broad field for a potential imagined market.

Table 6.1 Ottaviano Petrucci's First Five Motet Prints, Venice, 1502–1508
(174 pieces, 355 *partes*. Oblong quarto format, c. 16 × 23 cm).

RISM no. *(Boorman no.)*	*Title. Date. Edition.*
1502[1] (B 3) [1505[7]] (B 19)	*Motetti A numero trentatre*. 9 May 1502. 2nd edition, 13 February 1505 (n.s.) (not in RISM).
1503[1] (B 7)	*Motetti De passione De cruce De sacramento De beata virgine et huiusmodi B*. 10 May 1503.
1504[1] (B 15)	*Motetti C* (partbooks). 15 September 1504.
1505[2] (B 21)	*Motetti libro quarto* (partbooks). 4 June 1505.
1508[1] (B 46)	*Motetti a cinque Libro primo* (partbooks). [28 November 1508.]

THE IMAGINED MARKET

Like any entrepreneur who sets out to sell something, Petrucci had to imagine the people to whom he would sell his product. Unlike many entrepreneurs, however, Petrucci was selling a brand-new product (printed polyphonic motets), so he had to imagine a market for the motets based on his experience in a number of areas. We can speculate about how he imagined that market by looking at three different kinds of information:

1. the market for other *comparable printed products,*
2. functions for and consumers of motets, as indicated by late fifteenth-century *manuscripts containing motets,* and
3. the *format and layout of the motet prints,* as a guide to Petrucci's ideas about potential buyers.

Comparable Printed Products

Earlier Music Prints

Many of Petrucci's technical achievements were based on the work of earlier music printers, whose music incunabula contained liturgical plainchant. Some of his financial backers had also been involved in these earlier projects.[5] But did the market for the earlier chant prints provide a useful model for Petrucci?

The most common type of printed music book was the missal, which contained the parts of the Mass read and sung by the priest.[6] The market for this kind of book was thus clearly defined. Almost every priest in Western Christendom needed such a book in order to perform Mass, and as manuscript copies wore out and populations grew, printed missals proved to be more affordable and reliable than manuscripts. The priests using printed missals, however, would rarely or never have been involved in singing motets.

The books of chant used by the choir (the Gradual, containing chants for Mass, and the Antiphonal, containing chants for the Office) were printed much less frequently.[7] Most parish churches did not have professional choirs singing the ornate chants of the liturgy; the relatively small numbers of monasteries and major churches with professional choir members had the resources to pay for new manuscripts, and the professional singers were also expert in copying music. Nevertheless, some of the printed Graduals and Antiphonals are among the most spectacular books ever printed, and late fifteenth-century Venice was an important center for their production.[8] The institutional market for these chant books must have formed part of Petrucci's imagined market for the Mass and motet prints.

Printed Books

Of the many kinds of book printed and sold in Venice circa 1500, two seem particularly relevant to Petrucci's motet prints: books of hours, and classical humanist texts such as those published by Aldus Manutius. Both kinds of books had Latin texts, like the motet prints; the first, like the motet books, was devotional; the second was aimed at a sophisticated international republic of letters for which Latin was a common language.

Books of Hours

When most people think of books of hours, they imagine ornate illuminated manuscripts owned by members of the aristocracy, such as the *Très riches heures du Duc de Berry*. With the advent of printing in the mid-fifteenth century, however, ownership of a book of hours was possible for a much broader group of people. There may have been more printed books of hours than any other type of book in the late fifteenth and sixteenth centuries. If you owned only one book, it was likely to be a book of hours.[9] People read the book daily, or several times a day. Even people who could not understand Latin used such books: They could pronounce the words, and the act of saying the text out loud was efficacious as a prayer, even if the speaker did not understand the exact syntax or meaning.[10]

Many of the motets in Petrucci's motet books set texts found in books of hours—texts that many people read aloud on a daily basis for much of their lives.[11] The motet prints could therefore be used to perform personal devotions. Some people may have bought the motet books purely as anthologies of prayers to be said aloud, or to be sung by a single voice. Others may have sung motets as part of family devotions, or as part of communal devotions in confraternities.[12] The devotional market would probably have enjoyed the simpler homorhythmic settings of texts found in books of hours. Professional singers hired by the confraternities could have sung the more complex pieces for an audience that included owners of books of hours; members of that audience may have wanted to acquire the music and sing it at home or with friends.

It may seem odd to discuss the quintessentially private book of hours in relation to the *public* for the motet prints. But certainly Petrucci would have seen the potential for overlap between the market for books of hours and the market for his motet prints. In the case of printed books of hours we can posit two kinds of virtual publics. The first has to do with the market. Purchasers of books of hours must have seen themselves as members of a book-buying public: They may have met other buyers in bookshops, compared books with friends and relatives, given books to young relatives, and bought more elaborate books when finances allowed.

The second has to do with the nature of devotional practice during the period. The act of repeating a prayer assumed (or called into being) the community of the faithful. Marian devotions, central to books of hours (normally entitled *Officium beatae Mariae virginis*), called upon the Virgin to intercede with God for both the individual and the group. Another standard set of texts found in books of hours was the Office of the dead, as well as other prayers that were sung to reduce the time in purgatory of dead friends and relations. Some books of hours even included indulgenced prayers that promised reductions of hundreds or even thousands of years off the time in purgatory for each repetition of the text.[13] We can call the communities of the living faithful on earth and the repentant faithful in purgatory virtual publics, present in the imagination each time a book of hours was used.[14] Similarly, the people performing the texts and music in the motet books—whether alone, with a small group, or with a larger choir of amateurs or professionals—and the people listening to the motets, would have called into being these same virtual publics.

Latin Humanist Writings

Roughly speaking, Petrucci's music prints can be divided into two different types: those in Latin and those in the vernacular. His prints with Italian texts—eleven *frottola* and two *lauda* prints—were presumably aimed at a local market (it is striking how vernacular musical genres exploded in almost every European country within the first three decades after Petrucci introduced printed polyphony). But the Petrucci prints with Latin texts had the potential to sell in an international market, not limited by any local vernacular. As such, they resembled the humanist Latin publications of Aldus Manutius and others, whose octavo classical texts in the new italic font were embraced so enthusiastically by the republic of letters.[15] Like the octavo classics, Petrucci's prints featured an elegant new type face that was clear and easy to read, in a new smaller format.[16] The books are also remarkably free from errors, an essential feature for amateur singers without the musical skills required to correct mistakes. Sacred music such as motets and Masses had previously been found mostly in large choirbooks or bulky miscellaneous anthologies. The Petrucci prints provided a carefully selected group of pieces that was easy to sing from and to transport. The music lovers who bought the octavo classics might have enjoyed the Petrucci motets that set unusual or classicizing texts, as well as more complex musical settings, including works with multiple texts, *cantus firmi*, and canons.

One member of the republic of letters with an interest in music is Hartmann Schedel. Nuremberg medical doctor, humanist, and author of the illustrated *Weltchronik* (the *Nuremberg Chronicle*), Schedel also collected music during his student days (1460s), copying chansons and motets into a personal manuscript. As a source for performance, the manuscript is almost useless: There are too many mistakes. Thus even musically literate intellectuals did not have the training or the experience to copy music accurately. Schedel, and others like him, would have been eager purchasers of the Petrucci motet prints: clear copies of carefully selected Latin-texted music that had previously been available almost solely to professional musicians.[17]

*   *   *

When Petrucci began printing polyphonic music he must have looked around at other printers in Venice and at the various kinds of printed goods for sale there, and calculated the extent to which the purchasers of earlier music prints and books might also be interested in buying printed music. These included the owners of chant books, especially large Graduals and Antiphonals; the owners of printed books of hours; and the owners of Latin humanist texts. Many of these people would have been musically literate, and the pressure to become so increased as the sixteenth century wore on. Castiglione's *Cortegiano* (published in 1528, but set in 1508) requires that courtiers be able to read music. Both courtiers and upwardly mobile people all over Europe took this advice to heart and sought out music books.[18]

Fifteenth-Century Manuscript Sources

Petrucci's first print, entitled *Harmonice musices odhecaton A,* was a collection of ninety-six textless chansons. There are numerous surviving manuscript *chansonniers* from late fifteenth- and early sixteenth-century Italy, as well as in France and indeed across Europe; they were the kind of music manuscript most likely to be owned by nonprofessionals.[19] The chansonnier was as close as Petrucci could get to a sure thing: There was clearly an amateur market for the chansonnier in Northern Italy and beyond.

Petrucci's second print was the first of our motet prints. The manuscript antecedents for this kind of music book are almost nonexistent. In surviving fifteenth-century manuscripts, motets are always found with other genres (see Table 6.2, penultimate column). Although there were some precedents for the motet anthology, such as motet sections in manuscripts of sacred music, Petrucci's *Motetti A* is the first surviving collection from the Renaissance exclusively devoted to the motet.[20] The creation of a new kind of music book suggests that Petrucci was already imagining a new market for the motet, and in fact the motet anthology (print and manuscript) would go on to become the dominant type of sacred music collection for the rest of the sixteenth century.

The first potential customers Petrucci must have thought of were the people already involved and interested in motets, including the people from whom he obtained repertoire. One way to find out who they were is to look at the earlier manuscript sources that contain motets printed by Petrucci (see Table 6.2). I have focused on sources that contain two or more concordances with our Petrucci prints.

Table 6.2   Earlier MS Sources Containing More Than One Concordance

No. of con.	Dates	Provenance	Siglum	Source name	Size, cm	Type of source	Format
2a: Large Italian institutional choirbooks							
5	1492–1500	Italy, Milan	Milan 3	Milan, Archivio della Veneranda Fabbrica del Duomo, Sezione Musicale, Librone 3 (olim 2267)	48 × 34	Mixed sacred	choirbook
4	1484–90	Italy, Milan	Milan 1	Milan, Archivio della Veneranda Fabbrica del Duomo, Sezione Musicale, Librone 1 (olim 2269)	64 × 45	Vespers	choirbook
3	1487–99	Italy, Rome	CS 35	Rome, Vatican City, Biblioteca Apostolica Vaticana, MS Cappella Sistina 35	55 × 43	Masses and motets	choirbook
12	1495–97	Italy, Rome	CS 15	Rome, Vatican City, Biblioteca Apostolica Vaticana, MS Cappella Sistina 15	55 × 41	Vespers	choirbook
9	1500	Italy, Verona	Verona 758	Verona, Biblioteca Capitolare, MS DCCLVIII (758)	45 × 34	Vespers	choirbook
2b: German and East-European anthologies of mixed sacred music							
3	1466–1511	Austria	Munich 3154	Munich, Bayerische Staatsbibliothek, Musiksammlung, Mus. MS 3154 (Chorbuch des Nikolaus Leopold)	31 × 22	Mixed sacred	choirbook
3	1492–1504	Germany, Leipzig	Leipzig 1494 (Apel)	Leipzig, Universitätsbibliothek, MS 1494 (Nikolas Apel Codex)	32 × 21	Mixed sacred	choirbook
6	1485–1500	Germany, Leipzig?	Berlin 40021	Berlin, Staatsbibliothek - Preussischer Kulturbestiz, MS Mus. 40021	31 × 21	Mixed sacred	choirbook

5	Czech, Silesia, Bohemia	1495–1500	Warsaw 2016	Warsaw, Biblioteka Uniwersytecka, MS Mf. 2016 (formerly Breslau/Wroclaw)	33 × 23	Mixed sacred	choirbook
6	Czech; Prague	1480–1500	Spec	Hradec Králové, Museum, Hudebni oddelini, MS II.A.7 (Speciálník Codex)	38 × 28	Mixed sacred	choirbook

2c: Other sources

4	Nether-lands, Brussels	1497–1507	Chigi	Rome, Vatican City, Biblioteca Apostolica Vaticana, MS Chigi C VIII 234 (Chigi Codex). Alamire.	36 × 28	Masses and motets	choirbook
4	Spain, Toledo	1495–7; 1500–1503?	Segovia	Segovia, Archivio Capitular de la Catedral, MS s.s.	29 × 22	Mixed sacred and secular	choirbook
3	France, Paris	1500	Paris 1597	Paris, Bibliothèque Nationale de France, Département des Manuscrits, f.fr. 1597 (Lorraine Chansonnier)	28 × 20	Chansons	choirbook

As we see in Table 6.2, these sources can be divided into three groups:

- 2a: Italian institutional choirbooks (from cathedrals or the papal chapel): large choirbooks, for use in church on Sundays and feast days.[21]
- 2b: German collections of mixed repertoire, often collected over an extended period by school teachers and choir masters. These are smaller manuscripts with more varied contents. Clearly Germany had an appetite for the western European repertoire, making it a good potential market.
- 2c: Other manuscripts: a retrospective presentation manuscript from the Netherlands of Masses and motets; a Spanish mixed anthology similar to the German manuscripts; and a French chansonnier that contains some motets.

Taken together these sources suggest a potential international market, including major church choirs, German and Spanish choir masters, and court musicians.

The Format and Layout of Petrucci's Motet Prints

Our last source of information about Petrucci's imagined market is the visual appearance of the motet prints. As Roger Chartier observes, the "meanings [of texts] are dependent on the forms through which they are received," their "material forms." "The very structure of their books was governed by the way that book publishers thought that their target clientele read."[22]

For his music books Petrucci introduced a new format, known as oblong quarto format: a midsize book (around 16 × 23 cm) that turned the paper on its side and put the spine on the short side. This was the first use of oblong format for printed books of any kind.[23] *Motetti A* and *B* (like the *Odhecaton*) arranged the music on the page in choirbook format, meaning that all four voices were shown on one opening (see Figure 6.1).

Figure 6.1   Choirbook layout for Petrucci's *Motetti A* and *Motetti B*.

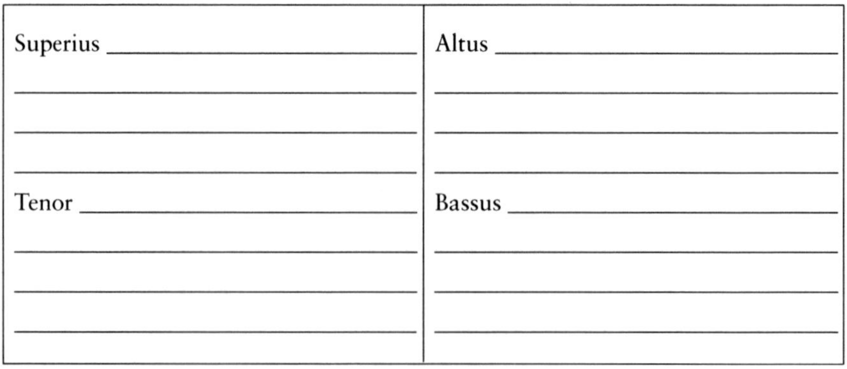

Church choirs normally sang from large manuscript choirbooks (a single page could be as large as 64 × 45 cm). Petrucci's quarto choirbooks were probably too small to sing from, even for one singer on a part.[24] He introduced partbooks (still oblong quartos) for his first book of Masses, published in September 1502, and began using them for motets beginning with *Motetti C* in September 1504. In partbooks there is an individual book for each part, and each singer sees only his or her part on the page. They solve the legibility problem, making it easy for four or eight people to see the music (one or two people for each partbook in four-voice music), and feasible for twelve (with three per partbook). Partbooks became standard for printed motet collections for the rest of the century.

Why did Petrucci choose the brand-new oblong quarto format? His very first book, the *Odhecaton*, was a secular collection of textless chansons. I suspect that when Petrucci began printing he identified the most common type of music manuscript owned by individuals in Northern Italy—the textless chansonnier.[25] A common format for early sixteenth-century chansonniers was oblong quarto.[26] Petrucci used this format for all his later music prints, including the motet books, even though almost all earlier manuscripts of sacred music were in upright format, and significantly larger (see Table 6.2). The choice of a format previously used almost exclusively for chansonniers, and the later decision to switch to partbook format, may have been a deliberate attempt to secularize the motet and attract a new market made up of amateur musicians.[27]

We can be fairly confident, then, that while Petrucci hoped to sell his motet books to the institutions and professionals already involved in the performance of motets, he was also hoping to expand his market to include a growing number of amateurs, including the owners and users of printed books of hours, Latin humanist texts, and manuscript chansonniers.

THE ACTUAL MARKET

Two kinds of evidence can tell us about the actual market for Petrucci's motet books in the sixteenth century: the surviving information about who owned the books and the transmission history of the pieces.

Owners of the Books (see Table 6.3)[28]

The kinds of institutional owners (Table 6.3 A) resemble the types of earlier sources for the motets (Table 6.2): church choirs, largely in Italy, but also in Germany and the Iberian Peninsula. The Italian owners, however, tend not to be the large cathedrals or the papal choir, but rather court chapels (Ferrara, Mantua, and Savoy) and the Accademia Filarmonica, an academy especially concerned with music that included both aristocratic amateurs and musicians among its members.[29]

Table 6.3   Sixteenth-Century Owners of the Petrucci Motet Prints
(Including the Later Motet Series, *Motetti de la Corona* I–IV)

A) Institutions (from Boorman, *Catalogue*, 343–4)
    Ferrara, chapel of Cardinal Ippolito I d'Este: unspecified books
      published before 1508
    Loreto, Casa Santa (unspecified motets), bought at book fair in
      Recanati, Sept. 1515
    Mantua, Santa Barbara: *Motetti 4*
    Rome, S. Luigi dei Francesi: *Motetti a 5*
    Verona, Accademia filarmonica: *Corona III*
    Monte Cenis (Col du), Savoy; house of Mauritani: *Motetti a 5*
    Neuburg, Ottheinreich's Court Chapel: *Corona I–IV*
    Lisbon, library of João IV (?; *Corona*)
B) Individuals (from Boorman, *Catalogue*, 346–8)
    Collectors
        Fernando Colón (*Motetti B, C, 4*, and *a 5*)
        Fugger family (*Motetti A, C,* and *4*);
            they also possibly used the books for performances
        Arundel, Earl of, and John, Lord Lumley (*Corona II–IV*)
        Bottrigari (*Motetti A and B*)
    Music theorists (see Boorman, *Catalogue*, 369, and Judd, *Reading*)
        Italian
                Aaron (1525, 1529)
                Zacconi (1592)
        German/Swiss
                Heyden (1537, 1540)
                Glareanus (1547)
                Wilphingseder (1554)
                Finck (1556)
    Miscellaneous people, including clerics and musicians,
      from Italy, Germany, and Switzerland.

Among the individual owners (Table 6.3 B) we see some actual members
of the market that Petrucci could not have imagined: book and music collectors, like Fernando Colón, and music theorists, like Glareanus (more on
the theorists later). Before Petrucci's music prints, collectors of polyphonic
music had to copy music themselves, commission manuscripts, or obtain
manuscripts previously copied for someone else. There was not a ready
market for music manuscripts: The number of available manuscripts was
limited, and few individuals retained trained music copyists, who normally
worked for court chapels or major churches in any case. Only with the
advent of music printing did it become possible for an individual to be
a music collector. The miscellaneous people who owned the prints lived
across Europe, and included both professional musicians and amateurs.

Later Transmission History of the Motets

Another way to track the market for the motet books is to look at how the
repertoire was disseminated. I have compiled a list of music manuscripts

and prints copied or published after our Petrucci prints, and containing two or more of the pieces included in the first five Petrucci motet prints (see Appendix and Table 6.4).[30] Some of these later music books include pieces that were copied directly from the Petrucci prints (shown by boldface for siglum in the Appendix).[31] These music books thus provide additional information about what kinds of people were interested in the repertoire found in our Petrucci books.

Looking first at the provenance of the manuscripts and prints listed in the Appendix (column 3), we can see that motets from the Petrucci prints were copied into many types of sources all over Western Europe. It is truly an international repertoire.

I have grouped the music books into categories, summarized in Table 6.4. The first three groups—(a) Italian sacred choirbooks, (b) German mixed sacred choirbooks, and (c) other choirbooks—contain the kinds of music manuscripts we saw in the earlier sources listed in Table 6.2. The kinds of musical institutions from whom he got his repertoire became part of his market, especially the large Italian churches, whose choirbooks contain quite a few copies from Petrucci.[32]

The next two categories—(d) French *chansons* and (e) Italian *frottole* and *laude*—contain motets alongside predominantly secular music. The Italian manuscripts also contain largely Italian-texted devotional laude, which were sung by amateurs and professionals in Italian confraternities. The presence of our motets in this kind of source suggests that Petrucci succeeded in selling his music to the amateur market and to the confraternities; once again his imagined market seems to have materialized.

Another new kind of music book is listed in category (f): sacred partbooks, manuscript and print. While there were partbooks before Petrucci, they were uncommon; after Petrucci partbooks became the standard format for printed music, and more and more common for manuscripts.[33] The books listed here are in a format very similar to Petrucci's, and two of

Table 6.4 Later Manuscripts and Prints Including More Than One Piece Found in the First Five Petrucci Motet Prints (for Details, See Appendix)

(a) Italian sacred choirbooks (8; 3 include copies from Petrucci)

(b) German mixed sacred choirbooks (4)

(c) Other choirbooks (7, from the Netherlands, Spain, Eastern Europe, and France; 1 Spanish copy of Petrucci)

(d) French *chansons* (6)

(e) Italian *frottole* and *laude* (4; 1 includes copies from Petrucci)

(f) Sacred partbooks, manuscript and print (11; 2 include copies from Petrucci))

(g) Tablature (3; 1 includes copies from Petrucci)

(h) Music theory treatises (5; 4 include copies from Petrucci)

(i) MSS associated with Glareanus (2; both include copies from Petrucci) the German manuscripts contain pieces copied from the Petrucci prints. Partbooks may have been used occasionally in major churches, but the evidence suggests that such institutions generally used big choirbooks. The partbooks are more likely to have been used for minor devotions in side chapels, in confraternities, or by amateurs or instrumentalists.[34] Here we see how the form of the later Petrucci motet books had a major impact on later music prints and manuscripts.

Category (g) includes print and manuscript collections of intabulations: arrangements of music for keyboard or lute in lute or keyboard tablature (special notations designed for instruments playing polyphonic music). The Sicher organ tablature contains fourteen of the Petrucci motets, often in the same order, and Sicher is believed to have intabulated the pieces directly from the Petrucci prints.[35] These sources prove that the motets moved into the instrumental repertoire.

Our last two categories—(h) music theory treatises and (i) manuscripts associated with Glareanus—show the importance of the Petrucci prints for two kinds of sixteenth-century music theorist. The Protestant pedagogues like Heyden and Wilphingseder included musical examples to teach school boys to read music.[36] Aaron and Glareanus, however, were more interested in finding new ways to describe music, and aimed their treatises at other intellectuals. Glareanus was definitely part of the international republic of letters; he was part of Erasmus's circle, and published widely on many topics (he even published a set of instructions for making globes).[37] All four of these theorists depend very heavily on Petrucci's motet prints for their musical examples, as Cristle Collins Judd has shown: Aaron refers to pieces in the prints, often in print order; Heyden, Glareanus, and Wilphingseder copy pieces from the prints into their treatises as musical examples.[38] The manuscripts associated with Glareanus in category (i) include copies from the Petrucci prints, with annotations about the modal theory that was the subject of Glareanus's treatise, as well as signs indicating page layout for the typesetter of the treatise.[39] The presence of a repertoire that was broadly disseminated in print form transformed music theory, making it possible to refer to specific compositions available to a broad range of people, and providing a common repertoire—a proto-canon—from which to take examples.

Evidence about owners of the motet books and about the transmission history of the motets confirms our hypotheses about the market Petrucci imagined, but also suggests that there were buyers of his books whom he did not predict. Major churches, such as those who bought the big printed Graduals and Antiphonals, or those that had large choirbooks with motet sections, did occasionally purchase the motet books, and copied pieces from the motet prints back into the big choirbooks. But this segment of the market—the most predictable segment—did not predominate. If Petrucci's choice of format looks toward the amateur market, it seems to have worked, judging by the presence of the motets in secular collections. The presence of the motets in collections of laude used in popular devotions suggests an overlap with the market for books of hours. The pan-European provenance of the later manuscripts including the Petrucci motets (as shown in the Appendix) suggests that the Latin texts appealed to an international audience, at least some of whom may have been members of the republic of letters.

Two segments of the market, however, may have come as a pleasant surprise to Petrucci. One was the collectors, who seem to have acquired books more for the sake of ownership than of performance. Petrucci may have had some inkling of this kind of buyer, but music collectors on the scale of Colón or the Fuggers probably did not occur to him when he started out. The other was the theorists who published treatises aimed at students, music teachers, and intellectuals, and whose books could refer to or include a widely disseminated common repertory established in the first instance by Petrucci.

PETRUCCI'S PUBLICS

Petrucci's imagined market is a hypothetical construct. However, the process of imagining his imagined market allowed us to identify groups of people, some of which were part of the actual market, and some of which (such as the devotional group, or the republic of letters) may have been publics for the motet. Petrucci's actual market seems to have included groups of people that Petrucci probably did not imagine, such as the collectors and the music theorists. Petrucci's publics, I suggest, are the groups of people who felt themselves to be part of the public(s) for the motet books, whether or not they actually owned a copy.

The way I have just described this third group comes out of what I perceive as essential to membership in a public: a self-conscious awareness of belonging to a group.[40] That sense of belonging could come from the act of deciding whether to buy a printed book, which might cause the buyer to think about the other people who might buy it; it could come from the act of communicating with other people about the motets and the motet books;[41] it could come from knowing people who bought the books; or it could come from planning/wanting/hoping to acquire/perform/study the music, in relation to other people. The publics for the motet books are thus both groups of real people and virtual communities called into existence by people interested in the books who perceive themselves as part of those interest communities.[42]

Given the existence of publics for the motet books, can we go on to say that the books had social agency, and brought new publics into being? Chartier frames the underlying question as follows: "How did increased circulation of printed matter transform forms of sociability, permit new modes of thought, and change people's relationship with power?"[43] In order to answer this question, and to understand more clearly the relationship between Petrucci's market and his publics, we will return to the segments of the market for the books as outlined previously and think about their status as publics.

Major Church Choirs

Major church choirs were part of Petrucci's imagined market: He must have obtained much of his music from singers in these institutions, and they were also the market for some of the liturgical incunabula (the big Graduals and Antiphonals). The church musicians and choirs were also part of Petrucci's actual market, since his books were owned by institutions, and motets from Petrucci's books were copied into the big choirbooks. We can call the musicians in these choirs a public for the motets, since they would have been interested in the new music made available by Petrucci; they would have discussed the pieces and selected the ones for copying, and they would have perceived themselves as members of a larger group of musicians working in similar institutions. They are not, however, a new public. Professional musicians continued to live in a predominantly manuscript culture. Their institutions might buy the books and copy some pieces into the big choirbooks, but the Petrucci prints functioned for them like manuscripts.

Amateur Singers and Players

Amateur singers and players were part of Petrucci's imagined market, if we judge by his format (the oblong quarto format associated with secular music), and by some of the comparable printed products already available—books of hours, devotional prints, and the international republic of letters. Amateur musicians also became part of Petrucci's actual market, since we find the Petrucci motets in a wide range of printed partbooks and manuscript sources containing secular music. The amateurs can be divided up into many overlapping segments: confraternities performing communal devotions; families using the motet books as part of their own devotional practice; and groups of friends who got together to sing or play music for fun, or in a more formalized setting, such as a salon or an academy. Some of these amateurs belonged to the merchant class or to the international republic of letters.

   Polyphonic music is more conducive to the creation of publics, however, than are printed books of hours or even classical texts. Performance of motets requires a group of people, and those groups are constantly shuffling and re-forming, so the public extends further than the group gathered together on one evening. The public is local, but also international—merchants, musicians, and courtiers travel and find new groups of people with whom to sing or play.[44] As acquisition and performance of motets become leisure activities, people make choices about what to buy and perform in relation to that larger group.

This is a new public, made possible by the existence of the motet books. As we have seen, most amateurs were not skilled enough to copy their own polyphonic music, and it took both money and access to repertoire to get a professionally copied music manuscript. Access to affordable, clear, and accurate printed music made it possible for people of moderate musical skill to get together and sing or play through music. Access to music in significant quantities and in a range of styles and difficulty levels also made it possible to improve musical skills. To go back to Chartier, printed motet books may have even changed "people's relationship with power." Increased access to music enhanced some kinds of social mobility—thanks to printed music, members of the merchant classes could develop the musical skills required of a courtier, make good marriages, and gradually move into court circles.

Private Collectors of Music

Private collectors of music may not have been part of Petrucci's imagined market. They were part of his actual market, however, since the survival of copies of the prints often depends on the survival or the records of those collections. Major collectors now are aware of the status of their collections in relation to others; I suspect that was true also in the sixteenth century. As such, the collectors were part of a new public made possible by the existence of the printed music books.

Music Theorists

While theorists certainly existed before music printing, they referred to specific pieces infrequently, and often included examples composed for the occasion rather than to preexistent repertoire. Petrucci probably did not originally imagine theorists as part of his market. They were however part of his actual market, drawing on the prints for many of their examples. This new kind of music theorist constitutes yet another new public made possible by the motet prints. They also promoted the growth of other publics for the motet prints, providing a model for language and evaluative criteria for communicating about the motets.

* * *

Petrucci's decision to print the motet books, and what the books looked like, depended on his imagined market. The actual market extended well beyond that imagined market. The publics for the motet books extended even further, including all those who saw themselves as part of a virtual community interested in motets. Petrucci's motet prints, therefore, not only provided music for the older public of professional church musicians, they also gave rise to new publics: an expanding group of amateur musicians, collectors, and music theorists. These new publics developed new forms of association, new channels for social mobility, and new kinds of language for talking about music.

Appendix   Later Manuscripts and Prints Including More Than One Piece Found in the First Five Petrucci Motet Prints
Bold sigla contain pieces probably copied from Petrucci.
Sigla consisting of dates are for printed sources (dimensions are not given).

No. of con.	Dates	Provenance	Siglum	Source name	Size, cm	Type of source	Format
(a) Italian sacred choirbooks							
5	1505	Italy, Milan	Milan 4	Milan, Archivio della Veneranda Fabbrica del Duomo, Sezione Musicale, Librone 4 (olim 2266; partly destroyed)	40 × 30	Mixed sacred	choirbook
7	1505	Italy, Siena	**Siena K.1.2**	Siena, Biblioteca comunale degli intronati, MS K.1.2	44 × 29	Vespers	choirbook
13	1503–12	Italy, Rome	CS 42	Rome, Vatican City, Biblioteca Apostolica Vaticana, MS Cappella Sistina 42 Motets in calendrical order	56 × 42	Motets	choirbook
4	1508–27	Italy, Rome	CS 46	Rome, Vatican City, Biblioteca Apostolica Vaticana, MS Cappella Sistina 46	55 × 42	Motets	choirbook
16	1515	Italy, Florence	Florence II.I.232	Florence, Biblioteca Nazionale Centrale, MS II.I.232 (olim Magliabecchi XIX.58)	43 × 30	Motets	choirbook
2	1520–30	Italy, Modena	Modena IV	Modena, Duomo, Biblioteca e Archivio Capitolare, MS Mus. IV	41 × 28	Mixed sacred	choirbook
4	1522	Italy, Padua	**Padua A17**	Padua, Biblioteca capitolare, MS A 17	55 × 42	Motets	choirbook
6	1535–1545	Italy, Cividale	**Cividale 59**	Cividale del Friuli. Museo Archeologico Nazionale, MS 59	42 × 28	Mixed sacred	choirbook

(b) German mixed sacred choirbooks

4	1510–30	Germany, Annaberg	Dresden 1/D/505	Dresden, Sächsische Landesbibliothek, MS Mus. 1/D/505 (olim Annaberg 1248)	39 × 28	Mixed sacred	choirbook
4	1516	Germany, Frankfurt	Wrocław I.F.428	Wrocław, Biblioteka Uniwersytecka, MS I.F.428 (Grüner Codex; Viadrina Codex, formerly Breslau)	40 × 28	Mixed sacred	choirbook
2	1530–40	Germany, Munich	Munich 19	Munich, Bayerische Staatsbibliothek, MS Mus 19	51 × 37	Mixed sacred	choirbook
3	1540	Germany, Torgau	Berlin 40013	Berlin, Staatsbibliothek, MS 40013 (now in the Biblioteka Jagiellońska, Cracow).	47 × 36	Mixed sacred	choirbook

(c) Other choirbooks

3	1505	Netherlands, Brussels, Mechlin	Brussels 9126	Brussels, Bibliothèque Royale, MS 9126	38 × 27	Masses and motets	choirbook
2	1510; CC: 1520–35	Netherlands	Toledo 23	Toledo, Catedral, Obra y Fabrica, MS Reservado 23 (formerly MS 22)	60 × 40	Mixed sacred	choirbook
7	1500–10; 1520–25	Spain	Barcelona 454	Barcelona, Biblioteca Central de Cataluña, MS 454	31 × 22	Mixed Sacred	choirbook
2	1505	Spain	Barcelona 5	Barcelona, Biblioteca de l'Orfeó Catalá. MS 5 (shelfmark: 12-VI-12)	34 × 24	Mixed Sacred	choirbook
2	1505–1550	Czech, Hradec Kralove	Hradec 6	Hradec Králové, Krajske Muzeum, Knihovna, MS II.A.6 (Franus Cantionale)	66 × 43	Motets	choirbook
8	1505	France	London 1070	London, Royal College of Music, MS 1070	29 × 19	Motets	choirbook

continued

Appendix   continued

No. of con.	Dates	Provenance	Siglum	Source name	Size, cm	Type of source	Format
2	1530	France	Uppsala 76c	Uppsala, Universitetsbiblioteket, MS Vokalmusik I Handskrift 76c	29 × 20	Mixed	choirbook

(d) French chansons

No. of con.	Dates	Provenance	Siglum	Source name	Size, cm	Type of source	Format
2	1525	France, Lyons	Copenhagen 1848	Copenhagen, Det Kongelige Bibliotek, MS Ny Kongelige Samling 1848, 2°	29 × 20	Chansons and mixed sacred	choirbook
2	1502–6	Italy, Bologna	Bologna Q18	Bologna, Civico Museo Bibliografico Musicale, MS Q18	17 × 24	Textless, chansons, and frottole	choirbook, oblong
3	1512	Italy, Florence	Florence 107bis	Florence, Biblioteca Nazionale Centrale, MS Magliabecchi XIX.107bis	17 × 24	Chansons	choirbook, oblong
3	1510	Netherlands, Brussels, Mechlin	Florence 2439	Florence, Biblioteca del Conservatorio di Musica "Luigi Cherubini," MS Basevi 2439 (Basevi Codex)	17 × 24	Chansons and mixed sacred	choirbook, oblong
7	1519–23	Italy, Florence	Cortona/ Paris	Cortona, Biblioteca Comunale, MSS 95–96, and Paris, Bibliothèque Nationale de France, Département des Manuscrits, n. acq.fr. 1817	12 × 18	Chansons and motets	partbooks
2	1540	Italy, northern	Bologna R 142	Bologna, Civico Museo Bibliografico Musicale, MS R 142, S partbook	11 × 18	Motets and chansons	partbooks

(e) Italian frottole *and* laude

6	1508	Italy, Venice	1508/3	Laude libro secundo. Venice, Petrucci, 1508.	16 × 23	Laude	choirbook, oblong
15	1505–12	Italy, Florence or Mantua or Ferrara	**Florence 27**	Florence, Biblioteca Nazionale Centrale, MS Panciatichi 27	15 × 21	Laude & Frottole, motets	choirbook, oblong
3	1506	Italy, northern	Capetown 3.b.12	Capetown, South African Public Library, MS Grey 3.b.12	17 × 12	Laude & Frottole	choirbook
4	1520	Italy, Florence	Florence 164-7	Florence, Biblioteca Nazionale Centrale, MS Magliabecchi XIX.164–167	11 × 17	Frottole	partbooks

(f) Sacred partbooks, manuscript and print

2	1528	France, Paris	1528/2	*Motetz nouvellement composez.* Paris, Atta.ngnant		Motets	partbooks
3	1555	France, Paris	1555J	*Josquini Pratensis, musici praestantissimi, moduli.* In 4, 5, et 6 vocis distinctis. Paris, Le Roy & Ballard, 1555. = RISM J678		Motets	partbooks
2	1528–31	Netherlands, Brussels, Mechlin	Rome 1976-9	Rome, Vatican City, Biblioteca Apostolica Vaticana, MSS Palatini Latini 1976–79. 4 partbooks	16 × 21	Motets	partbooks
4	1542	Netherlands, Bruges	Cambrai 125-8	Cambrai, Bibliothèque de la ville, MSS 125–128 (olim 124)	20 × 28	Mixed	partbooks
7	1530–40	Germany	Ulm 237	Ulm, Münster Bibliothek, von Schermar'sche Familienstiftung, MS 237	10 × 14	Mixed	partbooks

continued

Appendix   continued

No. of con.	Dates	Provenance	Siglum	Source name	Size, cm	Type of source	Format
3	1539–48	Germany, Torgau	Nuremberg 83 795	Nuremberg, Germanisches Nationalmuseum, Bibliothek, MS 83 & 795. T&B partbooks. Copied by J. Walther	15 × 21	Mixed sacred	partbooks
2	1539–88	Germany	Greifswald 640-41	Greifs-wald, Universitätsbibliothek, MSS BW 640-41 (S&B partbooks only). MS additions to 1538/2	14 × 19	Mixed sacred +German	partbooks
2	1543	Germany, Augsburg	Munich 326	Munich, Universitatsbibliothek, MS 326 (A partbook only)	14 × 21	Mixed sacred +German	partbooks
4	1559	Germany	1559/2	*Tertia pars magni operis musici ... quatuor vocum.* Nuremberg, Montanus & Neuber, 1559		Motets	partbooks
3	1538	Germany, Nuremberg	1538/3	*Secundus tomus novi operis musici, sex, quinque, et quatuor vocum.* Nuremberg: Grapheus, 1538. Ed. J. Ott		Motets	partbooks
2	1538	Germany, Wittemberg	1538/1	*Selectae harmoniae quatuor vocum de Passione Domini.* Wittemberg, Rhau, 1538		Motets	partbooks

(g) Tablature

No. of con.	Dates	Provenance	Siglum	Source name	Size, cm	Type of source	Format
14	1512–31	Switzerland, St. Gall	**Sicher**	St. Gall, Stiftsbibliothek, MS 530 (Fridolin Sicher Orgeltabulatur)	32 × 21	Tablature, keyboard	tablature
2	1517	Italy, Venice	Capirola	Chicago, Newberry Library, Capirola Lute Tablature		Tablature, lute	tablature

						Type	Format
2	1520–24	Germany	Berlin 40026	Berlin, Staatsbibliothek. Mus. 40026 (Kleber Tabulatur)		Tablature, keyboard	tablature

(h) Music theory treatises

						Type	Format
3	1525	Venice	1525 Aron	Pietro Aron. *Trattato della natura . . . di tutti li tuoni di canto figurato.* Venice, Vitali, 1525. Lists pieces from *Motetti C*		Theory treatise.	treatise
3	1537	Germany, Nuremberg	1537 Heyden	Sebald Heyden. *Musicae, id est artis canendi.* 1537		Theory treatise	treatise
5	1540	Germany, Nuremberg	1540 Heyden	*De arte canendi, ac vero signorum in cantibus usu, libri duo,* auctore Sebaldo Heyden. Nuremberg, Petreius, 1540		Theory treatise	treatise
12	1547	Switzerland	1547 Glareanus	*Glareani Dodekachordon.* Petri, Basle, 1547		Theory treatise	treatise
2	1563	Germany, Nuremberg	1563 Wilphingseder	Wilphingseder, *Erotemata musices.* Nuremberg, 1563		Theory treatise	treatise

(i) MSS associated with Glareanus

						Type	Format
13	1527	Switzerland, Basel	Munich 322-25	Munich, Universitätsbibliothek, MSS 322-325 (Glareanus Partbooks)	13 × 20	Motets	partbooks
24	1540	Switzerland, Basel	St Gall 463	St. Gall, Stiftsbibliothek MS 463 (Tschudi Liederbuch)	15 × 22	Mixed	partbooks

NOTES

1. Stanley Boorman, *Ottaviano Petrucci: A Catalogue Raisonné* (Oxford: Oxford University Press, 2006). I would like to thank the McGill graduate student research assistants who helped with this paper: Geneviève Bazinet, Remi Chiu, Jane Hatter, and Edward Melson.
2. My sense of public has been formed through the discussions of the Making Publics group; by Michael Warner, "Publics and Counterpublics," *Public Culture* 14, (2002): 49–90; and by Roger Chartier's ideas about communities of readers in Roger Chartier, *The Order of Books: Readers, Authors, and Libraries in Europe between the Fourteenth and Eighteenth Centuries*, trans. Lydia Cochrane (Cambridge: Polity, 1994; first published in France as *L'ordre des livres*, Alinea, 1992).
3. Petrus Castellanus is mentioned in the dedicatory letter at the beginning of Petrucci's first print, the *Odhecaton*. See Bonnie J. Blackburn, "Petrucci's Venetian Editor: Petrus Castellanus and His Musical Garden," *Musica Disciplina* 49 (1995): 15–45; Bonnie J. Blackburn, "Lorenzo de' Medici, a Lost Isaac Manuscript, and the Venetian Ambassador," in *Musica Franca: Essays in Honor of Frank A. D'Accone*, ed. Irene Alm, Alyson McLamore, and Colleen Reardon (Stuyvesant, NY: Pendragon, 1996), 19–44; and Bonnie J. Blackburn, "The Sign of Petrucci's Editor," in *Venezia 1501: Petrucci e la stampa musicale; Venice 1501: Petrucci, Music, Print and Publishing; Atti del convegno internazionale di studi, Venezia, Palazzo Giustinian Lolin, 10–13 ottobre 2001*, ed. Giulio Cattin and Patrizia Dalla Vecchia (Venice: Edizioni Fondazione Levi, 2005), 415–29.
4. Cited and discussed in Julie E. Cumming, *The Motet in the Age of Du Fay* (Cambridge: Cambridge University Press, 1999), 42–44. For Cortese see Nino Pirrotta, "Music and Cultural Tendencies in Fifteenth-Century Italy," *Journal of the American Musicological Society* 19 (1966): 127–61, at 150–51 (Latin), 154–55 (Pirotta's translation).
5. Mary Kay Duggan, *Italian Music Incunabula: Printers and Type* (Berkeley and Los Angeles: University of California Press, 1992), 8, 14, 39–41, 73, 133; Boorman, *Catalogue*, 77, 86. The Venetian printer Scotto published music incunabula and was one of Petrucci's backers; see Jane A. Bernstein, *Print Culture and Music in Sixteenth-Century Venice* (Oxford: Oxford University Press, 2001), 20, 75.
6. See Kathi Meyer-Baer, *Liturgical Music Incunabula* (London: Bibliographical Society, 1962), and Duggan, *Italian Music Incunabula*, 1.
7. Duggan, *Italian Music Incunabula*, 1, 11–21. Over time printed chant books for the choir became more common. See the statistics page of the online catalog of printed liturgical books, *Renaissance Liturgical Imprints: A Census* (RELICS): http://www-ersonal.umich.edu/~davidcr/stats_classification.html (accessed July 12, 2007). Their (incomplete) list of liturgical books printed before 1600 includes 2,472 books of hours, 2,299 missals, 78 graduals, and 69 antiphonals.
8. The *Graduale* published by Emerich for Giunta (Venice, 1499) is believed to be the "largest book printed in the fifteenth century." See Duggan, *Italian Music Incunabula*, 1, 207–8; see 18–20, 71–73, and 99–151 on the importance of Venice.
9. Paul F. Grendler, "Form and Function in Renaissance Popular Books," *Renaissance Quarterly* 46 (1993): 451–85, at 467–71; Brian Richardson, *Printing, Writers and Readers in Renaissance Italy* (Cambridge: Cambridge University Press, 1999), 114–17; Eamon Duffy, *Marking the Hours: English People and Their Prayers 1240–1570* (New Haven: CT: Yale University Press, 2006).

10. Paul Saenger calls this "phonetic literacy" in Paul Saenger, "Books of Hours and the Reading Habits of the Later Middle Ages," in *The Culture of Print: Power and the Uses of Print in Early Modern Europe*, ed. Roger Chartier, trans. Lydia G. Cochrane (Princeton, NJ: Princeton University Press, 1989), 141–73, at 141–42. See also Grendler, "Popular Books," 470.

11. Preliminary research suggests that 65 of the 174 pieces found in the five Petrucci prints set texts found in Books of Hours. Sources searched include the index to Victor Leroquais, *Les livres d'heures, manuscrits de la bibliothèque nationale* (Paris: Bibliothèque Nationale, Département des manuscrits, 1927), and the following online resources: *A Hypertext Book of Hours*, based on an English Prymer of 1599 (http://www.medievalist.net/hourstxt/home.htm#contents, accessed December 2007), and a *Prymer of Salysbury vse* (Paris, 1531), STC (2nd ed.) 15973. Printed books of hours and printed motet books are both preselected anthologies of Latin texts, with an emphasis on Marian devotion (95 of the 174 motets in Petrucci's Venetian motet books are Marian).

12. See Jane Hatter, "The Marian Motets in Petrucci's Venetian Motet Anthologies" (master's thesis, McGill University, 2007), 32–36; Blake Wilson, *Music and Merchants: The Laudesi Companies of Republican Florence* (Oxford: Oxford University Press, 1992); and Jonathan Glixon, *Honoring God and the City: Music at the Venetian Confraternities, 1260–1807* (Oxford: Oxford University Press, 2003). On books of hours and motets see also Kate van Orden, "Children's Voices: Singing and Literacy in Sixteenth-Century France," *Early Music History* 25 (2006): 209–256.

13. Bonnie J. Blackburn, "For Whom Do the Singers Sing?" *Early Music* 25 (1997): 593–609; and Bonnie J. Blackburn "The Virgin in the Sun: Music and Image for a Prayer Attributed to Sixtus IV," *Journal of the Royal Musical Association* 124 (1999): 157–95. On books of hours and motets see also Kate van Orden, "Children's Voices: Singing and Literacy in Sixteenth-Century France," *Early Music History* 25 (2006): 209–256.

14. See Patrick J. Geary, *Living with the Dead in the Middle Ages* (Ithaca, NY: Cornell University Press, 1994); and Jacques Le Goff, *The Birth of Purgatory*, trans. Arthur Goldhammer (Chicago: University of Chicago Press, 1984).

15. Anthony Grafton, "The Humanist as Reader," in *A History of Reading in the West*, ed. Guglielmo Cavallo and Roger Chartier, trans. Lydia G. Cochrane (Amherst: University of Massachusetts Press, 1999), 184–86, 193; Elizabeth L. Eisenstein, *The Printing Revolution in Early Modern Europe*, 2nd ed. (Cambridge: Cambridge University Press, 2005), 184, 193.

16. There may have been a connection between Petrucci and Manutius. Francesco Griffo da Bologna created Manutius's Greek font. Petrucci used this Greek font in the second dedicatory letter in the *Odhecaton* (fol. [1]); Griffo may also have cut Petrucci's music font, and later worked with Petrucci in Fossombrone (Boorman, *Catalogue*, 35, 88–91). Duggan, on the other hand, claims that Ungaro cut Petrucci's music type (*Italian Music Incunabula*, 38–41).

17. See Hartmann Schedel, *Das Liederbuch des Dr. Hartmann Schedel*, das Erbe deutscher Musik (Kassel: Bärenreiter, 1978), 84; and Martin Kirnbauer, *Hartmann Schedel und sein Liederbuch: Studien zu einer spätmittelalterlichen Musikhandschrift (Bayerische Staatsbibliothek München, cgm 810) und ihrem Kontext*, vol. 42 (Bern: Peter Lang, 2001).

18. The Count says, "Gentlemen, you must know that I am not satisfied with our Courtier unless he be also a musician, and unless, besides understanding and being able to read music, he can play various instruments." Baldesar Castiglione, *The Book of the Courtier*, trans. Charles S. Singleton (Garden City, NY: Doubleday, 1959), 74.

19. For a list see Allan Atlas, *The Cappella Giulia Chansonnier* (Brooklyn: Institute of Medieval Music, 1975), 2:233, 258.

20. On fifteenth-century sources of the motet, see Cumming, *Motet*, 54–60, and Cumming, "From Chapel Choirbook to Print Partbook and Back Again," in *Cappelle musicali fra corte, stato e chiesa nell'Italia del rinascimento: Atti del convegno internazionale di studi, Camaiore, 21–23 ottobre 2005*, ed. Franco Piperno, Gabriella Biagi Ravenni, and Andrea Chegai (Florence: Olschki, 2007), 273–403, at 375–79.

21. Cumming, "Chapel Choirbook," passim.

22. Chartier, *The Order of Books*, 3, ix, 13, passim. Grendler emphasizes the extent to which content and format are linked in "Popular Books."

23. David Fallows, review of *Ottaviano Petrucci: A Catalogue Raisonné*, by Stanley Boorman, *Journal of the American Musicological Society* 60 (2007): 415–21, at 415.

24. See Stanley Boorman, "Did Petrucci's Concern for Accuracy Include Any Concern with Performance Issues?" *Basler Jahrbuch für historische Musikpraxis* 25 (2001): 23–37, at 30–31, and Boorman, *Catalogue*, 250; David Fallows, "Petrucci's Canti Volumes: Scope and Repertory," *Basler Jahrbuch für historische Musikpraxis* 25 (2001): 39–52, at 42; and Howard Mayer Brown, "The Mirror of Men's Salvation: Music in Devotional Life about 1500," *Renaissance Quarterly* 43 (1990): 744–73, at 745.

25. See Boorman, *Catalogue*, 250.

26. Quite a few oblong Italian chansonniers survive c. 1500. See Fallows, "Petrucci's Canti Volumes," 41–42; Boorman, *Catalogue*, 249.

27. Cumming, "Chapel Choirbook," 379–82.

28. This section is based on the work of Stanley Boorman, both his Tables 10–3 and 10–4, 343–44 and 346–48, and the discussion of those tables, 336–49. See also Iain Fenlon, *Music, Print and Culture in Early Sixteenth-Century Italy* (London: The British Library, 1995), 12–14. On the theorists, see Cristle Collins Judd, *Reading Renaissance Music Theory: Hearing with the Eyes* (Cambridge: Cambridge University Press, 2000).

29. See Giuseppe Turrini, *L'Accademia filarmonica di Verona dalla fondazione (maggio 1543) al 1600 e il suo patrimonio musicale antico* (Verona: La Tipografia Veronese, 1941).

30. Information on dates, provenance, and contents in Table 6.2 are derived from Charles Hamm and Herbert Kellman, eds., *Census-Catalogue of Manuscript Sources of Polyphonic Music: 1400–1550*, 5 vols., Renaissance Manuscript Studies 1 (Neuhausen-Stuttgart: Hänssler-Verlag, 1979–1988), except in the case of the layer of Siena K.1.2 containing the motets; here dates are taken from Timothy Dickey, "Rethinking the Siena Choirbook: A New Date and Implications for its Musical Contents," *Early Music History* 24 (2005): 1–52, at 3, 17–18. The total number of concordances between each source and our Petrucci motet prints is shown in the first column of the Appendix.

31. Variant readings among sources have allowed the following scholars to determine which prints and manuscripts copied motets from Petrucci. See Marilee J. Mouser, "Petrucci and His Shadow: A Study of the Filiation and Reception History of the Venetian Motet Anthologies, 1502–1508" (Ph.D. dissertation, University of California, Santa Barbara, 2003), 92, 108; George Warren Drake, "The First Printed Books of Motets, Petrucci's *Motetti A numero trentatre* (Venice, 1502), and *Motetti de Passione, de Cruce, de Sacramento, de Beata Virgine et huiusmodi B* (Venice, 1503)" (doctoral thesis, University of Illinois, 1972); George Warren Drake, ed., Ottaviano Petrucci, *Motetti de Passione, de Cruce, de Sacramento, de Beata Virgine et huiusmodi B,*

Venice, 1503, Monuments of Renaissance Music 9 (Chicago: University of Chicago Press, 2002); Dickey, "Reading the Siena Choirbook," 74–75, 111–23; and Timothy Dickey, "Rethinking the Siena Choirbook" (Ph.D. dissertation, Duke University, 2003), 17–19, 40–43; on Florence 27 see Jon Banks, *The Motet as a Formal Type in Northern Italy ca. 1500* (New York: Garland, 1993), 1:10–12, 73, 83; and Willem Elders et al., eds., *New Josquin Edition* (Utrecht: Vereniging voor Nederlandse Muziekgeschiedenis, 1987).

32. Cumming, "Chapel Choirbook," 382–97.
33. Bernstein, *Print Culture*, 36–40.
34. Cumming, "Chapel Choirbook," 380–82.
35. Boorman, *Catalogue*, 368; and Hans Joachim Marx, "Neues zur Tablatur-Handschrift St. Gallen Stiftsbibliothek, cod. 530," *Archiv fur Musikwissenschaft* 37 (1980): 264–91.
36. Judd, *Reading Renaissance Music Theory*, 90–108.
37. Iain Fenlon, "Heinrich Glarean's Books," in *Music of the German Renaissance: Sources, Styles, and Contexts*, ed. John Kmetz (Cambridge: Cambridge University Press, 1994), 74–102, at 76.
38. Judd, *Reading Renaissance Music Theory*, 52–81, 100.
39. Ibid., 138–58.
40. This idea resembles Warner's claim that "a public is constituted through mere attention," in Warner, "Publics and Counterpublics," 60–61.
41. As in Warner's idea that "a public is the social space created by the reflexive circulation of discourse" (ibid., 62–67); and Lesley Cormack's concept of the "discursive public" in her contribution to this volume (see Chapter 8).
42. My concept of Petrucci's publics is very different from Harold Love's eighteenth-century public for music: See Harold Love, "How Music Created a Public," *Criticism* 46 (2004): 257–71. Love is willing to call a group a public only when he can identify the members of that public with some certainty (through subscriber lists, etc.; 263, 265–66). For me, Love's public is already postpublic—it has become too institutionalized to be called a public. However, some of Love's proto-publics resemble my publics for the motet prints, particularly the Catch Clubs (265), writers about music (266), and his discussion of the "exchange of partbooks from one musical family to another" that "linked them into that larger kind of community" (261).
43. Chartier, *The Order of Books*, 3.
44. Antonfrancesco Doni describes a group of people who meet to talk and sing madrigals and motets in his *Dialogo della musica* of 1544. Although it is a work of fiction, almost all of the characters in the dialogue have been associated with real people. See Alfred Einstein, "The 'Dialogo della musica' of Messer Antonio Francesco Doni," *Music and Letters* 15 (1934): 244–53; James Haar, "Notes on the 'Dialogo della musica' of Antonfrancesco Doni," *Music and Letters* 47 (1966): 198–224, esp. 202–5; and Daniel Donnelly, "The Anti-Courtier: Music, Social Criticism, and the Academy in Antonfrancesco Doni's *Dialogo della musica*" (paper presented at the Medieval and Renaissance Music Conference, Bangor, Wales, 25 July 2008). Doni's characters are a mixed group of "noble patrons, gentle women, men of letters or musicians" (Haar, "Notes on the 'Dialogo,'" 203) associated with the Accademia Ortolana in Piacenza, and with Venetian circles. See editions by G. Francesco Malipiero (Vienna: Universal Edition, 1964; scores transcribed by Virginio Fagotto), and Anna Maria Monterosso Vacchelli, *L'opera musicale di Antonfrancesco Doni* (Cremona: Athenaeum Cremonense, 1969).

Much later, in the preface to *Musica Transalpina*, a collection of Italian madrigals with texts translated into English, we get a similar picture of people meeting to sing polyphony in England. Nicholas Yonge states, "Since I first began to keepe house in this Citie, it hath been no small comfort unto mee, that a great number of Gentlemen and Merchants of good accompt (as well as this realme as of forreine nations) have taken in good part such entertainment of pleasure, as my poore abilitie was able to affoord them, both by the exercise of Musicke daily used in my house, and by furnishing them with Bookes that kinde yeerely sent me out of Italy and other places." See Nicholas Yonge, *Musica Transalpina* (London: Thomas East, 1588), reprinted in *The English Experience: Its Record in Early Printed Books Published in Facsimile 496* (Amsterdam: Theatrum Orbis Terrarum, 1972).

7 Cultural Relations between London and the Provincial Towns

Portraiture and Publics in Early Modern England

Robert Tittler and Anne Thackray

One of the cardinal elements in the formation of publics as they are construed in this volume is the development and dissemination of a public taste or fashion for particular ideas or for the particular style of specific things. One might well see the operation of this process in regard to all sorts of things in early modern Europe. We have chosen to examine a particular material object, a rare and perhaps even unique surviving example of its type, which illuminates for us the dissemination of secular portraiture as fashionable innovation in early modern England. While England did come to adopt the fashion for secular portraiture emanating especially from the studios of professionally trained virtuoso artists, operating first in Italy and then in various parts of transalpine Europe, with its formal conventions of more naturalistic form, it did so later and perhaps less extensively than most other areas of Europe. This and other factors make portraiture in England an appropriate exemplar in the wider study of the formation of public taste. Indeed, as Habermas has suggested, artistic taste is one of the key originating factors of an organized and inclusive public life.[1]

What this essay adds to Habermas's account of how art "became an object of free choice and changing preference" and thereby an instrument of public making, is that art, taste, and public formation are also always and dynamically involved in formative relations between metropolitan and provincial culture and forms of publicity.

Our interest in secular portraiture in post-Reformation England also has therefore a geographic dimension. When applied to the reception and dissemination of Renaissance portraiture, the common assumption that fashions and tastes naturally spread from large, metropolitan centers to smaller and more remote locations proves more complex than it seems. This becomes apparent when we look at the cultural interface between London and the provincial scene; at the interaction of the formal, polite cultural conventions emanating from the continent with their traditional, artisanal, and regionally rooted native counterparts; and at the fluid dynamic by which these polarities of style and location influenced each other.

As will become clear in the course of our discussion, the critically important object that allows us a window on dichotomies here is a specific collection of prints and drawings compiled for study and instruction by working painters of a particular type: the visual commonplace book or album of the professionally trained herald painters Randle Holme and his son and namesake, both of them living and working in the relatively remote provincial center of Chester in the first half of the seventeenth century. Though this collection, which we refer to as the *Holme Album,* was not bound in its present form until the eighteenth century, its contents of prints and drawings were collected by the Holmes between about 1600 and 1650. A discussion of its context allows us best to appreciate its significance to our theme.

Our most likely assumption about cultural dissemination in post-Reformation England resembles that which has long been employed by economic historians, who have seen London as the "engine of economic growth" for the rest of the kingdom.[2] Roughly applied to cultural commodities, this model would describe the fashion for formal, polite expressions of such diverse media as, for example, drama, architecture, or language itself, extending outward from the court and metropolitan center and on to the rest of the realm, gradually overwhelming traditional, local, and regional forms of cultural expression as they did so, and often working toward a formal and distinctly English convention.

On the face of it, there is certainly much to recommend this model. By the year 1600 London was more than ten times as large as any other English city. It controlled well over three-quarters of the nation's foreign trade and thus dominated England's contacts with the continent. It hosted an affluent and lavishly displayed court culture; it drew migrants from elsewhere like a powerful electromagnet (often sending them back home again later on); and it controlled the nation's publishing industry. Its cultural authority accounts, for example, for the wide dissemination of the English Bible and Cranmer's Prayer Book, both working toward a standardized written English. We also see London's potential for receiving cultural conventions from abroad and disseminating them throughout the rest of the realm, for example in the Palladian principles of architecture conveyed from the London workshop of Inigo Jones to the country houses of the Home Counties and beyond. We see it, too, in the familiar picture of London shops and craftsmen catering by 1600 to consumer demand from all over the realm for luxury goods, many of them of continental origin.[3]

But appealing as this paradigm may be, it may not have been the only one at work. England outside of London was not some vast cultural desert waiting to be irrigated by ideas, models, styles, and other conventions emanating from the great metropolis. Cultural life throughout the realm simply teemed with all sorts of activity, and in modes and styles that had long been deeply rooted in particular local or regional traditions.

The strength of that regionality appears in all sorts of phenomena: in distinctive patterns of landscape and settlement, lordship and loyalty, custom and belief, production and consumption, and certainly in speech and mimetic expression. Such deeply rooted conventions proved much more durable, especially over the putative Reformation divide and beyond, than we might think. Post-Reformation England was still a highly regional realm in all sorts of ways, some of which, including regional speech, persist to the present day.

Regional production of arts and crafts proved strongest where vibrant cathedral and monastic institutions, with their enormous patronage, had flourished prior to the Reformation. This is not necessarily to suggest that the production of such objects for spiritual purposes and ecclesiastical settings wholly survived the deracinating iconoclasm of the Reformation, though it may often have done so. It is instead to recognize that the production of specific crafts tended to be passed down in the same families, that many of these families remained in more or less the same areas after the monastic dissolutions of the 1530s,[4] and that centers long known for such skills as, for example, wood or stone sculpture or sundry forms of painting thereby retained those occupations. Practitioners of these visual arts remained active into the seventeenth century and beyond in ecclesiastical centers like Canterbury, Gloucester, Bury St. Edmunds, Chester, Exeter, and Norwich. Many local craftsmen successfully adapted to the changing subject matter, and even to new media of expression, required by the Reformation. They similarly and successfully responded to the new sources of patronage deriving from the expanding and socially competitive landed and urban elites of the day. Yet doggedly insular in their outlook and training, they were much slower to take on board and master the emerging cosmopolitan, formal, and refined styles of the day, which had come to be required by the social elites of court and metropolis, and were mostly produced by the foreign-trained.

Despite its relatively cosmopolitan nature and the large proportion of foreign craftsmen working in and around court and city even at the end of the fifteenth century, even London-based portraiture had been slow to catch up to continental trends in style and technique. Only under Henry VIII, with his engagement of Hans Holbein, did the English royal court and its surrounding circle commission a significant number of portraits approaching, in their quality and style, those being widely produced in many other parts of Europe.

A permanent London resident by 1532, Holbein brought his brilliant mastery of Northern Renaissance naturalistic painting and drawing dramatically to enhance the aesthetic tastes of court and city circles. It has become a virtual commonplace to note how, with these elites naturally setting the tone, his influence percolated steadily to other social elites in many parts of the realm thereafter. Not only did Holbein do more than anyone else to establish a formal style and an aesthetic standard to be emulated elsewhere, but he also did more than anyone else of his time to ensure the role of portraiture itself, however construed in stylistic terms, as a coveted cultural commodity among the competitive and materialistic elites of the day.[5]

By the time the Holmes began their collecting activity, these formal and polite traditions of portraiture (with variations) had been carried forth by a litany of other painters who set the tone for the London court and the English aristocracy: painters like Nicholas Hilliard, Isaac Oliver, Marcus Gheeraerts the Elder and Younger, William Larkin, Robert Peake, and Jan De Critz, and on to Daniel Mytens, Cornelius Janssen, Peter Paul Rubens, and Anthony Van Dyck.

But can we say that this consequent English consumer demand for portraits, a burgeoning public anxious to employ this new medium as a form of self-fashioning in a post-Reformation era, needed to rely on men of this caliber and fame, working in the formal and polite idiom of their time, to supply its needs? Were there even a sufficient number of painters trained in portraiture, if not necessarily in the most fashionable styles, to satisfy that demand? And did such willing patrons even have to rely on *London* artisans and workshops? Or were there other options?

Especially if we look at the rapidly growing patronage extended in the second half of the century by the *middling* elites (country gentry, urban professionals, and merchants) or by civic institutions (such as schools, charitable institutions, town and city governments, and university colleges), the answer to these questions must be "no." Such a London-centered model would ignore that home-grown English variety of portraiture, deeply rooted in the provinces, and undoubtedly more resilient to change outside the metropolis than within.

This is the visual imagery mostly produced, at least through the sixteenth century, by those native English craftsmen trained in such associated genres as heraldic painting, manuscript illumination, glass painting, wood and stone carving, metalworking, staining, and so forth. It is true that the capabilities of such practitioners fell far short, in both the professional and the aesthetic sense, of formal portraiture exemplified by men like Holbein. We may refer to these "makers" as craftsmen, artisans, "painters," or "painter-stainers," which is how they thought of themselves, but we cannot call them "artists" in the sense that had become common in the "Renaissance" world that produced Holbein. They little understood either the techniques or the stylistic conventions that would have allowed them to create Holbein's naturalistic illusions of three-dimensional imagery. They had none of the professional credentials or social standing of such continental virtuosi, nor did they think of themselves in those terms. They were as likely to paint an inn sign or a ship's prow or a staircase as a portrait, and no more likely to sign their work than a brickmaker to sign a brick.

Their work did reflect strong continuities with older, widely dispersed, visual craft traditions. These had certainly been concentrated in provincial urban centers as well as in London, and many of them remained in place over a long period.[6] The long-standing and very accomplished tradition of gold- and silversmithing in and around the city of Exeter, for example, remained sufficiently vigorous throughout this era to be recognized by the

Goldsmiths of London, eventually to be granted an assay office of the royal mint, and to spawn Nicholas Hilliard, whose father Richard was a prominent member of that Exeter industry.[7] Regional offices of the College of Arms such as that in Chester attracted and employed generations of herald painters, both post and pre-Reformation—men as adept at illumination and related visual techniques as they were at reconstructing genealogies and presiding at the funerals of the armigerous sort. As former ecclesiastical patronage dried up after the mid-1530s, these craftsmen took on the growing demand for portrait work as best they could: Their livelihoods depended upon it. The result was portraiture produced locally and regionally by anonymous native English craftsmen whose lack of skill and sophistication relegated their production to what we think of as the vernacular rather than to the formal and polite mode. Yet the still-novel desire to own a portrait at that time seems to have preceded the aesthetic sophistication embraced in such a judgment, so that these modest abilities by no means ruled the work of such men out of the contemporary market being formed at that time. Until the early seventeenth century, the conventions of contemporary, polite style in portraiture—many of which did ultimately originate on the continent and did disperse internally from the workshops and studios of London—made relatively slow headway among the middling elites and institutional patrons of provincial towns and cities, or among the middling gentry of the countryside outside the Home Counties and the more sophisticated south.

Though of course all these urban centers were closely connected to London in most respects, their merchant elites and the institutions that served as their governing bodies had been even slower than the landed gentry and regional aristocracy to assimilate the visual fashions of the new, continentally derived styles. They (and especially the institutional patrons among them) were not as engaged in the sort of one-upmanship so characteristic of contemporary landed society that required the construction of great country houses and bigger long galleries, with more paintings on display therein, than those of their neighbors. Nor did they clamor for the latest fashions to the same degree. Instead, they clung for quite a while to their pre-Reformation traditions and even styles of visual craftsmanship, and tended to resist—for reasons of both principle and expense—the intrusion by the fashionably informed, foreign-born, academically trained newcomers who had become established in the great metropolis as Holbein had done.

Then too, though it is now clear that examples of the new fashions that could serve as models for patrons or producers did somehow come to the attention of master masons, wood and stone carvers, and others in this era,[8] one cannot assume that they were readily or universally accessible in print form even by the end of the sixteenth century. There was little actual production in Elizabethan times of independent prints, beyond the crudity of woodcuts. The first dedicated print sellers to set up in London, and presumably the first the realm over, were the partners John Sudbury and George Humble, who established their shop at the sign of the White Horse, near Newgate, only in about 1600. It was only in the subsequent two decades that prints, especially in the sense of engravings incorporating a wider range of subjects, became widely produced and sold in England: considerably later than in most other parts of Western Europe.[9] And as for visual imitation based on the direct viewing of paintings, the lesser gentry who dominated much of rural society outside the Home Counties probably had limited access to the great houses of their social superiors, while regional craftsmen had even less.

Yet despite this relatively gradual dissemination of fashionable portraits, and the skills required to produce them, provincial patrons did not necessarily send to London for their portraits to be painted. When the governors of Christ's Hospital in Abingdon, Berkshire, wished to establish a portrait record of its founders and benefactors around 1600, they sent for Sampson Strong of Oxford, whose charming but rude vernacular portraits of several of that institution's founders and benefactors still grace its small hall. And even in the 1620s, a time when London had become well served by a substantial community of foreign-born and trained artists, the city fathers of Bristol sent for portraits of their civic benefactors both to Wiltshire and to Coventry, but not to London.[10]

Because local vernacular craftsmen, thinking of themselves as craftsmen, almost never signed their works, and because inscribed dates often cannot be trusted, it remains exceedingly difficult to attribute authorship or reliably to date particular paintings. Yet a quick survey of regional portraiture in the era at hand offers some examples. Norwich, with something like nineteen surviving portraits of its mayors, founders, and benefactors by the year 1640, had perhaps the best known local school of painters, and enjoys the highest survival rate of local work. Twenty-three men have been identified as plying the painter-stainers' craft there over approximately three generations.[11] Enough of their works survive for us even to detect some distinctive characteristics of modeling. Many of them, including portraits of John Marsham, Francis Moundford, Robert Jannys, and Augustine Steward, display a striking, broad-stroked, creamy appearance, especially in the working of clothing, and were carried out in a limited palette of mostly muted whites, grays, and blacks.[12]

Gloucester served as another center for civic portraiture, also in the vernacular idiom, and may well have hosted such activity for a very long time before. The city's twelve surviving portraits of local benefactors and officials, done from the 1590s to about 1620, were undoubtedly created by local painter-stainers. Quite possibly they were artisans whose families had been associated with the local abbey prior to the Reformation and with its successor, St. Peter's Cathedral, thereafter.[13] Here again, especially in depictions of, for example, Isabel Wetherstone, Joan Goldston, her husband William, or Gregory Wiltshire, we see a distinctive local vernacular at work, often marked by hunched shoulders, foreshortened arms, prominently outlined and rounded eyes, and lots of blacks, umbers, and reds in the palette.[14] Bury St. Edmunds, Canterbury, Leicester, and King's Lynn, none of them large cities even by the standards of the time, also served as centers of portrait production, as did both universities.

But perhaps the most interesting of all these regional centers is Chester. While we might perhaps expect affluent areas like Norwich, or Bury St. Edmunds or even Gloucester, with their populous and rich agrarian hinterlands, large and well-to-do gentry communities, and considerable aristocratic presence to provide ample support for local portraiture, Chester bore few of these advantages in the period at hand. Its hinterland of Flintshire, southern Lancashire, and western Cheshire remained economically deprived and poorly populated, with poor farmland and little industry, and (aside from the patronage of the Stanley earls of Derby) a local gentry community of distinctly modest pretensions. If a local school of portraiture could endure in Chester, one has to think it could presumably endure anywhere in England. And yet, such a local tradition *did* exist and seems to have thrived from at least the latter years of the sixteenth century right on into the eighteenth.

We also find surviving portraits in the city of Chester itself, done by anonymous and presumably local craftsmen in and after the period at hand, demonstrating that Chester maintained a tradition of vernacular panel portraiture well beyond the early seventeenth century. These include the images labeled (sometimes inaccurately) as those of William Offley, Sir Thomas White, John Vernon, and Richard Harrison, still on view in the mayoress's parlor of the town hall.[15] But the particular artifact that prompted this essay, which we refer to as the *Holme Album*,[16] allows us to look more closely at the Chester experience than others, and to use it as a window onto the process of the reception, assimilation, and dissemination of the newly fashionable, three-dimensional, and naturalistic painting over the course of several critical decades.

The Holme Album, one of several score volumes of surviving Holme manuscripts, consists of ninety-eight folios containing 126 drawings (mostly copies of paintings and other drawings) and prints. The prints appear to have been collected (some of them having been clipped from books), and the drawings produced, by the first two of the Holme family dynasty, Randle Holme the Elder (1570/1–1655) and his son, Randle Holme the Younger (1601–1659). Though almost none of the images have been labeled or identified in the album, many of them bear, albeit inconspicuously, the initials "rh i" and "rh ij" as marks of ownership, thus providing the essential clue to their provenance in the collection. As if further evidence were required, folios 17r, 28r, and several others have these initials extended as "RHolme." Though the album was bound in its current form only in 1843 (as is recorded by an archivist's pencil on the last page), both the images themselves and the marks of both Holmes suggest that all but one or two of its contents were assembled by the first two Holmes over a period of several decades centering on the 1620s to the 1640s. And, though some other contemporary herald painters kept visual commonplace books of one sort or another in which they recorded heraldic devices or techniques, and painter-stainers often kept pattern books for the convenience of their clients, we are not aware of other contemporary collections of this type, scope, and richness.[17]

We can only speculate where these images may have been acquired, but it is by no means a certainty that they were all acquired even indirectly from London. Most of the prints and drawings that can be identified are based on originals produced in the Low Countries; they could easily have come to Chester by sea. They could also have come overland from east coast ports with more extensive ties to the Dutch and Flemish cultural centers. We know, too, that Randle Holme the Elder had by 1626 a painful hernia that made it impossible to travel: so he told Charles I in explaining why he could not obey a command to come to court for the royal coronation.[18] Though he may have had others do it for him, it is unlikely that he himself could have acquired the later prints directly from London.

Both Holmes were locally trained herald painters. The elder, a blacksmith's son, apprenticed in both heraldry and heraldic painting with (and married the widow of) Thomas Chaloner, herald painter, poet, player, and deputy to the Norroy King of Arms. Randle the Younger apprenticed with his own father, eventually apprenticing his son, Randle Holmes III, in turn. Both remained resident in Chester for most or all of their working lives, held posts of their own in the College of Arms, and used their active membership in that city's Company of Painter-Stainers, Glasiers, Embroiderers and Stationers, founded in 1536,[19] as an avenue into local politics. Randle the Elder served as sheriff of Chester in 1615, and as mayor in 1630 and 1633; his son served as mayor of Chester in 1643–1644.

Most of the Holme manuscript volumes are taken up, as one might expect from men primarily engaged in that occupation, with aspects of heraldry. There are occasional visual references to heraldic painting in the album at hand, and the very act of collecting images, which could be used as models in, for example, hatchments or funeral monuments, is certainly essential to the herald painter's occupation. Perhaps the most famous of the four generations of Randle Holmes, Randle Holme III (1627–1700), is known for his work, *The Academy of Armory,* on that subject.[20] But this particular volume in the Holme corpus was clearly intended for other purposes. It is a collection of prints and drawings created in one version or another of contemporary, continentally derived, and naturalistic figurative representation, especially of the human form.

Some consideration of these images suggests further conclusions about the reasons for their collection, and the uses to which they may have been put. Although it can be very difficult to identify the prints of this era, and even more so the drawings, we have been able to identify almost all the engraved prints, and at least to examine the drawings so as to offer some working assumptions. Most of the prints before us will have been issued individually or as part of a set of prints. A few may have been cut from books and are thus more readily identified. Others may have been cut from sheets of prints, and still others may have been printed as frontispieces or title pages sheets but never bound.

The drawings and prints represent quite a diverse series of subject areas. Along with a few emblematic images of material objects such as might be employed in heraldic devices, there are religious themes (both Catholic and Protestant); figures and scenes from classical mythology; narrative allegorical scenes of hunting, warfare, or other dramatic activities; figure drawings both clothed and quite often nude; and portraits—a series and several individual images of English monarchs, several mostly female saints, and at least one series of *The Sibyls,* suitably clothed.

Some subjects are notably lacking: architectural images (though some of these appear in other Holme MS. volumes), maritime scenes (a little surprising considering Chester's importance as a port), land- and cityscapes, the natural world of plants and—save for some horses in military scenes and emblematic birds—animals. Some of the images are quite rare today and most probably were somewhat rare at the time. William Rogers's print of *Queen Elizabeth I Standing in a Room with a Latticed Window* (fol. 8r) is only the third known impression of this particular print, one of the finest produced in Tudor England, to come to light.[21]

We cannot be at all sure that the Holmes undertook this activity primarily for the sake of displaying their possessions, following the fashion for collecting and displaying material objects that is often seen as a fundamental feature of the Italian Renaissance,[22] and which had made its way to England by the mid-sixteenth century.[23] Thomas Chaloner, to whom Holme the elder had apprenticed, had also collected prints, and it had become common practice to place favorite prints on the walls of homes. But we find little evidence of the use of the pins or glue that would have affixed this album's prints and drawings to a wall. The very fact of their survival suggests that these images were kept relatively safe, away from exposure to light, damp, smoke, and other damaging pollutants.

On the whole the diversity of both the prints and drawings in the album seem more likely to reflect an active curiosity about newly fashionable forms of imagery, and of the skills required to produce such imagery, than with any pressing requirement of the herald's occupation. While the latter could be acquired through a traditional apprenticeship, the former remained the purview of the continental drawing academies, providing training still unavailable in England. This curiosity manifests itself in the album's life drawings, and by the unusually and artistically challenging poses of the human body featured in several of the prints, as well as by other images that were not being much produced or seen in England at that time.

In the seventeenth century, drawing, and especially life drawing, was being formalized and promoted in the art academies of Paris, Rome, and

Figure 7.1   Queen Elizabeth I Standing in a Room with a Latticed Window by William Rogers, c. 1590–1603. Engraving. British Library Harleian MS. 2001, image no. 10. © The British Library Board. All Rights Reserved 27/02/2009.

Antwerp. The concept of the painter as a virtuoso artist, a "history painter" identifiable by his education in the liberal arts and his accomplished technique, had at last begun to dawn in England. So had the aspirations of English artists to enjoy a higher status than that of mere craftsmen. This album suggests that the Holmes sought to enlarge their own artistic knowledge and enhance their technical training. This in turn suggests that they were ambitious to enjoy the abilities and reputation of virtuoso artists, marked out as such by their skill, their celebrity, and their academic as well as manual education.

The collection also responds to the requirements of those hoping to serve an expanding market for portraiture and other forms of painting: a consumer demand that, on the evidence of surviving regional portraits of that time, had begun to reach Chester and its hinterland at this time. It may also have responded to the likely interests of apprentices who came to work with the album's compilers in the hope of developing their own practices as regional portrait painters, a point to which we will return later. In sum, we see this collection as a snapshot of the sorts of images and forms of modeling that were lacking in the traditional vernacular, and that characterized the newer, formal, and polite fashions exemplified in this era by engravers like Renold Elstrack in London and Hendrick Goltzius in the Netherlands, or by court painters like Rubens and Van Dyck, whose fame extended across Europe.

A last question to consider is what impact this album, and the models it contained, may have had on the circles of painters and patrons extant in and around Chester in these years. Do the Holmes and their collection make for an interesting but inconsequential vignette, or might they have served—and might they serve us—as a view onto something larger? As with almost all regions of England, Chester and its hinterland obviously saw an emerging public for the appreciation of portraiture in the early years of the seventeenth century, which was to endure right into modern times. Most of the surviving seventeenth-century portraits associated with that area, themselves probably constituting but a fraction of what once existed, are unattributed to any particular painter. This alone makes it impossible confidently to identify portraits that the Holmes may have done themselves.

Yet it is obvious from their work as heraldic painters, and as masters and leading figures in Chester's amalgamated Company of Painters, Glasiers, Embroiderers and Stationers, that the Holmes remained continually active through these years. If the ability to abandon their occupations for a year at a time to serve in civic office—a standard requirement of mayoral office—is any indication, their work remained lucrative as well. The company itself included roughly six to eight master painters out of a total of twenty or so masters in all at any one time, making the painters the largest component of that amalgamated brotherhood throughout this era.[24] Both Holme the elder and the younger took on apprentices at a steady rate, though rarely more than one at a time. Holme the elder's earliest apprentices included Thomas

Chaloner's son, and then his own son and namesake. Holme the younger saw Daniel King, later one of England's leading engravers and associate of both Wenceslaus Hollar and William Dugdale, through his long apprenticeship.[25] But the most successful of those who apprenticed with either Holme was undoubtedly the widely regarded regional painter John Souch, apprentice to Randle the Elder from 1607 to 1617, and both friend and fellow guildsman to both Holmes.

John Souch (1594–1645) is an especially important figure in the context of our theme. He trained at Holme's elbow for ten years and forged that apprenticeship into a very successful career as a regional portrait painter to the country gentry of the Chester hinterland. Most importantly, a number of his portraits survive. Some fifteen have been attributed to him with some degree of confidence, almost all of them depicting members of the regional gentry in and around Chester.[26] Six of them have been signed. This very act—virtually never employed by vernacular craftsmen at this time—constitutes an affirmation of Souch's self-image as an artist rather than a craftsman: a man who had come to stand on a nearly equal social footing with the country gentry who sat for him.

His portraits show very clearly an attempt to span the stylistic distance between the two contemporary schools of visual depiction, and the sorts of people who were drawn to each: the regional vernacular of the Chester craftshop, and the formal, polite idiom, the taste for which became firmly established throughout the realm during Souch's lifetime. For example, his best known work, *Sir Thomas Aston at the Deathbed of his Wife* (1635),[27] certainly aspires to the formal and polite idiom. His subject is a family scene in a domestic setting (albeit a highly contrived one), aiming to convey an emotionally intense narrative: Sir Thomas clings to his wife's hand after she has died in childbirth, one of his children observing the scene from the left. The depiction of light and the modeling of clothing, facial features, and flesh convey the artist's efforts to depict a naturalistic scene, as if he were emulating effects that could well have been seen in the Holmes' prints and drawings. He has also at least attempted to adopt a consistent single point perspective, though he is more successful with single figures than with the composition as a whole.

And there are vernacular elements here, too, some of them right out of the heraldic playbook. The scene records the passage of generations, which was of prime concern to a herald painter. Its placement of figures and objects seems to follow a symbolic order, which makes the painting as a whole something of a genealogical record. The figures themselves are awkwardly posed, with laconic reminders of the event; for example, Sir Thomas is shown in his mourning suit. The painting displays the combined arms of Sir Thomas and his wife, several symbolic and perhaps emblematic objects (a surveying instrument, cradle, lute, and globe), and a Latin inscription appropriate to the occasion: "*Qui spem carne seminat Metat ossa.*"[28]

It remains impossible to determine whether Souch made direct use of the prints and drawings being collected by his master and lifelong associates, the Holmes, in striving toward this new form of visual imagery, or even if he imparted these ideas to his own apprentices. But by capturing and putting to use the forms and visual ideas that happen also to have been brought together in the album, his work suggests how new visual conventions were received and transmitted, even in such a provincial center as Chester. Taken together, the Holmes' work in assembling their collection and their almost certain use of it as a model book for teaching, coupled with Souch's stylistically hybrid production as a portrait painter, offer an important glimpse into the formation of a public for formal, fashionable portraiture in the provincial England of their time.

What can we make of this sort of evidence? Provincially-based portraiture, done by native-English painters and initially highly vernacular in appearance, needs to be explored much further if we are to arrive at a comprehensive picture of an emerging English public, or publics (to be more precise) for portraiture at this time, or of the cultural transmission of that idiom. So far the evidence from portraiture seems to suggest not one but several explanatory models of transmission operating at this time. Certainly, London acted as a conduit for foreign-born styles, conventions, and painters themselves making their way into England. It did so through the work of London-based, foreign-born painters from Holbein through Van Dyck, as well as the itinerant painters, also often foreign-born, who worked their way outward from London and from one provincial center and country house to the next. In time, it did so through the production and dissemination of printed materials, which were consumed or at least actively appreciated by patrons and craftsmen throughout the realm. And it undoubtedly did so by the direct example of formal paintings seen in the long galleries of royal residences and aristocratic halls, first by the court and aristocracy, and then by a regional gentry thus inspired to emulate the example of their more sophisticated neighbors. The royal galleries, we might say, belong to public art on a grand scale, while the vernacular portraits of the Holmes and also Souch's wonderfully hybrid *Sir Thomas Aston* were of a piece with a provincial art public, one that seems to have kept a certain distance from the continental style of royal and aristocratic public portraiture.

By the early seventeenth century, it is true, we see the emergence of formal, polite, and continentally derived concepts of portraiture as the current fashion over much wider areas and among a more inclusive sector of the population. Interest in portraiture also became more sophisticated and more self-consciously engaged in its appreciation and, often, in its acquisition. Part of this process of public formation must also be found on the supply side of the equation. Portrait makers responded to this burgeoning interest by opening up to new ideas and fashions, becoming more sophisticated and more professional in their work as they did so. And yet, as is the case with vernacular speech, the regional vernacular traditions do seem also to have survived. Men like John Newman of Cambridge, who worked a three-county area in the sixteenth century,[29] Gilbert Jackson in the early seventeenth,[30] or the Vicar of Wakefield's limner, who "traveled the country and took likenesses for fifteen shillings a head" in the eighteenth, continued to thrive on the provincial scene for a long time after our period.[31] This suggests to us that publics of this era, which formed out of an attraction for particular cultural forms, could be, and often were, marked by such dynamic interactions in which, for example, regionally specific traditions and wider mainstream expressions, typically if not necessarily emanating from great urban centers, engaged in a continuing, fertile, and sometimes oppositional relationship, each leaving some imprint on the other.

NOTES

1. Jürgen Habermas, *The Structural Transformation of the Public Sphere*, trans. Thomas Berger (Cambridge, MA: MIT Press, 1989), 39–40.
2. This tradition stems mainly from two seminal essays: F. J. Fisher, "London as an Engine of Economic Growth," first published in *Britain and the Netherlands*, vol. 4, *Metropolis, Dominion and Province*, ed. J. S. Bromley and E. H. Kossman (The Hague: Nijhof, 1971), 3–16; and E. A. Wrigley, "A Simple Model of London's Importance in Changing English Society and Economy, 1650–1750," *Past and Present* 37 (1967): 44–70.
3. Linda Levy Peck, *Consuming Splendor: Society and Culture in Seventeenth Century England* (Cambridge: Cambridge University Press, 2005).
4. Janis C. Housez, "The Impact of the Dissolution of the Monasteries on Patronage Structures in Yorkshire and East Anglia" (Ph.D. dissertation, McGill University, 1997).
5. On the significance of Holbein in the history of English portraiture, see Christopher Lloyd and Simon Thurley, *Henry VIII: Images of a Tudor King* (Oxford: Phaidon Press, 1990); Susan Foister, *Holbein and England* (New Haven, CT: Yale University Press, 2004); and Susan Foister, *Holbein in England* (London: Tate; New York: Harry N. Abrams, 2006).
6. Representative studies of such provincial craft traditions include Sally-Beth MacLean, *Chester Art: A Subject List of Extant and Lost Art Including Items Relevant to Early Drama* (Kalamazoo, MI: Medieval Institute Publications, Western Michigan University, 1982); and Peter Lasko and N. J. Morgan, eds., *Medieval Art in East Anglia, 1300–1520* (London: Thames and Hudson, 1974).
7. *Exeter and West Country Silver*, no. 86 (Exeter: Exeter Museum Publications, 1978), 3–4.
8. See especially Anthony Wells-Cole, *Art and Decoration in Elizabethan and Jacobean England: The Influence of Continental Prints, 1558–1625* (New Haven, CT: Yale University Press, 1997).
9. Leonie Rostenberg, *English Publishers in the Graphic Arts, 1599–1700: A Study of the Printsellers and Publishers of Engravings, Art and Architectural Manuals, Maps and Copybooks* (New York: B. Franklin, 1963), 1–3.
10. Bristol Record Office, Audit Books, 1624 and 1625, MSS.F/Au/1/19, 294; and F/Au/1/20, 25, 30, 44.

11. Virginia Tillyard, "Painters in Sixteenth and Seventeenth Century Norwich," *Norfolk Archaeology* 37 (1980): 315–16; Habermas, *Structural Transformation*, 39–40; also Andrew Moore and Charlotte Crawley, eds., *Family and Friends: A Regional Survey of British Portraiture* (London: HMSO, 1992), esp. 21–30.

12. As reproduced in Moore and Crawley, *Family and Friends*, 196–7.

13. Brian Frith, *Twelve Portraits of Gloucester Benefactors* (Gloucester, 1972), 5–6 passim.

14. On display at the Gloucester City Museum (double portrait of *John and Joan Cooke*), and the Folk Life and Regimental Museum at Gloucester. See also Frith, *Twelve Portraits*, 11, 17, 18, 19.

15. On-site visit of July, 7, 2005, facilitated through the kindness and expertise of Mr. Peter Boughton, Keeper of Art and Architecture, Chester Museums.

16. British Library Harleian MS. 2001, one of nearly three hundred volumes of heraldic drawings and notes compiled by Randle Holme the elder, his son, grandson, and great-grandson, all sharing his name and working as herald painters in the Chester area. Most but not all of these volumes rest in the British Library Harleian MSS.

17. Perhaps the closest in form to the *Holme Album* are the Trevilian volumes, though these differ in that they combine pictures and text, and seem to have been designed as finished books, intended for family reading, information, and entertainment. As true commonplace books, they are not collections assembled by professional painters for reference and training, unlike the *Holme Album*. See Thomas Trevilian, *The Trevelyon Miscellany of 1608: A Facsimile of Folger Library MS. V.b232*, ed. Heather Wolfe (Washington, DC, 2007); and Thomas Trevilian, *A Facsimile from the Manuscript in the Wormsley Library. With a Study by Nicholas Barker. For Presentation to the Members of the Roxburghe Club* (London, 2000).

18. *Oxford Dictionary of National Biography* (Oxford: Oxford University Press, 2004), vide "Holme, Randle I."

19. See a copy of the Company's 1536 charter in the British Library, Harleian MS. 2054, fol. 88a.

20. Randle Holme, *The Academy of Armory* (Chester: Printed for the author, 1688). It exists in two modern editions: in print as Randle Holme, *Academy of Armory, 1688* (Menston, UK: Scolar Press, 1972); and as an electronic resource as N. W. Alcock and Nancy Cox, *Living and Working in Seventeenth-Century England: An Encyclopedia of Drawings and Descriptions from Randle Holme's Original Manuscripts for the Academy of Armory* (London: British Library CD-ROM, 2000).

21. For this print see Freeman O'Donoghue, *Catalogue of Engraved British Portraits Preserved in the Department of Prints and Drawings in the British Museum* (London, 1910), 2:151 (no. 88); and A. M. Hind, *Engraving in England in the Sixteenth and Seventeenth Centuries* (Cambridge, 1952), 1:263–64, no. 8.

22. Paula Findlen, "Possessing the Past: The Material World of the Italian Renaissance," *American Historical Review* 103, no. 1 (1998): 86.

23. See, for example: Edward Chaney, *The Evolution of English Collecting* (New Haven, CT: Yale University Press, 2003), *passim*; Elizabeth Goldring, "The Earl of Leicester and Portraits of the Duc d'Alençon," *Burlington Magazine* 146 (2004): 108–11; Elizabeth Goldring, "An Important Early Picture Collection: The Earl of Pembroke's 1561/62 inventory and the Provenance of Holbein's *Christina of Denmark*," *Burlington Magazine* 144 (2002): 157–60.

24. Chester Record Office, Accounts of the Painters . . . Company, MS ZG/17/1, *passim.*

25. Daniel King (c. 1616–1661) remained part of the Chester circle until the mid-1650s, returning to it at the end of his life. In addition to his own engravings, he wrote on the art of limning and on local antiquities. See *Oxford Dictionary of National Biography,* vide "King, Daniel."

26. Based on the census maintained in the Witt Library of the Courtauld Institute of Art, vide "Souch, John."

27. Manchester City Art Gallery acc. no. 1927.150. Oil on canvas, 79 $^7/_8$ × 84 $^5/_8$ inches (203.2 × 215.1 cm.), signed *Jo:Souch Cestren[s] Fecit* . . . (Manchester City Art Gallery ref. Sept. 30/16/3/5). For reproductions, see the website for Manchester City Art Gallery (http://manchestergalleries.org); Ellis Waterhouse, *Painting in Britain 1530 to 1790,* 4th ed. (Harmondsworth: Penguin Books, 1978), 63, fig. 46; or Clare Gittings, "Venetia's Death and Kenelm's Mourning," in *Death, Passion and Politics: Van Dyck's Portraits of Venetia Stanley and George Digby,* ed. Ann Sumner (London: Dulwich Picture Gallery, 1995), 54–68, 55, fig. 1.

28. "Whoso soweth in the flesh will reap in the bones." This description is based in part on the notes accompanying the reproduction of the painting filed in the Witt Library, the origin or author of which have not been indicated. The Latin inscription is reminiscent of St. Paul's warning: "Quoniam qui seminat in carne sua, de carne et metet corruptionem; qui autem seminat in spiritu de spiritu metet vitam eternam" ["For whoever sows in his flesh from the flesh, he shall also reap corruption. But whoever sows in the spirit, from the spirit, shall reap eternal life"] (1 Galatians 6:8). A counterweight to the heraldic elements in the painting, the inscription reminds viewers of the primacy of spiritual growth over sensuality and worldly hopes of dynastic succession.

29. Margaret Statham, ed., "Accounts of the Feoffees of the Town Lands of Bury St. Edmunds, 1569–1622," *Suffolk Record Society* 46 (2003): lii, 239; Henry Peacham, *The Art of Drawing with the Pen* (1606; reprint: Amsterdam: Theatrum Orbis Terrarum, 1970), 26–27; Thomas Walker, *A Biographical Register of Peterhouse Men* (Cambridge, 1927 and 1930), 2:294.

30. *Oxford Dictionary of National Biography,* vide "Jackson, Gilbert."

31. As cited in Oliver Millar, *The Age of Charles I: Painting in England, 1620–1649* (London: Tate Gallery, 1972), 89.

8 Glob(al) Visions
Globes and Their Publics in Early Modern Europe

Lesley B. Cormack

INTRODUCTION

> Globes of themselves with their use (which is most singular of all
> other mathematical Instruments) are more delightfull to the eie then
> profitable to the professor thereof.[1]

So said Thomas Hood, in 1592, discussing the uses of the Molyneux
Globes, the first English-manufactured globes. There are several things to
notice about this quotation. First, Hood suggests that globes were to be
seen first and foremost as mathematical instruments—that is, instruments
used to measure the natural world—rather than as philosophical instruments (those used to understand the underlying essences of things) or as
aesthetic objects. Second, such instruments were not, in and of themselves,
self-evident in their use. That use needed to be articulated by mathematicians and other instructors. Thus, these globes needed a community of
scholars and consumers already aware of their importance and the globes
in turn had a function in creating a larger public, since they required a
range of people interested in their manufacture and use, in order to have
meaning.

The first engraved terrestrial and celestial globes began to appear in
Europe in the early sixteenth century. At first specialty items, with a limited and esoteric clientele, by 1600 globes were widely manufactured and
distributed, especially in northern Europe. These globes were impressive
technological, scientific, and aesthetic objects, depicting both the stars
in the heavens and the lands on the earth. The engraved gores allowed
the standardization of this information for significant numbers of globe
owners and viewers, while the handmade attention to the roundness of
the globes and their painted faces made them beautiful objects as well.
In order for these globes to be created, admired, used, and discussed,
however, a multivalent and ever-changing set of publics had to develop
and grow. Globe construction and use did not spring up from nothing,

but rather had to be nurtured and developed by people sharing an interest in these objects. This globe-focused group does not seem coherent and cohesive enough to claim as a single public however. In this chapter, I want to explore the concept of publics in this early modern period by positing that three different, interactive publics sprang up around these innovative instruments: a constructing public, a discursive public, and a consuming public.[2] These three networks interacted and overlapped at important points, but had different goals and different socioeconomic status. I want, therefore, to use this focus on globes to pull apart the different publics that existed within these overlapping interests and across these material spaces.

The constructing public of these globes would include engravers, cartographers, explorers, and astronomers, as well as the merchants interested in funding the enterprise. This group of men was both cooperative and fiercely competitive. They were motivated by a range of political, social, and economic concerns, and through their combined efforts, made large globes an important consumer good, mathematical instrument, and pedagogical tool.

But as Thomas Hood told us, the use of these globes for their owners and viewers was not self-evident. They might be mathematical and scientific instruments, or aids to exploration and navigation. Equally, these globes might be predominantly pedagogical tools. Or perhaps they are more appropriately understood as aesthetic objects or images of empire. Those who wrote treatises about these globes claimed the mathematical utility of these instruments. Thus, the discursive public for these globes, as characterized by the treatise writers, had an investment in understanding and measuring the real globe in the interests of navigation and trade, with some claim to controlling the larger oceans. Or at any rate, they constructed a "normative public," a sense of how people ought to interact with these globes.

The consuming public, of course, might disagree. The most elusive of the three publics focused on these early modern globes was that group of people interested in owning and using these artifacts. Why did they buy them? Where did they use them? We need to understand how they interacted with the first two communities, in order to create a group of scholars, virtuosi, merchants, and politicians who valued these objects of beauty and precision, and to determine whether they read these material artifacts as potential political narratives.

These three publics provide a case study for the formation of publics around material artifacts and in market conditions. In order to be more than interest communities, it seems to me, we need to argue that these publics joined together to advance particular innovative projects, be they intellectual, social, or political. We need to pay attention to whether they were open to strangers who would be united through these shared interests, and whether they encouraged any forms of debate or discussion.

THE CONSTRUCTING PUBLIC

The creation of multi-copy, engraved globes was an innovation of the sixteenth century. These globes could be produced only with the advent of print and copper-plate engraving, and so should be seen, even more than the compass or the printing press itself, as an authentically new artifact of early modern Europe.[3] The first globes were made in Germany, beginning with the mathematical rendering of round projections on the gored flat map, followed by the actual creation of round globes.[4] From the 1530s, the center of globe construction moved to the Low Countries, first to the Flemish area and latterly to Amsterdam. England was an insignificant player until the eighteenth century, except for the unparalleled and unrepeated construction of the Molyneux Globes in 1592, and even this globe was engraved by a Dutchman.[5]

An early glimpse of a globe- and map-constructing community can be seen in the life of Gerard Mercator. Mercator began his globe-making career in 1534 under the guidance of Gemma Frisius, professor of mathematics at Louvain. While Mercator was less interested in and adept at the full university curriculum, he soon mastered mathematics, teaching Louvain students and constructing mathematical instruments for them.[6] Frisius was impressed with Mercator's skill, both at mathematics and, especially, at the precision of his humanist script for engraving. Since Frisius was trying to produce an impressive new globe to maintain his charter from Charles V (Frisius had himself earlier produced the first Flemish globes, probably inspired by Schöner's[7]), he needed Mercator's skill as an engraver and instrument maker. Mercator worked with Frisius, the instrument maker Gaspar van der Heyden, and the cartographer Maximilianus Transylvianus to produce Frisius's impressive 1537 globe.[8] Mercator's most important contribution was his innovative engraving technique.[9] Soon after, Mercator began to create globes on his own, particularly his 1541 terrestrial and 1551 celestial globes.

Mercator's globes introduced some important changes to Frisius's earlier globes. First, Mercator had perfected his engraving techniques and his now-famous *cancelleresca* script appeared throughout. Second, Mercator added the loxodromic or rhumb lines of wind and compass direction, crisscrossing the entire surface, thereby stressing the mathematical nature of the globe and its potential for navigational use. Finally, Mercator's globes were one-eighth larger than Frisius's (at sixteen inches in diameter); this meant that the surface area to engrave was 25 percent larger, with a concomitant increase in detail.[10]

So far, everything I have described sounds like a closed apprentice system, as far removed from a public as one could imagine. But what makes Mercator a potential transitional figure in the development of a globe-making public is his interaction with a larger cartographical, astronomical, and mathematical Republic of Letters.[11] Throughout his life, Mercator

Figure 8.1   Mercator, Gerardus (Gerard) (1512–1594), Celestial globe. 1551. Map Division. Staatsbibliothek zu Berlin, Stiftung Preussischer Kulturbesitz, Berlin, Germany. Photo Credit: Bildarchiv Preussischer Kulturbesitz / Art Resource, New York.

communicated with many important cartographers, explorers, and mathematicians in Europe, some personally known to him and others unknown. For example, he kept up a lifelong correspondence with John Dee, whom he had known well during Dee's three-year sojourn in Louvain in the 1540s.[12] Ortelius, who himself had a wide network of correspondents throughout Europe, included Mercator in that circle; Ortelius and Mercator exchanged geographical and mathematical information, even as they competed for a market share in their map production and sales.[13] Especially interesting is Mercator's correspondence with Johanne Vivianus in Antwerp, a self-professed "lover of learning." In 1573, Vivianus asked Mercator to contribute to his *Album amicorum,* a cross between an autograph book and a commonplace. This shows Mercator's status among "amateurs" as well as professional mathematicians.[14] Mercator's voluminous correspondence reveals a community of men, interested in geographical and mathematical knowledge, willing to share important information and yet holding back some material, for reasons of state or for market competition. Some were lovers of learning; some were men of business. The transnational Republic of Letters is a complex space.

Of course, most of this information sharing was directed, not toward the construction of a new globe, since Mercator did not alter his 1541/1551 globes, choosing rather to manufacture and sell unaltered globes for the rest of his life. Instead, Mercator was collecting and exchanging information for his great magnum opus, his *Atlas.*[15] At this point, we need to see those manufacturing globes as part of a transnational mathematical public, rather than completely focused on globe making. Still, this shows the contacts, interactions, and shared concerns of this community, which crossed confessional, professional, and national boundaries in its pursuit of innovative and accurate geographical and astronomical information. This potential public of letter writers relied on the trust associated with scholarly or social status to determine the credibility to be granted to the information received.[16]

From the 1580s, the center of European globe manufacture moved to Amsterdam, providing a much more developed example of a globe-constructing public. Three Dutch globe manufacturers competed for this important market: Jacob Florisz van Langren (and sons), Jodius Hondius, and Willem Jansz Blaeu. And the competition was fierce.[17] At first, these manufacturers vied to have the most accurate celestial and terrestrial observations. Van Langren consulted with Rudolph Snellius, professor of mathematics at Leiden University. Hondius used fellow countryman (and co-religionist) Peter Plancius's map, which contained all the new discoveries of many northern European nations, especially those of the Dutch and Portuguese.[18] Soon, all three began to use the southern observations of the stars, especially from the Portuguese passage around the Cape of Good Hope in 1595. This passage and the observations brought back at the behest of Plancius were used by Hondius for his 1598 celestial globe, on which he depicts twelve new southern constellations, all devised by Plancius—the first modern constellations.[19]

Meanwhile, Blaeu had spent 1595 with Tycho Brahe, an aristocratic Danish astronomer widely held to have produced the best star chart in Europe, only to be superseded by others who had the help of the telescope (and even then, only once Flamsteed's chart finally appeared at the end of the seventeenth century). Blaeu used Brahe's star information to create his 1598 globe.[20] Sadly for Blaeu, this was trumped by Hondius's southern constellations, but for the north, Blaeu clearly had the superior charts. Blaeu quickly recovered by using new southern information from a fellow citizen, Frederick de Houtman, who ventured into the Pacific.[21]

After 1600, these Dutch globe manufacturers stopped trying to find and report new discoveries on their globes; instead they turned their attention to the aesthetic, hiring new artists to develop new more ornate ways to depict the constellations on the celestial globes and new cartouches and embellishments on the terrestrial.[22] Constellations took on more three-dimensional forms, in an Italianate style, which while beautiful, made them less useful to compare with the skies at night. Rhumb lines were removed from both globes, and depictions of imagined peoples, flora, and fauna on the terrestrial globe made them more interesting than accurate. As the competition became more and more about artistic quality, the globes became less important as mathematical and pedagogical instruments, and eventually less valuable to consumers, shown by the loss of the market to other manufacturers. Eventually the torch for globe manufacture was passed to Vincenzo Coronelli in Italy, loxodromic lines disappeared, and Amsterdam lost its position of prominence in the globe market.

Even more than with Mercator's involvement in the Republic of Letters, we can see in Amsterdam that globes revolved around a significant constructing community. Engravers, cartographers, explorers, and astronomers were all interconnected in the pursuit of the globe most likely to attract the attention of a buying public. Many of them knew each other, either as collaborators or as competitors. They were convinced that globes provided the best way of articulating the new knowledge of the earth and the skies to a paying public and that it was important that these instruments be accurate, beautiful, and profitable. Given that we have left behind the guild shop, in the production of something seen as modern, involving new and highly skilled contributions, there is at least an argument to be made that this group constitutes a public in this proto-capitalist moment. On the other hand, the motivations of this group seem pretty firmly fixed on the market, and the potential for strangers to enter the community is dubious. It is therefore not clear that this group of players constitutes a public. Let us return to this identification question once we have looked at the other two publics I have identified as involved with globes.

DISCURSIVE PUBLICS

Beautiful and impressive as these globes were, they could not exist by themselves, since their uses were not self-evident to their owners or viewers. Rather, treatises had to be written to accompany these globes, either explicitly or implicitly. Throughout the sixteenth century and continuing well into the seventeenth century, there was an explosion of *De globis* treatises, explaining the construction and use of these beautiful mathematical instruments.[23] Some were written by mathematical practitioners and instrument makers, hoping to encourage consumers to buy their knowledge or goods. Some were written by courtiers, gentlemen, or virtuosi, interested in the globes for their pedagogical, aesthetic, political, or economic value. A few were written by scholars, interested in the underlying philosophical model of the universe they provided.

An interesting example of the diversity of interests of *De globis* authors is shown by the four treatises written to accompany Emery Molyneux's globes of 1592. Four men, from different social, cultural, and economic communities, produced these treatises: Thomas Hood, a mathematical practitioner in London, writing for the merchant community; Robert Hues, an Oxford don, writing in Latin for a scholarly and international market; Thomas Blundeville, a courtier writing for that courtly and gentlemanly audience; and John Davis, a practicing seaman, writing for investors and navigators.[24] Each was working to create a public for the globes (and for their expertise), through their treatises and their mathematical view of the world.

All four authors argued that the globes were useful. These globes were useful, however, not principally because one could understand the placement of continents or oceans or see the new discoveries, but because these globes could be used to understand the overall cosmographical divisions of the world, to orient the globe to one's location, and to use the globe to find local time and place. Secondarily, they were useful in plotting the mariner's path as he sailed around the world.

Virtually all the *De globis* treatises, whether in Latin or the vernacular, covered the same issues concerning the use of these globes. First, all the treatises pointed out the imaginary lines running around the globes, especially the terrestrial, and explained the function of the equator, the tropics, the Arctic and Antarctic circles, and of course the longitude and latitude lines. Once these were established, the globe could be used. The user first needed to "set" the globe, making sure, as Thomas Blundeville suggested, "the Horizon stands alwaies levell . . . then with your 2 hands laying holde of the 2 next pillars, turne the foote of the Globe until it stand right North and South."[25]

Sometimes this could be done using the built-in compass in the stand. The user then needed to adjust the declination for the correct latitude and longitude of his location. Indeed, this is the reason to have the globe in a moving stand. It in no way suggested that the earth rotated on its axis, but rather allowed the user to rotate the globe until it corresponded with the stationary earth beneath its feet.[26] Following this, Blundeville lays out three types of propositions to be answered with the globes: the first concerning the "universal map" on the globe (which you could use to discover what types of people lived directly beneath your feet, for example); the second examining the sun, the length of days, and time; and the third regarding the stars.[27] These three categories encompassed the vast majority of issues discussed in all these treatises, and the second type—showing how to tell the length of days at specific times of the year, at different latitudes, the difference in lengths of days at different latitudes, and so forth—comprised the largest single group of problems for all the authors.[28] These problems are followed by such operations as how to find the distance between any two places, or the difference in latitude or longitude between places. Joseph Moxon, in 1659, suggested using globes to solve problems such as, "The Rhumb you have sailed upon, and the latitudes you departed from, and are arrived to, given, to find the Difference of Longitude, and the number of Leagues you have sailed."[29] In other words, if you know two of these four variables—direction, distance, difference in latitude, or difference in longitude—you can find the other two. This type of problem was repeated by every *De globis* treatise writer. Further, Moxon suggested keeping

> A Journal of the Ships Way by the Globe. By some of these foregoing problemes, you may Daily (when observations can be made) find both the Longitude and Latitude on the Globe, of the Place you have arrived to, and also the Way the ship hath made, and make Pricks on the Globe in their proper Places for every days Voyage, so truly, and so naturally, that if you kept your reckoning aright, you make sure you cannot miss any thing of the Truth it self.[30]

This seems to suggest a very utilitarian use for the globe, as a physical space to plot one's voyage. This, after all, is what we would expect such artifacts to be used for. It is, however, striking how little space these treatise writers give to such use and, by contrast, how much emphasis they place on the globes as calculational devices. Perhaps the globes weren't as useful in navigation as the authors claimed them to be.

Some of the problems described in these treatises demonstrate the value of these instruments in school mathematics. These are the mathematical problems claiming to be based on true-life situations:

> A merchant Man being in the latitude of 43d. falls into the hands of Pyrates, who amongst other things take away his Sea-Compass, but when he is gotten clear, he sails away as directly as he can, and after 2 days meets with a Man of War, who also had been the day before in the latitude of 43d and had sailed thence SE by S 37 leagues. He being desirous to find these Pyrates, the Merchant Man tells him he left them lying to and fro where they took him, and he had Sailed since at least 64 leagues between the South and West, what course shall the Man of War shape to find these Pyrates?[31]

These globes, in other words, were most useful as a tool in understanding our place on the globe and how to measure from one place to another. The treatises assumed that their readers would have personal access to a globe and so imagined and helped create a public that shared such ownership and an interest in the mathematical utility of these objects. This public, at least in the characterization by the treatise writers, would have an interest in understanding and measuring the real globe in the interests of navigation and trade, with some claim to controlling the larger oceans (as seen in the last mathematics problem). Often, the treatise writers assumed that at least some of their readers would be taking these globes on shipboard and actively using them in navigation.

This discursive public was thus in many ways a normative public. That is, the treatise writers wanted their audience to be a group of people united in their interest in the betterment of their country through trade and exploration, and who understood the need of better mathematics training and understanding to achieve this goal. Equally, many of these treatise writers were selling their expertise (and sometimes their instruments), so their goals were economic, as well as intellectual or ideological. Finally, while these writers may acknowledge that owning globes was an elite venture, they never make claim to the aesthetic value of these globes or their importance as objects of status or desire. Globes were useful, and the people buying them were to be motivated by concern for the public good, as well as their financial success.

CONSUMING PUBLICS

This normative public created by the treatise writers leads us to ask how the actual public for these globes was created? The globes themselves encouraged ownership and viewing, while the consumers spurred on globe construction to satisfy their demand for the items. In other words, this final public was created by both the actors and the artifacts, with each interacting with the other.[32]

In order to understand this consuming public, we need to discover just who owned these globes; that is, who constituted the market for these global visions and how did those owners interact with the artifacts and the normative values they putatively embodied? Were they navigators, ship owners, investors, natural philosophers, politicians, or virtuosi? Are they even classifiable as a group? The question of ownership turns out to be very difficult to answer, in part because the globes were fragile and probably thrown away as new ones came to the market. Few studies have been undertaken on globe ownership, in part because of the difficulty of doing so. In a larger study focusing on the Molyneux Globes, I have begun to collect instances of known globe ownership, which begins, in a very impressionistic way, to give us some insight into the demographics of that group.

There are a number of paintings depicting globes, but most are political portraits (for example, of Elizabeth I or Sir Francis Drake) and therefore do not give us any insight into ownership. Probably more interesting in this regard is Hans Holbein's 1533 double portrait, *The Ambassadors*.[33]

Figure 8.2   Hans Holbein the Younger, *Jean de Dinteville and Georges de Selve (The Ambassadors)*, 1533. Oil on oak, 207 × 209.5 cm. National Gallery, London, Great Britain. Photo Credit: © National Gallery, London / Art Resource, New York.

As John North has effectively shown, this picture is ideologically charged, so just as with the political portraits, the globes stand for something else.[34] However, Holbein used a variety of mathematical instruments in part because they resonated with the types of things available to these two French noblemen, and among them were two globes (not a pair)—a larger and more significant celestial globe and a smaller terrestrial one. Clearly it was possible for nobles to own globes, and for those viewing the painting to understand what they were.

In order to develop a picture of globe ownership, it is important to think about how many globes would have been made, something about which we know very little. We know, for example, that Mercator made and sold globes almost continuously for fifty years, but because he made globes to order, he produced fewer than five pairs a year, selling them for twenty to thirty florins for the pair.[35] In the case of the Molyneux Globes, we know that the investor, William Sanderson, paid the instrument maker Emery Molyneux one thousand pounds to make these globes.[36] It took him over two years to do so. The globes sold for between two pounds and twenty pounds a piece.[37] Was Sanderson expecting to make back his investment? If so, they must have thought they could sell at least fifty and perhaps as many as five hundred globes (of course, they would be sold in pairs, so that would be twenty-five to two hundred and fifty pairs). And yet, to date, I have traced only ten instances of Molyneux Globe ownership. Of course, if Molyneux anticipated that, like Mercator, he would use the plates over a long period, this plan was foiled by Molyneux's move to the Netherlands in 1597 and his death the next year.

Among the owners of the Molyneux Globes were Thomas Blundeville; Elizabeth I; the Earl of Northumberland; the Bodleian Library, Oxford; Shewsbury College; and All Souls College, Oxford.[38] Sanderson probably also had a pair, and at least two pairs have ended up in Germany.[39] There is also an extant pair at Middle Temple Library, which probably belonged to one of the members of the Inn (perhaps Thomas Crashawe).[40] We also know that John Dee and Sir Thomas Knyvett (later Baron Knyvett) owned Mercator Globes, so could add them to our list of early English globe owners.[41]

What unites all these owners is a certain level of wealth and power (not surprisingly), an interest in cosmology, mathematics, or natural philosophy, and an engagement with the wider world of trade, exploration, and nascent empire building. Of course, if it is true that Molyneux constructed smaller globes for the "meaner sort," that characterization could be modified. (We know, for example, that Sanderson sent his cousin John Jones with the smaller globes to Lord Burghley and that Thomas Hood says, in 1592, that "they [Molyneux globes in general] are now in the hands of many with whom I have to do."[42]) Equally, some of the globes, especially those owned by the two Oxford institutions, would have been seen by many more people than those belonging to individual gentry. Clearly we need to think of the group of people touched by globe ownership to be significantly larger than the small company of elite collectors.

HOW WERE THESE GLOBES USED?

This is a very difficult question. If they were used as the treatises suggest, they would have been on shipboard, with navigators plotting locations.

As an eighteenth-century treatise put it:

> And as the Terrestrial Globe only would be necessary in this case and there is Room enough in the Cabins of all large Ships to dispose of such a Globe with Conveniency, it is a wonder that any Masters, Captains, or Commanders of ships should ever go to sea without them.[43]

Figure 8.3   Title page of Thomas Hood, *T'Ghebruyck vande Zeecaert*. Amsterdam: Cornelis Claesz., 1602.

There is some evidence to suggest that this might have been the case, even in the sixteenth and seventeenth centuries. Lists of contents to be taken on Martin Frobisher's and Thomas James's voyages include a globe, for example, and recent archaeological work on VOC shipwrecks produced the brass scales to indicate there might have been globes on board, although these were more likely to have been celestial rather than terrestrial globes.[44] However, they are unlikely to have been accurate enough to have been useful, and they would have been hugely cumbersome.

Globes owned by those with serious mathematical interests may have been used as the treatises suggested, as calculational and pedagogical devices. John Dee may have used his globe as he pondered what advice to give to explorers searching for the Northwest and Northeast Passages. Northumberland might have had his in the tower, where he discussed natural philosophy with his coterie of esoteric scholars. Sir Thomas Knyvett was an important courtier and probably had his in his house in Westminster, perhaps in the library or long gallery, although it is not clear from his biography what he might have been doing with it.[45] He did lend it to Thomas

Blundeville, who used the globe to write his treatise, before purchasing the Molyneux Globes himself.[46]

It is hard to escape the feeling that those who owned globes saw them as meaningful artifacts, if not imbued with the meaning the treatise writers intended. The political portraits make clear that a terrestrial globe showed a mastery of the world; and even more than with a map on the wall, a globe would have given its owner a sense of knowledge and power of the world. Even on shipboard, globe owners did not necessarily interact with globes as the expected normative public. If Hood's woodcut gives us any indication, the globe seems more like window dressing than like a useful instrument, since the navigators are not even looking at it as they plot their course. When globes became more prevalent on board ship (in the eighteenth century), it may have been for their image of global control rather than for any actual utility they might have possessed.

CONCLUSION: PUBLICS CREATED

The explosion of globe manufacture in the sixteenth and seventeenth centuries tells us that there was tremendous interest in this new representation of the earth and the universe. The cutthroat competition by the Amsterdam globe makers demonstrates that the stakes were high and the potential rewards significant. Similarly, the new genre of *De globis* treatises and the significant number of books generated suggest that there was a market for global information, a market to be tapped—and one to be instructed and constructed. Finally, the ownership of globes and the related treatises indicates that market was real and growing. No wonder, by the eighteenth century, that globe manufacturers began to produce pocket globes by the dozen, to provide a more affordable—and enticing—version of the world at one's fingertips.

Do these globes indicate the presence of publics in early modern Europe? Did they help to create such publics, or at least provide some point of connection for publics already in existence? Yes, although we need to be careful about how we think of this.

The group of people who came together in the constructing of these globes was a heterogeneous group, moving out of an earlier artisanal structure to a new entrepreneurial one. A variety of different skills and knowledge was needed to effectively create a marketable globe, and so this process brought together mathematicians, cartographers, engravers, geographers, explorers, and astronomers. They potentially shared a goal of creating accurate and accessible information, of bringing the new discoveries and understanding of the world to a wider audience. But I think we would be ill-advised to call this a public. This was largely a closed community, connected through personal contact, focused on particular information. While Mercator's participation in the mathematical "Republic of Letters" might be seen as participation in a public, it was only coincidentally connected to the globes.

More satisfactory are publics imagined by the *De globis* treatise writers. Through these treatises, authors sought to conjure a public, a group of individuals united by their interest in mathematics, navigation, and trade, that would understand the use of globes and seek to use them in an expanding set of circumstances. Of course these treatises were not written naively. The authors wished to sell their ability to teach mathematics, their instruments, their concept of empire or nation, their idea of utility and the common good. Nevertheless, this was a public, both imagined and real, with an agenda of progress and expansion.

Finally, those who actually owned, used, or had contact with the globes constituted a small but important public. This is a particularly interesting public, since the artifacts themselves constitute a significant player in its creation and continuation. One could consider this public a subset of a virtuosi public, given that globes were often part of cabinets of curiosities and that the aesthetic nature of the globes became increasingly more important over time, or of a navigational/exploratory public, given the rhetorical importance of globes to navigating new geographical space. Particularly for the virtuosi, exemplified in someone like Gabriel Harvey, globes provided concrete access to new knowledge. They linked the virtuosi world of disinterested learning with the wider concerns of measuring the globe and exploiting its resources, while at the same time displaying beauty and craftsmanship for the connoisseur. The significance of these globes, for this consuming public, was twofold. As the treatise writers told them, these globes gave them ways to measure, dissect, and conceptualize a world gridiculed by longitude and latitude, and circumnavigated by loxodromic lines. Equally, as their participation in the social and political world of early modern Europe grew, globes gave them a sense of mastery, patriotism, and control, a glimpse at empire imagined.

NOTES

1. Thomas Hood, *The Use of Both the Globes, Celestiall, and Terrestriall, most plainely delivered in forme of a Dialogue* (London: 1592), A4a.
2. Given the focus of this volume, I don't need to rehearse the entire history of talking about publics here. I have been most influenced by Peter Lake and Steven Pincus, "Rethinking the Public Sphere in Early Modern England," *Journal of British Studies* 45 (2006): 270–92; Brian Cowan, *The Social Life of Coffee: The Emergence of the British Coffeehouse* (New Haven, CT: Yale University Press, 2005); Benedict Anderson, *Imagined Communities: Reflections on the Origin and Spread of Nationalism* (London: Verso, 1983); Michael E. Gardiner, "Wild Publics and Grotesque Symposiums: Habermas and Bakhtin on Dialogue, Everyday Life and the Public Sphere," *Sociological Review* 52 (2004): 28–48; and Michael Warner, *Publics and Counterpublics* (New York: Zone Books, 2003).

3. Bacon saw the compass and printing press as authentically modern. Francis Bacon, *The Advancement of Learning* (London: 1605). Many historians have discussed these technologies, including of course Elizabeth Eisenstein, *The Printing Press as an Agent of Change* (Cambridge: Cambridge University Press, 1980). For a basic history of globe making, see Elly Dekker and Peter van der Krogt, *Globes from the Western World* (London: Zwemmer, 1993); Edward Luther Stevenson, *Terrestrial and Celestial Globes; Their History and Construction*, 2 vols. (New Haven, CT: Public for the Hispanic Society of America by the Yale University Press, 1921). These texts remain very useful, even if now dated.

4. The earliest post-antique globe was the Behaim globe of 1490, best known because it was a pre-Columbian globe, and because it was used by the Portuguese in their dispute with Spain over ownership of the Spice Islands. See Jerry Brotton, *Trading Territories: Mapping the Early Modern World* (Ithaca, NY: Cornell University Press, 1998), for a wonderful discussion of this. The first multiple-manufactured globe was probably created by Johannes Schöner in 1515, using woodblocks. Dekker and Van der Krogt, *Globes*, 23; Günter Oestmann, "On the Construction of Globe Gores and the Preparation of Spheres in the Sixteenth Century," *Der Globusfreund* 43–44 (1995): 121–31, discusses the early German contributions.

5. Helen M. Wallis, "The Molyneux Globes," *B. M. Quarterly* 16 (1952): 89–90; "'Opera Mundi': Emery Molyneux, Jodocus Hondius and the first English Globes," in *Theatrum Orbis Librorum*, ed. Ton Croiset van Uchelen, Koert van der Horst, and Günter Schilder (Utrecht: Hes Publishers, 1989), 94–104.

6. Nicholas Crane, *Mercator: The Man Who Mapped the Planet* (London: Weidenfeld and Nicolson, 2002), 64.

7. Peter van der Krogt, *Globi Neerlandici: The Production of Globes in the Low Countries* (Utrecht: Hes Publishers, 1993), 60.

8. Crane, *Mercator*, 64–69.

9. Ibid., 73–75. For an old but highly useful history of engraving, see Arthur M. Hind, *A History of Engraving and Etching: From the Fifteenth Century to the Year 1914* (London, 1923).

10. Crane, *Mercator*, 135.

11. For some interesting work on the Republic of Letters, particularly as it affects natural philosophers, see Lorraine Daston, "The Ideal and Reality of the Republic of Letters," *Science in Context* 2 (1991): 367–86; Laurence Brockliss, *Calvet's Web: Enlightenment and the Republic of Letters in Eighteenth-Century France* (Oxford: Oxford University Press, 2002); Maarten Ultee, "The Republic of Letters: Learned Correspondence 1680–1720," *Seventeenth Century* 2 (1987): 95–112; and Robert Mayhew, "Mapping Science's Imagined Community: Geography as a Republic of Letters, 1600–1800," *British Journal for the History of Science* 38, no. 1 (2005): 73–92.

12. Crane, *Mercator*, 145–49. Some of the correspondence is printed in W. Shumaker, ed. and trans., *John Dee on Astronomy* (Berkeley and Los Angeles: University of California Press, 1978), esp. 112–13.

13. Crane, *Mercator*, 223.

14. M. van Durme, ed., *Correspondence Mercatorienne* (Antwerp, 1959), 107. Amateurs were lovers of learning for its own sake, for the love and wonder of that knowledge. For an interesting distinction between amateurs and virtuosi, see Walter E. Houghton Jr., "The English Virtuoso in the Seventeenth Century," *Journal of the History of Ideas* 3 (1942): 51–73.

15. Gerard Mercator, *Atlas sive cosmographicae meditationes de fabrica mundi* (Düsseldorf, 1595). Unfinished at his death, the *Atlas* made money for the

later globe maker, Jodius Hondius, after he purchased the plates from Mercator's estate. Hondius tried to make this look more like a personal transaction by reengraving the frontispiece for the 1619 edition to show Mercator and Hondius working together. Crane, *Mercator*, 288–89.

16. The literature on early modern trust and credibility is vast. Undoubtedly the place to start would be Steven Shapin, *A Social History of Truth: Civility and Science in Seventeenth-Century England* (Chicago: University of Chicago Press, 1994); contrasted with Barbara Shapiro, *Probability and Certainty in Seventeenth-Century England: A Study of the Relationships between Natural Science, Religion, History, Law, and Literature* (Princeton, NJ: Princeton University Press, 1983).

17. Peter van der Krogt, "Globe Production in the Low Counties and Its Impact in Europe, 1525–1650," *Globe Studies: The Journal of the International Coronelli Society* 49–50 (2002): 45–60.

18. Plancius was the first official cartographer to the Dutch East India Company (VOC) following its formation in 1602. Dekker and Van der Krogt, *Globes*, 42.

19. The first four southern constellations, constructed in 1589, were the Southern Cross, the Southern Triangle, the Magellanic Clouds, and Nubecula Major and Minor. In 1592, the following were added: Apus, Bird of Paradise, Chamealeon, Dorado, the Goldfish, Grus, the Crane, Hydrus, the Small Water Snake, Indus, the American Indian, Musca, the Fly, Pavo, the Peacock, the Phoenix, Tucana, the Toucan, Volans, the Flying Fish, and Columba, the dove from Noah's Ark. Dekker and Van der Krogt, *Globes*, 44.

20. John Robert Christianson, *On Tycho's Island: Tycho Brahe and His Assistants, 1570–1601* (Cambridge: Cambridge University Press, 2000); Elly Dekker, *Globes at Greenwich. A Catalogue of the Globes and Armillary Spheres in the National Maritime Museum, Greenwich* (Oxford: Oxford University Press, 1999), 278. See Lisa Jardine, *Ingenious Pursuits: Building the Scientific Revolution* (New York: Little, Brown, 1999), for an interesting telling of the development of this latter chart.

21. Dekker and Van der Krogt, *Globes*, 46.

22. Ibid., 48.

23. Robert Recorde's *The Castle of Knowledge* (London, 1556) was the first of this genre in English. Others include: Charles Turnbull, *A perfect and easie treatise of the use of the caelestil globe written as well for an introduction of such as bee exercised in the art of navigation* (London, 1585); Edward Wright, *The Description and use of the Sphaere* (London, 1613); Mauritus Huberinus, *Globorum Coelestis et Terrestris Fabrica et Usus* (Nürnberg, 1615); Robert Tanner, *A brief Treatise of the Use of the Globe Celestiall and Terrestriall* (London, 1630); A. A. Metius, *De genuino usu utriusque globi Tractatus* (Amsterdam, 1626); Willem Janszoon Blaeu, *Institutio Astronomica: De use globorum et sphaerarum caelestium ac terrestrium* (Amsterdam, 1634); R. T., *A brief treatise of the use of the globe celestiall and terrestriall wherein is set downe the principles of the mathematicks fit for all travelers, navigators* (London, 1647); W. Grent, *The Antiquity and excellency of globes* (London, 1653); Joseph Moxon, *A Tutor to Astronomie and Geographie. Or an Easie and Speedy way to know the Use of both the Globes, Celestial and Terrestriall* (London, 1659); R. P. Bourdin, *Le cours de mathematique: Contenant de plus un traité de l'usage du globe terrestre* (Paris, 1661); William Leybourne, *Panorganon: or, A Universal Instrument, performing all such conclusions Geometrical and Astronomical as are usually wrought by the Globes, etc.* (London, 1672); Roger Castlemaine, *The English Globe: Being a Stabil and Immobil One* (London,

1679); Nicolas Bion, *L'usage de globes celestes et terrestres, et des spheres suivant let differens systemes du monde* (Paris, 1699); and Benjamin Martin, *The Description and Use of both the Globes, the Armillary Sphere, and Orrery* (London, 1763).

24. Hood, *Use of the Globe;* Robert Hues, *Tractatus de globis et eorum usu* (London, 1592); Thomas Blundeville, *His Exercises, containing sixe Treatises* (London: 1594); and John Davis, *The Seamans Secret* (London: Thomas Dawson, 1595). The latter is less explicitly written about Molyneux's globes, but contains important references to it.

25. Blundeville, *His Exercises,* fol. 209b.

26. Elly Dekker, "The Doctrine of the Sphere: A Forgotten Chapter in the History of Globes," *Globe Studies: The Journal of the International Coronelli Society* 49–50 (2002): 25–44.

27. Blundeville, *His Exercises,* fol. 211a.

28. For example, Robert Recorde states that in Calicut, "if they bee a quarter of the earth more toward the east than we, they must see the Son 6 houres sooner than wee." Recorde, *Castle,* 71.

29. Joseph Moxon, *Tutor to Astronomie,* 114.

30. Ibid., 118.

31. William Pickering, *The Marrow of the Mathematicks* (London, 1686), 278.

32. See Bruno Latour, *Reassembling the Social: An Introduction to Actor-Network-Theory* (Oxford: Oxford University Press, 2005), for a good explanation of this idea of actor network theory.

33. It is possible Schöner's globe was depicted in Hans Holbein's painting. See John North, *The Ambassadors' Secret: Holbein and the World of the Renaissance* (London: Hambledon and London, 2002), for a full discussion of this painting.

34. Ibid.

35. Crane, *Mercator,* 215, 230–31. Perhaps the best information concerning Mercator's sales comes from Plantin's catalog, which show that Mercator sold, through Plantin, three single globes from 1558 to 1562 and twenty-two pairs from 1564 to 1569. C. A. Campan, *Mémoires de Francisco de Enzinas: texte latin inédit avec la traduction Française du XVIe siècle en regard 1543–1545* (Brussels, 1862), 2:302, n. 3.

36. Helen M. Wallis, "The First English Globe: A Recent Discovery," *The Geographical Journal* 117 (1951): 275.

37. The difference in price was probably due to the finishing used, whether it was in a case, had a cover, or, in the instance of the Bodleian globe, was attached to a mechanism to hoist it to the ceiling. Wallis, "First English Globe," 285. We know from accounts that the All Souls globe cost two pounds, but the entire cost was two pounds, eight shillings, and five pennies, including lodgings for the purchaser.

38. Helen M. Wallis, "Globes in England," *Geographical Magazine* 35 (1962): 267–79.

39. There were pairs of Molyneux globes at the Hessisches Landesmuseum in Kassel and The Germanisches Nationalmuseum in Nuremberg. In both locations, the terrestrial globes have disappeared in the twentieth century.

40. Sir Edmund Craster, "Elizabethan Globes at Oxford," *Geographical Journal* 117 (1951): 24–26; R. M. Fisher, "William Crashawe and the Middle Temple Globes 1605–15," *Geographical Journal* 140 (1974): 105–12.

41. Dee names the Mercator globe among his possessions destroyed when his home is ransacked. Julian Roberts and Andrew G. Watson, eds., *John Dee's Library Catalogue* (London, 1990), 99. Knyvett is named by Blundeville as an owner of this globe. Blundeville, *His Exercises,* fol. 205b.

42. Anna Maria Crino and Helen Wallis, "New Researches on the Molyneux Globes," *Der globusfreund* 35–37 (1987): 12; Hood, *Use of the Globe,* fol. B1a.
43. Benjamin Martin, *The Description and Use of both the Globes* (1763), 158.
44. Wayne Davies, *Writing Geographical Exploration: James and the Northwest Passage 1631–33* (Calgary: University of Calgary Press, 2003), 190; Wallis, "Globes in England," 272; Peter van der Krogt, "Seventeenth-Century Dutch Globes: Navigational Instruments?" *Der globusfreund* 38–39 (1990): 67–76; C. A. Davids, "The Use of Globes on Ships of the Dutch East India Company," *Der Globusfreund* 35–37 (1987): 67–78. I owe the latter observation to Peter van der Krogt.
45. *Oxford Dictionary of National Biography* (Oxford: Oxford University Press, 2004), vide "Thomas-Knyvett, Baron Knyvett." Knyvett had land in Yorkshire, and the globes could have been there, but his significant service to Elizabeth and later James (Knyvett was the discoverer of Guy Fawkes in 1605) suggests that he spent much of his time in town.
46. Blundeville, *His Exercises,* fol. 205b.

Part III
Forms of Knowledge

9   Richard Hakluyt and His Publics, c. 1580–1620

David Harris Sacks

"*Printing, gunpowder* and the *compass*," writes Francis Bacon. "These three have changed the whole face and state of things throughout the world; the first in literature, the second in warfare, the third in navigation; whence have followed innumerable changes, in so much that no empire, no sect, no star seems to have exerted greater power and influence in human affairs than these mechanical discoveries."[1] Nowhere is the collective potential of these modernizing inventions more apparent than in the history of oceanic navigation and overseas discovery, most especially in the published stories of exploration and encounter they engendered. There the power of print not only revealed the utility of the compass and the effectiveness of gunpowder, but promoted the creation of a public for further exploration and encounter. In Bacon's time, there could have no more important example of this phenomenon than Richard Hakluyt's *Principal Navigations of the English Nation*, whose first edition appeared in one large volume in 1589 and whose second, three-volume edition was published, one volume a year, between 1598 and 1600.[2]

For J. A. Froude, who called Hakluyt's book "the Prose Epic of the modern English nation," this massive work of historical and geographical learning represented a celebration of the origins of the British Empire, which Froude saw encapsulating the central features of English civilization—its devotion to Protestantism and enterprise, its spirit of endeavor and improvement.[3] He equated the book's cultural force for the English, especially its emphasis on the English contribution to newly discovered lands and trade routes, with what Homer represented for the Greeks, Virgil for the Romans, and the Norse sagas for the Vikings.[4] This aspect of Hakluyt's activities focused significantly on his role as one of the first citizens of the Atlantic world and the empire engendered within it.

But Hakluyt was also something more. From the very start of his public career around 1580, he acted frequently as an expert consultant on a host of practical matters concerning trade, navigation, and colonial enterprise.[5] In keeping with this role, he served in the mid-1580s as a diplomat and government intelligence officer in Paris while acting as chaplain to Sir Edward Stafford, Elizabeth I's ambassador. While there, he collected information about new overseas discoveries, international affairs, and internal French politics as well as witnessing the renewal of Europe's savage Wars of Religion. This experience deeply affected his views of the historical place of geographical discovery and colonization in bringing peace and unity in the world.[6] Later, during the last decades of his life he helped bring the Virginia Company into existence and advised its council on practical matters of logistics and settlement; he played a similar role as an expert consultant for the East India Company as well.[7]

Most important of all, perhaps, the humanist-geographer was also a clergyman—"Preacher of the Word of God," or just "Preacher," as he frequently identified himself[8]—and for the last fourteen years of his life he was a very active canon of Westminster, that "showcase" for "the English cathedral ethos" as Diarmaid MacCulloch has put it.[9] There he served at different times as archdeacon, steward, and treasurer as well as regularly attending the frequent chapter meetings.[10] In these capacities he found himself a partisan in the divisions over theology, liturgy, and ecclesiology that roiled the Church during his years of service. As we shall see, Hakluyt's big book also spoke to these issues as it sought to pave the way to the Last Judgment.

THE PUBLIC, THE PUBLIC GOOD, AND PUBLICS

As an Oxford don, expert consultant, and ecclesiastical official, Hakluyt was an active citizen in England's "monarchical republic" laboring to advance what he regarded as the public good.[11] In this sense, he was a "public man" whose career exemplifies the "publicness" to which Jürgen Habermas drew the attention of historians and political commentators in his *The Structural Transformation of the Public Sphere.*[12]

The word "public" is among the most commonly used terms in English. But, as Habermas emphasized, the usage of the word in modern discourse is particularly fraught. The concept of the "public sphere," he says, "betrays a multiplicity of concurrent meanings," going "back to various historical phases," which, when applied under the conditions of bourgeois society, "fuse into a clouded amalgam."[13] We often speak of public places, persons, policies, opinion, and debates; of the public sector of the economy and of the public trading of stocks and bonds; of appearing or going out in public; and of making public things that previously had been hidden from view or secret. We say that particular forms of cultural production, and of different genres within them, have their distinct and several publics, sometimes overlapping and sometimes competing, as do individual practitioners and performers, including politicians. There are connections among these diverse usages, but they do not form a hierarchically ordered, unified, and seamless whole.

It was not always so, at least not conceptually! In the ancient Greek and Roman world, and under commonwealth ideals in the Renaissance, a plurality of publics would have been thought absurd, although a plurality of commonwealths was not. Subsidiary communities—the family, the guild or similar corporation, the village, the town—were sometimes called "little commonwealths." They were construed as components of the commonwealth as a whole, supporting its goal of achieving the good, not as competing with each other or with it. For believing Christians, the ultimate community was the universal church—the Christian commonwealth—within which autonomous kingdoms and principalities each played their roles and made their contributions. In this conception, a unitary and universal doctrine of the public good trumped any modern notion of state sovereignty. In addition, every subsidiary commonwealth was understood to be Janus-faced, looking inward to its own affairs and outward to the larger commonwealth within which it was nestled.[14]

In present usage, the varied meanings and applications of the term "public" are grounded in the long history of ordinary speech. In a useful analogy, Wittgenstein identified this everyday language "as an ancient city: a maze of little streets and squares, of old and new houses, and of houses with additions from various periods," which he contrasted with the specialized languages of the sciences and technical disciplines as the equivalent of planned suburbs surrounding the city's heart: "a multitude of new boroughs with straight regular streets and uniform houses."[15] At the core of the historic urban center, we might say, is the archaic agora, which in its first manifestation was simultaneously the center for the dance, the native cult, the *ekklesia* or political assembly, and judicial processes as well as market exchange, and that gave birth to the drama, making it probably the site of the first theater. Over time, however, as the emergence of bureaucratic institutions, the sovereign state, and market capitalism challenged those ancient ideals of commonwealth, these activities diverged to find multiple and often overlapping publics, only some of which, and not always the most important, were engaged directly with "public policy" or government decision making. The resulting publics do not typically organize themselves neatly into a single coordinated system, and their existence at times contradicts Habermas's emphasis on "the public as carrier of public opinion" and his definition of "the public sphere . . . as a specific domain—the public domain versus the private" where public opinion "functions as a critical judge" of official actions.[16]

By what method then should we study such "publics"? Treating the complex "amalgam" as made up of dialectically juxtaposed publics and counterpublics,[17] risks being reductive, while disaggregating its components can become a sterile exercise in taxonomy. However, since we are dealing with what Wittgenstein called "family resemblances,"[18] we need to see the form or idea that interests us in its family relations with the other publics with which it coexisted. In the case of Richard Hakluyt and his publics, the focus will be mainly on the "politic public" in its relation to its religious, commercial, and literary kin.

THE COMINGS AND GOINGS OF THE MANY

Although the ideal of a seamless public life has long persisted, the capacity to sustain the good of unity began seriously to founder in the sixteenth century, with the transformation of the ancient city of everyday discourse into a burgeoning modern metropolis, where—as was said of early modern London—not even the tolling bells could agree on the hour.[19] Among those unity-shattering developments, we might single out the early modern period's Wars of Religion, which had occupied Hakluyt during the earlier stages of his career. This more than century-long sequence of upheavals left Europeans with neither common agreement on theological doctrine, nor a single church in which to worship, and eventually made it undesirable— even impossible—to imagine the establishment of a universal Christian commonwealth in the world. But we should also take note of three others: first, the rise of sovereign nation-states, which created political structures to displace the ideal of a universal commonwealth in favor of distinct and several principalities and republics, each enjoying a monopoly of rule over their territories and subjects and each competing with the others for dominion and resources; second, the development of the printing press and print culture, which not only made it possible rapidly to spread information as well as vituperation, but assisted in the advancement of vernacular literatures, including translations of the Bible, and promoted the creation of publics for different genres and diverse works in the vernacular; and third, the European discovery of the so-called New World, which not only contributed to a remarkable increase in knowledge of lands, peoples, and useful commodities and a burgeoning desire among the new European states to control the newly discovered territories, but added to the expansion of learning already under way and ushered in a period of new methods and new findings in natural philosophy and natural history.

On this last point Francis Bacon had much to say. For him, Atlantic discoveries from Columbus onward were the harbinger of history's end-time. "We must not forget," he said, "the prophecy of Daniel concerning the last ages of the world: that *Many shall go to and fro and knowledge shall be increased,* which manifestly hints and signifies that it was fated (that is, Providence so arranged it), that thorough exploration of the world (which so many long voyages have apparently achieved or are presently achieving) and the growth of the sciences would meet in the same age."[20] For Bacon, this growth of the sciences entailed the increase of the public good. One of the "signs" of philosophy's worth, he argued, is that it is productive of "fruits and works"—he meant useful outcomes that might be applied to alleviate social and political ills, advance general and personal welfare, improve health, and extend life. Their "discovery guarantees and underwrites the truth of philosophies."[21] Subsequently, in *New Atlantis,* he envisioned the existence of a research institute to organize the necessary experiments and journeys of exploration.[22]

Before going further, then, I want to suggest that the making of modern publics depends significantly on the development of this Baconian form of the advancement of learning. According to it, the creation of works is cumulative and incremental; public good moves forward piecemeal through the diverse and sometimes competing agency of the many, and the test of any particular truth is pragmatic or utilitarian rather than transcendental or metaphysical. In consequence, each discovery has the capacity to create its own particular public alongside the multiple publics committed to the promotion of exploration more generally, with supporters of the latter attracted by one or more of the following potential benefits: its immediate and tangible material returns; its role in advancing knowledge for its own sake; and, in the climate of the era's apocalyptical religious expectations, its contribution to the restoration of the world, or as Bacon would say its backing for the world's Great Instauration—*instauratio* being a Latin word for recapitulation, repetition, renewal, or in the case of architecture, rebuilding.[23]

When Bacon first connected the new geographical discoveries of his age with Daniel's prophecy, he almost certainly had in view Hakluyt's recently published second edition of *The Principal Navigations of the English Nation* with its nearly six hundred stories of the comings and goings of the many.[24] Its three volumes, containing diverse documents from different hands appealing to different tastes and interests, represent a compendium of publics in their own right. But they are arranged to tell a single story, which, to adapt T. S. Eliot's idea, is the "objective correlative" of Hakluyt's view of the history of the world as a coming together over time of multiple parts to form, or reconstitute, a unified whole.[25]

The completed volumes were the product of years of collecting from numerous mariners and navigators, antiquaries and scholars, geographers and cartographers, statesmen and great personages. Figures with these backgrounds populate one of the publics that he addressed. Publication also brought him into communication with many authors, editors, and collectors who had similar learned interests to his, and with publishers across Europe. Taken together, these groups make up a second broad public. And once in print, his book established his relationships with government officials, investors in trading and colonizing companies, and engaged readers of all sorts—yet another public or perhaps several.

READERS, READING PUBLICS, AND PUBLICS

I turn first to the readers of the two editions of *Principal Navigations*. Given Hakluyt's emphasis on trading commodities, those primarily interested in commerce were certainly among the most important of them.[26] But in the list of early owners we also find Lancelot Andrewes, who had been Bacon's friend since the latter's days as a student at Cambridge, and who, as Dean of Westminster between 1601 and 1605, was Hakluyt's near neighbor in the Abbey close.[27] Hakluyt and Andrewes each came from London merchant families, and had much in common including the patronage early in their lives of Sir Francis Walsingham and later of Sir Robert Cecil. Andrewes had a strong interest in geography and maps, which he conceived to have apocalyptic significance. Like Bacon, on whose preliminary studies for *Instauratio magna* he had commented, the bishop saw the knowledge represented in such works as presenting in visible form the instauration of the world evoked in 1 Ephesians 10—the gathering together again of all things into one in the fullness of time.[28]

A number of other commentators fit *Principal Navigations* into the classical tradition as having epic significance. The poet Michael Drayton speaks of Hakluyt in these terms in his ode "To the Virginian Voyage," first published in 1606. Writing to the adventures about to make their historic colonizing voyage—those "brave Heroique Minds . . . That Honour still pursue"—Drayton invokes the presence of "Industrious Hackluit, / Whose Reading shall inflame / Men to seeke fame" and asks him to attend their voyages and commend them "to after-Times" in the manner of a singer of tales.[29] In 1611, the East India Company sought to use *Principal Navigations* in similar terms to encourage its resident factors in the Indies. These were sent a copy along with editions of Foxe's *Book of Martyrs* and of William Perkins's *Works*. These texts, taken together, were to be read as remembrances of the purpose of their mission with Hakluyt specifically intended for the "better confort" of the company's agents, and "to recreate their spirittes with varietie of historie."[30]

By the early 1630s George Hakewill was asking to have *Principal Navigations* translated into Latin, not just for "the benefit that might redound to other Nations," but "for the honour of the English name" that it would spread on the continent.[31] As Hakluyt himself stressed, he was making public the knowledge he published in his massive book in part for just this reason—to acknowledge and to praise the heroic agency of the many English navigators and adventurers who had made original contributions to expanding what was then our knowledge of the world.[32]

But Hakewill's call for a Latin version shows that in presenting *Principal Navigations* only in English—a language little known, let alone used, elsewhere in Europe—Hakluyt aimed mainly to create a public in England itself for the multifaceted project of discovery. Just as in his youth he had become enthralled by the prospect of advancing geographical learning by observing the maps and cosmographies revealed to him by his cousin in his rooms at the Middle Temple, he hoped to use the new knowledge he printed and the tales he told to excite investment in projects of exploration and settlement, and, to promote, if possible, the establishment of a college for pilots and mariners to train them in the mathematics and astronomy as well as the practical sciences of winds, currents, and boat handling necessary for what John Dee had called the "perfect art of navigation."[33]

What can we say about the social makeup of Hakluyt's early readers? *Principal Navigations* was already a very large book in its single-volume first edition of 1589, filling more than 850 folio-size pages. Thomas Egerton, the future Lord Chancellor, seems to have paid nine shillings for his copy, and the copy that had been bought in 1590 by Robert Nicolson, a London citizen, probably a merchant, had cost him nine shillings, two pence. These prices amounted to more than a week's wages for a skilled craftsman at the time. It is likely that these copies were purchased unbound in sheets, but perhaps already in a sewn state. Other early owners of the 1589 edition of *Principal Navigations* paid somewhat more, which may reflect the fact and quality of the binding. Edward Wytt's copy cost him eleven shillings, six pence and another cost its owner sixteen shillings.[34]

The still more massive second edition in three volumes consisted of almost 2,100 folio-size pages. Printing it, even at the rate of one volume a year, would have been a labor-intensive and complicated task, demanding a major investment and the marshaling of considerable entrepreneurial skills. Over a ream of paper costing perhaps five shillings would have been used in printing the three volumes, suggesting that the cost of production counting the charge for engraving and printing the Wright-Molyneux map in the second volume would have been around ten shillings per set. From inscriptions on flyleaves, we also know something of the prices paid for copies of *Principal Navigations* itself, but it is usually uncertain whether the amount listed is for one volume or for more, and whether the copy in question was bound or unbound. For example, the first volume of the set belonging to Nicholas Howlett, of Caius College, Cambridge—he was later a prebendary of Norwich Cathedral—bears the price of twenty-one shillings. But Richard Punder, another Cambridge-educated clergyman, seems to have paid ten shillings for the first volume of his copy. The price difference probably reflects the fact that Howlett's copy was acquired in a good binding, while Punder's was originally purchased in sheets and bound later. In other words, it looks as though an unbound single volume might have sold for between ten and twelve shillings around the time of publication—a figure consistent with what we know in general of the cost of books at the time. This would suggest a cost per unbound set of between thirty and thirty-five shillings, almost a month's wages for a craftsman, and somewhere between six to nine pounds—that is, roughly two to three months' wages—for each bound set, depending on the binding.[35]

Neither edition went through more than one printing, no doubt because of the cost. Nor were large numbers in print. Their print runs probably were on the order of 750 copies, roughly the same as for Shakespeare's *First Folio*.[36] We know some of the names of the book's early owners from the inscriptions they left on the flyleaves of their copies or from inventories of their libraries.[37] Prominent public figures, ecclesiastical officials, learned scholars, and lawyers are especially evident among them. We have already mentioned Lancelot Andrewes and Thomas Egerton. In addition, as noted by Anthony Payne, "surviving copies include those of Robert Burton, . . . John Selden, John Whitgift, Lord Lumley (whose library was used by Hakluyt), Sir Robert Cecil, Sir Ferdinando Gorges, Prince Henry, George Wilmer (investor in the Virginia and East India Companies), the 'Wizard Earl' of Northumberland (that is, Henry Percy, Ninth Earl of Northumberland [1564–1632]), and Sir Edward Coke."[38] To this list we might add Anthony Rudd, Bishop of St. David's, chaplain to Queen Elizabeth I and after her death to King James I;[39] and Sir Henry Savile, sometime Warden of Merton College, Oxford and Provost of Eton, editor of the works of Xenophon and St. John Chrysostom, and translator of Tacitus.[40] Perhaps most notable of all, Sir Walter Raleigh, Hakluyt's early patron, had a copy in the extensive library he maintained while he was a prisoner in the Tower.[41]

Unsurprisingly, a number of individuals with strong interests in colonial enterprise also appear. Along with Wilmer and Gorges, singled out by Payne, we also find Sir William Berkeley, sometime governor of Virginia;[42] Sir Thomas Sherley, privateer, travel writer, and Virginia Company member;[43] and Henry Timberlake, a member of the East India Company, investor in the Somers Island plantation and in the search for the Northwest Passage, as well as a sometime pilgrim to the Holy Land.[44] However, because the list depends not just on which copies have survived, but also on which of their original owners had the habit of putting their names in their books, it is skewed toward great officers of state, noblemen and gentlemen, clergy, and successful lawyers rather than merchants and mariners, who must have been represented among the hundreds of early owners whose copies are unsigned or are now lost.[45]

Given Hakluyt's prominent role in the founding of the Virginia Company—his name appears third among the eight men named in its first charter of 1606[46]—we can perhaps take its investors as a model for this larger potential market. In 1609, under the company's second charter, its membership consisted of 812 individuals, headed by twenty noblemen, a bishop, and a hundred knights. The total of 196 peers, knights, and other gentlemen named in the charter amount to about a quarter of the company's first members. Merchants and large-scale luxury retailers, sea captains, shipwrights and other craftsmen, mainly from London, lawyers, physicians, civic, and ecclesiastical officials account for the rest.[47]

Extrapolating, we can perhaps take the body of early modern English commercial investors as a whole to represent the book's potential reading public. In studying these individuals, T. K. Rabb found that among 5,635 first-time memberships in the great companies of exploration and trade between 1575 and 1630, 979 (17 percent) came from among the nobility or gentry, while 3,461 (61 percent) were according to Rabb's designation "merchants."[48] Viewing investors as a whole, first-time or not, Rabb also discovered that peers accounted for nearly 3.5 percent of those he was able to classify, knights (including merchants elevated to the rank) almost 12 percent, other gentry a further 9.3 percent, professionals and those called "yeoman" 1.4 percent, and "merchants" 73.5 percent.[49] Although Rabb offers no more refined distinctions within his several categories, the general picture is almost certainly similar to the distribution of commercial occupations we observe among the Virginia Company's membership.

If investors in imperial enterprises indeed represent the core of Hakluyt's reading public, we might conclude that his main aim was to mobilize the ships and expertise in navigation, the credit and liquid capital, as well as the energies and entrepreneurial skills of England's commercial elite for his great project—to refashion them into adventurous knights eager for the lasting fame that would come with the advancement of learning and glory of discovery and not just for a profitable return on their company shares (which often proved illusory, and nowhere more so than in the Virginia Company). Indeed, Hakluyt modeled his methods in order to arouse the desires of these men for recognition of their achievements by emphasizing the individual agency of those whose narratives he printed.[50]

Since "publics" in the sense we have been using the term are nonexclusive, open-ended, voluntary associations based on common ideas, tastes, and interests, and not institutions with restricted memberships, it would seem that England's overseas trading companies, whose activities and privileges were closed to nonmembers, would not qualify. Hence insofar as an individual participated in a trade or craft under the aegis of a company's restrictive charter, he should not be classed as a member of a public. But many company investors were members of several companies,[51] while numerous others engaged in similar overseas enterprises outside of the company control.[52] Taken together, the collectivity of such investors can be said to have constituted a public, or key elements of one, for overseas enterprise, navigation, and discovery.

Were there then multiple publics present among Hakluyt's readers? I don't just mean did Hakluyt's book appeal in different ways to different types of investors, such as to passive ones, like the great noblemen in the list of the Virginia Company's members, and to active ones who engaged directly in trade or were governors and directors of the companies. I am equally interested in whether the opportunities of investment in geographical discovery might also have brought together diverse interests in a complex of overlapping publics. While market-oriented activities and the prospects of material gain motivated many of the participants, some also followed Bacon in seeking the great instauration of the world that would be gained through exploration. This motivation seems especially to account for the interest of the clergy, like Andrewes and Rudd, who owned Hakluyt's book, as well perhaps others among the learned such as Selden and Savile. Still others undoubtedly followed Bacon in putting their stress on useful knowledge capable of generating practical "works" to improve human welfare and build state power. Arguably these considerations underpinned the view of many of those company investors who held public offices. Similar ideas, no doubt, also help explain the presence of so many members of Parliament among company investors.[53] These motivations, however, were not mutually exclusive, since it was common for individuals to see no contradiction at all between the pursuit of knowledge of the world for philosophical and religious reasons and the pursuit of knowledge for the material improvement of their own lives and the benefit of their communities' welfare.

PATRONS, PATRONAGE, AND PUBLICS

Those persons who bore office were authorized to perform public business for the advantage of the commonwealth at large—the *res publica Anglorum*. To mobilize their energies, however, it was necessary for Hakluyt not just to lobby them for official support, but also to excite their personal passions and their self-interest in profit, glory, honor, and the production of new knowledge, thereby inducting them into a new public fellowship. In order to foster their collective interest, he relied significantly on the institution of patronage.

Hakluyt had many patrons, drawn from a wide spectrum in later Elizabethan and early Jacobean England, ranging from the Skinners' Company and the Clothworkers' Company in London to the Queen herself.[54] Over the course of his career he came to owe major debts of gratitude to Sir Francis Walsingham, to whom Hakluyt dedicated the first edition of *Principal Navigations* (1589); to Sir Philip Sidney, to whom he dedicated his *Divers voyages* (1582), and to Sidney's close friend Sir Edward Dyer, whom Hakluyt called "my Maecenas";[55] to the Earl of Leicester, Sidney's uncle, Chancellor of Oxford and the leading patron of Christ Church College, where Hakluyt was a fellow; to Sir Walter Raleigh, whose Virginia colony at Roanoke Island Hakluyt vigorously promoted; to Sir William Cecil, Lord Burghley, Elizabeth I's leading counselor; to Lord Charles Howard (the Lord Admiral), dedicatee of the first volume of the second edition of *Principal Navigations;* to Howard's close ally and Burghley's son Sir Robert Cecil, Earl of Salisbury, whose chaplain Hakluyt had become by 1601 and to whom he dedicated the second two volumes of *Principal Navigations;* and to Douglas, Lady Stafford and by her first marriage Countess of Sheffield (lover of the Earl of Leicester and mother of his child, the bastard Sir Robert Dudley). Lady Stafford was the sister of the Lord Admiral and the wife of Sir Edward Stafford, ambassador to Paris, whom Hakluyt served as chaplain and secretary; she was also the patroness of the parish of Wetheringsett with Blockford in Suffolk, where she appointed Hakluyt as rector.[56]

Hakluyt also relied heavily on the receipt of information and manuscript materials from a host of informants, including a number of mariners and merchants. Along with mentions of Raleigh and Dyer and his own cousin Richard Hakluyt the elder of the Middle Temple, he singles out Richard Staper, sometime Master of the Clothworkers and a Levant merchant; William Borough, a navigator and Clerk of the Queen's Navy, associated with the Muscovy Company; Anthony Jenkinson, the travel writer also associated with the Muscovy Company; William Sanderson, the Muscovy merchant; Sir John Hawkins, the merchant, naval commander and sometime privateer; Richard Garth, an official of the Exchequer; Walter Cope, feodary for the city of London and Middlesex and a client of Lord Burghley's; and Emery Molyneaux, the map- and globe maker, whose globes are discussed by Lesley Cormack in Chapter 8 of this volume.[57]

Hakluyt was also a patron in his own right. He was an ardent supporter, for example, of mapmakers and globe makers, book translators, and book publishers.[58] In addition to the books he himself edited and saw to publication, he was personally involved in influencing, and sometimes paying for, the publication by others of over twenty further books containing geographical knowledge, starting with John Florio's translation of Jacques Cartier's narrative of his discoveries in New France published in 1580,[59] and concluding with the works of Samuel Purchas, for which Hakluyt provided numerous documents.[60] Hakluyt's support for John Pory, sometime Fellow of Gonville and Caius College in Cambridge, is illustrative. In 1597, Hakluyt had taken Pory into his household as his pupil in "Cosmographie and forren histories." Three years later in the dedication of the third volume of *Principal Navigations,* Hakluyt—called, he said, to attend to his "profession of divinitie" and the care of his family—wrote to Cecil, his own patron, to recommend Pory, "my very honest, industrious, and learned friend," as a person "of speciall skill and extraordinary hope to perform great matters" in geographical study "and beneficial for the commonwealth." Pory, in the same year (1600), dedicated his edition of Leo Africanus's *A Geographical Historie of Africa* to Cecil, singling out Hakluyt as his "reuerend friend . . . who out of his mature iudgement . . . moued me to translate it." This in turn led Cecil and his own great friend Sir Walter Cope, whom Hakluyt earlier in his own career had acknowledged for his help, to use their patronage to secure Pory a seat in Parliament for the town of Bridgewater in Somerset. With this backing, Pory was able to begin a political career as a scholar-diplomat, acting much like Hakluyt himself had done during his five years of service in Paris.[61]

Hakluyt's incorporation of Pory into the patronage network in which he himself participated raises several important issues for our consideration of publics. Since patronage networks in the past typically had restricted memberships dependent on personal loyalties, we might wish to exclude them as irrelevant to our study. But many of them were also open-ended forms of association, capable of voluntarily including new members on the basis of their capacities to support one another in the pursuit of common interests, tastes, and goals. In this connection, they were traditionally deemed to play a vital role in the in the ancient ideal of the public, as is demonstrated in Aristotle's distinction between "virtue" friendship, where each party seeks the good of the other, and "use" friendship, where the parties seek advantage mainly for themselves. This second type provides the basis for reciprocity in gift exchange and patron-client relations. About it Aristotle said that it "seems to hold states together."[62] Similar ideas prevailed into the Renaissance.[63]

This conception of patronage blurred, without entirely erasing, the line separating the public from the private. Patronage singled out named individuals for specific benefits, whether these involved the granting of personal recognition or honor, or of power, office, or material profit. But it was possible to believe that such grants could provide private profits to some and still yield public benefit, general to all. As Queen Elizabeth put it in defending herself against criticism of the privileges she awarded to her councilors and courtiers: "Since I was Queen, yet, did I never put my Pen unto any Grant, but that, upon pretext and semblance made unto to me, that it was both Good and Beneficial to the Subject in general, though a private Profit to some of My Antient Servants, who had deserved well at My Hands."[64] Construed in this fashion, patronage created or reinforced bonds of mutual loyalty and the framework of social stability while simultaneously promoting activities—such as new inventions or trades, or new discoveries on land and sea—advantageous to the commonwealth.

Patronage, therefore, had a public function. Can we then think of the resulting clientage as a kind of public? To those excluded from the direct benefits of royal grants, a clientage was a faction. If the exchange of loyalty and goodwill was the great benefit of patronage, the risk of faction represented its potential for harm, as the English political nation would have been all too aware during the 1590s when relations between the rival networks behind the Earl of Essex and Sir Robert Cecil turned poisonous.[65] By the standards of ancient ethics and politics, a faction— an exclusive body seeking to use public power for selfish ends—was a conspiracy against the public good and intrinsically evil, what we might call an antipublic.[66]

However, whatever shortcomings there might be to factional competition, a faction was a social form systematically distinct from a social class or a status group. According to Max Weber's classic definitions, the former is constituted according to its "life chances" as "represented exclusively by economic interests in the possession of goods and opportunities for income . . . under the conditions of the commodity or labor markets." In contrast, the latter is constituted by social honor as expressed in the group's "specific style of life."[67] Neither of these forms seems well qualified for the status of a public or even of a "counterpublic" in Warner's sense.[68] Factions, however, have the character of "parties" in Weberian terms.[69] "'Parties,'" Weber says,

live in a house of power. Their action is oriented toward the acquisition
of social "power," that is to say, toward influencing a communal action
no matter what its content may be. . . . In individual cases, parties may
represent interests determined through "class situation" or "status situation." . . . But they need be neither purely "class" nor purely "status"
parties. In most cases they are partly class parties and partly status
parties, but sometimes they are neither.[70]

The term "party," as applied to politics, was a new one in the early
modern era. If it was used at all in ancient and Renaissance political discourse, it referred to one of the members or parts of the body politic, the
res publica, the commonwealth, which itself was understood to be composed of a number of parts, each of which contributed to the greater good
of the organic whole.[71] Weber however was thinking of something different, something more akin to the idea of "party" that arises within the law
of contract, where the "parties" are each understood to have distinct and
several interests that the exchange of material considerations brings into
arithmetic balance.[72] Weber was clear that "the communal actions of 'parties' . . . are always directed toward a goal which is striven for in a planned
manner." They involve what he called "a comprehensive societalization . . .
especially a political framework," without necessarily being "confined by
the frontiers of any individual political community."[73] That is, parties in
this modern sense typically represent open-ended and voluntary groupings of like-minded individuals, drawn from diverse classes and statuses,
engaged in the collective acquisition or appropriation of public power and
authority for the advancement of their goals, whether these are material
or intellectual or ideological. They remain parts of the body politic, to be
sure, but without necessarily carrying the additional implication that they
each contributed to advancing more than their own interests. For Weber,
moreover, they are "only possible within communities . . . which have some
rational order and a staff of persons available who are ready to enforce
it"—that is normally in a "state."[74] Hence, viewed as "parties," factions are
distinctively modern and rational institutions—publics in their own right.

It was important for Hakluyt and his mission to win the support of
those who commanded the English state and its resources, which in turn
required singling them out and treating them with special attention and
care. In other words, just as a heroic and noble passion for exploration
needed to be inculcated among the merchants, so too was it necessary to
instill in England's rulers a sense of the gains—religious and political as
well as material—to be won from successful voyages of discovery. English
public life, in other words, had become subject to forms of collective persuasion—practices that would only increase in the petitioning campaigns
and pamphlet wars that we witness later in the seventeenth and eighteenth
centuries. In the making of such publics, Hakluyt, in effect, had constituted
himself as one of the chief agents of the public for exploration and colonial

settlement. We are on our way, therefore, toward what would become a modern public—a coalition of interests brought into coordination in the pursuit of shared ends to contest with rivals for the resources and to achieve the policies that it believed would bring it success. In place of a commonwealth comprising diverse little commonwealths, we see a public composed of multiple publics.

NOTES

1. Francis Bacon, *The Instauratio magna Part 2: Novum organum and Associated Texts,* ed. Graham Rees and Maria Wakely (Oxford: Clarendon Press, 2004), 1:194–95, 1:168–69.
2. Richard Hakluyt, *The principall nauigations, voiages and discoueries of the English nation made by sea or ouer land* (London, 1589); Richard Hakluyt, *The principal nauigations, voyages, traffiques and discoueries of the English nation made by sea or ouer-land,* 3 vols. (London, 1599[1598]–1600).
3. D. B. Quinn, "Hakluyt's Reputation," in *The Hakluyt Handbook,* ed. D. B. Quinn (London: Hakluyt Society, 1974), 1:147–48; Richard Helgerson, *Forms of Nationhood: The Elizabethan Writing of England* (Chicago: University of Chicago Press, 1988), 175, 187.
4. James Anthony Froude, "England's Forgotten Worthies," in *Short Studies on Great Subjects* (London: Longmans, Green, 1886–1888), 1:446–47, 471–72.
5. For a summary of Hakluyt's career, see D. B. Quinn and A. M. Quinn, "A Hakluyt Chronology," in Quinn, *Hakluyt Handbook,* 1:263–331; the most recent biographical treatment is Peter C. Mancall, *Hakluyt's Promise: An Elizabethan's Obsession for an English America* (New Haven, CT: Yale University Press, 2007).
6. David Harris Sacks, "Richard Hakluyt's Navigations in Time: History, Epic, and Empire," *Modern Language Quarterly* 67, no. 1 (2006): 31–62; David Harris Sacks, "Discourses of Western Planting: Richard Hakluyt and the Making of the Atlantic World," in *The Atlantic World and Virginia, c. 1550–1624,* ed. Peter C. Mancall (Chapel Hill: University of North Carolina Press, 2007), 436–46.
7. See Mancall, *Hakluyt's Promise,* 92–94, 237–43, 250, 260–65, 270–72, 278–79, 292–94, 307–8.
8. See, for example, the title pages of the second edition of his *Principal Navigations* in D. B. Quinn, C. E. Armstrong, and R. A. Skelton, "The Primary Hakluyt Bibliography," in Quinn, *Hakluyt Handbook,* 2:501, 503, 505, 507, 509; see also Richard Hakluyt, *Analysis seu resolutio perpetua in octo libros politicorum Aristotelis,* 1583, BL, Royal MS 12 G. 18 f. 2.
9. Diarmaid MacCulloch, review of Stanford E. Lehmberg, *Cathedrals under Siege: Cathedrals in English Society, 1600–1700* (Exeter: University of Exeter Press, 1996) in *Journal of Ecclesiastical History* 48, no. 3 (1997): 581.
10. D. B. Quinn and A. M. Quinn, "Hakluyt Chronology," 1:317–18.
11. The term "monarchical republic" was introduced by Patrick Collinson in his "The Monarchical Republic of Queen Elizabeth I," *Bulletin of the John Rylands University Library of Manchester* 69, no. 2 (1987): 394–424.
12. Jürgen Habermas, *The Structural Transformation of the Public Sphere: An Inquiry into a Category of Bourgeois Society,* trans. Thomas Burger with

Frederick Lawrence (Cambridge: Polity, 1989); Richard Cust, "The 'Public Man' in Late Tudor and Early Stuart England," in *The Politics of the Public Sphere in Early Modern England* (Manchester, UK: Manchester University Press, 2007),116–43.
13. Habermas, *Structural Transformation,* 1.
14. David Harris Sacks, "Freedom to, Freedom from, Freedom of: Urban Life and Political Participation in Early Modern England," *Citizenship Studies* 11, no. 2 (2007): 137–38; P. J. Withington, *The Politics of Commonwealth: Citizens and Freemen in Early Modern England* (Cambridge: Cambridge University Press, 2005), 3–48.
15. Ludwig Wittgenstein, Aphorism 18, *Philosophical Investigations: The German Test, with a Revised English Translation,* trans. G. E. M. Anscombe, 3rd ed. (Oxford: Blackwell, 2001), 8e.
16. Habermas, *Structural Transformation,* 2.
17. Michael Warner, *Publics and Counterpublics* (New York: Zone Books, 2002).
18. Wittgenstein, Aphorism 67, *Philosophical Investigations,* 32.
19. David Harris Sacks, "London's Dominion: The Metropolis, the Market Economy, and the State," in *Material London, ca. 1600,* ed. Lena Cowen Orlin (Philadelphia: University of Pennsylvania Press, 2000), 20–21.
20. Italics in the original; Bacon, Aphorism 93, *Novum organum,* 1:151.
21. Ibid., Aphorism 73, 1:119.
22. Francis Bacon, *New Atlantis,* in *Francis Bacon: The Major Works,* ed. Brian Vickers (Oxford: Oxford University Press, 2002), 457–89.
23. Charles Whitney, *Francis Bacon and Modernity* (New Haven, CT: Yale University Press, 1986), 23–54; Charles Whitney, "Francis Bacon's Instauratio: Dominion of and over Nature," *Journal of the History of Ideas* 50, no. 3 (1989): 371–90.
24. Francis Bacon, *The Advancement of Learning,* ed. Michael Kiernan (Oxford: Clarendon Press, 2000), 70–71; see Charles Webster, *The Great Instauration: Science, Medicine, and Reform, 1626–1660* (London: Duckworth, 1975), 22–25.
25. T. S. Eliot, "Hamlet and His Problems," *The Sacred Wood: Essays on Poetry and Criticism,* 2nd ed. (1928; reprint, London: Faber, 1997), 85–86.
26. Richard Helgerson, *Forms of Nationhood: The Elizabethan Writing of England* (Chicago: University of Chicago Press, 1992), 171–81,
27. The Will of Lancelot Andrewes (1626), TNA, PROB 11/150, 151; D. D. C. Chambers, "A Catalogue of the Library of Bishop Lancelot Andrewes (1555–1626)," *Transactions of the Cambridge Bibliographical Society,* vol. 5 (1969–1970), part 2 (1970), 99–121 at 111; Paul A. Welsby, *Lancelot Andrews, 1555–1626* (London: S. P. C. K., 1958), 50, 73, 89, 160, 225–27.
28. Lancelot Andrewes, "A Sermon Preached before the Kings Maiestie, at *White-hall* on Thursday, the XXV. of *December,* A. D. MDXXXIII. being CHRISTMAS day," *XCVI Sermons,* 2nd ed. (London, 1632), 148–58. "Demands of (Lancelot Andrewes) Bishop of Chichester, for Stuff Left by Him (When Quitting the Deanery of Westminster) . . . circa 1605," Westminster Abbey MSS 41119, Westminster Abbey Library, London; Welsby, *Lancelot Andrewes,* 88–89; Sacks, "Discourses of Western Planting," 431–32.
29. Michael Drayton, "To the Virginian Voyage," in *Works,* ed. J. William Hebel (Oxford: Shakespeare Head Press, 1961), 2:363–64.
30. Commission of the Governor, Deputy, and Committees of the East India Company to John Sairis, chief commander, and Gabriel Towerson, captain of the *Hector,* et al., 4 April 1611, in *The Register of Letters, &c. of the*

Governour and Company of Merchants of London trading into the East Indies, 1600–1619, ed. George Birdwood with William Foster (London: Quaritch, 1893), 419.

31. George Hakewill, *An apologie or declaration of the power and providence of God in the government of the world,* 3rd ed. (London, 1635), 310–11; Quinn, "Hakluyt's Reputation," 1:136–37.

32. Richard Hakluyt, "To the Right Honorable Sir Francis Walsingham, November 17, 1589," *Principall nauigations,* sig. 2v; "Richard Hakluyt to the favourable reader," ibid., sig. 3v.

33. John Dee, *General and rare memorials pertayning to the perfect arte of nauigation annexed to the paradoxal cumpas* (London, 1577).

34. P. A. Neville-Sington and Anthony Payne, "An Interim Census of Surviving Copies of Hakluyt's *Divers Voyages* (1582) and *Principal Navigations* (1589; 1598/9–1600)," appendix to Anthony Payne, *Richard Hakluyt and His Books,* Annual Talk, 1996 (London: The Hakluyt Society, 1997), 36, 38, 39, 42.

35. Neville-Sington and Payne, "Interim Census," 47, 51. A set was bought for one pound, sixteen sterling from John Budge, the London Stationer in the early 1620s, for the use of the Virginia Company, Ferrar MSS, Magdelene College, Case 13, Miscellaneous 2, 1284, in D. B. Quinn, "A List of Books Purchased for the Virginia Company," *Explorers and Colonies* (London: Hambledon Press, 1990), 385; Anthony Payne, *Richard Hakluyt: A Guide to His Books and to Those Associated with Him, 1580–1625* (London: Quaritch, 2008), 44.

36. See Payne, *Hakluyt: A Guide,* 75, n. 134.

37. For the list, see Neville-Sington and Payne, "Interim Census," 32–76.

38. Payne, *Hakluyt: A Guide,* 43–44.

39. Notice of this copy appeared on the back page of the 10 October 2007, edition of *The New York Times Book Review* in an advertisement from Bauman Rare Books of Philadelphia and New York.

40. Neville-Sington and Payne, "Interim Census," 49, *Oxford Dictionary of National Biography,* online ed. (Oxford: Oxford University Press, 2004), vide: "Savile, Sir Henry (1549–1622)."

41. Walter Oakeshott, "Sir Walter Raleigh's Library," *The Library* 23, no. 4 (1968): 326.

42. Neville-Sington and Payne, "Interim Census," 50.

43. Ibid., 55; *Oxford Dictionary of National Biography,* vide: "Sherley, Sir Thomas (1564–1633/4)"; Theodore K. Rabb, *Enterprise and Empire: Merchant and Gentry Investment in the Expansion of England, 1575–1630* (Cambridge, MA: Harvard University Press, 1967), 376.

44. Neville-Sington and Payne, "Interim Census," 51; *Oxford Dictionary of National Biography,* vide: "Timberlake, Henry (d. 1625/6)."

45. Payne, *Hakluyt: A Guide,* 44.

46. William Waller Hening, ed., The First Charter of Virginia, 10 April 1606, in *Statutes at Large: Being a Collection of the Laws of Virginia, From the First Session of the Legislature, in the Year 1619* (Richmond, VA: Printed for the Editor by Samuel Pleasants, junior, printer to and for the Commonwealth, 1809–23), 1:57–66.

47. Second Charter of Virginia, 23 May 1609, ibid.,1:80–98.

48. Rabb, *Enterprise and Empire,* table 15, 120; the remaining 1,195 first-time investors in his list were members of the professions—lawyers, physicians, clergy, etc.—or self-identified as "yeoman," or not possible to be classified.

49. Ibid., table 1, 27. Among the 1,233 knights, 454 were merchants elevated to the status; ibid., table 11, 104.

50. Hakluyt, *Principal nauigations*, sig. 3v.
51. Rabb, *Enterprise and Empire*, table 3, 53.
52. See David Harris Sacks, *The Widening Gate: Bristol and the Atlantic Economy, 1450–1700* (Berkeley and Los Angeles: University of California Press, 1991), 54–127, 194–224; Robert Brenner, *Merchants and Revolution: Commercial Change, Political Conflict, and London's Overseas Traders, 1550–1653* (Princeton, NJ: Princeton University Press, 1993), 1–195.
53. Rabb, *Enterprise and Empire*, table 10, 94.
54. G. D. Ramsay, "Clothworkers, Merchant Adventurers and Richard Hakluyt," *E. H. R.* 92 (1977): 504–21.
55. François Hotman and Jean Hotman, *Epistolae* (Amsterdam: George Gallet, 1700), 292.
56. Payne, *Hakluyt: A Guide*, 3–21; Quinn and Quinn, "A Hakluyt Chronology," 1:266–69, 271–73, 278–81, 286, 292–93, 298, 303–4, 311.
57. Hakluyt, *Principal nauigations*, sig. 3v–4v; Quinn and Quinn, "A Hakluyt Chronology," 1:303.
58. See R. A. Skelton, "Hakluyt's Maps," in *Hakluyt Handbook*, 1:48–73; Quinn, Armstrong, and Skelton, "The Primary Hakluyt Bibliography," 2:528–75.
59. Jacques Cartier, *A shorte and briefe narration of the two nauigations and discoueries to the northwest partes called Newe Fraunce*, trans. John Florio (London, 1580).
60. C. R. Steele, "From Hakluyt to Purchas," in Quinn, *Hakluyt Handbook*, 1:74–96; L. E. Pennington, ed., *The Purchas Handbook: Studies of the Life, Times and Writings of Samuel Purchas, 1577–1626*, 2 vols. (London: Hakluyt Society, 1997); Mancall, *Hakluyt's Promise*, 233, 237, 275, 279, 388, 290, 304, 306, 359 n3.
61. William S. Powell, *John Pory, 1572–1636: The Life and Letters of a Man of Many Parts* (Chapel Hill: University of North Carolina Press, 1977), 9–25; Hakluyt, *Principal nauigations*, 3: sig. A3v; John Pory, "Sir Robert Cecil," unpaginated; "An approbation of the historie ensuing, by me Richard Hakluyt," Hakluyt, *Principal nauigations*, 3: 57–58; *Oxford Dictionary of National Biography*, vide: "Pory, John (bap. 1572, d. 1636?)."
62. *Nicomachean Ethics* .VIII:1:1155a21–25, trans. W. D. Ross, rev. J. O. Urmson in Aristotle, *The Complete Works of Aristotle: The Revised Oxford Edition*, ed. Jonathan Barnes (Princeton, NJ: Princeton University Press, 1984), 2:1825.
63. See Terence Ball, "Party," in *Political Innovation and Conceptual Change*, ed. Terence Ball, James Farr, and Russell L. Hanson (Cambridge: Cambridge University Press, 1989), 158–64.
64. Heywood Townshend, *Historical collections, or, An exact account of the proceedings of the four last parliaments of Q. Elizabeth of famous memory* (London, 1680: Wing), 264.
65. Paul E. J. Hammer, *Polarisation of Elizabethan Politics: The Political Career of Robert Devereux, 2nd Earl of Essex* (Cambridge: Cambridge University Press, 1999).
66. Ball, "Party," 159–61.
67. Max Weber, "Class, Status, Party," in *From Max Weber: Essays in Sociology*, ed. and trans. H. H. Gerth and C. Wright Mills (New York: Oxford University Press, 1946), 181, 187.
68. Warner, *Publics and Counterpublics*, 56–63.
69. Max Weber, "Class, Status, Party," in *From Max Weber: Essays in Sociology*, ed. and trans. H. H. Gerth and C. Wright Mills (London: Routledge, 1991), 180–95.

70. Ibid., 194.
71. Ball, "Party," 159.
72. Ibid., 166.
73. Weber, "Class, Status, Party," 194.
74. Ibid., 194; see Quentin Skinner, "The State," in *Political Innovation,* 90–131.

10 The "Confusion of Faces"

The Politics of Physiognomy, Concealed Hearts, and Public Visibility

Bronwen Wilson

> Using this veil [of dissimulation] is so necessary that only on the last day can one give it up. Then human interests will be finished, hearts will be more manifest than faces, souls exposed to public notice and thoughts examined by number and weight.[1]

Torquato Accetto's description of the Last Judgment comes toward the end of *Della dissimulazione onesta* (*Honest Dissimulation*), a short treatise written in 1641 in response to life at court. Employed as a secretary in Andria, a city ruled by the Carafa family, Accetto also wrote poems and traveled to Rome and Naples, then under Spanish control.[2] Otherwise little is known of the man whose obscurity may be in keeping with the voluntary concealment and the need to hide the bitterness of fortune he prescribes in his tract.[3] *Della dissimulazione onesta* describes those movements of the face and gestures that are the forms of expression that came to be used at court in the sixteenth and seventeenth centuries.[4]

The epigraph brings together the themes under consideration in this chapter: the divide between one's face and one's self and how that threshold was shaped by an emerging understanding of the public as a domain that both required and was conditioned by new modes of behavior and new forms of knowledge. Significantly, Accetto advances a new kind of political physiognomics, one that calls attention to the interests that others take in the body, and in so doing, one that reflected the social environment of the court even as it critiqued it. I use Accetto here to introduce the high stakes of the face, stakes that I argue were a symptom of a change in what it meant to do things in front of others, others who were increasingly understood as a diffuse group with their own particular opinions.

Any study concerned with the self and public formation in early modern Europe confronts an extensive literature. During the last three decades in particular, scholars have sought to redress Jacob Burckhardt's formulation of the Renaissance "individual" whose autonomous "will to power," as one scholar put it recently, was projected into portraits commissioned from artists in order to display oneself to others.[5] However already in the *Civilizing Process,* initially published in 1939 but relatively unknown until 1987 when it was published in *Die Gesellschaft der Individuen* (*The Society of Individuals*), Norbert Elias asked "Is the body the vessel which holds the true self locked within it? Is the skin the frontier between 'inside' and 'outside'?"[6] Against a priori assumptions about atomistic individuals, he argued for the historicity of social interaction (sociogenesis) and the interdependence of individuals and societies. Interiority, he proposes, is constituted by the "rise of an invisible wall of affects" that resulted from the imposition of social constraints described in courtesy books.[7] For Elias, the publication of Desiderius Erasmus's *De civilitate morum puerilium* (*On civility in children*) in 1530 signals a moment of change: Erasmus expresses a new concern with what one does in front of others, with "outward bodily propriety."[8] "Bodily carriage, gestures, dress, facial expressions," as Elias explains, are "the expression of the inner, the whole man."[9] Concerns with social behavior had already appeared in the medieval texts upon which Erasmus drew. What was new, however, was the interest in deportment prompted by his treatise, the kind of "active uptake" that Michael Warner ascribes to public formation.[10] This was certainly the case in sixteenth-century Italy; Baldassare Castiglione's *Il Cortegiano* (1528), Giovanni Della Casa's *Il Galateo* (1558), and Stefano Guazzo's *Civil conversatione* (1574, rev. 1579), to which I turn later in the chapter, are only the most famous examples of a genre that would become ubiquitous in seventeenth-century Europe.[11]

As Elias suggested, moreover, courtesy books contributed to increasing public awareness of inwardness, or better, to the "perception of bifurcated interiority," as Harry Berger has described it.[12] In studies of both courtesy books and portraits, Berger addresses the ways in which these genres were responses to the demands of the gaze, demands that were intensified by a culture of suspicion. Like Elias, he is concerned with how behavior was described and conditioned by representational technologies. One of these is *sprezzatura,* as he explains in *Absence of Grace,* that artful naturalness that is "also a normative demand: a demand for the performance of exemplary inwardness that's assumed to be inauthentic by the performers no less than by their audiences."[13] In *Fictions of the Pose,* Berger reiterates this "obligatory fictiveness or illusoriness of the 'self' conveyed by the performance."[14] The semblance of interiority went hand in hand with what he calls physiognomic idealism, the ideal image that sitters and courtiers endeavored to replicate by "transform[ing] faces and bodies into signs of the perfect mental and psychic grace denied them by nature."[15] This fictive "nature" was produced by "representation anxiety" that was intensified by "physiognomic skepticism," doubts about the truth of that nature by observers who had themselves been learning from courtesy books. Interiority was constituted by interests others showed in it, a process that forged a split between the character a person represents to others—as an object to be seen—and a remainder, a character or residue that is itself unrepresentable.[16]

It is precisely this divide where the politics of the face emerge, since the stakes of one's represented self were so high in the increasingly aristocratic context of late sixteenth-century Italy. Developing a facade had become urgent. Already in 1591, when Torquato Tasso responded to Castiglione's portrait of Urbino with his cynical portrait of the courtier's life at Ferrara in *Il Malpiglio overo de la corte* (The Malpiglio [bad air], or on the court), *sprezzatura* had been replaced by the more urgent *prudenza*.[17] The latter was an ethical imperative, according to John Martin, who contrasts prudence with sincerity in his account of interiority. Both modes of behavior, he argues, were bound to a new "understanding of the relation of one's thoughts and feelings to one's words and actions."[18] Both sincerity and prudence were ways of being that emphasized the threshold between one's heart and one's facade, but it was the political requirement for prudence, an ancient virtue given new urgency, as I emphasize here, that forged the opacity of that divide.

Physiognomy treatises—my focus in this chapter—overlap with courtesy books in their concern with what is visible on the body, with the latter providing instructions on how to construct a facade, and the former proffering knowledge about how to decipher it. As the humanist Pomponius Gauricus wrote in 1504, "Physiognomy is a way of observing by which we deduct those qualities of souls after traits that appear on the body."[19] Gauricus included a chapter on the topic in his book *De sculptura*, and indeed subsequent authors of physiognomy treatises sometimes compared their knowledge to that of artists.[20] Physiognomy was understood to be an innate cognitive faculty—and hence its connection to art—a form of natural visual literacy that was connected to the topos of the eyes as a window to the soul.[21] It was this kind of physiognomy of which Leonardo da Vinci approved—our ability to recognize, for instance, as he wrote in his *Trattato della pittura*, that "those who have horizontal lines strongly marked on their foreheads are men full of hidden and evident suffering."[22] As numerous authors claim—and by 1648 Honoré Nicquet would record 129 of them in his *Physiognomia humana libris*—physiognomy was knowledge that rendered interiority legible.[23] Conventional, classificatory, semiotic, and ubiquitous, the treatises fostered the culture of suspicion about faces they claimed to unveil, making the face a matter of concern.

The causes of this concern are multiple and complex, from the evolving political context of the courts and the change in affect identified by Elias, to religious conflicts and persecution that required the performance and expressions of faith but also the ability to conceal those beliefs.[24] I don't have space to address the complexity of the historical context here. Instead, this brief survey of texts endeavors to show how physiognomy, as a form of knowledge (however spurious it may strike us today), and an evolving understand of public life were mutually implicated. What is remarkable, on one side, is how little the purported uses, sources, and "science" of physiognomy changed over centuries, while on the other side, how radically different the stakes were in the seventeenth century when the face had changed from being something deemed to be relatively transparent to something opaque, a facade that was increasingly shaped by the interests friends and strangers took in it.[25] The notion of the public here, then, is a discursive one that developed in response to new kinds of social interactions and cultural representations in which attentiveness to faces was a crucial factor.[26] Considering changes in texts produced over several decades brings forward an understanding of public life as something distinct from earlier forms of association. This orientation is expressed in the texts themselves and through the discursive network in which they operated: the readers imagined by the authors, the academies in which they participated, and other kinds of social realignments—worldliness, in particular.

As already noted, Erasmus's emphasis on the observer's role was not new. According to the foundational *Physiognomics,* once attributed to Aristotle, physiognomy extends to "movements, gestures of the body, colour, characteristic facial expression, the growth of the hair, the smoothness of the skin, the voice, condition of the flesh, the parts of the body, and the build of the body as a whole."[27] Arabic authors developed the relation between astrology and physiognomy that was used for divination, a tradition—with chiromancy (palmistry) and metoposcopy (analogies between lines on the forehead and the stars)—that was criticized by the church, and by Pliny and Leonardo among many others, as false science.[28] Ideas about physiognomy didn't change substantially during the medieval period, according to Lucia Rodler, when it was used to reflect "on the social character of man and on his destiny," and for its political applications.[29] It was a means of assessing the character, as Gauricus informs readers, of potential spouses, instructors for one's children, and merchants, a recurring claim inherited from the Greek aristocrat and Sophist Polemon.[30]

While concerns about interpreting internal character from outward appearances go back to antiquity, the conflicted nature of this boundary emerges with particular force in the middle of the sixteenth century. Paolo Pinzio, for example, in his *Fisionomia,* published in 1550, contrasts the "clear and open" character of animals with humans who can conceal their vices and obfuscate their true natures.[31] Indeed, it was the ability of humans to veil their nature that caused a surge in interest and prompted men of diverse occupations to take up the pen.

One of these was Michelangelo Biondo, a Venetian physician and polymath, whose *De cognitione hominis per aspectum (On Knowledge of Men by Sight)* was published in Rome in 1544.[32] Dedicated to Francesco Venier, Biondo explains the practical value the book offers members of the Venetian Senate:

So analyzing men from their exterior aspect, you and the Senate will be able to protect and defend yourselves with great efficacy, since there is no mode easier than physiognomical judgment to recognize the innumerable deceptions with which a man can surround himself.[33]

Deceit is a crucial theme for Biondo, who begins the text by highlighting the difference between humans and animals. The enemies of the latter come from different species, whereas men, he observes, suffer at the hands of their own kind, the reason for practical instruction in recognizing the inclinations of others. Adding to the problem is the lack of sincerity:

In order to flee from human furor and to suffocate anxious fear of evil, one needs to observe some common and infallible norms that unveil even those dangers cloistered in the depths of hearts. With this same awareness, then, [readers] are able to understand individual comportment in a way that liberates them from dangers to pursue happily the destiny prescribed by the same nature. Let us practice, then, physiognomical conjecture to recognize more often honesty, and sometimes dishonesty.[34]

Biondo's interrogation of concealed dangers resonates with the political function he ascribes to physiognomy, and it connects also with his medical interests. Neither zoomorphism nor astrology is used here, since his pragmatic approach is based on observation and experience.[35] He proffers the deductive and scientific methods of his profession, "del tatto e della vista" (of touch and of sight), that draw on the Galenic and Hippocratic traditions of medicine and a concern with the body's natural complexion and its equilibrium.[36] The text is a reflection on the social value of physiognomy and the moral questions that accompany external appearances.

That knowledge of others facilitates self-reflection is central to Antonio Pellegrini's dialogue, a treatise that stages its orientation to the social world of professional civic life through its cast of interlocutors. *I segni de la natura e l'huomo* (*The Signs of Nature and Man*), first published in Venice in 1545, brings together the dialogue format of courtesy books with the indexing of facial features, types, and emotions that characterizes physiognomy treatises.[37] On the first day, Alessandro Dolce encounters the English ambassador and the Spanish consul at Murano where they talk about affects and inclinations based on the body's disposition. They reconvene the second day at Dolce's house, when they are joined by other Venetians—a doctor, a philosopher, and a theologian—with whom they debate the signs of human nature.[38] As Pellegrini explains at the beginning of the tract, the delight men take in learning about the differences between each other enables men to understand themselves.

Professional inclinations are also at the heart of Giambattista Della Porta's *De humana physiognomia,* first published in 1586, and famous for its use of zoomorphic resemblances. Since a raven pilfers food, for example, a man or woman with a raven's nose is likely a thief.[39] The theory that indicators of character are imprinted on the surface of bodies—the so-called Doctrine of Signatures—prompted Della Porta to visit "all the public prisons where there is always a large number of violent thieves, patricides, street assassins and other men with similar features," whose hands and feet are compared with those of animals, using the "the same method . . . in the *Fisonomia.*"[40] Not surprisingly, Della Porta advances his method for choosing one's friends.

Significantly, commensurability between physiognomy and character is demonstrated by the use of historical personages, sometimes illustrated, whose legendary personalities provide evidence for the theory. The bust-length countenance of the thirteenth-century tyrant Ezzelino, for instance, is adjusted to resemble the sharp snout, spiked collar, and raised brows of the adjacent hunting dog. An array of rulers, from the Roman emperors Servio Sulpicio Galba and Constantine, to the Ottoman sultans Mehmed II and Süleyman, provides similar evidence through the resemblance of their large noses to the beak of an eagle.[41] If the faces of the famous and the infamous attest to inclinations, Della Porta is also attentive to the fleeting nature of expressions, to the ways in which humans can alter their faces, and both concerns encourage the reader's scrutiny of others.

Indeed, this is why physiognomy "is loved by princes," as Giorgio Rizzacasa explains in his *Fisionomia,* first published in 1588, "since one can learn how to recognize inclinations to virtue and vice and those who will be faithful to the government."[42] In a dedication to Queen Elizabeth of unparalleled hyperbole, Rizzacasa praises his patron, sending his work into the world under her name because he has been "sweetly encouraged by the public saying that she has a great inclination to take pleasure in the loving and grateful acceptance of virtuous endeavors."[43] He begins with the "universal and infallible rule of physiognomy, [that] the just proportion and favorable disposition of our bodies uncovers and discloses always the nobility of the soul, integrity of its habits, prudence, and good judgment."[44] A beautiful exterior, significantly, depends upon prudence, the kind of judgment that enables a person to conceal his or her thoughts, the kind of private life that is forged in opposition to the sphere of speech and action that characterizes government, diverse professions, and public life. Physiognomy, to paraphrase Rizzacasa, is not only a tool for princes to elect faithful governors, it is similarly loved by captains who can surmise a courageous soldier in the absence of proof, celebrated by doctors, observed by philosophers, and admired by all men who are able to be more cautious about friendships and more prudent in all things.[45]

Physiognomy is harnessed to the demands of public life by Giovanni Ingegneri, bishop of Capo d'Istria, whose *Fisonomia naturale* appeared first in Milan in 1607. Cast as rational knowledge in opposition to the "fraudulent and false principles" of female intuition and chiromancy, physiognomy is "necessary for Orators and Princes." It makes a "clear argument about something present and occult through which one reads the inclinations of this or that other man."[46] "Long eyebrows toward the temples," for example, "signify an arrogant man," and "concave and small eyes signify that the man is inclined to evilness and betrayal."[47] Although proclivities toward vice can be remedied, "this is a rare thing," he observes, "especially when public training is lacking."[48] In the woodcuts that illustrate Pietro Discepolo's edition of Ingegneri's text, faces are cropped to single out the eyebrows, foreheads, and profiles. Published in Viterbo in 1612, the addition of images facilitates readers' perceptions, honing their rational skills for interacting with strangers, with "this or that other man," to repeat the author's words. Ingegneri is himself one of these new men, according to the publisher's dedication, "a character of celebrated doctrine and experience of the affairs of the world." This assessment is substantiated with a long list of compositions, notably, "the very useful *Trattato del Secretario*, and one on matters of the state."[49]

Perhaps no text conveys the breadth of interest in the topic as clearly as Cornelio Ghirardelli's *Cefalogia fisonomia*, a lengthy volume written with the participation of members of the Accademia dei Vespertini in Bologna where it was published in 1630.[50] The *Cefalogia* is populated by one hundred bust-length images of faces that appear to be portraits, an impression suggested by the elaborate frames that follow the convention of portrait-books.[51] The visual likeness is accompanied by a Latin epigram inscribed in a tablet, recalling the use of the parapet in Renaissance portraits and perhaps antique funerary statuary to which the convention looks back. The images are not portraits, however, but illustrations of the facial features analyzed in the text, which reiterates the familiar stereotypes, such as the porcine lack of discipline that characterizes men with small foreheads.[52] In contrast with most sixteenth-century illustrated treatises that solicit comparisons between paired faces, and in contrast with the use of historical personalities by Della Porta, the pictorial references to portraiture constitute a series of virtual encounters between readers and strangers, the kind of encounters that occur in public.

The trait depicted in the image, moreover, is described below it in the hundred sonnets written by some fifty poets, academicians, and members of Ghirardelli's circle, whose names appear at the bottom of the page.[53] Thus the *Cefalogia* brings together individuals of diverse interests and professions, including Lorenzo Campaggi, to whom the book is dedicated, Bologna's governor to Ancona, and Ghirardelli himself, a Franciscan and papal legate who participated in the election of Pope Gregory XV in 1621, and who also published on astrology.[54] Members of the Vespertini are identified by their nicknames, including the author, identified on the frontispiece as il Sollevato Academico Vespertino (the relieved one); l'Irresoluto (the indecisive one), who authored a sonnet on the nose;[55] and l'Inquieto (the restless one), also identified on the frontispiece, and who appended additions to the chapters. The latter may have been Ovidio Montalbani, professor of mathematics and astronomy at the university in Bologna, and founder of the Vespertini, in whose home they convened.[56] Thus the volume is a compendium of real and imagined individuals brought together by a shared interest in the legibility of the face.

This turn toward a broader social spectrum seen in the texts prompts consideration of Guazzo's *Civil conversatione,* mentioned earlier. There Guazzo describes citizenship as a form of association (conversatione), enabled by a change in the mind.[57] Peter Miller has called attention to the importance of the text in redefining citizenship and early modern public life. Focusing on seventeenth-century Venice, he argues that the concept of "citizen" evolved in response to ideas about friendship that were being discussed in political circles. The term had been used loosely earlier, following antique usage, to describe those who were subject to princes.[58] The publication of Guazzo's influential and widely translated text, however, contributed to a new understanding of the citizen and public life through the author's effort to describe "the complex network of ties between the unrelated, unconstrained, unequal members of modern society."[59] Guazzo was concerned, like Erasmus and others, with social behavior, but he was also attentive to the demands of one's performance with strangers and in diverse contexts in which status, education, or gender were mixed. For Miller, this is aligned with a shift in the notion of civility, one that redefines the terrain of the political debate of his case study. Instead of being related to the city or the prince, citizenship, for Guazzo, is an attribute of the individual, "of the qualities of the minde," the "manners and conditions which make [association] civile."[60] In this context, it is useful to underline the meta-topical structure that emerges from the treatises: the network that links the texts, with their orientation toward intersubjectivity; the paratext, which notes the worldly or political sphere of the author and the dedicatee; and the academies to which they belong, which are themselves proto-publics (as François Rouget's chapter in this volume demonstrates), and to which I turn now.

For the orientation toward sociability that I have been highlighting was also registered in the heterogeneity of professions of authors of physiognomy treatises and new forms of association in which they engaged. Ingegneri was a bishop, while others were mathematicians, poets, dramaturges, artists, lawyers, natural philosophers, physicians, and secretaries, among others. By the seventeenth century, many were members of academies or salons and part of the intelligentsia. For example, Della Porta became a member of the Accademia dei Lincei in Aquasparta (Umbria) in 1610; Giovanni Bonifaccio dedicates his *Arte de'cenni* (*The Art of Signs;* a key source for Accetto's *Dissimulazione*), to the Accademici Filarmonici in Verona; Agostino Mascardi and Marcello Giovannetti, to whom I will turn shortly,

were members of the academies of the Desiosi (poets and theorists), Umoristi, and Marinisti; and many, such as Della Porta and Montalbani, were
members of several academies. These different assemblies—the meetings
of academies, the collection of faces and the lists of names in Ghirardelli's *Cefalogia,* Pellegrini's inventive gathering of men of diverse rank and
profession in Dolce's house—bring forward the discursive nature of public
making, the process of generating one form of association out of another,
from one place into another.

The academic context of Ghirardelli's treatise points to what was a
larger epistemological shift toward a moral perspective that emerges in
Rome in the academies of the Desiosi and Umoristi. Mascardi, who delivered the inaugural oration to the Accademia dei Desiosi in 1625, was
cameriere d'onore to Urban VIII.[61] Mascardi's *Romanae dissertationes
de affectibus, siue perturbationibus animi, earumque caracteribus (The
Roman Discourses on the Emotions or the Disturbances of the Soul, and
their signs and how we recognize them from their external signs)* exemplifies the turn toward the transitory nature of human life and the somatic
signs that are registered in facial expressions, the voice, hair, clothes, and
movement.[62] Arguing against Galen, and the belief that the habits of the
soul are expressed in the body, Mascardi urges readers to distrust false
appearances of others and of oneself, a view that reflects a new understanding of interiority as a private, indecipherable space. This was a stoic
and Christian orientation concerned with care of the self. In this new
moral and sociological orientation, the (private) passions are analyzed in
relation to the public places of worldliness in a zone that unifies the intelligentsia with the court.[63]

I have been tracing the claim in the treatises, stated with increasing clarity, about the professional and political value of physiognomy, and its association with public life through the diverse pursuits of the authors and the
readers they solicit, and also through the encounters with others staged in
the texts and imagery. The ubiquity of these treatises, moreover, published
in numerous editions, translations, and formats, taken together with their
collective investment in interpreting both appearances and dissimulation,
participated in constituting the very nature of interiority itself. That is, I am
also arguing that physiognomy, by focusing attention on social behavior
and the legibility of the body, is itself implicated in establishing an understanding of the public in opposition to the private, and in focusing that
opposition in the face.

Evidence of this process comes forward in three early seventeenth-
century texts: Girolamo Aleandro, *Del modo che tener devono i saggi e
letterati cortigiani per non essere dalla corte (quasi da novella Circe) in
sembianze di brutti animale trasformati (On the manner that sages and
lettered courtiers have to conduct themselves [almost from the story of
Circe] in order not to be transformed to resemble nasty animals);* Girolamo
Rocco, *Della cognizione di se medesimo (Of knowledge of oneself);* and

Marcello Giovannetti, *Dello specchio* (*Of the mirror*). Developing an interior was a form of political pragmatism, as Rodler explains in her critical edition of these texts.[64] The need for prudence, as the titles imply, fostered a new kind of political physiognomy.

Against Della Porta's zoomorphism, Rocco asserts that people must mask their identity. Against the outside world and the politics of the court, interiority is both a place to hide one's vices through self-control, and a place of God.[65] As Rodler explains, a new kind of self-analytical domination of the instincts became "a way of arranging a physiognomic habit that is absolutely individual with which to face human behavior."[66] In *Dello specchio*, Giovannetti describes the self-analysis and increasing artifice that distance the author from his identity: "the confusion of faces made up from reflections sent back from many little mirrors with marvelous usury."[67] "There is no antidote," he writes, "more powerful against the veil of vice than the consideration of oneself in the mirror."[68] Inverting interiority—what Rodler describes as the "baroque death of the reflected image"—Giovannetti expresses the anti-narcissism that characterizes physiognomy when it is no longer yoked to status and associated instead with "a school that admits men of all classes, of all professions."[69] These three writers are particularly important here, for they indicate a moment of crisis around the visibility of the "universal man." As Rodler observes, with the "abandoning of the Aristotelian condition of psychophysical uniformity and transparency of virtue, the individual apprehends a sort of voluntary pragmatism that is a 'constant' interior."[70] Thus interiority emerges as an *effect* of the prudent making public of the private, an effect created by the splitting of interiority between what could be known by others, and the remainder that establishes the public in opposition to the private in the context of the individual human body.

This split, I think, is what distinguishes prudence from *sprezzatura* as the means to acquire grace and status. In the *Malpiglio*, mentioned earlier, Tasso contrasts the courtier's influence and performance in the *Cortegiano* with the impotence and conformity of his impoverished status at the end of the sixteenth century in Ferrara.[71] He was "reduced to the status of a mere technician," according to Virginia Cox, "a cipher to the prince, a morally neutral instrument of power."[72] Corruption of the court required what Tasso describes as the "ethics of disguise."[73] Wearing a mask had become more than self-protection; it had become a way of life. Where Tasso's interlocutor in the *Malpiglio* still asks the question "but does an honest man dissimulate," Accetto, with whom I began, argues that this is the only moral choice.[74] Simulation is dishonest, he explains, whereas "dissimulation is the industry of showing things as they are. One simulates what one is not; one dissimulates what one is."[75] Like Rocco and Giovannetti, Accetto believes the courtier can conform on the outside but still cultivate his interior. Dissimulation may be abandoned at the Last Judgment when "hearts are more manifest that faces, and souls are exposed to public notice," but "in this life one cannot always have a transparent heart." Hiding one's heart, he observes, "conforms to the moral condition" and the "order of the universe."[76]

Accetto's revision of the views that were established at the Council of Trent and published in 1566 as the Roman Catechism brings together the themes I have been considering in this essay: the divide between one's face and one's self and how that threshold was shaped by an emerging understanding of the public as a sphere that both required and was also conditioned by new modes of behavior and new forms of knowledge. According to the Catechism, character can be misrepresented and thus the final judgment will be—and it's important to underline the novelty of this terminology—both "public and general," not only of a person's "words and actions, but even of his most secret thoughts."[77] Fear of this unveiling, the authors posit, will encourage virtue among the laity. For Accetto, who questions the very premise that the human face is an expression of the soul, masking one's interests and thoughts is not only necessary, but also ethical; one cultivates one's interior self against the backdrop of public scrutiny.[78] Indeed, he uses the word frequently to account for the effects of one's actions: how one's gestures appeal to "public taste," accord with "public pomp," cause "public offense" and "public hatred."

Della dissimulazione onesta was written, as noted at the outset, under the rule of the Carafa in Andria and during Spanish control at the Neapolitan court. In this context, social interactions were complicated by what Gianfranco Borelli describes as the fracturing of time that constituted "a permanent state of tension and risk in intersubjective relations."[79] Intriguing evidence of this danger is expressed in Accetto's text through the use of animals. He translates the zoomorphic correspondences seen in earlier treatises into stereotypes; echoing the threat seen in Aleandro's tract—of courtiers "transformed into nasty animals"—Accetto warns of the wolves and lions encountered in public, and from whom dissimulation offers protection. One's position at court was no longer dependent on the eye of the prince alone, but on a public whose members were in flux and whose configuration was subject to shifting interests. One's face may have become a signature of the self,[80] but both that interior and exterior had become representations of the interests the public took in them. And with the splitting of interiority, the remainder—that unpresentable kernel—becomes a condition of privacy, and thus also constitutive of the alterity of public life.

By the second half of the seventeenth century, according to a recent study, physiognomy had been changed from a kind of knowledge into a form of play.[81] Perhaps this ludic turn might be understood as a symptom of anxiety wrought by the double bind of the politics of faciality, of the need for faces to conform on the one hand, and their failure, on the other, to be meaningful any longer.

NOTES

1. I am grateful for suggestions received from the anonymous readers and from the Making Publics team, especially Angela Vanhaelen and Paul Yachnin who read an earlier version of this essay. All translations are my own unless noted otherwise.

   On the epigraph: "È tanta la necessità di usar questo velo, che solamente nell'ultimo giorno ha da mancare. Allora saran finiti gl'interessi umani, i cuori piú manifesti che le fronti, gli animi esposti alla publica notizia, ed i pensieri esaminati di numero e di peso." Torquato Accetto, *Della dissimulazione onesta,* ed. Salvatore Silvano Nigro (Turin: Collana Biblioteca Einaudi, 1997), 18. On the tract, see Jean-Pierre Cavaillé, "Torquato Accetto, Les 'Ténèbres Honnêtes,'" in *Dis/simulations: religion, morale et politique au XVIIe siècle* (Paris: Champion, 2002), 332–69.

2. Brendan Dooley, ed., *Italy in the Baroque: Selected Readings* (New York: Garland, 1995), 368. Accetto's poems were published and known to Giambattista Marino, who with his father frequented the home of Giambattista della Porta, discussed later.

3. Cavaillé, "Torquato Accetto," 334.

4. Accetto is referring here to Giovanni Bonifaccio, *L'arte de'cenni con quale formandosi favella visibile, si tratta della muta eloquenza, che non è altro che un facondo silentio* (Vicenza: Francesco Grossi, 1616), 342–43.

5. Philippe-Alain Michaude, *Aby Warburg and the Image in Motion,* trans. Sophie Hawkes (New York: Zone Books, 2004), 31–32. Jacob Burckhardt, *The Civilization of the Renaissance in Italy: An Essay,* trans. S. G. C. Middlemore, revised and edited by Irene Gordon (New York: New American Library, 1960). On debates about Burckhardt see John Martin, "Inventing Sincerity, Refashioning Prudence: The Discovery of the Individual in Renaissance Europe," *The American Historical Review* 102, no. 5 (1997): 1308–42.

6. Norbert Elias, *The Civilizing Process,* trans. Edmund Jephcott (Oxford: Blackwell, 1996), 204. On the individual see esp. 202–6.

7. Ibid., 56.

8. Cited in ibid., 44.

9. Ibid.

10. Michael Warner, *Publics and Counterpublics* (New York: Zone Books, 2002), 87–89.

11. On Castiglione and Della Casa, see Harry Berger Jr., *The Absence of Grace: Sprezzatura and Suspicion in Two Renaissance Courtesy Books* (Stanford, CA: Stanford University Press, 2000); Peter Burke, *The Art of Conversation* (Cambridge: Polity, 1993).

12. Harry Berger Jr., *Fictions of the Pose: Rembrandt against the Italian Renaissance* (Stanford, CA: Stanford University Press, 2000), 149. For Berger's account of Elias, see 137–52.

13. Berger, *Absence of Grace,* 4.

14. Berger, *Fictions of the Pose,* 143.

15. Ibid., 102.

16. Ibid., 149–52.

17. Torquato Tasso, *Il Malpiglio overo de la corte* http://www.bibliotecaitaliana.it/xtf/view?docId=bibit000594/bibit000594.xml (Accessed September 2009).

18. John Martin, *Myths of Renaissance Individualism* (New York: Palgrave Macmillan, 2004), 113.

19. Pomponius Gauricus, *De sculptura,* ed. André Chastel and Robert Klein (Paris: Droz, 1969), 128–29.

20. See for example Antonio Pellegrini, *Fisionomia naturale* (Milan, 1622). On the impact of physiognomy on art theory, see Moshe Barasch, "Character and Physiognomy: Bocchi on Donatello's *St. George*, a Renaissance Text on Expression in Art," *Journal of the History of Ideas* 36, no. 3 (1991): 413–30.

21. Martin Porter, *Windows of the Soul: The Art of Physiognomy in European Culture 1470–1780* (Oxford: Clarendon Press, 2005), 19.

22. "Di fisonomia e chiromanzia. Della fallace fisonomia e chiromanzia non mi estenderò, perché in esse non è verità; e questo si manifesta perché tali chimere non hanno fondamenti scientifici. Vero è che i segni de' volti mostrano in parte la natura degli uomini, . . . e quelli che hanno le linee trasversali della fronte forte lineate sono uomini copiosi di lamentazioni occulte e palesi." Leonardo da Vinci, *Trattato della pittura*, ed. Angelo Borzelli (Carabba editore, 1947), 288. On Leonardo's interest in physiognomy and a possible treatise, see Michael Kwakkelstein, *Leonardo da Vinci as a Physiognomist: Theory and Drawing Practice* (Leiden: Primavera Press, 1994).

23. Honorat Nicquet, *Phisiognomia humana, libris IV* (Lugduni, 1648). For bibliography, see Peter Gerlach, *Physiognomik 1474–1979 in Europa*: www.peter-gerlach.eu. For a recent survey of the literature, see Porter, *Windows of the Soul*. This essay is indebted to the work of Lucia Rodler: Rodler, *Il corpo specchio dell'anima: teoria e storia della fisiognomica* (Milan: Mondadori Bruno, 2000); "La fisiognomica allo specchio," in *Esercizi fisiognomici* (Palermo: Sellerio, 1996); "Agostino Mascardi e la congettura fisiognomica," in *Mappe e letture: Studi in onore di Ezio Raimondi*, ed. A. Battistini (Bologna: Il Mulino, 1994); *I silenzi mimici del volto: studi sulla tradizione fisiognomica italiana tra Cinque e Seicento* (Ospedaletto, Pisa: Pacini, 1991).

24. Katharine Eisaman Maus, *Inwardness and Theater in the English Renaissance* (Chicago: University of Chicago Press, 1995), 5. A range of causes have been cited, including child-rearing practices, an expanding elite class concerned with strategies of social behavior, anatomy, and print technology. See, for example: Lacy Baldwin Smith, *Treason in Tudor England: Politics and Paranoia* (Princeton, NJ: Princeton University Press, 1986); Frank Whigham, *Ambition and Privilege: The Social Tropes of Elizabethan Courtesy Theory* (Berkeley and Los Angeles: University of California Press, 1984); Devon Hodges, *Renaissance Fictions of Anatomy* (Amherst: University of Massachusetts Press, 1985).

25. See Warner, *Publics and Counterpublics*, 74–76.

26. See ibid., 72. Ian Hacking, *The Social Construction of What?* (Cambridge, MA: Harvard University Press, 1999).

27. Aristotle, "Physiognomics," in *Minor Works* (Cambridge, MA: Harvard University Press, 1936). Cited in Porter, *Windows of the Soul*, 51.

28. Porter, *Windows of the Soul*, 19.

29. Michelangelo Biondo, *De cognitione hominis per aspectum/Conoscenza dell'uomo dall'aspetto esteriore*, ed. Lucia Rodler (Rome: Beniamino Vignola, 1995), 18.

30. Gauricus, *De sculptura*, 130–31. Porter notes the use of physiognomy by Protestant merchants in seventeenth-century England. On readership based on library records, see Porter, *Windows of the Soul*, 35–41. Polemon's *Physiognomy* was known through Adamantius's fourth-century Greek edition and also Latin, Syriac, and Arabic translations. On Polemon, see Simon Swain, *Seeing the Face, Seeing the Soul; Polemon's Physiognomy from Classical Antiquity to Medieval Islam* (Oxford: Oxford University Press, 2007).

31. Pinzio, *Fisionomia . . . raccolta da i libri di antichi filosofi* (Lyon: 1550), 50–51.

32. Michelangelo Biondo, *De cognitione hominis per aspectum* (Rome: Antonio Blado Asolano, 1544).

33. "Così, analizzando gli uomini dal'aspetto esteriore, Voi stesso e il Senato potrette proteggervi e difendervi con maggiore efficacia, giacché non esiste altro modo piú agevole del giudizio fisiognomico per riconoscere gli innumerevoli inganni tra i quali l'uomo si aggira." Biondo, *De cognitione*, 49.

34. "Per sfuggire al furore umano e soffocare il timore angoscioso del male, occorre osservare alcune norme comuni e infallibili che svelano persino le insidie rinchiuse nel fondo dei cuori. Con le medesime cognizioni poi, si possono comprendere i comportamenti individuali in modo tale da liberarisi dai pericoli e perseguire felicemente il destino prescritto dalla stessa natura. Pratichiamo dunque la congettura fisiognomica, per riconoscere piú spesso l'onestà, talvolta la disonestà." Ibid.

35. Rodler, in Biondo, *De cognitione*, 18–21.

36. Biondo, *De cognitione*, 55.

37. The book was published in Venice in 1545 and 1569, and in Milan in 1622 as *Fisionomia Naturale*. The 1622 edition was dedicated to Giovanni Dominico Peri, possibly the Genovese paper merchant (c. 1590–1666). Little is known of Pellegrini, who also published *De la vita solitaria* in Venice in 1568.

38. Pellegrini, *Fisionomia naturale.*

39. Giambattista della Porta, *De humana physiognomia/ Della fisonomia dell'uomo*, ed. Mario Cicognani, Biblioteca della Fenice (Parma: Ugo Guanda, 1988).

40. "Né hebbi minor pensiero a visitare tutte le carceri publiche, dove sempre è racchiusa gran moltitudine de' facinorosi ladri, parricidi, assassini di strada e d'altri uomini di simile fattezza, per vedere diligentemente le loro mani; doppo, contemplando i piedi e le mani de gli animali, conferii le loro figure con quelle de gli huomini, non senza naturali ragioni, e con l'istesso metodo del quale mi sono servito nella Fisonomia." Giambattista della Porta, *De ea naturalis physiognomoniae parte quae ad manuum lineas spectat libri duo: e in appendice Chirofisonomia*, ed. Oreste Trabucco (Naples: Edizioni scientifiche italiane, 2003), 92. His account of making wax figures from plaster casts of criminals begins on 91. See Louise Clubb, *Giambattista della Porta, Dramatist*, trans. Giambattista della Porta (Princeton, NJ: Princeton University Press, 1965), 40–41.

41. Della Porta, *De humana physiognomia*, 164.

42. Giorgio Rizzacasa, *La fisionomia . . . Non meno utile che dilettevole, si in morale che in naturale filosofia* (Carmagnola: Marc'Antonio Bellone, 1607). Dedicated in 1588, and unpaginated. "Ella carame[n]te, è amata da Principi si per il piacere che porta loro come perche da lei imparono à cognossere quali siano inclinati alle virtu & quali à vitii. Onde possono poi fare elettione do i fideli, è buoni per il fidele, sicure & buono governo dalla loro persona è de gli stati. È similme[n]te amata da i capitani de gl'eserciti poscia che senza il venire all'atto della prova, falor co[ng]iettura qual sia il valoroso soldato, quale il vi le, quale il fidele & quale il reo. Vien celebrata da i medici, perche (insieme co[n] il piacere) gli porta ancora non picciola utilità, conoscendo per lei la qualità de i temperamenti delle nostre complessioni. Osservate da Philosophi, & finalmente ammirata da tutti gli Huomini, percioche, divenuti con il mezzo di essa de gli animi humani conoscitori, possono essere piu cauti, nel congiongere le amicitie, piu prudenti nel conversare & in tutte le operationi." Proemio.

43. "Alletato dolcemente dalla publica voce di ogni uno della sua maggior' che grande inclinatione a compiacersi di amare & agradire l'opere virtuose." Dedication. My thanks to Elena Fumi for assistance with this translation.

44. "per regola universale, & gentil' dispositione di nostri corpi, scopri, & palesi sempre nobilità di animo, integrità di costumi, prudenza, & bontà di giudicio." Ibid.

45. See note 43.

46. "E perche quello, ch'è futuro contingente, . . . la qual cosa non è scienza, ma una divolgatissima intelligenza, commune alle femine, & à i fanciulli . . . & così i Chiromantici, & simili altri impostori . . . parte s'appoggia à principii falsi, & erronei. . . . Mà ben che la Fisonomia non sia tale, ch'ella possa guidare la nostra cognitione all'intelligenza delle cose future non necessarie, ella è nondimeno uno studio, per lo quale noi possiamo haver' assai chiaro argomento d'alcune cose presente, & occulte, come à dire, quali sieno l'inclinationi di questo, & di quell'altr'huomo." Giovanni Ingegneri, *Fisonomia naturale* (Milan, 1607), 1–3.

47. "Le ciglia lunghe verso le tempie significa l'huomo arrogante." "Gli'occhi concavi, e piccioli sono segno, che l'huomo sia inclinato alla malvagità, & al tradimento ancora." Ibid., 41, 50.

48. "quantunque le inclinationi di quegli huomini, che per natura sono accomodati al far male, si possano correggere, o d'impedire con buona institutione di vita; pare tuttavia, che questa sia rara cosa, massimamente dove manchi il publico ammaestramente." Ibid., 3.

49. "Personaggio di tanto celebre dottrina, & isperienza de gli affari del Mondo." Giovanni Ingegneri, *Fisonomia naturale* (Naples, 1606), 2r.

50. Cornelio Ghirardelli, *Cefalogia fisonomica diuisa in dieci deche, doue conforme a documenti d'Aristotile, e d'altri filosofi naturali, si esaminano le fisonomie di cento teste humane che intagliate si vedono in quest'opera* (Bologna, 1630).

51. On portrait books, see Bronwen Wilson, *The World in Venice: Print, the City, and Early Modern Identity* (Toronto: University of Toronto Press, 2005), 186–255.

52. Ghirardelli, *Cefalogia*, 92.

53. The British Library catalog lists fifty contributors.

54. Porter, *Windows of the Soul*, 162–63.

55. Ghirardelli, *Cefalogia*, 335.

56. http://213.225.214.179/fabitaliano2/dizionari/corpus/biografie/Montalbani_vita.htm. Accessed September 2009.

57. See "The Art of Conversation," in Burke, *The Art of Conversation*, 89–122.

58. Peter Miller, "Friendship and Conversation in Seventeenth-Century Venice," *The Journal of Modern History* 73, no. 1 (2001): 1–31.

59. Ibid., 3.

60. Ibid., 3–4.

61. Mario Biagioli, *Galileo, Courtier: The Practice of Science in the Culture of Absolutism* (Chicago: University of Chicago Press, 1993), 263–64. The oration was titled "That the practice of letters at Court is not only Appropriate but Necessary," and his writings include Agostino Mascardi, "Che la corte è vera scuola non solamente della prudenza, ma della virtù morale," in *Prose vulgari* (Venice: Baba, 1653), 349–67. On Mascardi see Rodler, "Agostino Mascardi."

62. Agostino Mascardi, *Romanae dissertationes de affectibus, siue perturbationibus animi, earumque caracteribus* (Paris, 1639). My thanks to John Martin for the English translation.

63. Rodler, "La fisiognomica allo specchio," 20–23.

64. Girolamo Aleandro, Girolamo Rocco, and Marcello Giovannetti, *Esercizi fisiognomici*, ed. Lucia Rodler (Palermo: Sellerio, 1996).
65. Ibid., 28.
66. Ibid., 19.
67. "O il composto di molti speglietti che per un volto che gli si mostri, con meravigliosa usura rimanda indietro una turba di volti." Ibid., 107.
68. "non vi è antidoto più possente contro il veleno del vizio che la considerazione di se stesso nello specchio." Ibid., 37.
69. "la morte barocca dell'immagine riflessa," Rodler in Ibid., 37. "Questa è una scuola ch'ammette gli uomini di tutte le classi, di tutte le professioni." Ibid., 111.
70. Ibid., 18.
71. Tasso, *Malpiglio*, 36.
72. Tasso states this in his *Gianluca or on Masks*, 1586. Virginia Cox, "Tasso's *Malpiglio overo de la corte: The Courtier* Revisited," *The Modern Language Review* 90, no. 4 (1995): 902.
73. Ibid., 910.
74. Tasso, *Malpiglio*, 37.
75. "La dissimulazion è una industria di on far veder le cose come sono. Si simula quello che non è, si dissimula quello ch'è." Accetto, *Dissimulation*, 51.
76. To have the heart hidden conforms to the "condizione morale." Ibid., 59, 79, 43.
77. See http://www.cin.org/users/james/ebooks/master/trent/tcreed07.htm. Accessed September 2009.
78. This chapter, then, argues against, at least for the early modern period, Michael Warner's assertion that the private has "no corresponding sense of public" as it relates "to the individual, especially to inwardness, subjective experience and the incommunicable." Warner, *Publics and Counterpublics*, 30.
79. Gianfranco Borrelli, ed., *Ragion di Stato: l'arte italiana della prudenza politica: catalogo della mostra* (Naples: Istituto italiano per gli studi filosofici, 1994).
80. See Wilson, *World in Venice*, 258.
81. Porter, *Windows of the Soul*, esp. 18, 35; Lucie Desjardins, *Le corps parlant: savoirs et représentation des passions au XVIIe siècle* (Laval: Les Presses de l'Université Laval, 2000).

11 Shakespeare's *Sonnets* and the Publication of Melancholy

Michael Bristol

Nothing is more idiosyncratic than melancholia, and yet nothing is more public and histrionic in its expression. "Idiosyncratic" comes from Greek ἴδιος—one's own, personal, private, peculiar, separate, distinct—and κρᾶσις commixture, tempering. It's a word with both medical and literary implications, referring to the physical or mental constitution peculiar to an individual, and also to the mode of expression peculiar to an author. Interestingly, there is a shared etymology with "idiot," from ἰδιώτης, referring to a private person, someone who is unsociable, lives a cloistered life, and takes no interest in the concerns of the polis. Melancholia is persistent ill-temper, groundless fear and anger, inexplicable despondency. Use of the word "melancholy" to identify a state of mind is a metonymic usage, substituting a cause for its effect. The cause is an excess of black bile, a bodily fluid that cannot actually be observed. And this fits well with what *can* be observed in melancholy people, who typically exhibit strong states of feeling that have no apparent cause at all.

Melancholy suffering may be private and idiopathic, but what is most characteristic of the melancholic is histrionic self-display. Adam Kitzes describes early modern melancholia as "ubiquitous and as hard to define as it was plain for anyone with eyes to see."[1] Hamlet acts out his grief with "windy suspirations of forced breath" and "dejected 'havior of the visage," upsetting his mother and everyone around him with his brooding unsociability. Asked to explain himself, he claims "I have that within that passeth show."[2] His suit of black is a conventional reference to his interior condition, but it is not a representation. But if nothing "can denote me truly," why does he go on about it so? What is the point in publicizing private misery in such creatively annoying ways? Most of Shakespeare's plays contain at least one reference to melancholy, and there is a "melancholy fellow" who turns up in many of them, usually dressed in black. He is often churlish, and prone to malevolent, unprovoked rage.

Early modern melancholics did not suffer in silence. Robert Burton thought that there was an "epidemic" of melancholia in his own time.[3] Lawrence Babb, writing from the perspective of several hundred years later, describes melancholia as a "fad."[4] Epidemics are diseases that suddenly become widely prevalent, affecting large numbers of people indiscriminately. Fads start out as idiosyncratic ways of doing something and then spread through a population by mimetic contagion. Both phenomena are forms of social disorder that attract public concern. But the pervasiveness of melancholia in early modern England is more socially articulate than an epidemic and more serious than a mere fad. Its features are delineated not only in drama and in medical treatises, but also in early modern lyric poetry. Shakespeare's *Sonnets,* first published in 1609, some of Donne's *Songs and Sonnets,* 1630, and George Herbert's *The Temple,* 1633, each express a highly idiosyncratic version of melancholia using a distinctively first-personal language. What public interest can there be for these intensely private expressions of memory, mourning, and loss? Can melancholia simply reflect a public interest prompted by mere worldliness and the wish to be *au courant?* In this chapter, however, I hope to argue for the existence of a melancholy public in some stronger sense, one that paradoxically grounds the public sphere in the strictly idiosyncratic experience of erotic desire and religious longing.

BLACK BEAUTY

There is no dark lady in Shakespeare's *Sonnets.* The "woman colored ill" in Sonnets 127–54 was not a lady and Shakespeare never refers to her using any such title of aristocratic privilege. She is referred to as "dark as night" only once, in Sonnet 147, where she is "black as hell, dark as night."[5] For what it's worth, there is no mention of a prodigal son in the King James Bible either. "Dark lady" and "prodigal son" are epithets belonging to traditions of exegesis, articulated by the creativity of audiences, readerships, and publics. "Prodigal son" seems apt in the way it captures what is salient in the parable of "a certain man had two sons."[6] "Dark lady" on the other hand is misleading. Colin Burrow refers to the expression as "a noxious piece of pseudo-gentility . . . to make her sound both sexy and upper-crust."[7] Edmund Malone was the first to identify a sexual liaison with a "woman colored ill" in the final twenty-eight sonnets in his edition of 1790. Since that time readers have made personal, at times highly fetishized investments in the *Sonnets,* focusing the story line first noted by Malone on the iconic figures of dark lady and beautiful boy. The dark lady is the creation of a big-time public; she stands in for everything else that escapes signification in the *Sonnets.* The phrase obscures what is actually said about her in the *Sonnets:* She was the poet's mistress and she was black. To imagine her as an actual woman with an intriguing sexual personality is an overspecification of the poetic imagery of black beauty.

They say it's always darkest before everything gets completely black. And the problem with the dark lady is just that; well, she really isn't dark enough. Part of what has been going on all these years is an awkward effort to make the mistress seem just a little lighter. Even the most sensible of Shakespeare's modern editors find it necessary to "clarify" what Shakespeare means by calling his mistress black. Burrow, for example, writes that "Sonnet 127 begins a group of sonnets which are chiefly about a mistress with dark hair and dark eyes whom Shakespeare never calls a 'lady' let alone the 'dark lady' favoured by his biographic critics."[8] On the facing page Sonnet 127 begins with the statement "in the old age black was not counted fair." The clarification has the unfortunate effect of displacing what is specifically black with what is only dark. Fantasizing about a sexy brunette might be getting in the way of seeing the real weirdness of the *Sonnets,* or at least noticing that other things are going on in describing the mistress as black. I'm not going to be talking about race, however, as other critics have already explored this aspect of the dark lady's story. I want to consider something even blacker than my Honda Civic, something so black you cannot even see it. In what follows I will interpret the *Sonnets* as a complex anatomy of black bile or melancholia, which flows unseen throughout the poetry.

Here is a list of things that are black in Shakespeare's *Sonnets:* night, ink, lines of type or text, the mistress's brows, her hair and her eyes as well as her deeds, hell, and beauty itself. Black is mentioned for the first time in Sonnet 27, a poem of sleeplessness brought about by "a journey in my head to work my mind." His "imaginary sight" presents him with the shadow of his beloved, which "makes black Night beauteous and her old face new." Black and beauty are also linked in Sonnets 63 and 65 on the power of time and the decay of beauty. Sonnet 73 links black to night, "death's second self." In Sonnet 127 the paradox of black and beauty is more fully developed. Helen Vendler refers to this sonnet as "the first Dark Lady sonnet," which she describes as "a myth of origin." "How did a black-haired, black-eyed woman come to be the reigning heir of beauty?"[9] Vendler sees this as parallel to the question of how the poetic subject could have fallen in love—mistakenly in her view—with a beautiful boy.

The focus on sexual melodrama downplays the poem's character as a rhetorical paradox. "In the old age black was not counted fair," according to Sonnet 127, because black and fair were for the people of the past logically contradictory expressions. The sonnet draws attention to the equivocal usage of common, ordinary words and to the expansive possibilities of wordplay with these signifiers, and with related binaries of fair and foul, natural and false.

The paradox of black beauty is a conventional topos that turns up earlier in Sidney's sonnet on Stella's "black eyes":

Whereas black seams beauty's contrary,
She even in black doth make all beauties flow:
But so and thus, she minding love should be
Placed ever there, gave him his mourning weed:
To honour all their deaths, who for her bleed.[10]

Although it seems paradoxical, the blackness of Stella's eyes is precisely what makes beauty flow. But it is also the mourning garment worn by Eros for all the unrequited lovers, including Astrophel himself. The same association of the mistress's black eyes with mourning appears in Shakespeare's Sonnet 127. It is developed more fully in Sonnet 132, which exploits the pun on mourning, comparing his mistress's eyes to the "morning sun of Heaven," which can also be the *mourning son* of heaven. The suggestion of penitential sorrow registers more sharply in later poems.

The paradox of black beauty appears without using the heuristic device of a woman or a mistress in Edward Herbert's "Sonnet of Black Beauty":

> Black beauty, which above that common light,
>> Whose Power can no colours here renew,
>> But those which darkness can again subdue,
> Do'st still remain unvary'd to the sight.
> And like an object equal to the view,
>> And neither chang'd with day, nor hid with night,
>> When all these colours which the world call bright,
> And which old Poetry doth so persue,
> Are with the night so perished and gone,
>> That of their being there remains no mark,
> Thou still abidest so intirely one,
>> That we may know thy blackness is a spark
> Of light inaccessible, and alone
>> Our darkness which can make us think it dark.[11]

Herbert resolves the paradox in terms of the physics of light, suggesting that what we know as "black" is simply the manifestation of our own "inner darkness" that leaves us unable to see the "oneness" of beauty, or God, or truth, or whatever the paradox of black beauty is supposed to express. This is consistent with neo-Augustinian theology, with its sense of a God or "light inaccessible" who is "so black you can't even see him." On this view, "all these colours which the world call bright" correspond to narrow sectarian beliefs.[12] But Herbert's depiction of "black beauty" is also consistent with a theory of melancholia, another kind of "light inaccessible" that might give access to a deeper awareness of beauty.

Shakespeare has a rather different treatment of the dialectic of inner darkness and light inaccessible. In Sonnet 63 he can fortify himself "against confounding ages' cruel knife" with the thought that the friend's "beauty shall in these black lines be seen." Here it's no longer beauty that is black, but rather the brightness of black ink that preserves an otherwise ephemeral beauty from being the "spoil" of time. But in Sonnet 147 the notion that something black can be bright is repudiated as a kind of delusional fantasy:

Past cure I am, now Reason is past care,
And, frantic-mad with evermore unrest,
My thoughts and my discourse as madmen's are,
At random from the truth vainly express.
    For I have sworn thee fair, and thought thee bright,
    Who are as black as hell, as dark as night. (9–14)

And here, finally, almost at the very end of the 1609 volume, the pure, unmixed blackness of the mistress finally lightens up a little bit to become something a little less black than hell, to become, in short, dark. The word "dark" echoes Sonnet 43, with its doubling of dark and bright, of shadows, and of sleeplessness. In Sonnet 27, an earlier sleeplessness poem, the mental image of the beautiful boy "makes Black night beauteous"(12). In Sonnet 43 a dream of the beautiful boy makes the restless speaker's "nights bright days" (14). And in Sonnet 65 the speaker hopes for a miracle: "in black ink my love will still shine bright"(14). By a bizarre and wonderful coincidence, there is a *Treatise on Melancholy* that Shakespeare may have known; its author is Timothie Bright.[13]

To interpret the trope of dark and bright as a reference to a book whose title and author's name are an example of the trope would be extremely far-fetched, although in a way that is exactly why it would be convincing. Shakespeare was himself a notorious far-fetcher. Even if he didn't think of it himself, it's the sort of thing he would have wanted readers to notice. But it is not altogether necessary for the darkness-brightness trope to be activated through a reference to Timothie Bright's book. It is already there in Sonnet 43, where the speaker's eyes, closed in sleep, see the beautiful boy "and darkly bright, are bright in dark directed." Interestingly, the same figure appears in scripture: "Woe unto them that call evil good, and good evil; that put darkness for light, and light for darkness; that put bitter for sweet, and sweet for bitter!"[14] The figure used in both texts is antimetabole—"turning about in opposite directions," prompting readers to look forward and backward. The first bright thing is mentioned in Sonnet 1, the beautiful boy's eyes, directed narcissistically at himself. In Sonnet 130 the mistress's eyes are "nothing like the sun" (1) and maybe they're nothing like the son either. The mistress's black eyes are "loving mourners . . . looking with ruth upon my pain" (Sonnet 132, 3).

Sonnet 43, where this complicated figure of turning about in opposite directions is situated, immediately precedes two sonnets that lay out the scheme of the four elements that constitute the body. Sonnet 44 imagines that "nimble thought can jump both sea and land" far-fetching the lover back from the "injurious distance" of his absence (7). But the beautiful boy has taken with him the lighter elements of air and fire.

    My life, being made of four, with two alone
    Sinks down to death, oppressed with melancholy. (Sonnet 45, 7–8)

Melancholy, which appears here for the first and the only time in the entire sonnet sequence, is placed at the end of the second quatrain, very near the center of the poem. The elements of "slight air and purging fire" are "present absent"—they "are gone / In tender embassie of love to thee." In the sestet "those swift messengers return'd from thee . . . come back again" to reassure the speaker of the boy's "fair health." And in the couplet the phrase is repeated as "I send them back again and straight grow sad." The movement of turning about in opposite directions is displaced in Sonnet 45 with an image of coming back to a fixed center, the heavy, dull subject of melancholy itself.

The mistress sonnets thematize the emotional complexity of melancholy in poems of self-revilement and self-contempt as in Sonnet 129, "the expense of spirit in a waste of shame is lust in action," or in Sonnet 137, "thou blind fool love," with its echo of Sir Philip Sidney. There are fantasies of sexual domination in Sonnet 133 and also Sonnet 135. And there is a pervasive atmosphere of suffering and torment, along with misogynistic resentment echoed almost everywhere in the critical tradition, especially in the narrative pursuit of the dark lady's identity. Sonnet 143 is a farcical and dreamlike expression of infantile anxieties of maternal abandonment:

> Loe as a carefull huswife runs to catch
> One of her feathered creatures broke away,
> Set's down her babe and makes all swift dispatch
> In pursuit of the thing she would have stay,
> Whilst her neglected child holds her in chase
> Cries to catch her whose busy care is bent
> To follow that which flies before her face
> Not prizing her poor infant's discontent. (1–8)

This is a more complicated variant of the *fort-da* game described so vividly by Freud, except that no mastery of the mother's absence is achieved. Instead he can only plead helplessly for the absent mother/mistress to "turn back and my loud crying still" (Sonnet 143: line 14). The subject of melancholy here has been reduced to the pathetic status of a little crybaby. But the feelings of helplessness and loss expressed here are explicitly linked to the melancholy subject as a grown man in Sonnet 45 through the couplet imagery of coming back, sending back, turning back.

In both Sonnet 45 and Sonnet 143 an abandoned self cries out to a beloved object to turn back to a center of emotional distress. That center is addressed in Sonnet 146:

> Poor soul, the center of my sinful earth,
> Feeding these rebel pow'rs that thee array,
> Why dost thou pine within and suffer dearth,
> Painting thy outward walls so costly gay?

Why so large cost, having so short a lese,
Dost thou upon thy fading mansion spend? (1–6)

Burrow identifies this as a reference to 2 Corinthians, 5:1: "For we know that, if our earthly house of this tabernacle were dissolved, we have a building of God, a house not made with hands, eternal in the heavens." The appearance of a religious meditation in a sonnet sequence has been confusing for many readers, but perhaps this is because, like the speaker, they have been morbidly—even sinfully—preoccupied with the mistress. But for early modern readers, the appearance of a penitential sonnet in this context would not be terribly surprising. Melancholy provoked by erotic desire is by no means unrelated to a deep consciousness of sin.

THE METAPHYSICS OF BLACK

In Sonnet 146, Shakespeare's "poore soule" is the center of his sinful earth, obsessed with the prospect of an impending "death that feeds on men." In the sestet, however, the soul itself will be fed by living upon the "servant's loss," or the death of the body. "Within be fed, without be rich no more." John Donne's soul in the second of his *Divine Meditations* is just plain black, a fugitive that doesn't know where to turn:

Oh my blacke Soule! Now art thou summoned
By sicknesse, deaths herald, and champion;
Thou art like a pilgrim, which abroad hath done
Treason, and durst not turne to whence hee is fled.
Or like a thiefe, which till deaths doome be read,
Wisheth himselfe delivered from prison;
But damn'd and hal'd to execution
Wisheth that still he might be imprisoned;
Yet grace, if thou repent, thou canst not lacke;
But who shall give thee that grace to beginne?
Oh make thy self with holy mourning blacke,
And red with blushing, as thou art with sinne;
Or wash thee in Christs blood, which hat this might
That being red, it dys red soules to white.[15]

But, as with the poor soul of Sonnet 146, this black soul can hope for grace in and through repentance. And that repentance takes the form of a transformation of the blackness of sin to the blackness of mourning. Once there is true contrition for sin, something that is both black and also red, the soul becomes white through the sacrament of Christ's blood.

The complicated color scheme here links the blackness of melancholia to the red and white that characterizes the desired woman of the early modern love-sonnet tradition. Divine meditation is an attempt at transubstantiation in which erotic desire is converted into fear of God's judgment. According to Timothie Bright, this state of mind closely resembles the condition of natural melancholy:

> I have layd open howe the bodie, and corporall things affect the soule, & how the body is affected of it againe: what the difference is betwixt natural melancholie, and that heavy hande of God upon the afflicted conscience, tormented with remorse of sinne and fear of his judgement.[16]

Bright's *Treatise* devotes considerable space to the role of diet and other physiological elements in the treatment of melancholia, as do many other writers in the early modern medical profession.[17] But Bright is also concerned with explaining how "the learned sort" might use a more philosophical orientation to understand their condition if they "knowe the grounds and reasons of their passions, without which they might receave more discomfort."[18]

The distinction between the morbid pathology of melancholia and the similarly painful feelings of an afflicted conscience is crucial to understand, even if it is extremely difficult to recognize.

> Many are of opinion that this sorrow for sinne is nothing els but a melancholike passion: but in trueth the thing is farre otherwise, as may appeare in the example of David: who by all coniectures was least troubled with melancholie, and yet never any tasted more deeply of the sorrowe and feeling of Gods anger for sinne than he did, as the booke of the Psalmes declareth. And if any desire to know the difference, they are to be discerned thus. Sorrrow for sinne my bee where health reason, senses, memorie and all are sound: but Melancholike passions are where the bodie is unsound, and the reason, senses, memorie, dulled and troubled.[19]

Bright and William Perkins both clearly insist on a distinction between a medical condition characterized by physical as well as emotional derangement and a spiritual suffering where the mind is in a state of health. Donne would clearly have understood this, if not from reading these treatises, then certainly from the tradition of neo-Augustinian spirituality in which he was immersed throughout his life. The problem, which Donne also understood, is how to tell these states apart from each other. Although it would seem that contrition of heart can transform melancholia into repentance, in actual fact the transformation might also go in the other direction.

For Shakespeare the black mistress was a courtesan, "the bay where all men ride." For Donne the black mistress is a paragon, a woman one would desire except that she is beyond the possibility of desire. The paradox emerges against a background of misogynistic resentment pervasive in the

Songs and Sonnets.[20] For Donne, the object of devotion is deliberately contrasted with others of that "perverse sex, where none is true but she." The woman worthy of love can be imagined only in fantasies of death, loss, and emotional destitution. This is vividly expressed in Donne's "A Nocturnall upon St. Lucie's Day."[21] It has been suggested by Sir Herbert J. C. Grierson that Lucy, Countess of Bedford, must have been the subject of the poem. Helen Gardner is a bit more judicious: "If so, the poem far transcends its original conception and has become the most profound expression of the sensation of utter and irremediable loss."[22]

> Blasted with sighs, and surrounded with tears,
>   Hither I come to seek the spring,
>   And at mine eyes, and at mine ears,
> Receive such balms, as else cures everything;
>   But O, self-traitor, I do bring
> The spider love, which transubstantiates all,
>   And can convert manna to gall.
> And that this place may thoroughly be thought
> True Paradise I have the Serpent brought. (1–9)

The crucial image here is the remarkable idea of a transubstantiation of "manna to gall." Gall here has the biblical sense of bitterness of spirit and can even mean the causeless anger closely associated with melancholia. If manna is taken as a metaphor for divine grace, or more specifically for the saving grace of repentance, then the gall is an antisacramental substance, not the body and blood of Christ, but the black bile of a sick soul.

In "Mourning and Melancholia" Freud somewhat ruefully maintains that the depressed patient who persists in this kind of self-indictment may in fact be on to something.[23] The resentful self-disappointment and low self-esteem are in some sense more "realistic" than the rather more delusional forms of what is called a "strong ego." I rather think that Donne would agree with the general drift of Freud's argument here, but he would certainly have grounded his analysis in his religious understanding rather than a secular, therapeutic, and psychoanalytic context. But the sense of an irreparable loss of something that was never actually possessed, of a wound or trauma that cannot be healed, is certainly recognizable in both settings. The question I would pose here is whether depression and melancholia are both the symptom of and punishment for one's total lack of faith or, contrariwise, whether a morbid preoccupation with sin and an accompanying fear of hellfire are just rather colorful and overly self-dramatic symptoms of the ordinary, everyday bummer of chronic depression.

I have sometimes wondered if this question ever occurred to George Herbert, the supposedly serene and simple man of faith, as he enjoyed his retirement from life at court as a country parson. Interpreting Herbert's *The Temple* in the context of melancholia is a bit unusual, and perhaps controversial. It's more common to discuss his work as the expression of orthodox belief within the dispensation of the Church of England. Stanley Fish reads the poems as a sort of catechism. "What is crucial is not the dialogue in the poem, but the dialogue the poem is in, and that, in turn, is a function of the way these poems characteristically engage their readers."[24] Fish is interested in the priestly character expressed in *The Temple,* but he tends to disregard what Vendler and others regard as expressions of personal religious experience. Like Fish and also Richard Strier, however, Vendler regards the personal experience as itself basically orthodox. I'm not going to contest this assessment. Yes, definitely, for sure, Herbert's poetry is in conformity with the Book of Common Prayer and the various articles of Christian faith.[25] But at the same time his "faith" is characterized by a keen and painful sense of God's absence. God exists, to be sure, but appears somehow apathetic, uncaring, and distant.

The poet's love of God is not in question, but this is an unrequited love, not really so different from the erotic disdain complained of by sonneteers. In "Deniall" it's clear that God is basically either indifferent to prayer or else actually deaf.

> O that thou shouldst give dust a tongue
>   To cry to thee,
> And then not hear it crying! All day long
>   My heart was in my knee,
>   But no hearing. (11–15)[26]

The poet is forsaken, and his verse as well as his spirit is broken. The recurring image in *The Temple* of something broken is taken from Psalm 31:14: "I am forgotten as a dead man out of mind: I am like a broken vessel." The broken vessel is a crucial image for Herbert's "personal experience of God," occurring several times in the sequence of "Affliction" poems, along with related metaphors of sickness, restlessness, and even torture.

Another way to see what I'm getting at here is to look at a poem called "Love Unknown," an extended narrative of the subject's troubled and troubling relationship with a certain Lord to whom he brings "a dish of fruit one day" in which he has placed his heart.

> Dear Friend, sit down, the tale is long and sad:
> And in my faintings I presume your love
> Will more comply, than help. (1–3)

The friend—the poet's therapist?—listens to a series of dreamlike incidents in which the heart is washed, wrung dry, then thrown into a cauldron. After escaping from these bizarre discomforts he escapes to his bed, which he finds is stuffed with thoughts, or, actually, with thorns. The poet's dialogue partner sees that the heart given to the lord was foul, hard, dull, and that it needed to be made "new, tender, quick."

> All did but strive to mend, what you had marr'd.
> Wherefore be cheer'd, and praise him to the full
> Each day, each houre, each moment of the week,
> Who fain would have you be new, tender, quick. (68–71)

Now isn't that just like your shrink? You go in with a big sob story, you've got all this great dream material, and all he can do is interrupt a few times to remind you how screwed up you are. Do these therapeutic insights actually help or do they just comply with the conventional, catechistical, and orthodox way of looking at things?

Herbert, I think, is too astute a theologian to believe in a God whose business is to answer prayers, to come when he is called, to respond to loving overtures, or to take any kind of interest in the suffering of human beings, whatever orthodox beliefs they might profess. A being who could be induced to do our bidding would be decidedly un-godlike. Spinoza will aspire to *Amor deus intellectualis,* advising his readers that it is possible to love God, but only on the express condition that one does not expect to be loved in return. Whether God actually exists as something separable from the larger nature of things remains an open question for Spinoza, and for this he was condemned as an atheist. But for Spinoza the compassionate acceptance of other people's lives and of the world they all inhabit is the only way God could possibly be loved.[27] Herbert's own "atheism" is the obverse of this. His poems work against the background of a redeemer God who really is constant and loving, constantly hoping for the redemption of the poet. But it's not the poet's love for God that is unrequited, but perversely the other way around. God is terribly undervalued, misunderstood by the poet, who is unable to believe in his own *amor deus.* What is bracketed is not the God term, but the possibility of anything like *amor deus intellectualis,* the very attitude privileged throughout Spinoza's *Ethics.*

Herbert's religiosity is "orthodox," but it may be related to the tradition of fideism that wants somehow to derive faith from doubt or skepticism. Blaise Pascal is perhaps the best known early modern thinker in this tradition, suggesting first that any belief in the existence of God is groundless, but no more so than belief in his nonexistence. The way out of the paradox is Pascal's famous "wager."[28] If I were God I might find this all a bit too crass. I might in fact prefer Herbert's expression of profound theological blues—"I gave you my heart and you let your servants throw it in the frying pan." *The Temple* is clear, lucid, unadorned love poetry, but it is also very much concerned with obscurity, remoteness, the sheer recalcitrance of the beloved. Like Donne's poems of grief over the loss of a perfect woman or Shakespeare's *Sonnets* in their longing for the beautiful boy, *The Temple* expresses the feeling of intense love for an object always already lost to the lover. Julia Kristeva calls this permanently lost and intensely desired object a person's "Thing" and she maintains it is the crucial element in the diverse, idiosyncratic phenomena of melancholia.[29] Herbert's poetry is different from *The Sonnets* in its representation of longing in the sense that the object of desire is unquestionably worthy of his love. Reflecting on the consolations of prayer and the observance of the sacraments can alleviate his melancholy. But melancholia provides consolations of its own, and in an important sense it is indistinguishable from faith.

LET THERE BEE GAULLE ENOUGH IN THY INKE. . . . A MELANCHOLY PUBLIC?

When Toby Belch advises Sir Andrew Aguecheek "let there be gall enough in thy ink," he is engaging in a bit of complex metaphysical wit. Gall in this context refers to the bitterness of Andrew's rage, to the boldness or effrontery of his challenge, but also to the oak gall that was used in making the kind of ink used with a goose-quill pen. W. G. Sebald, in "Constructs of Mourning," claims that in the sixteenth century black bile "was a synonym for the ink with which the writer draws his circles."[30] The connection is never made explicitly in the poetry discussed in Sebald's essay. Still, ink is black; some kinds of ink are made out of oak galls; gall is bile; things equal to the same thing are equal to each other; the writer's medium is literally melancholia, QED. Sebald is aware that this is in some ways dangerous: "A writer who uses black bile as a medium for creative work risks taking on the misunderstood depression of those for whom he writes."[31] But who are the people for whom one writes and why is their depression misunderstood? Is writing the symptomatic expression of melancholia, my own or someone else's? Or is it the other way around?

You have to use a lot of gall to make ink dark enough to read, and even at that it takes a few days of exposure to oxygen before the writing becomes really black. You can make the ink darker by adding burnt paper or parchment to the solution. Gum arabic is then added to improve the flow of the ink. Recipes for making ink from oak galls and copperas (iron sulphate) are known from ancient times and they are still easy to find on many websites. Oak gall ink, which is generally "homemade," is the traditional material used in making Torah scrolls. Knowledge of these techniques is also useful in a variety of other fields, including textual editing and bibliographical description. And there are occult or esoteric applications as well. If you use an infusion of pure gall, the writing will be completely invisible until you sponge it over with iron sulphate. "From the ancient world until recent times," as R. D. Wood explains, "there has been a universal familiarity with the reaction of gallotannins with metal salts, in relation to the chemistry of inks, and even more widely with techniques in many fields as a means to reveal the invisible."[32]

The poetry I have discussed in the preceding sections was first written down for circulation in manuscript form, partly as a "means to reveal the invisible." In every case the poetry was then published "after the fact" at the initiative of someone other than the author, and in the case of Donne and Herbert publication was posthumous. Here I'm adopting the contemporary usage of publication in the narrow sense of the mechanical reproduction and the circulation of printed books in the commercial market place. But of course "publication" can also refer to other means of "making public." The poems in question were initially composed for more esoteric and personal modes of distribution in the form of hand-copied manuscripts, using vellum and oak gall ink. At a later stage in their history they were edited and published as bound volumes made of paper and carbon-based printer's ink, a substance with very different chemical and physical properties. Handwritten copies can be understood as confessional or even autobiographical texts; the people for whom one writes are after all friends and personal acquaintances. Melancholia is communicated with the expectation of a sympathetic response. The printed volumes derived from these manuscript sources are produced by and for total strangers. The reflection of the poets' "misunderstood depression" addresses and constitutes a real public.

The 1609 printed text of the *Sonnets* is dedicated to the "onlie begetter," and it makes sense to read the poems as addressed to this person, whomever he might have been. But if the fictive addressee is the beautiful boy, it's also clear that Shakespeare has other readers in mind, for otherwise why does he make so many promises to the boy that his beauty will be preserved by the verse in the minds of future readers? According to Francis Meres, Shakespeare's "sugared sonnets" were already being read by his "private friends" long before the appearance of the 1609 text. *The Sonnets* were published during Shakespeare's lifetime, but the circumstances of their preparation and their release for the general public is one of the many maddening obscurities that surround the work. On the other hand, Shakespeare's *Sonnets* are intensely concerned with publicity, fame, and the possibility of future readers. Indeed everything claimed for the power of the verse would clearly depend on publication precisely in the sense of mechanical reproduction of printed books. What else could the promise that "in black ink my love will still shine bright" possibly refer to? And yet Shakespeare appears to be quite embarrassed at having to earn his living by writing plays, deploring the "public means which public manners breeds" in a medium addressed to the public. Finding your own livelihood deplorable is just one of the many forms of self-revilement found in the *Sonnets*. John Updike describes Shakespeare's theatrical career as "dirty work . . . though lucrative."[33] The publication of the *Sonnets* in 1609 would presumably have been lucrative as well, though maybe not for Shakespeare.

Donne's *Songs and Sonnets* are mostly about women, but they are best read as addressed to a male friend or intimate companion. The poetry makes the most sense when read as examples of private, man-to-man utterance, whether the woman referred to is being demeaned or idealized. Thanks to the wonderfully thorough work of Arthur Marotti, we now know that Donne's poems were composed specifically for manuscript circulation among a coterie of private readers.[34] The published texts, including all modern editions, are based on this manuscript tradition, with no real assurance that we are reading exactly what Donne wrote. Donne was no stranger either to publicity or to publication during his lifetime, but he evidently did not consider the material later collected as the *Songs and Sonnets* to be suitable for public consumption. Herbert's poems can also be read as addressed to a male friend, though in this case the "friend" seems to be Jesus. But of course for Herbert, Jesus was not like an imaginary playmate, and the poems are probably best characterized as soliloquies, both in the ordinary sense of someone talking to himself and in the more technical sense of a private utterance directed toward God. Although *The Temple* was not actually published during Herbert's lifetime, there is evidence that a manuscript or "little book" was entrusted to Nicholas Ferrar shortly before the poet's death. Modern editors think that this may well have been *The Temple,* which appeared in book form close to the actual date of Herbert's death.

The poetry transcribed in these volumes expresses dark and difficult feelings with extraordinary ingenuity. But who reads this stuff? Happy, well-adjusted people are, presumably, not much interested in hearing about melancholia; it's too depressing. The publication of such a melancholy poetry suggests the existence of a melancholy public. But why is this public melancholy and in what way might it be representative of early modern publics considered more broadly? What Burton described as an "epidemic of melancholia" comes about through an obscure awareness that there are important existential losses connected with newer modes of making publics. Publics are no longer closely embedded in the traditional estates or local communities or religious congregations, already seen as disappearing from the political landscape. The people for whom one writes are melancholy because they are not truly or fully members of any public in this traditional sense. The "bourgeois public sphere" described by Jürgen Habermas is paradoxically grounded in personal, familial life and in the slightly more detached self-awareness of consumers of new kinds of literary products available in the cultural marketplace.[35] Hannah Arendt describes this as a displacement of the classical sense of "publics" by an expansion of what she calls the "social."[36] New habits of consumption provide a false or inadequate public life, in which people have get-togethers, but only to talk about the conditions in which they live their private lives. Since what has been lost can scarcely be noticed, let alone acknowledged, it is hardly surprising that they are melancholy.

The "epidemic of melancholy" also correlates with the discovery of interiority. As Bronwen Wilson argues in relation to the "science" of physiognomy (in Chapter 10 of this volume), this discovery appears first as its own obverse in a heightened awareness of dissimulation, the everyday self-fashioning that enables an ambitious upward mobility among middle-class men. But the deployment of a false face becomes necessary for self-protection, especially in conditions of inquisitorial scrutiny and violent religious persecution in England and throughout Europe.[37] Descartes assumed he would have to wear a mask when he went out in public, in order to avoid social opprobrium: "Just as comedians are counseled not to let shame appear on their foreheads, and so put on a mask, so likewise, now that he is about to mount the stage of the world, where he has so far been a spectator, young Renatus Cartesius comes forward in a mask."[38] The social mask expresses an easygoing or at least unthreatening conformity as a mode of resistance to intrusive public scrutiny of what is not or cannot be shown. But it's not altogether clear what this mask of Descartes might look like. Is the wish to avoid the "appearance of shame" best achieved with a smiley face or is it better to look melancholy with the hope of being taken seriously?

Descartes's discovery of his own interiority proceeds from a prior awareness of exteriority, the sense that one's public self is just a mask concealing or protecting, to use Hamlet's words, "that within which passeth show" (1. 2, 85). But why does Descartes compare himself to a comedian and what is the shameful inner condition he has to conceal? Juliana Schiesari has suggested that the pervasiveness of early modern melancholia is just a self-serving pose adopted by ambitious scholars and men of letters to privilege their "suffering" as the sign of genius. It's a way of showing off, dramatizing ordinary and mediocre discomforts to make them seem genuinely important. But she also connects melancholia with "the rise of a subjectivism that finds its source of identity within melancholy, an identity whose contours proceed from the ambiguous point of intersection between clinical limitation and philosophical (spiritual) transcendence."[39] This analysis suggests that melancholia is dissimulation and also identity, the social mask and the core of interiority that cannot be shown. The poetics of melancholy are contrasted with the more confident and productive poetics of public making as the pursuit of new kinds of knowledge. Melancholia more often than not leads to confusion and despair rather than to any kind of deeper understanding.

Melancholy is not about knowledge and not about self-knowledge either, but about what cannot be known. "I have of late—but wherefore I know not—lost all my mirth" (2.2.293). If Hamlet really knew what was bothering him he might be mournful but he wouldn't be melancholy and he wouldn't have to fake it either. Hamlet wears "an inky cloak" to express what can never actually appear in public. And he displays at one point a kind of mania for writing things down, so that he can "remember" what his father's ghost has told him. The same obsession with exhaustively writing down everything is a characteristic of many books about melancholy, from Timothie Bright's *Treatise* and Robert Burton's *Anatomy of Melancholy* to Andrew Solomon's *The Noon Day Demon: An Atlas of Depression*.[40]

The publication of such encyclopedic volumes is warranted as a kind of public service, motivated by a concern with public health or public morality. But even the most comprehensive treatment of the subject has a more idiosyncratic and self-reflexive purpose very similar to what is found in the more condensed forms of the personal lyric. Reading about someone else's melancholia can have a therapeutic value, even if no reliable knowledge can be gained through an imagined experience of suffering. In this sense it is possible to make a public for melancholia, consisting of writers, theologians, physicians, anyone who might have a contingent interest in the subject. But there is also another sense in which lyric poetry speaks to a melancholy public.

In a way melancholia seems fundamentally incompatible with public life. Even the melancholy genius is in some sense marginal, a point made in "Problem 30," a text traditionally ascribed to Aristotle but probably written by someone else. Max Pensky, in his book on *Melancholy Dialectics: Walter Benjamin and the Play of Mourning,* thinks that "genius itself is incompatible with integration into the polis," even though its characteristic "alienation [is] necessary to gain insight into the critical structure of society itself."[41] Melancholy seems profoundly incompatible with what I would call the sociable side of public life, its openness, animation, purposefulness. But a public is a network of relationships among people who are strangers to each other and it can be constituted through mere attention given to something. The publication of poetry of melancholia suggests that a public might be composed of solitary, isolated subjects connected only by the attention given to the expressive lives of others. Readers who recognize themselves as singular personalities through the imagined experiences in powerful works of art may form a public in the most generic sense of this elusive notion. There are actual techniques for restoring faded oak-gall ink and for bringing out the latent images of lost meanings. And this is a nice analogue for psychoanalysis and for the enterprise of hermeneutics. So maybe it's even possible to see what is so black you cannot even see it in the sonnets of Shakespeare, or the elegiac lyrics of Donne, or the religious verse of Herbert. Their poetry is thematically concerned with many different kinds of erotic objects, and, at the same time, with the invention of new kinds of poetic subjectivity. Such preoccupations articulate and reveal the presence of a self in its radical condition of solitude—the poor soul at the center of its sinful earth. The readers imagined in these poems are representative of early modern publics in their anonymity and in their self-conscious awareness of radical singularity. They form a public composed of solitary, private persons who go about suitably masked and thus opaque, even to themselves. Emanuel Levinas brings these ideas together with precision: "The fact of finding oneself settled in the world, occupied with things, attached to them, and even the aspiration to dominate them, is not merely depreciated in the experience of solitude, but explained by a philosophy of solitude."[42]

The individual solitude expressed in this poetry is the strong articulation of a first-personal point of view; it valorizes the singularity of one's own personhood. Hamlet is alone when he says "Now I am alone," and everyone in the theater can hear him say it. His utterance speaks to a collectivity that will judge him and discuss his actions. Theatergoers present at the performance are constituted as a public in the sociable sense; they share an interest in going to the theater and appreciating dramatic performances. But Hamlet, in speaking to himself, also speaks to the perspective of the playgoers' own melancholy privateness. His melancholia, imperfectly signified in his inky cloak, is articulated fully in Shakespeare's *Sonnets*. But it's not idiocy and it's not something than one can usefully repent. The melancholy public in this sense is like God; it is everywhere and it is nowhere, or more precisely it is everyone and it is no one. It defines the basic condition of possibility for participation in public life.

NOTES

1. Adam Kitzes, *The Politics of Melancholia from Spenser to Milton* (New York: Routledge, 2006), 9.
2. William Shakespeare, *Hamlet*, ed. G. R. Hibbard (Oxford: Oxford University Press, 1987), 1.2.76–85. All further references to *Hamlet* are given in the text.
3. Robert Burton, *The anatomy of melancholy vvhat it is. VVith all the kindes, causes, symptomes, prognostickes, and seuerall cures of it. In three maine partitions with their seuerall sections, members, and subsections. Philosophically, medicinally, historically, opened and cut vp. By Democritus Iunior. With a satyricall preface, conducing to the following discourse* (Oxford: Iohn Lichfield and Iames Short, for Henry Cripps, 1621).
4. Lawrence Babb, *The Elizabethan Malady; A Study of Melancholia in English Literature from 1580 to 1642* (East Lansing: Michigan State College Press, 1951).
5. Colin Burrow, ed., *Complete Poems and Sonnets by William Shakespeare* (Oxford: Oxford University Press, 2002). All further references to Shakespeare's *Sonnets* are given in the text.
6. Matt. 21, Luke 15.
7. Burrow, "Introduction," in *Complete Poems and Sonnets*, 131.
8. Ibid., 634.
9. Helen Vendler, *The Art of Shakespeare's Sonnets* (Cambridge, MA: Belknap Press, 1997), 540.
10. Sir Philip Sidney, "Astrophel and Stella," in *Complete Poems*, ed. William Ringler (Oxford: Clarendon Press, 1962).
11. Herbert of Cherbury, *Poems English and Latin*, ed. G. C. Moore Smith (Oxford: Clarendon Press, 1923).
12. Michael Bristol, "Sacred Literature and Profane Religion: The Modernity of Herbert of Cherbury," in *The Witness of Times: Manifestations of Ideology in Seventeenth Century England*, ed. Katherine Z. Keller and Gerald J. Schiffhorst (Pittsburgh, PA: Duquesne University Press 1993), 29.
13. Timothie Bright, *A treatise of melancholy Containing the causes thereof, and reasons of the strange effects it worketh in our minds and bodies: with*

the physicke cure, and spirituall consolation for such as haue thereto adi-oyned afflicted conscience (London: Vautrolier, 1586),

14. Isa. 5:20.
15. John Donne, *Divine Poems,* ed. Helen Gardner (Oxford: Clarendon Press, 1956).
16. Bright, *Treatise of melancholy,* iii.
17. Angus Gowland, "The Problem of Early Modern Melancholy," *Past and Present* 191 (2006): 77–121; Jeremy Schmidt, "Melancholy and the Thera-peutic Language of Moral Philosophy in Seventeenth-Century Thought," *Journal of the History of Ideas* 65, no. 4 (2004): 583–601.
18. Bright, *Treatise of melancholy,* iii.
19. William Perkins, *A Treatise Tending Unto a Declaration, Whether a Man Be in the Estate of Damnation or in the Estate of Grace* (London: Printed by the Widow Orwin, for Iohn Porter, 1597), 159.
20. Janel Mueller, "Women among the Metaphysicals: A Case, Mostly, of Being Donne for," *Modern Philology* 87 (1989): 142–58.
21. John Donne, *The Elegies and the Songs and Sonnets,* ed. Helen Gardner (Oxford: Clarendon Press, 1965), 84–85.
22. Donne, 251.
23. Sigmund Freud, "Mourning and Melancholia," in *The Standard Edition of the Complete Psychological Works,* ed. J. Strachey (London: Hogarth, 1957), 14:245.
24. Stanley Fish, *The Living Temple: George Herbert and Catechizing* (Berkeley and Los Angeles: University of California Press, 1978), 35.
25. Richard Strier, "John Donne Awry and Squint: The 'Holy Sonnets,' 1608–1610," *Modern Philology* 86 (1989): 357–84.
26. George Herbert, *The Complete English Poems,* ed. John Tobin (Oxford: Oxford, University Press, 1991). All further references to Herbert's poetry are given in the text.
27. Benedictus de Spinoza, *Ethics,* trans. George Henry Radcliffe Parkinson (Oxford: Oxford University Press, 2000).
28. Blaise Pascal, *Pensées,* translated with an introduction by A. J. Krailsheimer (London: Penguin Books, 1995), 55.
29. Julia Kristeva, *Black Sun: Depression and Melancholia* (New York: Colum-bia University Press, 1989).
30. W. G. Sebald, "Constructs of Mourning," in *Campo Santo,* ed. Sven Meyer, trans. Anthea Bell (London: Hamish Hamilton, 2005), 120.
31. Ibid.
32. R. D. Wood, "The Daguerreotype and Development of the Latent Image: 'Une Analogie Remarquable,'" *Journal of Photographic Science* 44 (1996): 165.
33. John Updike, "Late Works: Writers and Artists Confronting the End," *New Yorker,* August 7, 2006, 77.
34. Arthur Marotti, *John Donne, Coterie Poet* (Madison: University of Wiscon-sin Press, 1986).
35. Jürgen Habermas, *The Structural Transformation of the Public Square,* trans. Thomas Burger with the assistance of Frederick Lawrence (Cambridge, MA: MIT Press, 1992), 43–51.
36. Hannah Arendt, *The Human Condition* (Chicago: University of Chicago Press, 1958), 38–50.
37. See also Katharine Eisaman Maus, *Inwardness and Theater in the English Renaissance* (Chicago: University of Chicago Press, 1995).
38. "Ut comœdi, moniti ne in fronte appareat pudor, personam induunt, sic ego hoc mundi teatrum consensurus, in quo hactenus spectator exstiti, larvatus

prodeo." René Descartes, *Œuvres de Descartes*, Publiées par Charles Adam et Paul Tannery sous les auspices du minstère de l'instruction publique (Paris: L. Cerf, 1897–1910), 10:213, 4–6.

39. Juliana Schiesari, *The Gendering of Melancholia: Feminism, Psychoanalysis and the Symbolics of Loss in Renaissance Literature* (Ithaca, NY: Cornell University Press, 1992).

40. Andrew Solomon, *The Noonday Demon: An Atlas of Depression* (New York: Touchstone, 2002).

41. Max Pensky, *Melancholy Dialectics : Walter Benjamin and the Play of Mourning* (Amherst: University of Massachusetts Press, 1993), 33.

42. Emmanuel Levinas, *Time and the Other*, trans. Richard A. Cohen (Pittsburgh, PA: Duquesne University Press, 1987), 59.

12 Specifying Unknown Things
The Algebra of *The Merchant of Venice*[1]

Shankar Raman

INTRODUCTION

For most people, mathematics and questions about privacy and publicity seem worlds apart, entirely incommensurable. This essay seeks to reverse that impression. In Jürgen Habermas's influential account of how voluntary associations among people led to the emergence of a public sphere,[2] the emphasis falls on the contributions of literary publics to the new institutional bases of civil society.[3] As a corrective, my work on Renaissance algebra stresses the contributions of mathematics, not only to modes of discourse increasingly deemed appropriate in the domain of the public, but also to the rise of the very category of the "private" that underpins this developing "publicity." For the private in Habermas's formulation does not simply point to some sort of average everyday individuality that all human beings share. Rather, it is an abstraction through which individuals constituted themselves "voluntarily" in and through their aggregations as private people. Such abstraction was achieved through the conjunction of mathematics with literature, economics, natural philosophy, and law.

While it is doubtful that "a" public sphere emerged between the sixteenth and eighteenth centuries, Habermas's concept remains useful as a model as well as a means of locating broad transformations in the social categories constitutive of empirically existing publics and/or public spheres. He himself emphasizes the trajectory leading from "the publicness . . . of representation" to "the sphere of public authority." High medieval notions of the public involved displaying status; the publicity of representation remained inseparable from "the lord's concrete existence, that, as an 'aura,' surrounded and endowed his authority."[4] By the end of the seventeenth century, however, a line between state and society had been drawn, demarcating two domains of public life. On the side of the state, the public sphere was coextensive with public authority, which was identified with "the functioning of an apparatus with regulated spheres of jurisdiction and endowed with a monopoly over the legitimate use of coercion."[5] Alongside—and included within the private realm—emerged an "authentic 'public sphere,'" in the sense of being "constituted by private people."[6]

In what follows, I offer a very abbreviated account of how mathematical transformations in algebra helped lay the foundation for emerging concepts of privacy upon which notions of the public sphere would come to rest. My essay argues that the changing conception of algebraic things in the early modern period was correlated with the shifting construction of legal personhood. More specifically, it locates a shift from representing things—be they commodities, people, or algebraic unknowns—as determinate-but-unknown to representing them in their merely potential determinateness, leaving their ontological specification to different locations (the courtroom and the concrete equation) within which such valuation or determination dynamically occurs. And *The Merchant of Venice* articulates precisely this nexus of mathematics and the law, rendering visible the interdependent historical shifts occurring in what otherwise seem quite diverse fields.

TRAFFICKING IN UNKNOWN THINGS

Shakespeare's *The Merchant of Venice* famously opens with a profession of sadness whose cause is so concealed it escapes detection even by the person most privy to its effects:

> In sooth, I know not why I am so sad.
> It wearies me, you say it wearies you;
> But how I caught it, found it, or came by it,
> What stuff 'tis made of, whereof it is born,
> I am to learn;
> And such a want-wit sadness makes of me
> That I have much ado to know myself.[7] (1.1.1–7)

There has been no shortage of attempts to identify the "why" of Antonio's sadness, but the merchant himself remains resolute in his ignorance of causation—and, by his own extension, of his self. While the effect—the sadness—is not in doubt, the manner of its acquisition, the "stuff" of its composition, and its genealogy remain hidden. There is a privacy of motive at work here that eludes and baffles all efforts at extracting a root cause.

The failure of causal investigations is perhaps best expressed by the proliferation in this scene of indexical terms that stand for a cause without, however, specifying its nature, namely—words like "it," "thing," and "this." Antonio opens the play with a sevenfold iteration of the "it" he cannot name, and even Salerio's attempt to name the unnameable becomes infected by the language of unspecifiability:

> And in a word, but even now worth this,
> And now worth nothing? Shall I have the thought
> To think on this, and shall I lack the thought

That such a thing bechanced would make me sad?
But tell not me; I know Antonio
Is sad to think upon his merchandise. (1.1.36–41)

The shifting referents of Salerio's "this"es—the first an unspecified measure of worth, the second both indicating the change in worth from this
to nothing, and anticipating the "thing bechanced"—suggest that his own
identification of "this" with Antonio's "merchandise" is perhaps a little
over-hasty, as Antonio himself immediately confirms by denying the proposed equation ("Believe me, no. I thank my fortune for it" [1.1.42]).

I have opened with how Antonio as it were traffics in unknown things
in order to establish in *The Merchant of Venice* the echo of an increasingly
important early modern mathematical discipline: what was called either
the art of the coss or—the term more familiar to us—algebra. Indeed, the
shared concern with unknown things and causes is signaled by these very
names. Reviewing its history, John Wallis's 1685 *Treatise of Algebra* tells
us that the art of the coss—or the cossick art—acquired its name from the
Italian use of "cosa" for the unknown root in an algebraic equation (that
is, for the "x" in an equation such as $3x^2 + 4x = 8$):

> Now what we call the Root . . . being by . . . [the Italians] called *Res,*
> the Thing, which is (in their language) *Cosa,* (a word corrupted from
> the Latin *Causa* whence also comes the French *Chose*) hath given occa-
> sion to the name of *Cossick* numbers . . . and the rule of *Coss,* that is,
> *Regula Cosa* or *Regula Rei.*[8]

The proposed connection between things and unknowns can be found in a
range of European mathematical texts.[9]

The now more common—and older—name, algebra, offers yet another
route into Shakespeare's play, this time in terms of mathematical procedure. According to Wallis, "algebra" abbreviates the Arabic *al-gjabr w'al-
mokabla,* which combines the Arabic word *Gjabara*—for "to restore, and
(more especially) to restore a broken bone or joint"—with the word *Kabala,*
which "signifies to oppose, compare or set one thing against another."[10]
This combination offers him an apt description for algebraic procedure as
such. "The true import of the Arabic name given to this art," he says, is
the following:

> A quantity, as yet unknown . . . is supposed (by such Additions, Sub-
> ductions, Multiplications, Division, and other like Operations as is
> proposed) to be so changed, as at length to become equal to a known
> quantity, compared with it, or set over against; which comparing, is
> commonly called an Equation: And by resolving such Equation, the
> Root (so changed, transformed, or luxated) is (as it were) put in joynt
> again, and its true value made known.[11]

Wallis's formulation of the algebraist's task rests upon a text that was, as we shall see, crucial to the development of modern algebra, François Viète's 1591 *In Artem Analyticem Isagoge*. Viète understands this branch of mathematics as central to what the Greeks called analysis, that is, a "way of seeking the truth" that "tak[es] the thing sought as granted and proceed[s] by means of what follows to a truth that is uncontested."[12]

Something akin to such an analytic procedure is evident in the different approaches adopted by Antonio's friends to "resolve" the unknown cause of his melancholy, and by so doing, to put him "in joint" again. Taking for granted Antonio's unknown "it," Salerio proceeds to solve for it by substituting Antonio's mind for his "argosies with portly sail"; the mind's unease is explained by its "tossing on the ocean" as his ships do (1.1.8ff). Solanio's reasoning, by contrast, identifies the hidden cause of Antonio's sadness with the hidden dangers of the world so that "every object that might make me fear / Misfortune to my ventures, out of doubt / Would make me sad" (1.1.15ff). Building on this equation, Salerio in turn argues that it is not only those objects capable of generating fear that contribute to Antonio's depression; rather, even quotidian objects and actions come to stand for unknown perils, conducing to a vivid, internal realization of an imagined end: the wind cooling his broth becomes the "wind too great" at sea, the hourglass's sand evokes the "shallows and flats" upon which the ship beaches, and the stones of the church conjure up the "dangerous rocks, / Which touching but my gentle vessel's side / Would scatter all her spices on the stream, / Enrobe the roaring waters with my silks" (1.1.32–5).

Of course, Antonio accepts none of these analyses, but their litany nonetheless suggests the play's concern with how unknown causes are related to sensible phenomena. And in this sense, its opening scene echoes the analytic emphasis of Viète's *Isagoge*, whose algebraic sections are ultimately concerned less with the actual solution for the "thing sought," that is, with making known its true value, than with the general mathematical operations through which an unknown *res* "hidden under the wrappings of what is given in the problem"[13] can be expressed in terms of an equation or proportion connecting known and unknown quantities. As Jacob Klein puts it, Viète is interested "less in the 'truths' themselves which are to be found than in the *finding of 'correct finding.'*"[14]

It is not, I hope, too much of a leap to suggest that the finding of a correct finding is central to the venture of the three caskets. Moreover, Shakespeare explores this issue in ways that go well beyond the obvious challenge of identifying which casket to select. Upon choosing correctly, Bassanio launches into a blazon inspired not so much by Portia herself as by the vision of "fair Portia's counterfeit," the "picture" hitherto "locked" in lead. Pulling himself up short in midflow, Bassanio develops a complex proportion intended to convey the radical disproportion between the thing-in-itself and the sign that stands for it.

> Yet look—how far
> The substance of my praise doth wrong this shadow
> In underprizing it, so far this shadow
> Doth limp behind the substance. (3.2.129–32)

There are two substances here–the praise and Portia herself—which are brought into a relationship by the mediating form of Portia's picture, the "shadow" that stands for her and is simultaneously the referent of the blazon that precedes these lines. The equation set up here does not seek to specify the unknown substance that is Portia, but rather to establish the correct relationship among the three terms in a manner that allows the "correct finding" to be made.

To specify Portia's "substance" as the determinate value associated with the shadow that stands for her requires a legal validation by the object of desire herself, so Bassanio continues to "stand" (3.2.149) "doubtful whether what I see be true / Until confirmed, signed, and ratified by you" (3.2.150–51). And it is precisely to the justness of this relationship that Portia responds, in "convert[ing]" (3.2.170) herself and her possessions into Bassanio's care.[15] Through this abdication, she indeed passes into his possession, her status changing to mirror that of her "fair picture," which is already in Bassanio's hands. As the scroll tells Bassanio:

> If you be well pleased with this,
> And hold your fortune for your bliss,
> Turn you where your lady is
> And claim her with a loving kiss. (3.2.138–41)

Portia's ratification of the "claim" specifies the "this" being held, and produces the determinate value that it denotes—thereby resolving the equation that has been set up, and confirming the "correctness" of its finding.

SPECIOUS LOGIC

As well as illuminating *The Merchant of Venice*'s dramatic logic, these attempts to specify the referent of the sign confirming the venture's success bespeak a change fundamental to mathematics: a major shift across the early modern period in how to understand the algebraist's task. In order to comprehend the nature of this change, we need first to step back to consider the Western origins of algebra. These are generally traced to a founding Greek text, Diophantus's *Arithmetic* (c. 250 AD). As Paul Tannery, Thomas Heath, and others have shown, one of the principal contributions of Diophantine arithmetic lay in its designation of the unknown and its exponential powers by signs that stood in their place. Diophantus defines the unknown quantity as "an undefined number of units" [*plethos monadon aoriston*], and refers to it in verbal descriptions as *arithmos,* the Greek word for number. Crucially, however, in representing and solving a particular equation, Diophantus designates the unknown by a form of σ, an abbreviation apparently derived from the final consonant of *arithmos.*[16]

Two connected features of Diophantus's *Arithmetic* are of especial importance here: the concept of number underlying the treatise, and the relationship between the sign and the unknown it stands for. As Klein has convincingly shown, Diophantus's understanding of *arithmos* is very different from the idea of number that developed across the early modern period (and to which we all are heir). For the Greeks, *arithmos* meant "a definite number of definite things" or "a numbered assemblage." In other words, number was always a counting number, so that counting, say, "dogs, horses, and sheep . . . yield[ed] as results a definite horse-, dog-, or sheep number."[17] Diophantus, too, restricts himself to countable numbers; that is, a valid solution to an equation must be either a positive integer or a ratio of two positive integers. This limitation becomes especially evident in those equations whose solution leads to a negative or irrational number. According to Heath:

> of a negative quantity *per se,* i.e., without some positive quantity to subtract it from, Diophantus had apparently no conception. Such equations then as lead to surd [that is, irrational], imaginary, or negative roots he regards as useless for his purpose: the solution in these cases is *adunatos,* impossible.[18]

When faced with these arithmetical impossibilities—that is to say, impossibilities for his notion of *arithmos*—Diophantus quite remarkably retraces his steps to find out how his equation had arisen and how he may, by altering the previous work, substitute another equation that would yield a result that is numerically permissible.

This fundamental dependence of number upon concrete enumeration has consequences, too, for how Diophantine arithmetic understands the connection between an unknown number and the sign that denotes the type or kind of number it is (its *eidos*). Notably, the unknown number is *not* understood as indeterminate: Any numerical *eidos* always intends a determinate number of monads—whether the *eidos* be of the type designating the unknowns, or of the class designating the squares of the unknown. But this implicit determinacy means that the signs for unknown numbers are shorthand or "word abbreviations" with a purely instrumental significance: The sign signals a completely determinate number, but simply one whose value we do not yet know. In this sense, it is "a mere tachygraphic abbreviation [that is, a contraction] and not an algebraic symbol like our x, though discharging much of the same function"[19]

Just such a Diophantine understanding of unknown numbers underlies Bassanio's response to his own success. As his elaborate blazon of praise indicates, he seeks to "prize" or assess the value of the "substance" that the portrait stands for. Throughout, his attitude implies an understanding that the unknown substance does have a determinate value and can therefore be correctly appraised. Recall, for instance, how he describes the venture to Antonio in 1.1: "In Belmont is a lady richly left, / . . . / Her name is Portia, nothing undervalued / To Cato's daughter, Brutus' Portia" (1.1.164ff). Here, too, the actual value remains unknown, but the economic language of comparison nevertheless implicitly posits Portia as embodying a determinate value that is as yet concealed. That he now stands "doubtful whether what [he] see[s] be true" marks his hesitation as a problem of *knowing* what the value is, against a background assumption that the sign referring to the substance does indeed stand for a determinate value. As with Diophantus's σ, "Fair Portia's counterfeit" is simply a shorthand, an abbreviation, for the thing it represents—hence the blazon's initial insistence upon likeness— "What demigod / Hath come so near creation?" (3.2.118–19)—before it veers off to consider the gap between sign and unknown substance.

But even as Portia "confirm[s], sign[s], ratif[ies]" Bassanio's choice, she does so through an elaborate equation of her own, which suggests a very different attitude toward the problem of how to assign herself a value:

> You see me, Lord Bassanio, where I stand,
> Such as I am. Though for myself alone
> I would not be ambitious in my wish
> To wish myself much better, yet for you
> I would be trebled twenty times myself—
> A thousand times more fair, ten thousand times
> More rich; that only to stand high in your account
> I might in virtues, beauties, livings, friends
> Exceed account. But the full sum of me
> Is sum of something, which to term in gross
> Is an unlessoned girl, unschooled, unpracticed;
> Happy in this, she is not yet so old
> But she may learn. (3.2.152–63)

Portia's language is imbued with the arithmetical operations of multiplication and addition to which equations are subjected in the process of solving for unknowns: The tautological "I" that ostensibly stands simply for itself ("where I stand / such as I am") becomes subjected in her imagination to being "trebled twenty times," her fairness and wealth taking on additional ciphers that multiply their worth. Yet the aim of her imaginative arithmetic is not to establish a fixed value; rather, she seeks to "exceed account," to escape a logic that assigns her a determinate value that can be counted and thereby accounted for. And even this unaccountable excess is not the central issue in this account of herself. For, underlying (and indeed enabling) these imagined transformations in her value is a more radical indeterminacy. What is the nature of the I that simply stands such as it is? Its "full sum," she suggests through a resonant homonym, remains fundamentally unknown, essentially indeterminate: "the sum of something." This is not to say that the unknown (some)thing cannot be given a determinate value—it can, and she herself does so repeatedly. But her determinateness is always thought of only as *a merely potential determinateness,* rather than—as Bassanio's algebra would have it—an in-itself enumerated and determinate "something" whose specific value happens to be unknown. In short, what characterizes the unknown something that is Portia is that it can always be determined as some *other* thing: She is, after all, "not yet so old / But she may learn." Small surprise, then, that the declarative act by which she "ratifies" Bassanio's "fortune," converting herself from subject to object, is preceded by a proliferation of subjunctives and conditionals: She "would not" be ambitious for herself, yet for him she "would be trebled," so that she "might" exceed account—all these potential transformations resting upon the something she is, which "may" be "schooled" into something else.

This difference between Bassanio's and Portia's views regarding the status and value of the unknown thing that is Portia parallels a shift in the history of algebra, reflected in Viète's reconceptualization of Diophantine arithmetic. In the manner typical of the Renaissance, Viète presents innovation as renovation—he borrows terms directly from the ancient mathematical tradition and interprets his own deviations as mere developments of that tradition. Yet, his deceptively simple contribution marks a profound transformation of the two central features of the earlier algebra emphasized above: the concept of number, and the relationship between sign and unknown. Essentially, Viète does no more than introduce a new notation wherein the determinate or given coefficients of an equation are also designated by letters. Thus, rather than working with, say, $3x^2 = 4x = 8$, Viète operates with a version of the more general form we know today: $ax^2 + bx = c$, where x is the unknown to be found, while a, b, and c represent the coefficients that multiply the individual powers of x. On the basis of this alphabetic notation he arrives at a mode of calculation, a *logistice speciosa* carried out entirely in terms of these "species of number" (lending algebra yet another name in the process: specious arithmetic).

Unlike Diophantus, however, Viète leaves the question of "how many" entirely indeterminate. That is, rather than conceive number as a determinate (if unknown) counting number, he posits as the basis of algebra a notion of number that is indifferently applicable to numbers of any kind and to geometric magnitudes alike. This universalization of the concept of number marks the emergence of a mathematical formalism that is (in principle at least) free of ontological commitment, and in particular of any intuitive ontology of the physical world.[20] It is impossible to see determinate numbers in the isolated letter signs Viète uses, except through the syntactic rules for their combination.

This changed understanding of number has as its consequence a transformation in the relationship between the sign and the unknown it stands for. No longer simply an abbreviation for a determinate value, the alphabetic sign represents the unknown—as the other alphabetic signs do the coefficients in the equation—in its general character of being a number. The being of the "species" that one multiplies or adds is understood as *symbolic,* and the analytical procedures allow one to treat these symbols, these merely potential objectivities, *as if* they were actual objectivities. In other words, given an equation of the form $ax^2 + bx = c,$ we can solve for the unknown x in terms of a, b, and c. But to do so is not to fix the value of x, but simply to express it as potentially determinable *depending on the particular values we assign to a, b and c.* The actual value of x—what it will be—depends on its mathematical relationships to the other species in the equation, and to the determinate values that accrue to these when they become fixed.

To return, then, to Portia, and read the final lines of her speech against this background: If she "converts" herself into a determinate object—comprising "this house, these servants, and this same myself"—for Bassanio to "lord" it over, this self-specification is immediately undercut by the symbolization that follows:

> I give them with this ring,
> Which when you part from, lose, or give away,
> Let it presage the ruin of your love
> And be my vantage to exclaim on you. (3.2.174–77)

Unlike the portrait as a sign for the unknown—which rests upon likeness and hence an underlying determinacy—the ring stands for her as a symbol indicating her "merely possible determinateness." Not only does the ring undo the revaluation that has just been carried out by pointing to its future reversal ("when you part from, lose or give away"), but it also symbolically represents Portia's "substance," who she is, as an unknown thing whose "being" is not specifiable in advance; rather, it emerges retroactively through the various theatrical operations in which she participates. While ratifying her escape from a previous specification—"so is the will of a living daughter," Portia had earlier complained, "curbed by the will of a dead father"—her circular symbolization here ratifies, too, the dynamic fluidity of a determination that is always only provisional. Only a short while ago, she had stood, she insisted, "for sacrifice"; a little later she stands for herself; and not very much later she will stand as Balthazar to specify with mathematical exactitude the nature of the "substance" that Shylock may demand of Antonio:

> If thou tak'st more
> Or less than a just pound, be it so much

As makes it light or heavy in the substance
Or the division of the twentieth part
Of one poor scruple—nay if the scale do turn
But in the estimation of a hair—
Thou diest and all thy goods are confiscate. (4.1.336–43)

Respecifying the penalty, "expressing" (see 4.1.268 and 315) the law to the letter, Portia-as-Balthazar ensures that the pound of Antonio's flesh not take with it the unknown substance that inheres in it and that Shylock's penalty symbolizes: his life.

THE ALGEBRA OF JUSTICE

I have shown how the language of proportionality and algebraic equations permeates in particular Bassanio's and Portia's responses to the "hazard" of choosing the right casket. That scene is far from exceptional. But rather than multiply instances, I wish to shift terrain in order to suggest that the *Merchant*'s investment in this language expresses as well a fundamental connection between law and mathematics. This alliance was not invented by Shakespeare, for its roots extend at least as deep as Aristotle's discussion of justice in Book V of the *Nicomachean Ethics*. After distinguishing lawful or universal justice from fair and equal [*ison*] or particular justice, Aristotle turns his attention to the genus and specific differences characterizing the latter; it is here that mathematics enters the scene. The two forms of particular justice he identifies are distinguished by their mathematical procedures of equalization—though what equalization means and how it operates is different in each case.

To begin with the second of these, rectificatory (or commutative) justice: This form applies, says Aristotle, to transactions of an economic nature (such as purchase and sale, loans, deposits, and so on) as well as of a criminal nature (theft, adultery, assault, etc.). What is fundamental is that the law attends only to the "distinctive character of the injury," and not to the actual worth of the two parties. Justice seeks to correct the inequality caused by an unjust act, which had resulted in "the suffering and the action [being] unequally distributed."[21] The judge restores equality arithmetically, taking away or subtracting the excessive "gain" of one party and adding or giving it to the other to reach an equality that corresponds to their anterior status as equals before the law.

Against this "arithmetical proportion," Aristotle offers geometric proportionality as the model appropriate to distributive justice. Distributive equalization is not absolute but relative, the task being to apportion goods according to the respective merits of the receivers. Hence, equality does not mean that the individuals involved get equal amounts. It obtains instead between two proportions or ratios connecting the relative rights of the two persons to their relative shares in the "things in which [the just] is manifested."[22] And Aristotle again draws out the mathematical relationships at some length: "As the term A, then, is to B, so will C be to D, and therefore, *alternando,* as A is to C, B will be to D. . . . The conjunction . . . of the term A with C and of B with D is what is just in distribution, and this species of the just is intermediate, and the unjust is what violates the proportion; for the proportional is intermediate, and the just is proportional."[23]

That the early modern period remained attentive to this Aristotelian conjunction of mathematics and justice is evident in the work of the mathematician Robert Recorde (c. 1510–1558), whose numerous introductory books on arithmetic, algebra, and geometry were regularly reprinted in the sixteenth and seventeenth centuries. In the versified claim that, by "measur[ing] all truly," geometrical proportionality yields "the full right to every man justly,"[24] Recorde's *The Pathway to Knowledge* evokes the two central precepts of equality and proportionality that constitute the conceptual bridge between algebra and law. His preface to *The Whetstone of Witte*—the earliest algebraic work in English—makes his appreciation of Aristotle explicit:

> In Law two kinds of Justice are the sum of the study: Justice Distributive, and Justice Commutative, which terms I use, as best known in that art. But what is any of them both without number? I have said in another place (as I learned of that noble Philosopher Aristotle) that if the knowledge and distinction of Geometrical and Arithmetical proportion be not well observed, there can no Justice be well executed. And how often the ministers of Law use aid of Number, I need not repeat, because none but mad men doubt of it.[25]

Early modern algebra drew directly upon the Greek analysis of proportion [*analogia*] bequeathed by Books V and VII of Euclid's *Elements* (which in turn encapsulated the inheritance of the Pythagoreans and Aristotle).[26] This lineage persisted even as algebra emerged as the mathematical discipline concerned with analyzing equations rather than geometrical proportions since, as Viète put it, "a proportion can be called the composition (constitutio) of an equation, an equation the resolution (resolutio) of a proportion."[27]

The proximity between law and early modern algebra is especially intimate in Viète's case, who pursued his interests as an amateur mathematician alongside a professional legal (and political) career. His mathematical contributions ebb and flow in roughly inverse relation to the political demands upon him. From 1564 to 1571, his post as private secretary to Antoinette d'Aubeterre allowed him the time to work on the ambitious tables of trigonometric functions (published in his *Canon Mathematicus* and *Universalium Inspectionum Liber Singularis*, 1579). A hiatus that parallels the turmoils in the wake of the Religious Wars ends with his important work on algebra from about 1584 onward, leading to the publication of *In Analyticem Isagoge* or *The Analytic Art* in 1591. His work was disseminated in England through the circle of scholars surrounding Henry Percy, Earl of Northumberland, and in particular through Nathaniel Torporley, a student of Viète's who was employed by Percy upon return to England and later put in charge of collating and publishing Thomas Hariot's mathematical work.[28]

While it is probably impossible to establish direct connections between Viète's politico-legal and mathematical personae, John Wallis at least was willing to hazard just such an assertion. Looking back on the history of algebra from his perch in the seventeenth century, Wallis claimed to discern the dependence of Viète's mathematics upon his legal training:

> The name of *Specious Arithmetick* is given to it (I presume) with respect to a sense wherein the Civilians [that is, lawyers trained in Civil Law] use the word *Species;* for whereas it is usual with our Common Lawyers to put *Cases* in the name of *John-an-Oaks* and *John-a-Stiles* or *John-a-Down,* and the like (by which names they mean any person indefinitely, who may be so concern'd) and of later times (for brevity sake) of J. O. and J. S. or J. D., (or yet more shortly) of A, B, C etc. In like manner, the Civilians make use of the Names of Titus, Sempronius, Caius, and Mevius, or the like, to represent indefinitely, any person in such circumstances. And cases so propounded, they call *Species.*
>
> Now with respect hereunto, *Vieta* [sic] (accustomed to the language of Civil Law) did give, I suppose, the name of *Species* to the letters A, B, C etc. made use of by him to represent indefinitely any Number or Quantity, so circumstanced as the occasion required. And accordingly, the accommodation of Arithmetical Operations to Numbers or other Quantities thus designed by *Symbols* or *Species,* was called *Arithmetica Speciosa* or *Specious Arithmetic;* the word *Species* signifying what we otherwise call *Notes, Marks, Symbols,* or *Characters,* made use of for the compendious expressing or designating of Numbers or other Quantities.[29]

The Latin word "species" itself communicates the convergence of legal and mathematical terminology since Viète adopts it to translate—as was standard practice in medieval translations of Aristotle—the Greek *eidos,* which Diophantine arithmetic used when speaking of the sign for the unknown in an algebraic equation. *Eidos* in these instances refers to species not as the contrasting term to genus (as Aristotle tends to use the word in his biological works) but denotes rather the *form* predicated of the matter of which a substance is composed (corresponding to Aristotle's metaphysical usage). In Roman and Civil law, too, "species" had at least two different senses. It could mean "an individual thing, to be distinguished from *genus* = a kind, sort of things, with common qualities . . . [and was] also used of a specific legal problem submitted for a decision or discussion." In connection with legal institutions, however, "*species* mean[t] the legal form in which the act was performed."[30] Wallis himself stresses the latter sense: Just as a particular letter in algebra denotes a multitude or magnitude in its formal quality as number or quantity in an equation of a certain type ("so circumstanced as the occasion required"), so too does the letter of the law denote an individual in his or her formal quality of personhood in a certain legal situation ("to represent indefinitely, any person in such circumstances").

While Wallis seeks a clear distinction between the individual *qua* individual and the individual as standing in for all individuals in a similar situation, both the Aristotelian *eidos* and legal *species* preserve the tension between token and type. In *Merchant,* this implicit duality becomes apparent, for instance, when Salerio expresses his disbelief that Shylock would seek to hold Antonio to the terms of the bond: "I am sure if he forfeit thou wilt not take his flesh. What's that good for?" Shylock's reply—"To bait fish withal"—takes up the terms of Salerio's question by treating the flesh as material substance that can be put to use. But he replies, too, to the question behind Salerio's question—"what use is killing Antonio?"—with "what good is taking his life?" In response, Shylock offers another use: "If it will feed nothing else, it will feed my revenge" (see 3.1.42ff). The flesh is always thought of as something concrete, but its concreteness is also always a placeholder, substituting for or standing for something else: life. In the trial scene, too, Shylock's legal process stumbles when Portia remakes the facts in the case by producing anew the thing at its heart, revealing the unexpected gap between the pound of flesh he (thinks he) has demanded and what the legal process retroactively determines that thing to be. This reversal suggests a constitutive tension inhering in the very relationship between material things and the legal causes, resulting in things themselves moving between what they "are" and what they "stand for."

Such an ambiguity already inheres in the numerical logistics to which Viète's symbolic algebra was to give a decisive turn. Even in early algebras such as Gerolamo Cardano's 1545 *Ars magna,* which used actual numbers to designate the given or known coefficients in an equation, the algorithm leading to a fixed numerical value for the unknown *res* was thought of as being *generally* applicable, regardless of the actual numbers in the equation being analyzed. Hence, while the specific numbers were actual multitudes, they also stood or substituted for actual multitudes (in the sense of pointing to processes that would hold true for any multitudes chosen).

With Viète's "specious arithmetic," this implicit distinction is made explicit by separating mathematical form from its numerical instantiation. But in so doing, Viète's symbolic method crucially sidesteps the question of what *species* are. While the *species* stand for numbers and are manipulated as if they were numbers, the ontology of the numbers being represented is a matter of indifference, since the very idea of number has (in principle at least) been generalized to include different kinds of numbers—be they geometrical magnitudes, integers, real numbers, and so on. The "actual multitudes" to which the symbols refer is specified by the situation that the equation is designed to represent. If the problem concerns the arrangement of an army, then the numbers represent individual soldiers; if the division of a mercantile partnership, then money, and so on. What a number *is* depends, then, upon producing the algebraic form appropriate to a given situation (namely, the right kind of equation), and upon applying it to the "facts" of the situation as they are taken up within that equation. *The Merchant of Venice* projects a similar relationship between the *species* of legal actions and the determination of intentions in a particular legal situation. But to follow this algebraic logic through to its conclusion, we need to look more closely at the play's final judgment: Portia's verdict in the case of the missing rings.

THE RING'S THE THING

> Well, while I live I'll fear no other thing
> So sore as keeping safe Nerissa's ring. (5.1.324–25)

The ring as the symbol for the algebraic thing is neatly expressed by Gratiano's bawdy rhyme that closes *The Merchant of Venice*. But before the play can end, the whereabouts of the ring must be ascertained, another legal dispute resolved. In the event, Portia's return home first produces a remarkable avian proportionality:

> The crow doth sing as sweetly as the lark
> When neither is attended; and I think
> The nightingale, if she should sing by day
> When every goose is cackling, would be thought
> No better musician than the wren. (5.1.109–13)

To indulge in Euclid-talk, we might redescribe the lines thus: Crow : Lark as Nightingale : Wren. The simplicity of the structure is complicated, however, by the negations that run through it, qualifying each of the terms. The somewhat vertiginous quality of Portia's ruminations marks the increasingly unstable boundary between things as they are and things as they are when surrounded by other things. Leah Marcus's edition helpfully glosses Portia's sententious preamble to this analogy—"Nothing is good, I see, without respect" (5.1.106)—as nothing is good "except in relation to things around it." True, but this relation is as much one of perspective as one concerning the nature of things. After all, etymologically, to respect is to see again, to look at things anew, to respecify their nature. And the return to Belmont is entirely about the difference that context seems to produce within (and with respect to) things. At such moments, it seems, things are not what they are.

And neither are identities, intentions, and desires. When Bassanio swears his fidelity to Portia "even by thine own fair eyes, / Wherein I see myself," Portia pounces upon his utterance by exposing its inherent duplicity: "Mark you but that! / In both my eyes he doubly sees himself, / In each eye one" (5.1.255ff). People, too, are internally divided, both themselves and other. Portia's ring expresses the play's double-dealing. On the one hand, as a thing that stands for or seals a contractual obligation, it harks back to the roots of contracts in Roman law. As Adolf Berger's *Dictionary* tells us, the ring or *anulus* was connected to "the old Roman custom that freeborn men wore rings *signandi causa*, i.e., for sealing written instruments they made or witnessed." This custom leads to its connection with the legal *symbolum*, defined as "[a] sign of recognition (e.g., a ring = *anulus*), a proof of authorization (a document provided with a seal). A messenger or creditor had to prove by a *symbolum* to the debtor that he was authorized to receive payment."[31] In the casket scene, Portia herself uses the ring as a proof of authorization in telling Bassanio: "and even now, but now, / This house, these servants, and this same myself / Are yours, my lord's. I give them with this ring" (3.2.172–74).

On the other hand, Portia's immediate qualification of her gift also shifts the ring's mode of symbolization toward Viète's appropriation of the legal *symbolum* to denote algebraic symbolization. Rather than simply stopping with the gift of the ring, she continues to specify its significance: "which, when you part from, lose, or give away, / Let it presage the ruin of your love, / And be vantage to exclaim on you" (3.2.175–77). Bassanio accedes to these supplemental terms: "But when this ring / Parts from this finger, then parts life from hence. / O, then be bold to say Bassanio's dead" (3.2.186–88). If in the first instance the ring acts as *quid* for a transaction in *re*—the transfer of house, servants, herself—here the ring acts as consideration for an executory promise, namely, that Bassanio will refrain from acting in such and such a way in the future or face the consequences.[32] Thus, in addition to authorizing the material transfer of things, the ring symbolizes, too, the future promise or intention that is imported by the transaction.

But the ring's symbolic function has consequences. For Bassanio and Gratiano at the play's close, this means that the actual circumstances and considerations that led them to their breach of faith cannot—as Renaissance lawyers might put it—be traversed; that is, these cannot be entered into as facts material to the case. Thus, neither Gratiano's claim that the ring was of negligible material value—"a paltry ring / . . . whose posy was / . . . like cutler's poesy / Upon a knife" (5.1.159–61)—nor Bassanio's detailing the psychology of his obligation—"to whom," "for whom," "for what," and "how unwillingly I left the ring" (5.1.206ff)—are accepted by Nerissa and Portia as having any bearing on the issue at hand. The agreement symbolized by the rings attaches no consequence to motivations and intentional causes *except* insofar as they have led to the promises being broken. The only fact admitted as material is that, as Bassanio is constrained to admit, "my finger / Hath not a ring upon it. It is gone" (5.1.199–200). As Portia tells Gratiano, he is to blame for having parted with his wife's gift, "[a] thing stuck on with oaths upon your finger, / And so riveted with faith unto your flesh" (5.1.179–80).

Facts that can be pleaded are brought together here with the facts that can be established, and willy-nilly intentions and actions follow these facts. The absence of the rings places Bassanio and Gratiano in breach of faith, whatever their original justifications might have been. And Portia has no hesitation in imputing intentions that are quite contrary to those that Bassanio had had: "I'll die for't, but some woman had the ring." Nor does she hesitate in awarding herself the damages: "Let not that doctor come near my house. / . . . / I will become as liberal as you. / I will not deny him anything I have—/ No, not my body nor my husband's bed!" (5.1.236ff). Rather than the ring representing an already given intention, it expresses the status of intention as potentially determinable, its actual determination depending not upon the invisible interiority of the person but upon the facts as they are established in the case at hand. Who Bassanio is depends only upon the *species* of action and the only fact of legal relevance (the absence of the ring). As is true for Viète's conception of an unknown, personhood is simply the "x" that the legal equation solves for.

It is curious, then, that this situation is resolved by Antonio's being bound again, swearing his "soul upon the forfeit, that your lord / Will never more break faith advisedly" (5.1.267–68). This would seem a return to a world where a defendant can wage his law, relying upon oath takers who vouch for his probity. Indeed, this scene is full of oaths and swearing. Even as she sets Bassanio up, Portia herself turns compurgator:

> I gave my love a ring and made him swear
> Never to part with it; and here he stands.
> I dare be sworn for him he would not leave it. (5.1.181–83)

Tellingly, Portia does not return the ring herself. Instead, she asks Antonio, as Bassanio's "surety," to "give him this / And bid him keep it better than the other" (5.1.269–70). That resolving the conflict requires the oath of a third party signals the importance, Jill Ingram notes, of Bassanio's testing as a *public* one. At stake in the dispute and its settlement is the renegotiation of trust. And to this end Portia redirects the agonistic mechanism of the law displayed in the trial scene in order to re-create a form of "communal trust."[33] Her endeavor takes shape as a new arrangement of people and things, which nonetheless clothes itself in the vestments of an older covenant: Portia repeatedly invokes the older dispensation of the wager of law (linked to debt actions), which culminates in her gifting herself anew, with the ring that Antonio returns to Bassanio. However, the ostensible return takes place under changed conditions that rearticulate the bases of trust: This trial extracts from Bassanio the public concession of Portia's manhood (and thus of her formal equivalence to him): "Sweet doctor, you shall be my bedfellow. / When I am absent then lie with my wife" (5.1.300–1).

From this perspective, Shylock's original bond can also be understood as a means of renegotiating his relationship to Antonio, and to the Christian world of Venice more generally. He seeks to bridge the gap between his resentment of Antonio—on grounds mercantile, religious, and personal—and the need to establish trust (by gaining Antonio's "favor").[34] On the one hand, then, he demands the pound of flesh as forfeit, and on the other, offers an interest-free loan that seems almost certain to be repaid, and these unlikely bedfellows are bound together in a single contract. When Antonio responds by saying "there is much kindness in the Jew," his intended irony implicitly acknowledges the possibility that Shylock and he may be, against all appearances, of the same *kind*. This possibility will later be echoed in the question with which Balthasar/Portia opens the trial: "Which is the merchant here and which the Jew?" If the earlier attempt at renegotiation breaks down ultimately, it is at least in part because a theft intervenes: of daughter, of jewels, and of another ring that Shylock himself would not have sold "for a wilderness of monkeys" (3.1.104).

CONCLUSION

As noted earlier, rectificatory justice in Aristotle's *Nicomachean Ethics* tightly coupled the formal equality of persons before the law in general with their actual inequality before the law in a particular situation. The legal process aimed at restoring equality. The central principle of Germanic law, which lay at the heart of English common law, was also rectificatory, since its different forms of action rested upon the nature of the relief sought; the two main writs of debt and trespass grew out of differing characterizations of what ought to be restored to an injured party to settle a dispute (specific relief versus compensation). But such "arithmetical" judgments in common law seeking a return to a *status quo ante* were—unlike in Aristotle—precisely judgments about *status*, about whom or what persons were. Hence, the compurgators' oaths in the wager of law attested not to the truth about the actual claim made by a defendant, but to his veracity: Because he is the kind of person whose word is generally to be believed, this particular claim should also be believed. (This sense is conveyed by the conditional in Portia's mock compurgation: "I dare be sworn for him, he *would* not leave it.") The facts of the defendant's case were thereby made to depend upon the status of the person asserting them. Restoring formal equality before the law meant reinstating the difference between them as (social) beings—one is believable, the other not. And in this sense, intentions were not treated as subjective or private but were instead absorbed into a person's objective status, to which the oath takers bore witness.

If we take a long view across the sixteenth and seventeenth centuries, the gradual transformation in how personhood was conceived involved the extraction and externalization of intention as a legal category. Already, with the fourteenth-century doctrine of *quid pro quo,* there had emerged the crucial principle that a determinate but unknown *causa* had to be represented by a material *res.* Only through such representation could intention emerge into the public space of the courtroom. But the sixteenth and seventeenth centuries further set in motion the process of separating the *species* or form of intention from the specification of its actual content. The logical end point is the treatment of intentional "content" as something retroactively produced via things and material facts; their determination in a specific legal situation allows one to "fill" the empty slot in an intentional structure. Personhood is posited thereby as an "x" that is always only potentially determinate. In the domains of both contract and criminal law, the legal process no longer seeks to subordinate intention to the status of the person, or to reveal a given but as yet unknown intention that is privy to the person. Instead, privacy is itself construed as the ascription to a person of a *formal* intention, which acquires its concrete manifestation as individual will or voluntariness only when a trial or a set of actions specifies the actual natures of things and material facts.[35]

The long, intertwined histories of the diverse words used to denote (and to distinguish among) different spheres of social life—such as "republic" (from the Latin *res publica* or public things), "*publicum,*" "commonwealth," "property," "propriety," "privy," and so on—remind us of the complexity of the processes that brought the recognizably modern domains of privacy and publicity into being. Their histories emphasize, too, the impossibility of conceiving publics without correlate notions of personhood and the private. That literature and law played important parts in this mutual determination seems an unexceptional claim: They visibly fashion public spaces of participation (courtrooms and theaters, for example) along with permissible modes of individual participation (for example, as plaintiffs and defendants, witnesses and audiences). But to unfold the implications of such constructions, it is necessary to cast our nets much wider, and to consider their close relationship—especially in the early modern period—to the mathematical discourses and forms of knowledge that were reshaping the world. And here, as I suggest, the abstract, relational, and transactional identities projected by mathematics were central for the emergence of new forms of public life. Modern republics would be built on unknown things.

Perhaps, then, the unknown *cosa,* the "x" that troubles Antonio in the play's opening scene, is impossible to specify not because it is something hidden so deep that it is impossible to uproot. Its unknowability may mark instead the very constitution of that thing, that is, of "privacy" itself as an indeterminacy that is always only made determinate. If so, it is no surprise that Antonio cannot truly "know" himself—from this point on, nobody would. People had long been arithmetical; they must now become algebraic.

NOTES

1. My thanks to Diana Henderson and Paul Yachnin for their numerous constructive suggestions and comments.
2. See Jürgen Habermas, *The Structural Transformation of the Public Sphere* (Cambridge, MA: MIT Press, 1989), 30.
3. Science has often been noted as an important omission in Habermas's influential work. See, for example, David Zaret, "Religion, Science, and Printing in the Public Spheres in Seventeenth-Century England," in *Habermas and the Public Sphere*, ed. Craig Calhoun, (Cambridge, MA: MIT Press, 1992), 212–35.
4. Habermas, *Structural Transformation*, 7.
5. Ibid., 18.
6. Ibid., 30.
7. William Shakespeare, *The Merchant of Venice*, ed. Leah S. Marcus (New York: Norton, 2006). I indicate subsequent citations by act, scene, and line number in the body of the essay.
8. John Wallis, *Treatise of Algebra* (London: 1685), 3. I lightly modernize the quotations from his book.
9. See Pietro Antonio Cataldi, *Algebra discorsiva, numerale et lineale* (Bologna: 1618), 5. One can multiply such instances indefinitely.
10. Wallis, *Algebra*, 2.
11. Ibid.
12. I cite Jacob Klein's translation of the Latin text edited by F. van Schooten in *Francisi Vietae Opera Mathematica* (Leiden, 1646), 1–12. The translation is appended to Klein's *Greek Mathematical Thought and the Origin of Algebra* (New York: Dover, 1968), 320.
13. Ibid., 339.
14. Klein's emphasis. Ibid., 166.
15. On Portia's "conversion," see Karen Newman, "Portia's Ring and Structures of Exchange in *The Merchant of Venice*," *Shakespeare Quarterly* 38 (1987): 19–33.
16. He likewise develops signs that stand for the unknown raised to the second and third powers, as well as a sign (an inverted psi) to indicate subtraction (Diophantus's term is *lepsis*, meaning "negation" or "wanting"). The standard translation of (and commentary on) Diophantus's text is Thomas L. Heath, *Diophantus of Alexandria: A Study in the History of Greek Algebra*, 2nd ed. (Cambridge: Cambridge University Press, 1910), esp. 33 and 39–41. Paul Tannery, *La géométrie grecque* (Hildesheim: Georg Olms, 1988).
17. Klein, *Greek Mathematical Thought*, 47.
18. Heath, *Diophantus*, 53.
19. Ibid., 36.
20. See Michael Sean Mahoney, *The Mathematical Career of Pierre de Fermat (1601–1665)* (Princeton, NJ: Princeton University Press, 1973), 35–36.
21. Aristotle, *The Nicomachean Ethics*, trans. David Ross (Oxford: Oxford University Press, 1980), 115.
22. Ibid., 112.
23. Ibid., 113.

24. Robert Recorde, *The Pathway to Knowledge* (London, 1551), t1v.

25. Robert Recorde, *The Whetstone of Witte* (London, 1557), b1v–b2r.

26. For instance, Euclid uses the term *alternando* to indicate—as Aristotle does in his discussion of geometric proportionality—the procedure of "taking antecedents in relation to antecedents, and consequents in relation to consequents." Euclid, *The Elements*, trans. Sir Thomas L. Heath (New York: Dover, 1956), 2: 114.

27. Viète, *Analytical Art*, in Klein, *Greek Mathematical Thought*, 324.

28. The Torporley connection is summarized in Jacqueline Stedall's introduction to her collation and translation of Hariot's algebraic manuscripts: Jacqueline Stedall, *The Greate Invention of Algebra: Thomas Hariot's Treatise on Equations* (Oxford: Oxford University Press, 2003).

29. Wallis, *Algebra*, 66.

30. Adolf Berger, *Encyclopedic Dictionary of Roman Law*, in *Transactions of the American Philosophical Society*, new series, 43.2 (1953): 712.

31. Berger, *Dictionary*, 364, 727.

32. David Harris Sacks offers an excellent account of how the legal notion of consideration developed: David Harris Sacks, "Promise and Contract in Early Modern England: Slade's Case in Perspective," in *Law and Rhetoric in Early Modern Europe*, ed. Victoria Kahn and Lorna Hutson (New Haven, CT: Yale University Press, 2001), 41ff.

33. Jill Phillips Ingram, *Idioms of Self-Interest: Credit, Identity, and Property in English Renaissance Literature* (London: Routledge, 2008), 115.

34. For a different reading of this renegotiation, see Charles Spinosa's "The Transformation of Intentionality: Debt and Contract in *The Merchant of Venice*," *English Literary Renaissance* 24, no. 2 (1994): 392–97.

35. See Luke Wilson, *Theaters of Intention: Drama and Law in Early Modern England* (Stanford, CA: Stanford University Press, 2000), 43–50.

Publics
A Bibliographic Afterword

Yael Margalit

Broadly conceived, the bibliographic context for this volume extends back to Aristotle's *Politics,* for it was there that the philosopher stated, "Only a beast or a god would live outside the *polis*" (1253a 27–29). A considerable swath of bibliographic history separates Aristotle's polis from this volume's conception of publics, yet the two ideas are linked. Given the Renaissance commonplace that the classical past has intellectual authority in explaining and understanding the present, the recourse to Aristotle would seem appropriate. There is also a sense, however, that publics were forward-looking, as they in some ways anticipate the social formations that took a more institutional shape in the eighteenth century and persist today. The Janus-faced nature of early modern publics indeed fostered a productive tension between the tenacious voices of the ancient past and sixteenth- and seventeenth-century encounters with new ideas, places, objects, and technologies. As the concept of early modern publics has its basis in a vast period of history—not to mention a reticular network of people, things, and forms of knowledge—the bibliographic contexts for this volume's contributions are themselves diverse. I will preface this account of the diverse public-making catalysts that operated in the early modern period—print culture, different modes representation (music, pictorial images, literature, and performance), religion, the production and circulation of objects, science, comportment, and rhetoric—with a brief comment on the contexts for the concept of plural publics.

Aristotle's definition of the human as an essentially political animal in the *Politics* and political philosophers' subsequent work on sociability, self-organization, civil society, public office, and public opinion are relevant to the work in this volume. It is worth exploring the bibliographic history of these themes, in part to show the limitations of concepts that often presume the existence of a unified and institutionalized social entity. The social formations under consideration in this volume—the loosely organized, dynamic, and individuated *publics*—recall the identity-conferring, social capacity of Aristotle's polis. Both publics and the classical polis provide individuals with a larger and ultimately more influential, more far-reaching platform upon which to associate with others. Whereas the idealized membership of the classical polis is rather general (that is, as a mortal human or a politically viable citizen), the membership of publics is more idiosyncratic, which is to say more invested with what Aristotle would likely have regarded as *private* content. This volume in many cases addresses the social and public relevance of private, individual thought, which is one feature of the early modern public that sets it apart from the Aristotle's polis.

David Sacks observes in Chapter 9 that the commonwealth ideals of republican Rome and medieval Europe differed rather significantly from the plural forms of public life that emerged in the early modern period. As Bronwen Wilson and Paul Yachnin discuss at the outset of this volume, it was Jürgen Habermas who described the emergence of a public sphere comprised of private, opining individuals as an eighteenth-century (and notably English) phenomenon. A number of contributors in this volume note that the plurality of early modern publics differs from the unified, monolithic concept of the bourgeois public sphere that Habermas identifies as a late seventeenth-century and more enduringly eighteenth-century phenomenon, in both its chronological origination and its philosophical content. Habermas's project is indeed occupied with such eighteenth-century concerns as the democratic exercise of instrumental reason, the role of government, the political implications of individual autonomy, and the role and formation of public opinion. The rash of late seventeenth- and early eighteenth-century works (not to mention the succeeding nineteenth-century ideas of Hegel and Marx) that addresses these topics—Thomas Hobbes's *Leviathan* (1651), John Locke's *Two Treatises of Government* (1690), David Hume's *A Treatise of Human Nature* (c. 1740) and his *Essays and Political Discourses* (c. 1752), baron of Montesquieu's *On the Spirit of the* Laws (1748), Adam Smith's *Theory of Moral Sentiments* (1759), Jean-Jacques Rousseau's *The Social Contract, Or Principles of Political Right* (1762), Immanuel Kant's *What Is Enlightenment?* (1784)—do not enter explicitly into the chapters of this volume, but they are enfolded into the problematic touchstone that is Habermas's concept of the public sphere. Thus reflections on the classical polis and the work in eighteenth-century political thought in a sense bookend the *Making Publics* volume, although most contributors probably would not regard these contexts as constraints on their thinking. The early modern publics' orientation toward the past and the future is indeed embedded in an early modern culture that was at once beholden to antiquity and advancing new forms of knowledge and ideas.

The contributions in this volume share with Habermas's notion of the public sphere, and even Aristotle's concept of the polis, the claim that public life has its basis in an idea, an imaginary or virtual dimension: a polis, the public sphere, or publics are defined by their anonymous membership and by their potentially unbounded nature. A number of recent political theorists have addressed the imaginary, virtual, and creative dimensions of public and political entities. Significant works on the thought content of social life include Cornelius Castoriadis's *The Imaginary Institution of Society* (1975), Benedict Anderson's book on nationalism, *Imagined Communities (1991),* and Charles Taylor's *Modern Social Imaginaries* (2004). These works, however, are more concerned with the emergence of political institutions and ideas such as democracy or nationalism than the agency of culture. Steven Mullaney, Angela Vanhaelen, and Joe Ward's essay on the Dutch house church (Chapter 1), as well as Yachnin's essay on the "social thing" created by the play *Hamlet* (Chapter 2), draw on theoretical contexts that discuss publics in terms of their cultural rather than political agency. Of particular relevance to both essays is Michael Warner's *Publics and Counterpublics,* especially his discussion of the "poetic world making" capacity of a public.[1] Craig Calhoun's essay, "Imagining Solidarity: Cosmopolitanism, Constitutional Patriotism, and the Public Sphere," also remarks that public making is a creative endeavor, as new "ways of imagining identity, interests, and solidarity make possible new material forms of social relations."[2] The imaginary and intellectual dimension of public making of course contributed to and was in turn conditioned by pivotal material developments in technology, chiefly in the invention of the printing press.

PUBLICS AND PUBLICATION

More than half of the essays in this volume deal explicitly with the relationship between a burgeoning sixteenth- and seventeenth-century print culture and the formation of publics. The growth and identity of some publics studied in this volume depend more peripherally on print than others, but in most cases the technology of print had a direct role in the constitution of publics. Antoine de Marcourt's religious pamphlets (Chapter 2), the manuscripts that some participants in French salons eventually chose to publish (Chapter 3), Aretino's and Nashe's satirical work (Chapter 4), the many editions and textual afterlife of *Hamlet* (Chapter 5), Petrucci's motet prints (Chapter 6), the prints among the commonplace books and albums produced by the herald painters Randle Holme and his son (Chapter 7), the printed gores of globes and their treatises (Chapter 8), Richard Hakluyt's travel narratives (Chapter 9), courtesy books and physiognomy treatises (Chapter 10), and English poetry heavy with melancholy (Chapter 11): all of these were public-making artifacts. In each case, the printed text's capacity for widespread dissemination helped to cultivate new forms of association, many of which were based on personal taste, interest, and belief.

Others have written about the cultural changes (or "structural transformation," in Habermas's terminology) heralded by print. For a general account of the radical effect of print on society and culture, see Elizabeth L. Eisenstein's *The Printing Revolution in Early Modern Europe.* "Publishing the Private," Chapter 2 of Michael McKeon's *The Secret History of Domesticity: Public, Private, and the Division of Knowledge,* addresses the role of print in the expression of inwardness and interiority, a topic covered here by Michael D. Bristol (Chapter 11) and Wilson (Chapter 10). For a discussion of the political, economic, and ultimately public-making effects of print capitalism, see David Zaret's *Origins of Democratic Culture: Printing, Petitions, and the Public Sphere in Early-Modern England,* Alexandra Halasz's *The Marketplace of Print: Pamphlets and the Public Sphere in Early Modern England,* and Craig E. Harline's *Pamphlets, Printing, and Political Culture in the Early Dutch Republic.* There are also bodies of work devoted to the effect print had on modes of representation that were not literary, such as music, the pictorial image, and performance. Tessa Watt's *Cheap Print and Popular Piety,* for example, discusses the increasing musical and visual literacy created by the widespread circulation of ballad broadsides and woodcuts featuring popular iconography. Some modes of representation, however, required more specialized knowledge than others. In *Print Culture and Music in Sixteenth-Century Venice,* Jane A. Bernstein argues that music printing appealed to a rarefied niche market, a claim that Julie Cumming gently challenges in this volume (Chapter 6). The anthology *Music and the Cultures of Print,* edited by Kate van Orden, includes a section on "Music in the Public Sphere." Also relevant to the print culture of music is Harold Love's article "How Music Created a Public," although it focuses on the eighteenth century. In Chapter 7 of this volume, Robert Tittler and Anne Thackray discuss the public-making capacity of printed images, some of which had a vernacular origin and some of which were based on continental conventions. For more discussion on the intracontinental traffic in printed images, see Anthony Wells-Cole's *Art and Decoration in Elizabethan and Jacobean England: The Influence of Continental Prints, 1558–1625.* Although his consideration of visual culture has less to do with print than it does other media, Tittler's book *The Face of the City: Civic Portraiture and Civic Identity in Early Modern England* is a good source on the autonomous emergence of English forms of association, forms expressed in the vernacular, artisanal production of civic portraiture. For a related consideration of the relationship between printed images, a sense of the world, and a sense of the self, see Wilson's *The World in Venice: Print, the City, and Early Modern Identity.*

LITERATURE, THEATRICAL PERFORMANCE, AND AESTHETIC VALUE

A number of the publics discussed in this volume deal with literary or theatrical forms of association and publication. Yachnin (Chapter 5) and Shankar Raman (Chapter 12), for example, discuss Shakespeare's drama as a site of public making. François Rouget (Chapter 3), Wes Folkerth (Chapter 5), and Michael Bristol (Chapter 11) discuss publics that were distinctly literary. The work of philosophers of art who stress the collaborative creation and transmission of aesthetic value might be of relevance where theatrical and literary publics are concerned, not to mention the publics that formed around musical works and portraiture (as in Chapters 6 and 7). Such work on the collaborative production of aesthetic value includes Michael Baxandall's *Patterns of Intention,* Gregory Currie's "Imagination and Make-Believe," Howard Becker's *Art Worlds,* and Arthur Danto's *The Transfiguration of the Commonplace.* For a more explicit discussion of the limited application of Habermasian ideas about the public sphere and communicative action to theories of aesthetic value, see Pieter Duvenage's *Habermas and Aesthetics.*

As the emergence of print is a key variable in the formation of theatrical and literary publics, historiographical work on print culture has relevance here, especially where such work takes into account the combined aesthetic and social effect of print. This is not to say, however, that there was a strict dichotomy of print as public and manuscript as private; on the contrary, print and manuscript cultures overlapped in terms of public formation. Print could in fact be a more conservative, limiting medium than manuscript because fixed printed texts were often directed at specific groups while manuscripts might be even more widely circulated through public readings and performances. For more information about the overlap of print and manuscript cultures, see Brian Richardson's *Print Culture in Renaissance Italy: The Editor and the Vernacular Text 1400–1600* and *Printers, Writers, and Readers in Renaissance Italy,* especially Chapter 4, "From Pen to Print: Writers and Their Use of the Press." The public dimensions of performance and print, as well as the public and private signification of manuscript, are also addressed in the anthology of essays edited by Arthur E. Marrotti and Michael D. Bristol, *Print, Manuscript, and Performance: The Changing Relations of the Media in Early Modern England.* William B. Worthen also addresses the dialectic between print and performance in *Shakespeare and the Authority of Performance.* In *Shakespeare and the Book,* particularly in the chapter "From Playhouse to Printing House; Or, Making a Good Impression," David Scott Kastan considers the formation of Shakespeare's reading public in light of his claim that text and performance are "dissimilar and discontinuous modes of production."[3] With attention to popular seventeenth-century entertainments such as street pageants and the work of Augustan women's writing, Paula R. Backscheider argues in *Spectacular Politics: Theatrical Power and Mass Culture in Early Modern England* that a political public coalesced around a distinctly theatrical and literary culture.

Rouget's chapter in this volume on the "literary public sphere" shows that some forms of early modern association indeed grew from smaller, more elite coteries to associations with a more expansive membership and a more far-reaching influence. For more discussion of the ultimately public aspect of the French salon, see Elizabeth C. Goldsmith and Dena Goodman's anthology *Going Public: Women and Publishing in Early Modern*

France, Julie D. Campbell's *Literary Circles and Gender in Early Modern Europe: A Cross-Cultural Approach*, and Faith E. Beasley's *Salons, History, and the Creation of Seventeenth-Century France*. The individual writer's particular position and identity vis-à-vis the collective formation of the literary public is also a germane topic here. For more attention to the public persona of the literary author, see Kevin Pask's *The Emergence of the English Author*, in the last chapter of which Pask discusses how the private life of a poet takes on public significance.

RELIGION

The relationship between individual and collective life, of private self-examination and public expression and ritual, is also at stake in the discourse and conflict created by early modern religion. The commonplace perception of a binary of Catholicism as a public practice and Protestantism as a private one (or, conversely, of a binary of Catholicism as authoritarian and hierarchical and Protestantism as egalitarian and vernacular) has been challenged by a number of authors. The chapters on religious publics in this volume, namely, Chapters 1 and 2, show how publics that form around religious ideas are in fact difficult to pin down in terms of their membership, interests, and relationship to hegemonic parts of the culture. Revision of the reductive binaries of public and private in the history of early modern religion is taken up in Ramie Targoff's *Common Prayer: The Language of Public Devotion in Early Modern England* and Wim Janse and Barbara Pitkin's anthology *The Formation of Clerical and Confessional Identities in Early Modern Europe*. Mullaney, Vanhaelen, and Ward's essay in this volume (Chapter 1) also resists a reductive account of early modern religion, as it describes the rather complex public of the huiskerk (house church) that "occupied a paradoxical place in Dutch society." The chapter shows that forms of social association can emerge from attitudes of dissent and difference, and not just from the Habermasian paradigm of reason and consensus building. Likewise, in a response to the claim that the Reformation was a fundamentally divisive movement, Gregory Hanlon's *Confession and Community in Seventeenth-Century France* suggests that interactions between Catholics and Protestants, when fostered by attitudes of tolerance, in fact created new forms of sociability and community. In *Faith on the Margins: Catholics and Catholicism in the Dutch Golden Age*, Charles H. Parker points out that the Dutch Counter-Reformation was met with violence, but also with "interludes of concord," which contributed "to a way of ordering religious difference and maintaining public unity in a pluralistic environment."[4] For additional material on the public-making role of Dutch tolerance and dissent, see Benjamin J. Kaplan's "Fictions of Privacy: House Chapels and the Spatial Accommodation of Religious Dissent in Early Modern Europe" and Ronnie Pop-chia Hsia and Henk F. K. van Nierop's anthology *Calvinism and Religious Toleration in the Dutch Golden Age*.

The public under discussion in Chapter 1 of this volume is unique in that its formation is only indirectly related to print culture. Other religious publics, such as the one identified by Torrance Kirby in Chapter 2, relied more crucially on the production and circulation of printed material. Indeed, as many religious historians have observed, the Reformation and its subsequent forms of affiliation were made possible by the printing press. For a discussion of the relationship between print and the Reformation, see Mark E. Edwards's *Printing, Propaganda, and Martin Luther,* Jean-François Gilmont's *The Reformation and the Book,* Francis Higman's collected essays *Lire et découvrir: la circulation des idées au temps de la réforme,* and both Andrew Pettegree's article "French Books at the Frankfurt Fair" and his book *Reformation and the Culture of Persuasion.* In the article "Religion, Science, and Printing in the Public Spheres in Seventeenth-Century England" and later in a more sustained study, *Origins of Democratic Culture: Printing Petitions, and the Public Sphere in Early-Modern England,* David Zaret argues that seventeenth-century centrist thinkers forged the "social authority of public opinion" by promoting the view that religion and reason were compatible.[5] The conclusions of Zaret's and Kirby's arguments are slightly different, as Zaret is more explicitly forward-looking in the connection he draws between modern democracy and the Reformation, but notably both Zaret and Kirby identify print culture and its participants (in Kirby's view, the propagandists, printers, and publishers) as key figures in the formation of public opinion.

PRODUCTION AND CIRCULATION OF OBJECTS

Printing was one mode of artisanal and increasingly entrepreneurial production, but there were others, as Tittler and Thackray demonstrate in Chapter 7, where they discuss the *Holme Album,* which included not just prints, but drawings as well. Tittler and Thackray suggest that the vernacular tradition of regional portraiture might have emerged in part from consultation of the *Holme Album.* Thus objects—and not just printed texts and ideas—have a rather prominent role in the formation of the public that Tittler and Thackray describe. Similarly, the globe is at the center of Lesley Cormack's inquiry in Chapter 8. The association of mathematicians, cartographers, engravers, geographers, explorers, and astronomers who contributed to the globe's production was, for the most part, a network of individuals known to each other, but not entirely open to public participation. Nonetheless, the globe still has a high profile in what Cormack identifies as the more expansive public of *De globis* treatise writers. The circulation and prominence of the object is also relevant wherever artworks help to form networks within publics. This is to say that the materiality of objects, along with people and their ideas, have an important role in the formation of publics.

Circulated objects operate as forms of publicity, just as printed texts do, but they also have additional significance in creating social affiliations. In his work on *Hamlet*'s "social thing" (Chapter 5), Yachnin refers to Bruno Latour's extension of social agency to things in *Reassembling the Social: An Introduction to Actor-Network Theory*. Latour suggests that any entity—human or otherwise—that makes a difference to some other agent's action is itself an agent. Many early modernists recognize how objects were indeed often the sources of the interests and concerns that brought people together. For more discussion of how one might think about the mutual implication of subjects and objects in early modern history, see Bill Brown's essay "Thing Theory," Julian Yates's "What Are 'Things' Saying in Renaissance Studies?" and John Plotz's "Can the Sofa Speak? A Look at Thing Theory." The turn toward objects and materiality is also apparent in the anthologies *Subject and Object in Renaissance Culture*, edited by Margreta De Grazia, Maureen Quilligan, and Peter Stallybrass, and *Things That Talk: Object Lessons from Art and Science*, edited by Lorraine Daston.

SCIENTIFIC KNOWLEDGE

The particular relationship between the artisan and the object indeed played an important role in the forms of knowledge understood by contemporaries as scientific endeavors. In *The Body of the Artisan*, Pamela Smith shows that early modern science owed as much to the artisan's practices and production of things as it did to new ideas and methods generated by scholars. Whereas scholars might have had abstract, philosophical ideas about nature, artisans had hands-on, practical knowledge borne of interacting with and manipulating the natural world. Moreover, Smith argues, the artisan's knowledge played a key role in the formation of early modern science. Developments in mathematics, natural philosophy, navigation, and cartography play a crucial role in public making, as discussed in the essays by Cormack in Chapter 8, Sacks in Chapter 9, and Raman in Chapter 12. For more information about the early modern science that contributed to publics that formed around the production of globes, see Jerry Brotton's *Trading Territories: Mapping and the Early Modern World* as well as Brotton's "Terrestrial Globalism: Mapping the Globe in Early Modern Europe." Additional material about the public that formed around Richard Hakluyt's travel narratives, as described by Sacks in Chapter 8, can be found in David Livingstone's *The Geographical Tradition: Episodes in the History of a Contested Enterprise*, Joyce E. Chaplin's *Subject Matter: Technology, the Body, and Science on the Anglo-American Frontier, 1500–1676*, and Cormack's *Charting an Empire: Geography at the English Universities, 1580–1620*. The history of math with which Raman works in Chapter 12 is elaborated in Jacob Klein's *Greek Mathematical Thought and the Origins of Algebra*, which includes one of Raman's main primary sources—Francois Viète's *Introduction to the Analytic Art*— as an appendix. In *On the Shoulders of Merchants: Exchange and the Mathematical Conception of Nature in Early Modern Europe,* Richard Hadden asserts an historical connection between mercantile and mathematical assessments of value, a connection that proves central to Raman's argument in Chapter 12. For another discussion of the social relevance of the relationship between early mercantilism and empiricism, see Mary Poovey's *A History of the Modern Fact: Problems of Knowledge in the Sciences of Wealth and Society.*

While the particular fields discussed in the sources cited previously are indeed central to many of the publics featured in this volume, it is notable that in each case the public's forms of knowledge are characteristically diverse: in Cormack's case, the public of treatise writers would not have been possible without artisans, court geographers, mathematical practitioners, and others; in Sacks's chapter, both Francis Bacon's reflections on the growth of the sciences as well as Hakluyt's diverse network of patrons played a role in the formation of Hakluyt's public; and in Raman's chapter, the contingencies of mercantilism, new articulations of legal intention, and the algebraic concept of variables together contributed to a new concept of the public. Many historians and sociologists of science have discussed how early modern science was indeed a community-based enterprise. For more information about the collaborative, public-making basis of early modern science, see David S. Lux and Harold J. Cook's essay "Closed Circles or Open Networks? Communicating at a Distance during the Scientific Revolution," Mordechai Feingold's *The Mathematicians' Apprenticeship: Science, Universities and Society in England, 1560–1640,* Steven Shapin's *A Social History of Truth: Civility and Science in Seventeenth-Century England,* and the aforementioned *Reassembling the Social: An Introduction to Actor-Network-Theory,* by Latour.

COMPORTMENT AND RHETORIC

Whereas the previous sections of this bibliographic essay are about what is needed for people to come together to create a public, this section is about what is needed for people to recognize each other as belonging to the same public. Just as the scientific communities discussed earlier were established in part through social discourse and collaboration, so were other publics. The early modern occupation with how one should speak and act in certain situations is yet another important variable in the formation of publics. This topic raises an interesting duality at the heart of publics: a double emphasis on the core and periphery. Members of publics need something around which to congregate, but they also need something to define themselves against. A particular public's rules of comportment and conventions of rhetoric, for example, might reveal that publics can sometimes be exclusionary, that they can tell us that some members belong, while others do not.

The focus on the effect of rhetoric in public making occurs in Chapter 2, where Kirby discusses the culture of persuasion out of which Antoine de Marcourt's *Livre des marchans* grew, and in Chapter 4, where Folkerth points out that Aretino and Thomas Nashe shape their reading publics by altering their discourse, particularly their styles of address. In both cases, rhetoric was used to play upon how one imagined the community of which one was a part. Chapters 2 and 4 also demonstrate that rhetorically defined publics provide their members with a common sense of purpose, a purpose according to which one might organize one's actions. For more discussion of the relationship between imagined community and rhetoric, see Geoff Baldwin's "The 'Public' as a Rhetorical Community in Early Modern England." Jennifer Richards's *Rhetoric and Courtliness in Early Modern Literature* also addresses the rhetorical dimension of early modern forms of sociability, but with a particular inquiry into the role of conversation, manners, and codes of conduct. Richards argues that while the art of familiar conversation was promoted in such sixteenth-century works as Castiglione's *The Courtier,* social and political discourse remained apart, for there was a "perceived bifurcation in the late seventeenth century between the public and private spheres, between a sphere which encouraged negotiation among free, prudential and self-interested individuals and a sphere regarded as sentimental, feminine and outside public discourse."[6]

The current volume in some ways challenges Richards's claim about discrete spheres, especially in Chapters 10 and 11, where inwardness and selfhood take on public significance. Both Wilson's Chapter 10 and Bristol's Chapter 11 draw attention to the public expression of interiority, either through the representation of the face in social encounters (Chapter 10) or through the shades of melancholy expressed in early modern poetry (Chapter 11). In an argument that in some ways resembles Richards's in its focus on the social significance of conversation, Peter Miller's "Friendship and Conversation in Seventeenth-Century Venice" asserts that the private, intersubjective encounter that occurs in a friendship in fact helped to shape the early modern concept of "citizen," and thus produced a "third domain" of social life: civil society.[7] Wilson makes a similar argument about the interdependence of public expression and private selfhood, but with reference to Norbert Elias's sociological work *The Civilizing Process,* which suggests that individuals and collectivities or societies are indeed mutually constitutive. Wilson also draws on Harry Berger's *The Absence of Grace: Sprezzatura and Suspicion in Two Renaissance Courtesy Books,* where Berger shows that courtesy books serve in a paradoxical way to show an "exemplary inwardness" called for by the rhetorical situation of which such modes of representation were a part. In the same line of thinking, Bristol points out that displays of private, idiosyncratic melancholy were intended as exemplary, as signs to be interpreted by the particular speech community of which early modern poetry was a part. For more discussion of the public/ private paradox in shows of melancholy, see Juliana Schiesari's *The Gendering of Melancholia: Feminism, Psychoanalysis, and the Symbolics of Loss in Renaissance Literature* and Max Pensky's *Melancholy Dialectics: Walter Benjamin and the Play of Mourning.* A more general discussion on early modern inwardness, interiority, and subjectivity can be found in Michael Carl Schoenfeldt's *Bodies and Selves in Early Modern England: Physiology and Inwardness in Spenser, Shakespeare, Herbert, and Milton,* Katherine Eisaman Maus's *Inwardness and the Theater in the English Renaissance,* and Robert Cockcroft's *Rhetorical Affect in Early Modern Writing: Renaissance Passions Reconsidered.*

CONCLUSION: INTEGRATING KNOWLEDGE

The foregoing attention to rhetoric recalls some of the backward-looking aspects of publics: in the same way that early modern rhetoric had its main classical precedent in Aristotle's thought, the concept of publics stretches back to earlier, Aristotelian ideas about the polis and about the conditions that make sociability and ultimately politics possible. Rhetoric and politics—and in turn the early modern publics upon which this volume focuses—are similar in that they both make a virtue out of prudence, out of the deliberative thinking "about matters that are variable, indeterminate, or contingent."[8] In Eugene Garver's view in *Aristotle's Rhetoric: An Art of Character,* rhetoric can indeed be regarded "as a *civic* activity."[9] The persuasion of the rhetorician is thus as important as the deliberation—the prudence—of the rhetorician's audience. Early modern publics were thus formed as a rhetorical exercise in prudence, in the deliberation and judgment of individuals who exhibited a vast array of interests and tastes. The classical history of prudence bears on this volume's concept of publics, but so too do much more contemporary ideas about deliberative democracy and civil society. Thus the volume is also in some ways forward-looking, as where it suggests that early modern publics were precursors to a civil society in which rational debate—as well as expressive, passionate rhetoric—was foundational.

The forward- and backward-looking implications of the volume also speak to the multidisciplinary nature of early modern publics and of the early modern period generally. Early modern modes of representation, forms of knowledge, uses of space, and developments of technologies were usually not separable disciplines, which is to say that they formed in relation to each other rather than in isolation. Other scholars of the early modern period, many of whom refer to some of the same historical developments and figures discussed in this volume, make clear that an understanding of the period necessitates familiarity with a vast range of texts and discourses. Consider Peter C. Mancall's *Hakluyt's Promise: An*

Elizabethan's Obsession for an English America, where Mancall shows that Hakluyt's narrative strategies were as important as nautical science or the economics of imperialism. Elizabeth Spiller's *Science, Reading, and Renaissance Literature: The Art of Making Knowledge, 1580–1670* also shows that natural knowledge and literary art were considered to be a part of the same sphere of discourse. In Bronwen Price's anthology of essays, *Francis Bacon's New Atlantis,* the contributions have a disciplinary range that is as expansive as this volume's, for Francis Bacon's emerging public is best understood in the diverse terms of narrative context, rhetoric, developments in natural knowledge, theology, the politics of difference, and still other fields of experience and knowledge. Many of the publics discussed in this volume are made up of a motley crew of printers, artisans and artists, poets, conversationalists, actors, mathematical practitioners, huiskerkgoers, reading publics of different persuasions and levels of prudence, and so on. But at the same time that publics were loose affiliations with a diverse membership and an importantly notional or imaginary dimension, they also bore directly on such developments as the long afterlife of *Hamlet* (Chapter 5), the wide circulation of Petrucci's motets (Chapter 6), or the complex signification of faces (Chapter 10). This is to say that while early modern publics were entities in flux, entities in which change and invention were definitional, they also had a lasting—even transformative—effect on preexisting social entities.

NOTES

1. Michael Warner, *Publics and Counterpublics* (New York: Zone Books, 2002), 114.
2. Calhoun, "Imagining Solidarity: Cosmopolitanism, Constitutional Patriotism, and the Public Sphere," *Public Culture* 14, no. 1 (2002): 149.
3. David Scott Kastan, *Shakespeare and the Book* (Cambridge: Cambridge University Press, 2001), 7.
4. Charles H. Parker, *Faith on the Margins: Catholics and Catholicism in the Dutch Golden Age* (Cambridge, MA: Harvard University Press, 2008), 48.
5. David Zaret, *Origins of Democratic Culture: Printing Petitions, and the Public Sphere in Early-Modern England* (Princeton, NJ: Princeton University Press, 2000), 230.
6. Jennifer Richards, *Rhetoric and Courtliness in Early Modern Literature* (Cambridge: Cambridge University Press, 2003), 42.
7. Peter Miller, "Friendship and Conversation in Seventeenth-Century Venice," *Journal of Modern History* 73 (2001): 3.
8. James Jasinski, *Sourcebook on Rhetoric: Key Concepts in Contemporary Rhetorical Studies* (Thousand Oaks, CA: Sage, 2001), 463.
9. Eugene Garver, *Aristotle's Rhetoric: An Art of Character* (Chicago: University of Chicago Press, 1994), 79.

Contributors

Michael Bristol is Greenshields Professor of English Emeritus at McGill University. In addition to many articles and chapters, he is the author of *Carnival and Theater: Plebeian Culture and the Structure of Authority in Renaissance England* (Routledge, 1989), *Shakespeare's America / America's Shakespeare* (Routledge, 1990), and *Big Time Shakespeare* (Routledge, 1996). He is presently engaged in a project about Shakespeare and moral agency.

Lesley B. Cormack, Professor of History and Dean of the Faculty of Arts and Social Sciences at Simon Fraser University in Burnaby (British Columbia), is a historian of science, specializing in the history of geography and mathematics in early modern England. Her recent publications include *Charting an Empire: Geography at the English Universities 1580–1620* (University of Chicago, 1997) and *A History of Science in Society: From Philosophy to Utility* (Broadview, 2004; with Andrew Ede).

Julie E. Cumming is Associate Professor in the Schulich School of Music at McGill University. She has published a monograph on fifteenth-century music, *The Motet in the Age of Du Fay* (Cambridge University, 1999), as well as articles and reviews in *Speculum*, the *Journal of Musicology*, and *New Grove Opera*. She is currently working on a book, *The Motet in the Age of Josquin*. Other areas of interest include analysis of Renaissance music, music printing in the Renaissance, baroque opera, and performance practice.

Wes Folkerth is Associate Professor of English at McGill University. His publications include "Shakespeare in Popular Music," in *Shakespeares After Shakespeare: An Encyclopedia of the Bard in Mass Media and Popular Culture* (Greenwood, 2006); "Tempaurality in *Twelfth Night*," in *Aural Cultures* (YYZ Books, 2004); and *The Sound of Shakespeare* (Routledge, 2002). His current research focuses on Shakespeare in popular music from the Victorian era to the present day, and on sound and listening in Shakespeare in mass media.

Torrance Kirby is Professor of Church History at McGill University. His principal field of research is Reformation thought, especially of Richard Hooker, Peter Martyr Vermigli, Heinrich Bullinger, and other Protestant thinkers; he also works on the history of Christian Platonism, in the Patristic as well as in the late medieval and early modern periods. His most recent book is *The Zurich Connection and Tudor Political Theology* (Koninklijke Brill NV, 2007). He has published four books on the thought of Richard Hooker (including *Richard Hooker, Reformer and Platonist* in 2005), and various articles on aspects of Reformation thought including pieces on Vermigli, John Calvin, Bullinger, and Antoine de Marcourt.

Yael Margalit teaches English Literature at John Abbott College in Sainte-Anne-de-Bellevue, Québec. She received her Ph.D. in English from McGill University. Yael's current research explores the connections between early modern natural, material, and civic history, particularly in the representation of animality on the early modern stage.

Steven Mullaney teaches early modern literature at the University of Michigan in Ann Arbor. He is the author of *The Place of the Stage: License, Play, and Power in Renaissance England* (Chicago, 1988; rpt. Michigan, 1995) and essays on topics such as Elizabethan drama, first encounters between European and New World cultures, and the history of affect in the early modern period. He is currently completing *The Reformation of Emotion in the Age of Shakespeare* (for Chicago).

Shankar Raman is Associate Professor of Literature at MIT. His research focuses on late medieval and early modern literature and culture, and in particular on the intersection of colonialism, science, and economics. His first book, *Framing "India": The Colonial Imaginary in Early Modern Culture* (Stanford, 2002), investigates the relationship between colonialism and literature in sixteenth- and seventeenth-century Europe. It compares Portuguese, English, and Dutch colonial activity to examine the role of India as a figure through which these diverse European powers imagined and defined themselves. He is now completing a second book on the intersection of science and the aesthetic in sixteenth- and seventeenth-century Europe, tentatively entitled *Untimely Meditations: Crises of Representation in Early Modern Literature and Painting*.

François Rouget, Queen's National Scholar and Professor of French Literature at Queen's University (Ontario), has published eleven books, collections, and critical editions, including *L'apothéose d'Orphée: L'esthétique de l'ode en France au XVIe siècle de Sébillet à Scaliger (1548–1561)* (Droz, 1994); *Les trois premiers livres des odes d' Olivier de Magny* (Droz, 1995); *Poétiques de l'objet dans la poésie française du moyen* *âge au XXe siècle* (Champion, 2001; with J. Stout); and *L'arc et la lyre: Introduction à la poétique des odes (1550–1552) de Pierre de Ronsard* (Sedes, 2001).

David Harris Sacks is Richard F. Scholz Professor of History and Humanities at Reed College in Portland, Oregon. His books include *The Widening Gate: Bristol and the Atlantic Economy, 1450–1700* (California, 1993), an edition of Thomas More's *Utopia* (Bedford, 1999), and *The Historical Imagination in Early Modern Britain: History, Rhetoric, and Fiction, 1500–1800* (Cambridge, 2002; ed. with Donald R. Kelley).

Anne Thackray has worked in the curatorial departments of the National Gallery and National Portrait Gallery, London, and has taught courses in seventeenth- and nineteenth-century British art at the University of Edinburgh and the Open University. A former research fellow in European art at the National Gallery of Canada, she is currently preparing an exhibition of the Wenceslaus Hollar collection at the Thomas Fisher Rare Book Library, University of Toronto. Recent publications include "Elizabeth I as Empress: A Portrait Engraving in the National Gallery of Canada" (*National Gallery of Canada Review*, vol. 4) and "The Randle Holme Album" (*British Art Journal*, forthcoming; with Robert Tittler).

Robert Tittler (FRHistS; FSA) is Distinguished Professor of History Emeritus and Adjunct Professor of Art History at Concordia University, Montreal. His recent books include *The Face of the City, Civic Portraits and Civic Identity in Early Modern England* (Manchester, 2007); *A Companion to Tudor Britain* (Blackwells, 2004; ed. with Norman Jones); *Townspeople and Nation, English Urban Experiences, 1540–1640* (Stanford, 2001); and *The Reformation and the Towns in England* (Oxford/Clarendon, 1998). His current research concerns the social and economic context of portraiture in early modern England, and especially the making of publics for portraiture in that era.

Angela Vanhaelen, Associate Professor of Art History at McGill University, specializes in the study of seventeenth-century Dutch visual culture. She is the author of *Comic Print and Theatre in Early Modern Amsterdam: Gender, Childhood and the City* (Ashgate, 2003). Recent articles include "Utrecht's Transformations: Claiming the Dom through Representation, Iconoclasm and Ritual," *De Zeventiende Eeuw* (2005); and "Iconoclasm and the Creation of Images in Emanuel de Witte's Old Church in Amsterdam," *Art Bulletin* (2005). Her forthcoming book, *The Wake of Iconoclasm: Painting the Church in the Dutch Republic,* examines the changing status of art, artists, and viewers after iconoclasm.

Joseph Ward is Associate Professor and Chair of the History Department at the University of Mississippi. His publications include *Metropolitan Communities: Trade Guilds, Identity, and Change in Early Modern London* (Stanford, 1997), and three edited books: *Britain and the American South: From Colonialism to Rock and Roll* (Mississippi, 2003); *The Country and the City Revisited: England and the Politics of Culture, 1550–1850* (Cambridge, 1999; with Gerald MacLean and Donna Landry); and *Protestant Identities: Religion, Society, and Self-Fashioning in Post-Reformation England* (Stanford, 1999; with Muriel C. McClendon and Michael MacDonald). His current research includes two book projects—"From State to Nation: Londoners, Education, and Provincial Reform in Early Modern England and Wales" and "Cultural Exchange in Early Modern London."

Bronwen Wilson is Associate Professor in the Department of Art History, Visual Art, and Theory at the University of British Columbia. Her publications include *The World in Venice: Print, the City, and Early Modern Identity* (Toronto, 2005); "The Renaissance Portrait: From resemblance to representation," in *The Renaissance World* (Routledge, 2007); "*Foggie diverse di vestire de'Turchi*: Turkish Costume Illustration and Cultural Translation" in *The Journal of Medieval and Early Modern History* (2007); "Visual Knowledge/Facing Blindness" in *Seeing Across Cultures: Visuality in the Early Modern Period* (Ashgate, 2010); and a forthcoming book *Facing the End of the Renaissance: Portraits, Physiognomy, and Naturalism in Northern Italy (1500–1620)*. Her current book project is *Journeys to Constantinople: Inscription and the Horizon in Early Modern Travel Imagery*.

Paul Yachnin is Tomlinson Professor of Shakespeare Studies and Chair of the Department of English at McGill University. His books include *Stage-Wrights* (Pennsylvania, 1997), *The Culture of Playgoing in Shakespeare's England* (Cambridge, 2001; with Anthony Dawson), *Shakespeare and the Cultures of Performance* (Ashgate, 2008; ed. with Patricia Badir), and *Shakespeare and Character: Theory, History, Performance and Theatrical Persons* (Palgrave Macmillan, forthcoming 2008; ed. with Jessica Slights). He is one of the editors of the new Oxford *Complete Works of Thomas Middleton*. Work-in-progress includes an edition of *Richard II* (for Oxford) and a book-length study, *Shakespeare and the Social Thing: Making Publics in the Renaissance Theatre*.

Bibliography

PRIMARY SOURCES

Accetto, Torquato. *Della dissimulazione onesta*. Edited by Salvatore Silvano Nigro. Turin: Collana Biblioteca Einaudi, 1997.

Aleandro, Girolamo, Girolamo Rocco, and Marcello Giovannetti. *Esercizi fisiognomici*. Edited by Lucia Rodler. Palermo: Sellerio, 1996.

An answere to a letter. London: Thomas Godfray, 1535.

Andrewes, Lancelot. *XCVI Sermons*. 2nd ed. London, 1632.

Aretino, Pietro. *The Letters of Pietro Aretino*. Edited and translated by Thomas Caldecott Chubb. Hamden, CT: Archon, 1967.

Aristotle. *The Complete Works of Aristotle: The Revised Oxford Translation*. Edited by Jonathan Barnes. 2 vols. Princeton, NJ: Princeton University Press, 1984.

———. *The Nicomachean Ethics*. Translated by David Ross. Oxford: Oxford University Press, 1980.

———. "Physiognomics." In *Minor Works*. Cambridge, MA: Harvard University Press, 1936.

Armin, Robert. *A Nest of Ninnies*. London, 1608.

Atlas, Allan. *The Cappella Giulia Chansonnier*. 2 vols. Brooklyn, NY: Institute of Medieval Music, 1975.

A treatise concernynge the diuision betwene the spiritualtie and temporaltie. London: Thomas Berthelet, 1532?

Bacon, Francis. *The Advancement of Learning*. Edited by Michael Kiernan. Oxford: Clarendon Press, 2000.

———. *Francis Bacon's New Atlantis*. Edited by Bronwen Price. Manchester, UK: Manchester University Press, 2002.

———. *The Instauratio magna Part 2: Novum organum and Associated Texts*. Edited by Graham Rees and Maria Wakely. Oxford: Clarendon Press, 2004.

Beaumont, Francis. *The Knight of the Burning Pestle*. Edited by Michael Hattaway. 2nd ed. London: A and C Black; New York: Norton, 2002.

Bion, Nicolas. *L'usage de globes celestes et terrestres, et des spheres suivant les differens systemes du monde*. Paris, 1699.

Biondo, Michelangelo. *De cognitione hominis per aspectum / Conoscenza dell'uomo dall'aspetto esteriore*. Edited by Lucia Rodler. Rome: Beniamino Vignola, 1995.

Birdwood, George, with William Foster, eds. *The Register of Letters, &c. of the Governour and Company of Merchants of London trading into the East Indies, 1600–1619*. Quaritch, 1893.

Blaeu, Willem Janszoon. *Institutio astronomica. De usu globorum et sphaerarum caelestium ac terrestrium*. Amsterdam, 1634.

Blundeville, Thomas. *His Exercises, containing sixe Treatises.* London, 1594.

The Boke of Marchauntes, right necessarye vnto all folkes. Newly made by the lorde Pantapole, right expert in suche busynesse, nere neyghbour vnto the lorde Pantagrule. London: Thomas Godfraye, 1534.

Bonifaccio, Giovanni. *L'arte de'cenni con quale formandosi favella visibile, si tratta della muta eloquenza, che non è altro che un facondo silentio.* Vicenza: Francesco Grossi, 1616.

Bourdin, R. P. *Le cours de mathematique.... Contenant de plus un traité de l'usage du globe terrestre.* Paris, 1661.

Bright, Timothie. *A treatise of melancholy Containing the causes thereof, and reasons of the strange effects it worketh in our minds and bodies: with the physicke cure, and spirituall consolation for such as haue thereto adioyned afflicted conscience.* London: Vautrolier, 1586.

Burton, Robert. *The anatomy of melancholy vvhat it is. VVith all the kindes, causes, symptomes, prognostickes, and seuerall cures of it. In three maine partitions with their seuerall sections, members, and subsections. Philosophically, medicinally, historically, opened and cut vp. By Democritus Iunior. With a satyricall preface, conducing to the following discourse.* Oxford: Iohn Lichfield and Iames Short, for Henry Cripps, 1621.

Cartier, Jacques. *A shorte and briefe narration of the two nauigations and discoueries to the northwest partes called Newe Fraunce.* Translated by John Florio. London, 1580.

Castiglione, Baldesar. *The Book of the Courtier.* Translated by Charles S. Singleton. Garden City, NY: Doubleday, 1959.

Castlemaine, Roger. *The English Globe: Being a Stabil and Immobil One.* London, 1679.

Cataldi, Pietro Antonio. *Algebra discorsiva, numerale et lineale.* Bologna, 1618.

Chapman, George, Ben Jonson, and John Marston. *Eastward Ho!* Edited by R. W. Van Fossen. Revels Plays. Manchester, UK: Manchester University Press, 1979.

Clermont, Catherine de, and Maréchale de Retz. *Album de poésies.* Edited by Colette Winn and François Rouget. Paris: H. Champion, 2004.

da Vinci, Leonardo. *Trattato della pittura.* Edited by Angelo Borzelli. Carabba editore, 1947.

Davis, John. *The Seamans Secret.* London: Thomas Dawson, 1595.

Dee, John. *General and rare memorials pertayning to the perfect arte of nauigation annexed to the paradoxal cumpas.* London, 1577.

della Porta, Giambattista. *De ea naturalis physiognomoniae parte quae ad manuum lineas spectat libri duo: E in appendice Chirofisonomia.* Edited by Oreste Trabucco. Naples: Edizioni scientifiche italiane, 2003.

———. *De humana physiognomia / Della fisonomia dell'uomo.* Biblioteca della Fenice. Edited by Mario Cicognani. Parma: Ugo Guanda, 1988.

Donne, John. *Divine Poems.* Edited by Helen Gardner. Oxford: Clarendon Press, 1965.

Euclid. *The Elements.* Translated by Sir Thomas L. Heath. 3 vols. New York: Dover, 1956.

Foxe, John. *Actes and monuments of these latter and perillous dayes, touching matters of the Church, wherein ar comprehended and described the great persecutions [and] horrible troubles, that haue bene wrought and practised by the Romishe prelates, speciallye in this realme of England and Scotlande.* London: John Day, 1563.

Gauricus, Pomponius. *De sculptura.* Edited by André Chastel and Robert Klein. Paris: Droz, 1969.

Ghirardelli, Cornelio. *Cefalogia fisonomica diuisa in dieci deche, doue conforme a documenti d'Aristotile, e d'altri filosofi naturali, si esaminano le fisonomie di cento teste humane che intagliate si vedono in quest'opera.* Bologna, 1630.

Grent, W. *The Antiquity and excellency of globes.* London, 1653.

Hakewill, George. *An apologie or declaration of the power and providence of God in the government of the world.* 3rd ed. London, 1635.

Hakluyt, Richard. *Analysis sev resolutio perpetua in octo libros politicorum Aristotelis.* 1583.

———. *The principal nauigations, voyages, traffiques and discoueries of the English nation made by sea or ouer-land.* 3 vols. London, 1599–1600.

Hening, William Waller, ed. *Statutes at Large: Being a Collection of the Laws of Virginia, From the First Session of the Legislature, in the Year 1619.* 13 vols. Richmond: Printed for the Editor by Samuel Pleasants, junior, printer to and for the Commonwealth, 1809–1823.

Herbert, George. *The Complete English Poems.* Edited by John Tobin. Oxford: Oxford University Press, 1991.

Herbert of Cherbury, Lord Edward. *Poems English and Latin.* Edited by G. C. Moore Smith. Oxford: Clarendon Press, 1923.

Hobbes, Thomas. *Leviathan.* New York: Touchstone, 2008.

Hood, Thomas. *The Use of Both the Globes, Celestiall, and Terrestriall.* London, 1592.

Hotman, François, and Jean Hotman. *Epistolae.* Amsterdam: George Gallet, 1700.

Huberinus, Mauritus. *Globorum coelestis et terrestris fabrica et usus.* Nuremberg, 1615.

Hues, Robert. *Tractatus de globis et eorum usu.* London, 1592.

Hume, David. *A Treatise of Human Nature.* Oxford: Oxford University Press, 2000.

Ingegneri, Giovanni. *Fisonomia naturale.* Naples, 1606.

Kant, Immanuel. *What Is Enlightenment?* Upper Saddle River, NJ: Prentice Hall, 1995.

Leybourne, William. *Panorganon: or, A Universal Instrument, performing all such conclusions Geometrical and Astronomical as are usually wrought by the Globes, etc.* London, 1672.

Locke, John. *Two Treatises of Government.* New Haven, CT: Yale University Press, 2003.

Lodge, Thomas. *Wits Miserie, and the Worlds Madnesse Discouering the Deuils Incarnat of This Age.* London: Printed by Adam Islip, 1596.

Marcourt, Antoine. *Réformateur et pamphlétaire du Livre des Marchans aux Placards de 1534.* Geneva: Droz, 1973.

Martin, Benjamin. *The Description and Use of both the Globes, the Armillary Sphere, and Orrery.* London, 1763.

Mascardi, Agostino. *Dissertationes de affectibus sive perturbationibus animi.* Paris, 1639.

Mascardi, Antonio. "Che la corte è vera scuola non solamente della prudenza, ma della virtù morale." In *Prose vulgari,* 349–67. Venice: Baba, 1653.

Mercator, Gerard. *Atlas sive cosmographicae meditationes de fabrica mundi.* Düsseldorf, 1595.

Metius, A. A. *De genuino usu utriusque globi Tractatus.* Amsterdam, 1626.

Monconys, Balthasar de. *Journal des voyages de Monsieur de Monconys, conseiller du roi en ses conseils d'estat et privé. Seconde partie. Voyage d'Angleterre, Païs-Bas, Allemagne et Italie.* Lyon: Horace Boisat et Georges Remeus, 1666.

Montesquieu, Charles de Secondat, Baron of. *On the Spirit of the Laws.* Berkeley and Los Angeles: University of California Press, 1977.

Moxon, Joseph. *A Tutor to Astronomie and Geographie. Or an Easie and Speedy way to know the Use of both the Globes, Celestial and Terrestriall.* London, 1659.

Nashe, Thomas. *The Works of Thomas Nashe.* Vol. 2. Oxford: Basil Blackwell, 1958.

Niccholes, Alexander. *A Discourse of Marriage and Wiving*. London, 1615.
Nicquet, Honorat. *Phisiognomia humana, libris IV*. Lugduni, 1648.
Pellegrini, Antonio. *Fisionomia naturale*. Milan, 1622.
Perkins, William. *A Treatise Tending Unto a Declaration, Whether a Man Be in the Estate of Damnation or in the Estate of Grace*. London: Printed by the Widow Orwin, for Iohn Porter, 1597.
Pickering, William. *The Marrow of the Mathematicks*. London, 1686.
Pinzio. *Fisionomia . . . raccolta da i libri di antichi filosofi*. Lyon, 1550.
Prymer of Salysbury vse. Paris, 1531.
Recorde, Robert. *The Castle of Knowledge*. London, 1556.
———. *The Pathway to Knowledge*. London, 1551.
———. *The Whetstone of Witte*. London, 1557.
Rizzacasa, Giorgio. *La fisionomia. . . . Non meno utile che dilettevole, si in morale che in naturale filosofia*. Carmagnola: Marc'Antonio Bellone, 1607.
Rousseau, Jean-Jacques. *The Social Contract; or, Principles of Political Right*. London: George Allen and Unwin, 1920.
Salem and Bizance. London: Thomas Berthelet, 1533.
Schedel, Hartmann. *Das Liederbuch des Dr. Hartmann Schedel, das Erbe deutscher Musik*. Kassel: Bärenreiter, 1978.
Shakespeare, William. *The Merchant of Venice*. Edited by Leah S. Marcus. New York: Norton, 2006.
Sidney, Sir Philip. *Complete Poems*. Edited by William Ringler. Oxford: Clarendon Press, 1962.
Smith, Adam. *Theory of Moral Sentiments*. New York: Cambridge University Press, 2002.
Spinoza, Benedictus de. *Ethics*. Translated by George Henry Radcliffe Parkinson. Oxford: Oxford University Press, 2000.
Tanner, Robert. *A brief Treatise of the Use of the Globe Celestiall and Terrestriall*. London, 1630.
———. *A brief treatise of the use of the globe celestiall and terrestriall wherein is set downe the principles of the mathematicks fit for all travelers, navigators*. London, 1647.
Tasso, Torquato. 1591. *Il malpiglio: a dialogue on the court*. Translated by Dain A. Trafton. Hanover, NH: Dartmouth College in conjunction with English Literary Renaissance, 1973.
Temple, William. *Observations upon the United Provinces of the Netherlands, 1673*. Edited by George Clark. Oxford: Clarendon Press, 1972.
Townshend, Heywood. *Historical collections, or, An exact account of the proceedings of the four last parliaments of Q. Elizabeth of famous memory*. London, 1680.
Trapman, Johannes, ed. *De Summa der Godliker Scrifturen [1523]*. Leiden: Elve / Labor Vincit, 1978.
Turnbull, Charles. *A perfect and easie treatise of the use of the caelestil globe written as well for an introduction of such as bee exercised in the art of navigation*. London, 1585.
Tyndale, William. *The obedyence of a Chrysten man: and howe Chrysten rulers ought to gouerne, wherin also (yf thou marke dilygently) thou shalte fynde eyes to perceyue the craftye conueyaunce of all iugglers*. London: Thomas Godfray?, 1536.
Wallis, John. *Treatise of Algebra*. London, 1685.
Will of Lancelot Andrewes. 1626.
Wright, Edward. *The Description and use of the Sphaere*. London, 1613.
Yonge, Nicholas. *Musica transalpina*. In *The English Experience: Its Record in Early Printed Books Published in Facsimile 496*. Amsterdam: Theatrum Orbis Terrarum, 1972.

SECONDARY SOURCES

Anderson, Benedict. *Imagined Communities: Reflections on the Origin and Spread of Nationalism.* London: Verso, 1983.

Arendt, Hannah. *Between Past and Future.* Harmondsworth: Penguin, 1968.

———. *The Human Condition.* 1958, reprint, Chicago: University of Chicago Press, 1998.

Babb, Lawrence. *The Elizabethan Malady; A Study of Melancholia in English Literature from 1580 to 1642.* East Lansing: Michigan State College Press, 1951.

Backscheider, Paula R. *Spectacular Politics: Theatrical Power and Mass Culture in Early Modern England.* Baltimore: Johns Hopkins University Press, 1993.

Bakhtin, Mikhail. *Speech Genres and Other Late Essays.* Translated by Vern W. McGee. Edited by Caryl Emerson and Michael Holquist. Austin: University of Texas Press, 1986.

Baldwin, Elizabeth, Lawrence Clopper, and David Mills, eds. *Records of Early English Drama: Chester.* 2nd ed. 2 vols. Toronto: University of Toronto Press, 2007.

Baldwin, Geoff. "The 'Public' as a Rhetorical Community in Early Modern England." In *Communities in Early Modern England: Networks, Place, Rhetoric,* edited by Alexandra Shepard and Phil Withington, 199–215. Manchester, UK: Manchester University Press, 2000.

Ball, Terence, James Farr, and Russell L. Hanson, eds. *Political Innovation and Conceptual Change.* Cambridge: Cambridge University Press, 1989.

Balsamo, Jean. "Société et culture de cour au XVIe siècle." In *Histoire de la France littéraire, naissances, renaissances. Moyen âge-XVIe siècle,* edited by Frank Lestringant and Michel Zink. Paris: PUF, 2006.

Banks, Jon. *The Motet as a Formal Type in Northern Italy ca. 1500.* 2 vols. New York: Garland, 1993.

Barasch, Moshe. "Character and Physiognomy: Bocchi on Donatello's *St. George,* a Renaissance Text on Expression in Art." *Journal of the History of Ideas* 36, no. 3 (1991): 413–30.

Barker, Francis. *The Private Tremulous Body: Essays on Subjection.* New York: Methuen, 1984.

Baxandall, Michael. *Patterns of Intention.* New Haven, CT: Yale University Press, 1985.

Beasley, Faith E. *Salons, History, and the Creation of Seventeenth-Century France.* Burlington, VT: Ashgate, 2006.

Bec, Christian. *Précis de littérature italienne.* Paris: Presses Universitaires de France, 1982.

Becker, Howard. *Art Worlds.* Berkeley and Los Angeles: University of California Press, 2008.

Bellenger, Yvonne. "Des académies italiennes à celles de France au XVIe siècle." In *Rapporti e scambi tra umanesimo italiano ed umanesimo europeo,* edited by Luisa Rotondi Secchi Tarugi, 11–22. Milan: Nuovi Orizzonti, 2001.

Benedict, Philip. "The Wars of Religion, 1562–1598." In *Renaissance and Reformation France, 1500–1648,* edited by Mark Holt. Oxford: Oxford University Press, 2002.

Benjamin, Walter. *The Origins of German Tragic Drama.* Translated by John Osborne. London: NLB, 1997.

Berger, Adolf. *Encyclopedic Dictionary of Roman Law.* Transactions of the American Philosophical Society, n.s., 42, pt. 2. Philadelphia: American Philosophical Society, 1953.

Berger, Harry, Jr. *The Absence of Grace: Sprezzatura and Suspicion in Two Renaissance Courtesy Books.* Stanford, CA: Stanford University Press, 2000.

————. *Fictions of the Pose: Rembrandt against the Italian Renaissance.* Stanford, CA: Stanford University Press, 2000.

Bermingham, Ann. *Learning to Draw: A Cultural History of the Polite and Useful Art.* London: Published for the Paul Mellon Centre for Studies in British Art by Yale University Press, 2000.

Bernstein, Jane A. *Print Culture and Music in Sixteenth-Century Venice.* Oxford: Oxford University Press, 2001.

Berthoud, Gabrielle. *Antoine Marcourt: Réformateur et pamphlétaire du 'Livre des Marchans' aux placards de 1534.* Geneva: Droz, 1973.

Bhabha, Homi K. *The Location of Culture.* New York: Routledge, 1994.

Biagioli, Mario. *Galileo, Courtier: The Practice of Science in the Culture of Absolutism.* Chicago: University of Chicago Press, 1993.

Black, Joseph. "The Rhetoric of Reaction: The Martin Marprelate Tracts (1588–89), Anti-Martinism, and the Uses of Print in Early Modern England." *The Sixteenth Century Journal* 28, no. 3 (1997): 707–25.

Blackburn, Bonnie J. "For Whom Do the Singers Sing?" *Early Music* 25 (November 1997): 593–609.

————. "Lorenzo de' Medici: A Lost Isaac Manuscript, and the Venetian Ambassador." In *Musica franca: Essays in Honor of Frank A. D'Accone,* edited by Alyson McLamore, Irene Alm, and Colleen Reardon, 19–44. Stuyvesant, NY: Pendragon, 1996.

————. "Petrucci's Venetian Editor: Petrus Castellanus and His Musical Garden." *Musica disciplina* 49 (1995): 15–45.

————. "The Sign of Petrucci's Editor." In *Venezia 1501: Petrucci e la stampa musicale; Venice 1501: Petrucci, Music, Print and Publishing; Atti del convegno internazionale di studi, Venezia, Palazzo Giustinian Lolin, 10–13 ottobre 2001,* edited by Giulio Cattin and Patrizia Dalla Vecchia, 415–29. Venice: Edizioni Fondazione Levi, 2005.

————. "The Virgin in the Sun: Music and Image for a Prayer Attributed to Sixtus IV." *Journal of the Royal Musical Association* 124, no. 2 (1999): 157–95.

Boorman, Stanley. "Did Petrucci's Concern for Accuracy Include Any Concern with Performance Issues?" *Basler Jahrbuch für historische Musikpraxis* 25 (2001): 23–37.

————. *Ottaviano Petrucci: A Catalogue Raisonné.* Oxford: Oxford University Press, 2006.

Borrelli, Gianfranco, ed. *Ragion di stato: L'arte italiana della prudenza politica: Catalogo della mostra.* Naples: Istituto italiano per gli studi filosofici, 1994.

Boucaut, Audrey. "Utilisateurs et mécènes de la musique imprimée à Paris au XVIe siècle: Étude des dédicaces des éditions d'Adrian Le Roy et Robert Ballard." *Seizième Siècle* 2 (2006): 243–313.

Brenner, Robert. *Merchants and Revolution: Commercial Change, Political Conflict, and London's Overseas Traders, 1550–1653.* Princeton, NJ: Princeton University Press, 1993.

Brewer, J. S., J. Gairdner, and R. H. Brodie, eds. *Letters and Papers, Foreign and domestic of the reign of Henry VIII, 1509–1547.* 22 vols. Vol. 7. London, 1862-1932.

Bristol, Michael. *Big Time Shakespeare.* London: Routledge, 1996.

————, ed. *Print, Manuscript, Performance: The Changing Relations of the Media in Early Modern England.* Columbus: Ohio State University Press, 2000.

————. "Sacred Literature and Profane Religion: The Modernity of Herbert of Cherbury." In *The Witness of Times: Manifestations of Ideology in Seventeenth Century England,* edited by Katherine Z. Keller and Gerald J. Schiffhorst, 14–33. Pittsburgh, PA: Duquesne University Press, 1993.

Brockliss, Laurence. *Calvet's Web: Enlightenment and the Republic of Letters in Eighteenth-Century France*. Oxford: Oxford University Press, 2002.

Brotton, Jerry. "Terrestrial Globalism: Mapping the Globe in Early Modern Europe." In *Mappings*, edited by Denis Cosgrove, 71–89. London: Reaktion Books, 1999.

———. *Trading Territories: Mapping the Early Modern World*. Ithaca, NY: Cornell University Press, 1998.

Brown, Bill. "Thing Theory." *Critical Inquiry* 28, no. 1 (Autumn 2001): 1–22.

Brown, Howard Mayer. "The Mirror of Men's Salvation: Music in Devotional Life about 1500." *Renaissance Quarterly* 43 (1990): 744–73.

Brunel, Jean. *Un poitevin poète, humaniste et soldat à l'époque des guerres de religion. Nicolas Rapin (1539–1608)*. Paris: H. Champion, 2002.

Bruster, Douglas. "The Structural Transformation of Print in Late Elizabethan England." In *Print, Manuscript, Performance: The Changing Relations of the Media in Early Modern England*, edited by Arthur F. Marotti and Michael D. Bristol, 49–89. Columbus: Ohio State University Press, 2000.

Burckhardt, Jacob. *The Civilization of the Renaissance in Italy: An Essay*. Edited and revised by Irene Gordon. Translated by S. G. C. Middlemore. New York: New American Library, 1960.

Burian, Jarka. "Hamlet in Postwar Czech Theatre." In *Foreign Shakespeare: Contemporary Performance*, edited by Dennis Kennedy, 195–210. Cambridge: Cambridge University Press, 1993.

Burke, Peter. *The Art of Conversation*. Cambridge: Polity, 1993.

———. "L'homme de cour." In *L'homme de la renaissance*, edited by E. Garin, 167–72. Paris: Le Seuil, 2002.

Burnett, Mark Thornton. "Apprentice Literature and the 'Crisis' of the 1590s." *The Yearbook of English Studies* 21 (1991): 27–38.

Buron, Emmanuel. "Le mythe du salon de la maréchale de Retz." In *Henri III mécène des arts, des sciences et des lettres*, edited by Isabelle de Conihout et al., 306–15. Paris: Presses de l'Université de Paris-Sorbonne, 2006.

Burrow, Colin. "Introduction." In *Complete Poems and Sonnets by William Shakespeare*. The Oxford Shakespeare, 1–39. Oxford: Oxford University Press, 2002.

Calhoun, Craig. "Imagining Solidarity: Cosmopolitanism, Constitutional Patriotism, and the Public Sphere." *Public Culture* 14, no.1 (Winter 2002): 147–71.

Campan, C. A. *Mémoires de Francisco de Enzinas: Texte latin inédit avec la traduction Française du XVIe siècle en regard 1543–1545*. Vol. 1. Brussels, 1862.

Campbell, Julie D. *Literary Circles and Gender in Early Modern Europe: A Cross-Cultural Approach*. Burlington, VT: Ashgate, 2006.

Castoriadis, Cornelius. *The Imaginary Institution of Society*. Translated by Katherine Blamey. Cambridge, MA: MIT Press, 1987.

Cavaillé, Jean-Pierre. "Torquato Accetto, les 'ténèbres honnêtes.'" In *Dis/simulations: Religion, morale et politique au XVIIe siècle*, 332–69. Paris: Honoré Champion, 2002.

Certeau, Michel de. *The Writing of History*. Translated by Tom Conley. New York: Columbia University Press, 1988.

Chambers, D. D. C. "A Catalogue of the Library of Bishop Lancelot Andrewes (1555–1626)." In *Transactions of the Cambridge Bibliographical Society*, 5 (1969–1970): 99–121.

Chambers, E. K. *The Elizabethan Stage*. Vol. 4. Oxford: Clarendon Press, 1923.

Champion, Pierre. *Contribution à l'histoire de la société polie: Ronsard et Villeroy, les secrétaires du roi et les poètes d'après le manuscrit français 1663 de la bibliothèque nationale*. Paris: É. Champion, 1925.

Chaney, Edward. *The Evolution of English Collecting*. New Haven, CT: Yale University Press, 2003.

Chaplin, Joyce E. *Subject Matter: Technology, the Body, and Science on the Anglo-American Frontier, 1500–1676*. Cambridge, MA: Harvard University Press, 2001.

Chapman, George, Ben Jonson, and John Marston. *Eastward Ho!* Edited by R. W. Van Fossen. Revels Plays. Manchester, UK: Manchester University Press, 1979.

Chartier, Roger. *The Order of Books: Readers, Authors, and Libraries in Europe between the Fourteenth and Eighteenth Centuries*. Translated by Lydia Cochrane. Cambridge: Polity, 1994.

Chastel, André. *Marsile Ficin et l'art*. Geneva: Droz, 1975.

Christianson, John R. *On Tycho's Island: Tycho Brahe and His Assistants, 1570–1601*. Cambridge: Cambridge University Press, 2000.

Clubb, Louise. *Giambattista della Porta, dramatist*. Translated by Giambattista della Porta. Princeton, NJ: Princeton University Press, 1965.

Cockcroft, Robert. *Rhetorical Affect in Early Modern Writing: Renaissance Passions Reconsidered*. New York: Palgrave Macmillan, 2003.

Coldiron, A. E. B. "Public Sphere / Contact Zone: Habermas, Early Print, and Verse Translation." *Criticism* 46, no. 2 (Spring 2004): 207–22.

Collinson, Patrick. "The Monarchical Republic of Queen Elizabeth I." *Bulletin of the John Rylands University Library of Manchester* 69, no. 2 (1987): 394–424.

Cormack, Lesley. *Charting an Empire: Geography at the English Universities, 1580–1620*. Chicago: University of Chicago Press, 1997.

Cowan, Brian. *The Social Life of Coffee: The Emergence of the British Coffeehouse*. New Haven, CT: Yale University Press, 2005.

Cox, Virginia. "Tasso's *Malpiglio overo de la corte*: The *Courtier* Revisited." *The Modern Language Review* 90, no. 4 (1995): 897–918.

Crane, Nicholas. *Mercator: The Man Who Mapped the Planet*. London: Weidenfeld and Nicolson, 2002.

Craster, Sir Edmund. "Elizabethan Globes at Oxford." *Geographical Journal* 117, no. 1 (March 1951): 24–26.

Crino, Anna Maria, and Helen Wallis. "New Researches on the Molyneux Globes." *Der Globusfreund* 35–37 (1987): 11–20.

Crossley, Nick, and John Michael Roberts, eds. *After Habermas: New Perspectives on the Public Sphere*. Oxford: Blackwell, 2004.

Cumming, Julie. "From Chapel Choirbook to Print Partbook and Back Again." In *Cappelle musicali fra corte, stato e chiesa nell'Italia del rinascimento: Atti del convegno internazionale di studi, camaiore*, 21–23 ottobre 2005, edited by Franco Piperno, Gabriella Biagi Ravenni, and Andrea Chegai, 373–40. Florence: Olschki, 2007.

———. *The Motet in the Age of Du Fay*. Cambridge: Cambridge University Press, 1999.

Currie, Gregory. "Imagination and Make-Believe." In *The Routledge Companion to Aesthetics*. 2nd ed. London: Routledge, 2005.

Cust, Richard. "The 'Public Man' in Late Tudor and Early Stuart England." In *The Politics of the Public Sphere in Early Modern England*, edited by Peter Lake and Steven Pincus, 116–43. Manchester, UK: Manchester University Press, 2007.

Danto, Arthur. *The Transfiguration of the Commonplace*. Cambridge, MA: Harvard University Press, 1981.

Daston, Lorraine. "The Ideal and Reality of the Republic of Letters." *Science in Context* 4, no. 2 (1991): 367–86.

———, ed. *Things That Talk: Object Lessons from Art and Science*. New York: Zone Books; Cambridge, MA: MIT Press, 2004.

Davids, C. A. "The Use of Globes on Ships of the Dutch East India Company." *Der Globusfreund* 35–37 (1987): 67–78.

Davies, Wayne. *Writing Geographical Exploration: James and the Northwest Passage 1631–33*. Calgary: University of Calgary Press, 2003.

Dawson, Anthony, and Paul Yachnin. *The Culture of Playgoing in Shakespeare's England: A Collaborative Debate*. Cambridge: Cambridge University Press, 2001.

De Grazia, Margreta. *Hamlet without Hamlet*. Cambridge: Cambridge University Press, 2007.

———. "The Scandal of Shakespeare's Sonnets." *Shakespeare Survey* 46 (1994): 35–49.

De Grazia, Margreta, Maureen Quilligan, and Peter Stallybrass, eds. *Subject and Object in Renaissance Culture*. Cambridge: Cambridge University Press, 1996.

Dekker, Elly. "The Doctrine of the Sphere: A Forgotten Chapter in the History of Globes." *Globe Studies: The Journal of the International Coronelli Society* 49–50 (2002): 25–44.

———. *Globes at Greenwich: A Catalogue of the Globes and Armillary Spheres in the National Maritime Museum, Greenwich*. Oxford: Oxford University Press, 1999.

Dekker, Elly, and Peter van der Krogt. *Globes from the Western World*. London: Zwemmer, 1993.

Deramaix, Marc, Perrine Galand-Hallyn, Ginette Vagenheim, and Jean Vignes, eds. *Les Académies dans l'Europe humaniste: Idéaux et pratiques*. Geneva: Drosz, 2008.

Desjardins, Lucie. *Le corps parlant: Savoirs et représentation des passions au XVIIe siècle*. Laval: Les Presses de l'Université Laval, 2000.

Dickey, Timothy. "Rethinking the Siena Choirbook." Ph.D. diss., Duke University, 2003.

———. "Rethinking the Siena Choirbook: A New Date and Implications for its Musical Contents." *Early Music History* 24 (2005): 1–52.

Diller, George E. *Les dames des roches. Étude sur la vie littéraire à Poitiers dans la deuxième moitié du XVIe siècle*. Paris: Droz, 1936.

Donnelly, Daniel. "The Anti-Courtier: Music, Social Criticism, and the Academy in Antonfrancesco Doni's *Dialogo della musica*." Paper presented at the Medieval and Renaissance Music Conference, Bangor, Wales, 25 July 2008.

Dooley, Brendan, ed. *Italy in the Baroque: Selected Readings*. New York: Garland, 1995.

Drake, George Warren. "The First Printed Books of Motets, Petrucci's *Motetti A numero trentatre* (Venice, 1502), and *Motetti de Passione, de Cruce, de Sacramento, de Beata Virgine et huiusmodi B* (Venice, 1503)." Ph.D. diss., University of Illinois, 1972.

———, ed. *Ottaviano Petrucci*, Motetti de Passione, de Cruce, de Sacramento, de Beata Virgine et huiusmodi B, *Venice, 1503*. Vol. 11, *Monuments of Renaissance Music*. Chicago: University of Chicago Press, 2002.

Droz, Eugénie. "Marguerite de Valois's Album of Verse." In *Aspects of the Renaissance. International Conference on the Meaning of the Renaissance (1964)*, edited by Archibald Ross Lewis, 87–100. Austin: University of Texas Press, 1967.

Dubrow, Heather. *Shakespeare and Domestic Loss: Forms of Deprivation, Mourning and Recuperation*. Cambridge: Cambridge University Press, 1999.

Duffy, Eamon. *Marking the Hours: English People and Their Prayers 1240–1570*. New Haven, CT: Yale University Press, 2006.

———. *The Stripping of the Altars*. New Haven: Yale University Press, 1992.

Duggan, Mary Kay. *Italian Music Incunabula: Printers and Type*. Berkeley and Los Angeles: University of California Press, 1992.

Duke, Alistair. *Reformation and Revolt in the Low Countries*. London: Hambledon Press, 1990.

Duvenage, Pieter. *Habermas and Aesthetics*. Malden, MA: Blackwell, 2003.

Earwaker, J. P. "The Four Randle Holmes of Chester." *Journal of the Chester Archaeological and Historic Society* 4 (1892): 113–70.

Eck, Xander van. "The Artist's Religion: Paintings Commissioned for Clandestine Catholic Churches in the Northern Netherlands, 1600–1800." *Simiolus* 27, nos. 1–2 (1999): 70–94.

———. "Dreaming of an Eternally Catholic Utrecht during Protestant Rule." *Simiolus* 30, nos.1–2 (2003): 19–33.

Edmond, Mary. "Bury St. Edmunds: A Seventeenth Century Art Centre." *Walpole Society* 43 (1989 for 1987): 106–18.

Edwards, Mark E. *Printing, Propaganda, and Martin Luther.* Berkeley and Los Angeles: University of California Press, 1994.

Einstein, Alfred. "The 'Dialogo della musica' of Messer Antonio Francesco Doni." *Music and Letters* 15 (1934): 244–53.

Eisenstein, Elizabeth L. *The Printing Revolution in Early Modern Europe.* 2nd ed. Cambridge: Cambridge University Press, 2005.

Elders, Willem, et al., eds. *New Josquin Edition.* Utrecht: Vereniging voor Nederlandse Muziekgeschiedenis, 1987.

Eley, Geoff. "Nations, Publics, and Political Cultures: Placing Habermas in the Nineteenth Century." In *Habermas and the Public Sphere,* edited by Craig Calhoun, 289–339. Cambridge, MA: MIT Press, 1992.

Elias, Norbert. *The Civilizing Process.* Translated by Edmund Jephcott. Oxford: Blackwell, 1996.

Eliot, T. S. *The Sacred Wood: Essays on Poetry and Criticism.* 2nd ed. 1928; reprint, London: Faber, 1997.

Elton, G. R. *Reform and Reformation: England 1509–1558.* Cambridge: Harvard University Press, 1977.

Elwood, Christopher. *The Body Broken: The Calvinist Doctrine of the Eucharist and the Symbolization of Power in Sixteenth-Century France.* New York: Oxford University Press, 1999.

Enterline, Lynn. *The Tears of Narcissus: Melancholia and Masculinity in Early Modern Writing.* Stanford, CA: Stanford University Press, 1995.

Evans, G. Blakemore, ed. *The Riverside Shakespeare.* 2nd ed. Boston: Houghton Mifflin, 1997.

Fallows, David. "Petrucci's Canti Volumes: Scope and Repertory." *Basler Jahrbuch für Historische Musikpraxis* 25 (2001): 39–52.

———. "Review of *Ottaviano Petrucci: A Catalogue Raisonné,* by Stanley Boorman." *Journal of the American Musicological Society* 60 (2007): 415–21.

Farley-Hills, David. *Critical Responses to Hamlet, 1600–1790.* New York: AMS, 1997.

Feingold, Mordechai. *The Mathematicians' Apprenticeship: Science, Universities and Society in England, 1560–1640.* Cambridge: Cambridge University Press, 1984.

Fenlon, Iain. "Heinrich Glarean's Books." In *Music of the German Renaissance: Sources, Styles, and Contexts,* edited by John Kmetz, 74–102. Cambridge: Cambridge University Press, 1994.

———. *Music, Print and Culture in Early Sixteenth-Century Italy.* London: British Library, 1995.

Fineman, Joel. *Shakespeare's Perjured Eye: The Invention of Poetic Subjectivity in the Sonnets.* Berkeley and Los Angeles: University of California Press, 1986.

Fish, Stanley. *The Living Temple: George Herbert and Catechizing.* Berkeley and Los Angeles: University of California Press, 1978.

Fisher, F. J. "London as an Engine of Economic Growth." *Britain and the Netherlands.* Vol. 4, *Metropolis, Dominion and Province,* edited by J. S. Bromley and E. H. Kossman, 3–16. The Hague: Nijhof, 1971.

Fisher, R. M. "William Crashawe and the Middle Temple Globes 1605–15." *Geographical Journal* 140, no. 1 (February 1974): 105–12.

Foister, Susan. *Holbein and England.* London: Yale University Press, 2004.

——. *Holbein in England*. London: Harry N. Abrams, 2006.
——. "Paintings and Other Works of Art in Sixteenth Century Inventories." *Burlington Magazine* 123 (1981): 273–82.
Ford, Philip. "An Early French Renaissance Salon: The Morel Household." *Renaissance and Reformation/Renaissance et Réforme* 28, no. 1 (2004): 9–20.
Frémy, Édouard. *Origines de l'académie française. L'Académie des derniers Valois.* Paris: E. Leroux, 1887.
Freud, Sigmund. "Mourning and Melancholia." In *The Standard Edition of the Complete Psychological Works*, edited by J. Strachey, 14: 243–58. 24 vols. London: Hogarth, 1957.
Frijhoff, Willem. *Embodied Belief: Ten Essays on Religious Culture in the Dutch Republic*. Hilversum: Verloren, 2002.
Frith, Brian. *Twelve Portraits of Gloucester Benefactors*. Gloucester, UK, 1972.
Froude, James Anthony. *Short Studies on Great Subjects*. 4 vols. London: Longmans, Green, 1886–1888.
Gardiner, Michael E. "Wild Publics and Grotesque Symposiums: Habermas and Bakhtin on Dialogue, Everyday Life and the Public Sphere." *Sociological Review* 52 (2004): 28–48.
Garver, Eugene. *Aristotle's Rhetoric: An Art of Character*. Chicago: University of Chicago Press, 1994.
Geary, Patrick J. *Living with the Dead in the Middle Ages*. Ithaca, NY: Cornell University Press, 1994.
Gélis, François de. *Histoire critique des jeux floraux depuis leur origine jusqu'à leur transformation en académie, 1323–1694*. 1912; reprint, Geneva: Slatkine Reprints, 1981.
Gilmont, Jean-François. *The Reformation and the Book*. Brookfield, VT: Ashgate, 1998.
Glixon, Jonathan. *Honoring God and the City: Music at the Venetian Confraternities, 1260–1807*. Oxford: Oxford University Press, 2003.
Goldsmith, Elizabeth C., and Dena Goodman, eds. *Going Public: Women and Publishing in Early Modern France*. Ithaca, NY: Cornell University Press, 1995.
Gowland, Angus. "The Problem of Early Modern Melancholy." *Past and Present* 191 (2006): 77–121.
Grafton, Anthony. "The Humanist as Reader." In *A History of Reading in the West*, edited by Guglielmo Cavallo and Roger Chartier, translated by Lydia G. Cochrane, 184–93. Amherst: University of Massachusetts Press, 1999.
Grant, Patrick. "Augustinian Spirituality and the Holy Sonnets of John Donne." *ELH* 38 (1971): 542–61.
Greenblatt, Stephen. *Hamlet in Purgatory*. Princeton, NJ: Princeton University Press, 2002.
Grendler, Paul F. "Form and Function in Renaissance Popular Books." *Renaissance Quarterly* 46 (1993): 451–85.
Griffiths, Antony. *The Print in Stuart Britain, 1603–1689*. London: The British Museum, 1998.
Gros, Gérard. *Le poète, la vierge et le prince du puy: étude sur les puys marials de la France du nord du XIVe siècle à la renaissance*. Paris: Klincksieck, 1992.
Haar, James. "Notes on the 'Dialogo della musica' of Antonfrancesco Doni." *Music and Letters* 47 (1966): 198–224.
Habermas, Jürgen. *The Structural Transformation of the Public Sphere: An Inquiry into a Category of Bourgeois Society*. Translated by Thomas Burger. Cambridge, MA: MIT Press, 1989.
——. *Technik und Wissenschaft als "Ideologie."* Frankfurt am Main: Suhrkamp, 1968.

Hacking, Ian. *The Social Construction of What?* Cambridge, MA: Harvard University Press, 1999.

Hadden, Richard. *On the Shoulders of Merchants: Exchange and the Mathematical Conception of Nature in Early Modern Europe.* Albany: State University of New York Press, 1994.

Hadfield, Andrew. *Shakespeare and Republicanism.* Cambridge: Cambridge University Press, 2005.

Halasz, Alexandra. *The Marketplace of Print: Pamphlets and the Public Sphere in Early Modern England.* Cambridge: Cambridge University Press, 1997.

Hamel, Anton Gerard van. "L'album de Louise de Coligny." *Revue d'histoire littéraire de la France* 10 (1903): 232–55.

Hamm, Charles, and Herbert Kellman, eds. *Census-Catalogue of Manuscript Sources of Polyphonic Music: 1400–1550.* 5 vols. Renaissance Manuscript Studies 1. Neuhausen-Stuttgart: Hänssler-Verlag, 1979–1988.

Hammer, Dean. *Roman Political Thought and the Modern Theoretical Imagination.* Norman: University of Oklahoma Press, 2008.

Hammer, Paul E. J. *Polarisation of Elizabethan Politics: The Political Career of Robert Devereux, 2nd Earl of Essex.* Cambridge: Cambridge University Press, 1999.

Hanlon, Gregory. *Confession and Community in Seventeenth-Century France: Catholic and Protestant Coexistence in Aquitaine.* Philadelphia: University of Pennsylvania Press, 1993.

Harline, Craig E. *Pamphlets, Printing, and Political Culture in the Early Dutch Republic.* Boston: M. Nijhoff, 1987.

Hatter, Jane. "The Marian Motets in Petrucci's Venetian Motet Anthologies." Master's thesis, McGill University, 2007.

Heal, Bridget, and Ole Peter Grell, eds. *Reformation: Princes, Clergy and People.* Burlington, VT: Ashgate, 2008.

Heath, Thomas L. *Diophantus of Alexandria: A Study in the History of Greek Algebra.* 2nd ed. Cambridge: Cambridge University Press, 1910.

Hebel, William J. *Works.* Vol. 2. Oxford: Shakespeare Head Press, 1961.

Heidegger, Martin. "The Thing." In *Poetry, Language, Thought,* 163–80. New York: Harper & Row, 1975 [1951].

Helgerson, Richard. *Forms of Nationhood: The Elizabethan Writing of England.* Chicago: University of Chicago Press, 1992.

Hendrix, Harald. "The Construction of an Author: Pietro Aretino and the Elizabethans." In *Betraying Our Selves: Forms of Self-Representation in Early Modern English Texts,* edited by Henk Dragstra, Sheila Ottway, and Helen Wilcox, 31–44. Basingstoke, UK: St. Martin's, 2000.

Higman, Francis. *Lire et découvrir: La circulation des idées au temps de la réforme.* Geneva: Droz, 1998.

Hind, Arthur M. *Engraving in England in the Sixteenth and Seventeenth Centuries.* 3 vols. Cambridge, 1952–1964.

———. *A History of Engraving and Etching: From the Fifteenth Century to the Year 1914.* London, 1923.

Hirschkop, Ken. "Justice and Drama: On Bakhtin as a Complement to Habermas." In *After Habermas: New Perspectives on the Public Sphere,* edited by Nick Crossley and John Michael Roberts, 49–65. Oxford: Wiley-Blackwell, 2004.

Hodges, Devon. *Renaissance Fictions of Anatomy.* Amherst: University of Massachusetts Press, 1985.

Houghton, Walter E., Jr. "The English Virtuoso in the Seventeenth Century." *Journal of the History of Ideas* 3, no. 1 (January 1942): 51–73.

Hughes, Paul L., and James F. Larkin, eds. *Tudor Royal Proclamations.* 3 vols. New Haven, CT: Yale University Press, 1969.

Hutchinson, Robert. *Thomas Cromwell: the Rise and Fall of Henry VIII's most Notorious Minister.* London: Weidenfeld & Nicolson, 2007.

Hypertext Book of Hours. "Detailed Contents." Prepared by Glen Gunhouse. http://www.medievalist.net/hourstxt/home.htm#contents (accessed December 2007).

Ingrams, Jill Phillips. *Idioms of Self-Interest: Credit, Identity, and Property in English Renaissance Literature.* London: Routledge, 2008.

Isjewijn, Josef, Gilbert Tournoy, and Marcus De Schepper. "Jean Dorat and his *Tumulus Brynonis.*" In *Neo-Latin and the Vernacular in Renaissance France,* edited by Grahame Castor and Terence Cave, 129–55. Oxford: Clarendon Press, 1984.

Jackson, Stanley W. *Melancholia and Depression: From Hippocratic Times to Modern Times.* New Haven, CT: Yale University Press, 1986.

Janse, Wim, and Barbara Pitkin, eds. *The Formation of Clerical and Confessional Identities in Early Modern Europe.* Boston: Brill, 2006.

Jardine, Lisa. *Ingenious Pursuits: Building the Scientific Revolution.* New York: Little, Brown, 1999.

Jasinski, James. *Sourcebook on Rhetoric: Key Concepts in Contemporary Rhetorical Studies.* Thousand Oaks, CA: Sage, 2001.

Jones, Nicholas F. *The Associations of Classical Athens: The Response to Democracy.* New York: Oxford University Press, 1999.

———. *Politics and Society in Ancient Greece.* Westport, CT: Praeger, 2008.

Jouanna, Arlette. *La France de la Renaissance, histoire et dictionnaire.* Paris: Éditions Robert Laffont, 2001.

Judd, Cristle Collins. *Reading Renaissance Music Theory: Hearing with the Eyes.* Cambridge: Cambridge University Press, 2000.

Kaplan, Benjamin J. "Confessionalism and Its Limits: Religion in Utrecht, 1600–1650." In *Masters of Light: Dutch Painters in Utrecht during the Golden Age,* exhibition catalogue, edited by Joneath Spicer et al., 60–71. Baltimore: Walters Art Gallery; San Francisco, CA: Fine Arts Museum of San Francisco; New Haven, CT: Yale University Press, 1997.

———. "Fictions of Privacy: House Chapels and the Spatial Accommodation of Religious Dissent in Early Modern Europe." *American Historical Review* 1, no. 4 (October 2002): 1031–64.

Kastan, David Scott. *Shakespeare and the Book.* Cambridge: Cambridge University Press, 2001.

Keating, L. Clark. *Studies on the Literary Salon in France, 1550–1615.* Cambridge, MA: Harvard University Press, 1941.

Kirby, Torrance. "The Public Sermon: Paul's Cross and the Culture of Persuasion in England, 1534–1570." *Renaissance and Reformation / Renaissance et réforme* 31, no. 1 (2008): 3–29.

Kirnbauer, Martin. *Hartmann Schedel und sein Liederbuch: Studien zu einer spätmittelalterlichen Musikhandschrift (Bayerische Staatsbibliothek München, cgm 810) und ihrem Kontext.* Vol. 42. Bern: Peter Lang, 2001.

Kitzes, Adam. *The Politics of Melancholia from Spenser to Milton.* New York: Routledge, 2006.

Klein, Jacob. *Greek Mathematical Thought and the Origins of Algebra.* Translated by Eva T. Braun. North Chelmsford, MA: Courier Dover, 1992.

Klibansky, Raymond, Erwin Panofsky, and Fritz Saxl. *Saturn and Melancholy: Studies in the History of Natural Philosophy, Religion and Art.* London: Nelson, 1964.

Kooi, Christine. "'A Serpent in the Bosom of Our Dear Fatherland.' Reformed Reaction to the Holland Mission in the Seventeenth Century." In *The Low Countries as a Crossroads of Religious Beliefs,* edited by Arie-Jan Gelderblom, Jan L. de Jong, and Marc van Vaeck, 165–76. Leiden: Brill, 2004.

Kristeva, Julia. *Black Sun: Depression and Melancholia.* Translated by Leon S. Roudiez. New York: Columbia University Press, 1989.

Kwakkelstein, Michael. *Leonardo da Vinci as a Physiognomist: Theory and Drawing Practice.* Leiden: Primavera Press, 1994.

Lake, Peter. *The Antichrist's Lewd Hat: Protestants, Papists and Players in Post-Reformation England.* New Haven, CT: Yale University Press, 2002.

Lake, Peter, and Steven Pincus. "Rethinking the Public Sphere in Early Modern England." *Journal of British Studies* 45 (April 2006): 270–92.

Larsen, Anne. "Catherine Des Roches, the Pastoral, and Salon Poetics." In *Women Writers in Pre-Revolutionary France. Strategies of Emancipation,* edited by Colette Winn and Donna Kuizenga, 227–41. New York: Garland, 1997.

Latour, Bruno. *Reassembling the Social: An Introduction to Actor-Network-Theory.* Oxford: Oxford University Press, 2005.

———. "Why Has Critique Run out of Steam? From Matters of Fact to Matters of Concern." *Critical Inquiry* 30, no. 2 (2004): 225–48.

Le Goff, Jacques. *The Birth of Purgatory.* Translated by Arthur Goldhammer. Chicago: University of Chicago Press, 1984.

Leroquais, Victor. *Les livres d'heures, manuscrits de la bibliothèque nationale.* Paris: Bibliothèque Nationale, Département des manuscrits, 1927.

Le Van Baumer, Franklin. *The Early Tudor Theory of Kingship.* New York: Russell and Russell, 1966.

Levinas, Emmanuel. *Time and the Other.* Translated by Richard A. Cohen. Pittsburgh, PA: Duquesne University Press, 1987.

Livingstone, David. *The Geographical Tradition: Episodes in the History of a Contested Enterprise.* Cambridge, MA: Blackwell, 1993.

Lloyd, Christopher, and Simon Thurley. *Henry VIII: Images of a Tudor King.* Oxford: Phaidon Press, 1990.

Loewenstein, Joseph, and Paul Stevens. "Charting Habermas's 'Literary' or 'Precursor' Public Sphere." *Criticism* 46, no. 2 (Spring 2004): 201–5.

Love, Harold. "How Music Created a Public." *Criticism* 46, no. 2 (Spring 2004): 257–71.

Luciani, Isabelle. "Jeux floraux et 'humanisme civique' au XVIe siècle: entre enjeux de pouvoir et expérience du politique." In *L'Humanisme à Toulouse (1480–1596): Actes du colloque international de Toulouse (2004),* edited by Nathalie Dauvois, 301–35. Paris: H. Champion, 2006.

Lux, David S., and Harold J. Cook. "Closed Circles or Open Networks? Communicating at a Distance During the Scientific Revolution." *History of Science* 36 (1998): 179–211.

Lyons, Bridget Gellert. *Voices of Melancholy: Studies in Literary Treatments of Melancholy in Renaissance England.* New York: Barnes and Noble, 1971.

MacCulloch, Diarmaid. *The Reformation.* New York: Viking, 2004.

MacLean, Sally-Beth. *Chester Art: A Subject List of Extant and Lost Art Including Items Relevant to Early Drama.* Kalamazoo: Medieval Institute Publications, Western Michigan University, 1982.

Mahoney, Michael Sean. *The Mathematical Career of Pierre de Fermat (1601–1665).* Princeton, NJ: Princeton University Press, 1973.

Mancall, Peter C. *Hakluyt's Promise: An Elizabethan's Obsession for an English America.* New Haven, CT: Yale University Press, 2007.

Marotti, Arthur. *John Donne, Coterie Poet.* Madison: University of Wisconsin Press, 1986.

———. "Patronage, Poetry, and Print." *The Yearbook of English Studies* 21 (1991): 1–26.

Marotti, Arthur, and Michael D. Bristol, eds. *Print, Manuscript, and Performance: The Changing Relations of the Media in Early Modern England.* Columbus: Ohio State University Press, 2000.

Marshall, Cynthia. "The Doubled Jaques and Constructions of Negation in *As You Like It.*" *Shakespeare Quarterly* 49 (1998): 375–92.

Marshall, Peter, and Alex Ryrie, eds. *The Beginnings of English Protestantism.* Cambridge: Cambridge University Press, 2002.

Martin, John. "Inventing Sincerity, Refashioning Prudence: The Discovery of the Individual in Renaissance Europe." *The American Historical Review* 102, no. 5 (1997): 1308–42.

———. *Myths of Renaissance Individualism.* New York: Palgrave Macmillan, 2004.

Marx, Hans Joachim. "Neues zur Tablatur-Handschrift St. Gallen Stiftsbibliothek, cod. 530." *Archiv für Musikwissenschaft* 37 (1980): 264–91.

Maus, Katharine Eisaman. *Inwardness and Theater in the English Renaissance.* Chicago: University of Chicago Press, 1995.

Mayhew, Robert. "Mapping Science's Imagined Community: Geography as a Republic of Letters, 1600–1800." *British Journal for the History of Science* 38, no. 1 (2005): 73–92.

McConica, James Kelsey. *English Humanists and Reformation Politics under Henry VIII and Edward VI.* Oxford: Oxford University Press, 1965.

McGinn, Donald J. "Nashe's Share in the Marprelate Controversy." *PMLA* 59, no. 4 (1944): 952–84.

McKeon, Michael. *Secret History of Domesticity: Public, Private, and the Division of Knowledge.* Baltimore: Johns Hopkins University Press, 2007.

McLuskie, Kathleen, E. "The Poets' Royal Exchange: Patronage and Commerce in Early Modern Drama." *The Yearbook of English Studies* 21 (1991): 53–62.

Meyer-Baer, Kathi. *Liturgical Music Incunabula.* London: Bibliographical Society, 1962.

Michaude, Philippe Alain. *Aby Warburg and the Image in Motion.* Translated by Sophie Hawkes. New York: Zone Books, 2004.

Millar, Fergus. *The Roman Republic in Political Thought.* Hanover, NH: Brandeis University Press, 2002.

Miller, Peter. "Friendship and Conversation in Seventeenth-Century Venice." *The Journal of Modern History* 73, no. 1 (2001): 1–31.

Moore, Andrew, and Charlotte Crawley, eds. *Family and Friends: A Regional Survey of British Portraiture.* London: HMSO, 1992.

Mouser, Marilee J. "Petrucci and His Shadow: A Study of the Filiation and Reception History of the Venetian Motet Anthologies, 1502–1508." Ph.D. diss., University of California, Santa Barbara, 2003.

Mueller, Janel. "Women among the Metaphysicals: A Case, Mostly, of Being Donne for." *Modern Philology* 87, no. 2 (November 1989): 142–58.

Newman, Karen. "Portia's Ring and Structures of Exchange in *The Merchant of Venice.*" *Shakespeare Quarterly* 38 (1987): 19–33.

Nolhac, Pierre de. *Ronsard et l'humanisme.* Paris: H. Champion, 1966.

Norbrook, David. *Writing the English Republic: Poetry, Rhetoric and Politics, 1627–1660.* Cambridge: Cambridge University Press, 1999.

North, John. *The Ambassadors' Secret: Holbein and the World of the Renaissance.* London: Hambledon and London, 2002.

Oakeshott, Walter. "Sir Walter Raleigh's Library." *The Library* 23, no. 4 (1968): 285–327.

O'Donoghue, Freeman. *Catalogue of Engraved British Portraits Preserved in the Department of Prints and Drawings in the British Museum.* 3 vols. London: British Museum, 1910.

Oestmann, Günter. "On the Construction of Globe Gores and the Preparation of Spheres in the Sixteenth Century." *Der Globusfreund* 43–44 (1995): 121–31.

Parker, Charles H. *Faith on the Margins: Catholics and Catholicism in the Dutch Golden Age.* Cambridge, MA: Harvard University Press, 2008.

———. "Obedience with an Attitude: Laity and Clergy in the Dutch Catholic Church of the Seventeenth Century." In *The Low Countries as a Crossroads of*

Religious Beliefs, edited by Arie-Jan Gelderblom, Jan L. de Jong, and Marc van Vaeck, 177–96. Leiden: Brill, 2004.

Pask, Kevin. *The Emergence of the English Author*. Cambridge: Cambridge University Press, 1996.

Paster, Gail. *Humoring the Body: Emotions and the Shakespearean Stage*. Chicago: University of Chicago Press, 2004.

Payne, Anthony. *Richard Hakluyt: A Guide to His Books and to Those Associated with Him, 1580–1625*. London: Quaritch, 2008.

———. *Richard Hakluyt and His Books*. London: The Hakluyt Society, 1997.

Peck, Linda Levy. *Consuming Splendor: Society and Culture in Seventeenth Century England*. Cambridge: Cambridge University Press, 2005.

Pennington, L. E., ed. *The Purchas Handbook: Studies of the Life, Times and Writings of Samuel Purchas, 1577–1626*. 2 vols. London: Hakluyt Society, 1997.

Pensky, Max. *Melancholy Dialectics: Walter Benjamin and the Play of Mourning*. Amherst: University of Massachusetts Press, 1993.

Petey-Girard, Bruno. "Rêve académique, goût du prince et mécénat royal au XVIe siècle." *Travaux de littérature* 19 (2006): 96–110.

Pettegree, Andrew. "French Books at the Frankfurt Fair." In *The Impact of the European Reformation and the Culture of Persuasion*. Cambridge: Cambridge University Press, 2005.

———. "Printing and the Reformation: the English Exception." In *The Beginnings of English Protestantism*, edited by Peter Marshall and Alex Ryrie. Cambridge: Cambridge University Press, 2002.

———. *Reformation and the Culture of Persuasion*. Cambridge: Cambridge University Press, 2005.

Pirrotta, Nino. "Music and Cultural Tendencies in Fifteenth-Century Italy." *Journal of the American Musicological Society* 19 (1966): 127–61.

Plotz, John. "Can the Sofa Speak? A Look at Thing Theory." *Criticism* 47, no.1 (Winter 2005) 109–18.

Pollmann, Judith. "The Bond of Christian Piety: The Individual Practice of Tolerance and Intolerance in the Dutch Republic." In *Calvinism and Religious Toleration in the Dutch Golden Age*, edited by Ronnie Po-Chia Hsia and Henk Van Nierop, 53–71. Cambridge: Cambridge University Press, 2002.

Poovey, Mary. *History of the Modern Fact: Problems of Knowledge in the Sciences of Wealth and Society*. Chicago: University of Chicago Press, 1998.

Porter, Martin. *Windows of the Soul: The Art of Physiognomy in European Culture 1470–1780*. Oxford: Clarendon Press, 2005.

Post, Gaines. *Studies in Medieval Legal Thought: Public Law and the State, 1100–1322*. Princeton, NJ: Princeton University Press, 1964.

Powell, William S. *John Pory, 1572–1636: The Life and Letters of a Man of Many Parts*. Chapel Hill: University of North Carolina Press, 1977.

Prescott, Anne Lake *Imagining Rabelais in Renaissance England*. New Haven, CT: Yale University Press, 1998.

Quinn, D. B. *Explorers and Colonies*. London: Hambledon Press, 1990.

———. *The Hakluyt Handbook*. 2 vols. London: Hakluyt Society, 1974.

Rabb, Theodore K. *Enterprise and Empire: Merchant and Gentry Investment in the Expansion of England, 1575–1630*. Cambridge, MA: Harvard University Press, 1967.

Renaissance Liturgical Imprints: A Census (RELICS). "Books by Classificiation." http://www-personal.umich.edu/~davidcr/stats_classification.html (accessed July 12, 2007).

Rex, Richard. "The Crisis of Obedience: God's Word and Henry's Reformation." *The Historical Journal* 39, no. 4 (1996): 863–94.

Richards, Jennifer. *Rhetoric and Courtliness in Early Modern Literature*. Cambridge: Cambridge University Press, 2003.

Richardson, Brian. *Print Culture in Renaissance Italy: The Editor and the Vernacular Text 1400–1600*. Cambridge: Cambridge University Press, 2004.

———. *Printing, Writers and Readers in Renaissance Italy*. Cambridge: Cambridge University Press, 1999.

Roberts, Julian, and Andrew G. Watson. *John Dee's Library Catalogue*. London, 1990.

Rodler, Lucia. "Agostino Mascardi e la congettura fisiognomica." In *Mappe e letture: Studi in onore di Ezio Raimondi*, edited by A. Battistini, 133–52. Bologna: Il Mulino, 1994.

———. *Il corpo specchio dell'anima: Teoria e storia della fisiognomica*. Milan: Mondadori Bruno, 2000.

———. "La fisiognomica allo specchio." In *Esercizi fisiognomici*, 9–41. Palermo: Sellerio, 1996.

———. *I silenzi mimici del volto: Studi sulla tradizione fisiognomica italiana tra cinque e seicento*. Ospedaletto, Pisa: Pacini, 1991.

Rostenberg, Leonie. *English Publishers in the Graphic Arts, 1599–1700: A Study of the Printsellers and Publishers of Engravings*. New York: B. Franklin, 1963.

Rouget, François. "Marguerite de Berry et sa cour en savoie d'après son album de vers." *Revue d'histoire littéraire de la France* 1 (2006): 3–16.

Ryrie, Alec. "The Strange Death of Lutheran England." *Journal of Ecclesiastical History* 53, no. 1 (2002): 83-92.

Sacks, David Harris. "Discourses of Western Planting: Richard Hakluyt and the Making of the Atlantic World." In *The Atlantic World and Virginia, c. 1550–1624*, edited by Peter C. Mancall, 436–46. Chapel Hill: University of North Carolina Press, 2007.

———. "Freedom to, Freedom from, Freedom of: Urban Life and Political Participation in Early Modern England." *Citizenship Studies* 11, no. 2 (2007), 135–50.

———. "London's Dominion: The Metropolis, the Market Economy, and the State." In *Material London, ca. 1600*, edited by Lena Cowen Orlin, 20–54. Philadelphia: University of Pennsylvania Press, 2000.

———. "Promise and Contract in Early Modern England: Slade's Case in Perspective." In *Law and Rhetoric in Early Modern Europe*, edited by Victoria Kahn and Lorna Hutson, 28–53. New Haven, CT: Yale University Press, 2001.

———. "Richard Hakluyt's Navigations in Time: History, Epic, and Empire." *Modern Language Quarterly* 67, no. 1 (March 2006): 31–62.

———. *The Widening Gate: Bristol and the Atlantic Economy, 1450–1700*. Berkeley and Los Angeles: University of California Press, 1991.

Saenger, Paul. "Books of Hours and the Reading Habits of the Later Middle Ages." In *The Culture of Print: Power and the Uses of Print in Early Modern Europe*, edited by Roger Chartier, translated by Lydia G. Cochrane, 141–73. Princeton, NJ: Princeton University Press, 1989.

Satterthwaite, P. E., and D. F. Wright, eds. *A Pathway i[n]to the Holy Scripture [London: Godfray, 1536?]* Grand Rapids, MI: Eerdmans, 1994.

Schiesari, Juliana. *The Gendering of Melancholia: Feminism, Psychoanalysis and the Symbolics of Loss in Renaissance Literature*. Ithaca, NY: Cornell University Press, 1992.

Schilling, Heinz. "Confessional Europe." In *Handbook of European History, 1400–1600: Late Middle Ages, Renaissance and Reformation*. Vol. 2, *Visions, Programs and Outcomes*, edited by Thomas A. Brady et al., 641–70. Leiden: Brill, 1995.

Schmidt, Jeremy. "Melancholy and the Therapeutic Language of Moral Philosophy in Seventeenth-Century Thought." *Journal of the History of Ideas* 65, no. 4 (2004): 583–601.

Schoenfeldt, Michael. C. *Bodies and Selves in Early Modern England: Physiology and Inwardness in Spenser, Shakespeare, Herbert and Milton*. Cambridge: Cambridge University Press, 1999.

Sealy, Robert J. *The Palace Academy of Henry III*. Geneva: Droz, 1981.

Sebald, W. G. "Constructs of Mourning." In *Campo Santo*, edited by Sven Meyer, translated by Anthea Bell, 102–29. London: Hamish Hamilton, 2005.

Shagan, Ethan. "Clement Armstrong and the Godly Commonwealth: Radical Religion in Early Tudor England." In *The Beginnings of English Protestantism*. Cambridge: Cambridge University Press, 2002.

Shapin, Steven. *A Social History of Truth: Civility and Science in Seventeenth-Century England*. Chicago: University of Chicago Press, 1994.

Shapiro, Barbara. *Probability and Certainty in Seventeenth-Century England: A Study of the Relationships between Natural Science, Religion, History, Law, and Literature*. Princeton, NJ: Princeton University Press, 1983.

Shuger, Debora K. *Habits of Thought in the English Renaissance: Religion, Politics, and the Dominant Culture*. Berkeley and Los Angeles: University of California Press, 1990.

Shumaker, W., ed. and trans. *John Dee on Astronomy*. Berkeley and Los Angeles: University of California Press, 1978.

Smith, Lacy Baldwin. *Treason in Tudor England: Politics and Paranoia*. Princeton, NJ: Princeton University Press, 1986.

Smith, Pamela. *Body of the Artisan*. Chicago: University of Chicago Press, 2004.

Solomon, Andrew. *The Noonday Demon: An Atlas of Depression*. New York: Scribner, 2001.

Spaans, Joke. "Catholicism and Resistance to the Reformation in the Northern Netherlands." In *Reformation, Revolt and Civil War in France and the Netherlands 1555–1585*, Verhandelingen, afd. letterkunde, vol. 176, edited by Philip Benedict et al., 149–63. Amsterdam: Royal Netherlands Academy of Arts and Sciences, 1999.

———. "Violent Dreams, Peaceful Coexistence: On the Absence of Religious Violence in the Dutch Republic." *De zeventiende eeuw* 18, no. 2 (2003): 149–66.

Spiller, Elizabeth. *Science, Reading, and Renaissance Literature: The Art of Making Knowledge, 1580–1670*. Cambridge: Cambridge University Press, 2004.

Spinosa, Charles. "The Transformation of Intentionality: Debt and Contract in *The Merchant of Venice*." *English Literary Renaissance* 24, no. 2 (1994): 392–97.

Stedall, Jacqueline. *The Greate Invention of Algebra: Thomas Hariot's Treatise on Equations*. Oxford: Oxford University Press, 2003.

Stengers, Isabelle. "The Cosmopolitical Proposal." In *Making Things Public: Atmospheres of Democracy*, edited by Bruno Latour and Peter Weibel, 994–1003. Cambridge, MA: MIT Press, 2005.

Stern, Tiffany. "Watching as Reading: The Audience and Written Text in Shakespeare's Playhouse." In *How to Do Things with Shakespeare: New Approaches, New Essays*, edited by Laurie Maguire, 136–59. Oxford: Blackwell, 2008.

Stevenson, Edward L. *Terrestrial and Celestial Globes; Their History and Construction*. 2 vols. New Haven, CT: Public for the Hispanic Society of America by the Yale University Press, 1921.

Strier, Richard. "John Donne Awry and Squint: The 'Holy Sonnets,' 1608–1610." *Modern Philology* 86, no. 4 (May 1989): 357–84.

Swain, Simon. *Seeing the Face, Seeing the Soul: Polemon's Physiognomy from Classical Antiquity to Medieval Islam*. Oxford: Oxford University Press, 2007.

Swanson, Judith. *The Public and the Private in Aristotle's Political Philosophy*. Ithaca, NY: Cornell University Press, 1992.

Tambling, Jeremy. *Allegory and the Work of Melancholy: The Late Medieval and Shakespeare*. Amsterdam: Rodopi, 2004.

Tannery, Paul. *La géométrie grecque*. Hildesheim: Georg Olms, 1988.

Targoff, Ramie. *Common Prayer: The Language of Public Devotion in Early Modern England*. Chicago: University of Chicago Press, 2001.

Tarte, Kendall B. *Writing Places: Sixteenth-Century City Culture and the Des Roches Salon.* Newark: University of Delaware Press, 2007.

Taylor, Charles. *Modern Social Imaginaries.* Durham, NC: Duke University Press, 2004.

———. "Modern Social Imaginaries." *Public Culture* 14, no. 1 (2002): 91–124.

———. *A Secular Age.* Cambridge, MA: Harvard University Press, 2007.

Taylor, Gary. "*Hamlet* in Africa 1607." In *Travel Knowledge: European "Discoveries" in the Early Modern Period,* edited by Ivo Kamps and Jyotsna G. Singh, 211–48. New York: Palgrave, 2001.

Thomson, Patricia. "The Literature of Patronage, 1580–1630." *Essays in Criticism* 2 (1952): 267–84.

Tillyard, Virginia. "Painters in Sixteenth and Seventeenth Century Norwich." *Norfolk Archaeology* 37 (1980): 315–19.

Tittler, Robert. *The Face of the City: Civic Portraits and Civic Identity in Early Modern England.* Manchester, UK: Manchester University Press, 2007.

———. "Portrait Collection and Display in the English Civic Body, c. 1540–1640." *Journal of the History of Collections* 20, no. 2 (2008): 161–72.

Trevor, Douglas. *The Poetics of Melancholy in Early Modern England.* Cambridge: Cambridge University Press, 2004.

Turrini, Giuseppe. *L'Accademia filarmonica di Verona dalla fondazione (maggio 1543) al 1600 e il suo patrimonio musicale antico.* Verona: La Tipografia Veronese, 1941.

Ultee, Maarten. "The Republic of Letters: Learned Correspondence 1680–1720." *Seventeenth Century* 2 (January 1987): 95–112.

Vacchelli, Anna Maria Monterosso. *L'opera musicale di Antonfrancesco Doni.* Cremona: Athenaeum Cremonense, 1969.

van der Krogt, Peter. "Globe Production in the Low Counties and Its Impact in Europe, 1525–1650." *Globe Studies: The Journal of the International Coronelli Society* 49–50 (2002): 45–60.

———. *Globi Neerlandici: The Production of Globes in the Low Countries.* Utrecht: Hes Publishers, 1993.

———. "Seventeenth-Century Dutch Globes: Navigational Instruments?" *Der Globusfreund* 38–39 (1990): 67–76.

van Durme, M., ed. *Correspondence Mercatorienne.* Antwerp, 1959.

van Orden, Kate. "Children's Voices: Singing and Literacy in Sixteenth-Century France." *Early Music History* 25 (2006): 209–56.

———., ed. *Music and the Cultures of Print.* London: Garland, 2000.

Vendler, Helen. *The Art of Shakespeare's Sonnets.* Cambridge, MA: Belknap Press, 1997.

Viennot, Éliane. *Marguerite de Valois: 'La reine Margot.'* Paris: Perrin, coll. Tempus, 2005.

Wallis, Helen M. "The First English Globe: A Recent Discovery." *The Geographical Journal* 117 (1951): 275–90.

———. "Globes in England." *Geographical Magazine* 35, no. 5 (1962): 267–79.

———. "The Molyneux Globes." *B. M. Quarterly* (1952): 89–90.

———. "'Opera Mundi': Emery Molyneux, Jodocus Hondius and the First English Globes." In *Theatrum Orbis Librorum,* edited by Ton Croiset van Uchelen, Koert van der Horst, and Günter Schilder, 94–104. Utrecht: Hes Publishers, 1989.

Warner, J. Christopher. *Henry VIII's Divorce: Literature and the Politics of the Printing Press.* Woodbridge, UK: Boydell Press, 1998.

Warner, Michael. *Publics and Counterpublics.* New York: Zone Books, 2002.

———. "Publics and Counterpublics." *Quarterly Journal of Speech* 88, no. 4 (November 2002): 413–25.

Watt, Tessa. *Cheap Print and Popular Piety.* Cambridge: Cambridge University Press, 1991.

Weber, Max. *From Max Weber: Essays in Sociology,* Edited and translated by H. H. Gerth and C. Wright Mills. London: Routledge, 1991.

Webster, Charles. *The Great Instauration: Science, Medicine, and Reform, 1626–1660.* London: Duckworth, 1975.

Wells-Cole, Anthony. *Art and Decoration in Elizabethan and Jacobean England: The Influence of Continental Prints, 1558–1625.* London: Yale University Press, 1997.

Welsby, Paul A. *Lancelot Andrews, 1555–1626.* London: S. P. C. K., 1958.

Whigham, Frank. *Ambition and Privilege: The Social Tropes of Elizabethan Courtesy Theory.* Berkeley and Los Angeles: University of California Press, 1984.

Whitney, Charles. *Francis Bacon and Modernity.* New Haven, CT: Yale University Press, 1986.

———. "Francis Bacon's Instauratio: Dominion of and over Nature." *Journal of the History of Ideas* 50, no. 3 (July–September 1989): 371–90.

Williams, Raymond. *Keywords: A Vocabulary of Culture and Society.* London: Fontana, 1983.

Wilson, Blake. *Music and Merchants: The Laudesi Companies of Republican Florence.* Oxford: Oxford University Press, 1992.

Wilson, Bronwen. *The World in Venice: Print, the City, and Early Modern Identity.* Toronto: University of Toronto Press, 2005.

Wilson, Luke. *Theaters of Intention: Drama and Law in Early Modern England.* Stanford, CA: Stanford University Press, 2000.

Withington, P. J. *The Politics of Commonwealth: Citizens and Freemen in Early Modern England.* Cambridge: Cambridge University Press, 2005.

Wittgenstein, Ludwig. *Philosophical Investigations: The German Test, with a Revised English Translation.* Translated by G. E. M. Anscombe. 3rd ed. Oxford: Blackwell, 2001.

Wood, R. D. "The Daguerreotype and Development of the Latent Image: 'Une analogie remarquable.'" *Journal of Photographic Science* 44, no. 5 (September / October 1996): 165–67.

Worthen, William. *Shakespeare and the Authority of Performance.* Cambridge: Cambridge University Press, 1997.

Wrigley, E. A. "A Simple Model of London's Importance in Changing English Society and Economy, 1650–1750." *Past and Present* 37 (July 1967): 44–70.

Yachnin, Paul. "'The Perfection of Ten': Populuxe Art and Artisanal Value in *Troilus and Cressida.*" *Shakespeare Quarterly* 56, no. 3 (2005): 306–25.

———. *Stagewrights: Shakespeare, Jonson, Middleton, and the Making of Theatrical Value.* Philadelphia: University of Pennsylvania Press, 1997.

Yates, Frances. *The French Academies of the Sixteenth Century.* London: Warburg Institute, University of London, 1947.

Yates, Julian. "What Are 'Things' Saying in Renaissance Studies?" *Literature Compass* 3, no. 5 (2006): 992–1010.

Zaret, David. *Origins of Democratic Culture: Printing Petitions, and the Public Sphere in Early-Modern England.* Princeton, NJ: Princeton University Press, 2000.

———. "Religion, Science, and Printing in the Public Spheres in Seventeenth-Century England." In *Habermas and the Public Sphere,* edited by Craig Calhoun, 212–35. Cambridge, MA: MIT Press, 1992.

Index

Lightning Source UK Ltd.
Milton Keynes UK

172697UK00001B/49/P